ALPHA

Questions of Life

By the same author:
Why Jesus?
Why Christmas?
Searching Issues
A Life Worth Living
Telling Others
Challenging Lifestyle
The Heart of Revival
30 Days
Is God a Delusion?

ALPHA
Questions of Life

Nicky Gumbel

Alpha

First published 1993
Revised edition 1995
New edition 2001
New edition 2003
Revised in 2007

ISBN: 978 1 905887 77 4

1 2 3 4 5 6 Print / Year 12 11 10

Text illustrations by Charlie Mackesy

Published by Alpha International
Holy Trinity Brompton
Brompton Road
London SW7 1JA
Email: publications@alpha.org

Contents

Foreword

This book has come at exactly the right time. It fills a gap which has existed in Christian literature for several years. On the one hand, as recent well documented figures show, the church in England has been losing members at an alarming rate, particularly among young people under the age of twenty. While it is certainly true that a number of churches are showing very encouraging signs of growth, the overall picture in the country is still one of perceived dullness, decay and, as Nicky shows in this book, disillusion generally with church life. And yet . . . on the other hand there is beyond any question a very considerable new interest in spiritual things, together with a hunger and growing hope that somewhere, somehow, there may be found a contemporary answer to the age-old question, 'What is truth?'

Questions of Life is a sympathetic, fascinating and immensely readable introduction to Jesus Christ – still the most attractive and captivating person it is possible to know. Nicky Gumbel's intelligent, well researched and informed approach ensures that the search for Truth fully engages our minds as well as our hearts.

I am very glad that all the hard work that Nicky has put into the Alpha course at Holy Trinity Brompton, through which literally hundreds of people have been deeply affected, is now available to an even wider public. I have no hesitation in highly commending this readable and important book.

Sandy Millar
Former Vicar of Holy Trinity Brompton

Preface

There is today a new interest in the Christian faith, and more specifically in the person of Jesus. Nearly two thousand years since his birth he has approaching two billion followers. Christians will always be fascinated by the founder of their faith and the Lord of their lives. But now, there is a resurgence of interest among non-churchgoers. Many are asking questions about Jesus. Was he merely a man or is he the Son of God? If he is, what are the implications for our everyday lives?

This book attempts to answer some of the key questions at the heart of the Christian faith. It is based on 'Alpha', a course run at Holy Trinity Brompton for non-churchgoers, those seeking to find out more about Christianity, and those who have recently come to faith in Jesus Christ. We have watched in astonishment as Alpha has spread to over 18,000 courses in over 120 countries. Thousands of men and women of all ages have come on the course full of questions about Christianity, and have found God as their Father, Jesus Christ as their Saviour and Lord and the Holy Spirit as the one who comes to live within them.

I would like to thank all the people who have read and offered constructive criticisms on the manuscripts, and Cressida Inglis-

Jones who typed the original manuscript and almost all the revisions with great speed, efficiency and patience.

Nicky Gumbel

1

Is There
More to Life Than This?

For many years I had three objections to the Christian faith. First, I thought it was boring. I went to chapel at school and found it very dull. I felt sympathy with Robert Louis Stevenson who once entered in his diary, as if recording an extraordinary phenomenon, 'I have been to Church today, and am not depressed.' In a similar vein, the American humorist, Oliver Wendell Holmes, wrote, 'I might have entered the ministry if certain clergymen I knew had not looked and acted so much like undertakers.' My impression of the Christian faith was that it was dreary and uninspiring.

Secondly, it seemed to me to be untrue. I had intellectual objections to the Christian faith and, rather pretentiously, I called myself a logical determinist. When I was fourteen I wrote an essay in an RE lesson in which I tried to destroy the whole of Christianity and disprove the existence of God. Rather surprisingly, it was put forward for a prize! I had knock-down arguments against the Christian faith and rather enjoyed arguing with Christians, thinking I had won some great victory.

Thirdly, I thought that it was irrelevant. I could not see how something that happened 2,000 years ago and 2,000 miles away in the Middle East could have any relevance to my life in twentieth-century Britain. We often used to sing that much-loved hymn 'Jerusalem' which asks, 'And did those feet in ancient time walk upon England's mountains green?' We all knew that the answer was, 'No, they did not.' It seemed to be totally irrelevant to my life.

I realise, with hindsight, it was partly my fault as I never really listened and was totally ignorant about the Christian faith. There are many people today, in our secularised society, who don't know much about Jesus Christ, or what he did, or anything to do with Christianity. One hospital chaplain listed some of the replies he was given to the question, 'Would you like Holy Communion?' These are some of the answers:

'No thanks, I'm Church of England.'

'No thanks, I asked for Cornflakes.'

'No thanks, I've never been circumcised.'[1]

Christianity is far from boring, it is not untrue and it is not irrelevant. On the contrary, it is exciting, true and relevant. Jesus said, 'I am the way and the truth and the life' (John 14:6). If he was right, and I believe he was, then there can be nothing more important in this life than our response to him.

DIRECTION FOR A LOST WORLD

Men and women were created to live in a relationship with God. Without that relationship there will always be a hunger, an emptiness, a feeling that something is missing. Prince Charles once spoke of his belief that, for all the advances of science, 'there remains deep in the soul (if I dare use that word), a persistent and unconscious anxiety that something is missing, some ingredient that makes life worth living'.

Bernard Levin, perhaps the greatest columnist of this generation, once wrote an article called 'Life's Great Riddle, and No Time to Find Its Meaning'. In it he spoke of the fact that in spite of his great success as a columnist for over twenty years he feared that he might have 'wasted reality in the chase of a dream'. He wrote:

> To put it bluntly, have I time to discover why I was born before I die? . . . I have not managed to answer the question yet, and however many years I have before me they are certainly not as many as there are behind. There is an obvious danger in leaving it too late . . . why do I *have* to know why I was born? Because, of course, I am unable to believe that it was an accident; and if it wasn't one, it must have a meaning.[2]

He is not a Christian and on one occasion wrote, 'For the fourteen thousandth time, I am not a Christian.' Yet he seems to be only too aware of the inadequate answers to the meaning of life. He wrote some years earlier:

> Countries like ours are full of people who have all the material comforts they desire, together with such non-material blessings as a happy family, and yet lead lives of quiet, and at times noisy, desperation,

understanding nothing but the fact that there is a hole inside them and that however much food and drink they pour into it, however many motor cars and television sets they stuff it with, however many well balanced children and loyal friends they parade around the edges of it . . . it aches.[3]

Some people spend much of their lives seeking something that will give meaning and purpose to life. Leo Tolstoy, author of *War and Peace* and *Anna Karenina*, wrote a book called *A Confession* in 1879, in which he tells the story of his search for meaning and purpose in life. He had rejected Christianity as a child. When he left university he sought to get as much pleasure out of life as he could. He entered the social world of Moscow and Petersburg, drinking heavily, living promiscuously, gambling and leading a wild life. But it did not satisfy him.

Then he became ambitious for money. He had inherited an estate and made a large amount of money out of his books. Yet that did not satisfy him either. He sought success, fame and importance. These he also achieved. He wrote what the *Encyclopaedia Britannica* describes as 'one of the two or three greatest novels in world literature'. But he was left asking the question 'Well fine . . . so what?', to which he had no answer.

Then he became ambitious for his family – to give them the best possible life. He married in 1862 and had a kind, loving wife and thirteen children (which, he said, distracted him from any search for the overall meaning of life!). He had achieved all his ambitions and was surrounded by what appeared to be complete happiness. And yet one question brought him to the verge of suicide: 'Is there any meaning in my life which will not be annihilated by the inevitability of death which awaits me?'

He searched for the answer in every field of science and philosophy. The only answer he could find to the question 'Why do I live?' was that 'in the infinity of space and the infinity of time infinitely small particles mutate with infinite complexity'.

As he looked round at his contemporaries he saw that people were not facing up to the first order questions of life ('Where did I come from?', 'Where am I heading?', 'Who am I?', 'What is life about?'). Eventually he found that the peasant people of Russia had been able to answer these questions through their Christian faith and he came to realise that only in Jesus Christ do we find the answer.

Over one hundred years later nothing has changed. Freddie Mercury, the lead singer of the rock group Queen, who died at the end of 1991 wrote in one of his last songs on *The Miracle* album, 'Does anybody know what we are living for?' In spite of the fact that he had amassed a huge fortune and had attracted thousands of fans, he admitted in an interview shortly before his death that he was desperately lonely. He said, 'You can have everything in the world and still be the loneliest man, and that is the most bitter type of loneliness. Success has brought me world idolisation and millions of pounds, but it's prevented me from having the one thing we all need – a loving, ongoing relationship.'

He was right to speak of an 'ongoing relationship' as the one thing we all need. Yet no human relationship will satisfy entirely. Nor can it be completely ongoing. There will always be something missing. That is because we were created to live in a relationship with God. Jesus said, 'I am the way.' He is the only One who can bring us into that relationship with God that goes on into eternity.

When I was a child our family had an old black and white television set. We could never get a very good picture; it was always fuzzy and used to go into lines. We were quite happy with it since we did not know anything different. One day, we discovered that it needed an outside aerial! Suddenly we found that we could get clear and distinct pictures. Our enjoyment was transformed. Life without a relationship with God through Jesus Christ is like the television without the aerial. Some people seem quite happy, because they don't realise that there is something better. Once we have experienced a relationship with God the purpose and meaning of life should become clear. We see things that we have never seen, and it would be foolish to want to return to the old life. We understand why we were made.

REALITY IN A CONFUSED WORLD

Sometimes people say, 'It does not matter what you believe so long as you are sincere.' But it is possible to be sincerely wrong. Adolf Hitler was sincerely wrong. His beliefs destroyed the lives of millions of people. The Yorkshire Ripper believed that he was doing God's will when he killed prostitutes. He too was sincerely wrong. His beliefs affected his behaviour. These are extreme examples, but they make the point that it matters a great deal what we believe, because what we believe will dictate how we live.

Other people's response to a Christian may be, 'It's great for you, but it is not for me.' This is not a logical position. If Christianity is true, it is of vital importance to every one of us. If it is not true, Christians are deluded and it is not 'great for us' – it is very sad

and the sooner we are put right the better. As the writer and scholar C. S. Lewis put it, 'Christianity is a statement which, if false, is of *no* importance, and, if true, of infinite importance. The one thing it cannot be is moderately important.'[4]

Is it true? Is there any evidence? Jesus said, 'I am . . . the truth.' Is there any evidence to support his claim? These are some of the questions we will be looking at later in the book. The linchpin of Christianity is the resurrection of Jesus Christ and for that there is ample evidence. Professor Thomas Arnold, who as the headmaster of Rugby School revolutionised the concept of English education, was appointed to the chair of modern history at Oxford University. He was certainly a man well acquainted with the value of evidence in determining historical facts, and he said:

> I have been used for many years to studying the histories of other times, and to examining and weighing the evidence of those who have written about them, and I know of no one fact in the history of mankind which is proved by better and fuller evidence of every sort, to the understanding of a fair inquirer, than the great sign which God has given us that Christ died and rose again from the dead.

As we shall see later in the book, there is a great deal of evidence that Christianity is true. Yet, when Jesus said, 'I am . . . the truth,' he meant more than intellectual truth. The original word for truth carries with it the notion of doing or experiencing the truth. There is something more than an intellectual acceptance of the truth of Christianity, and that is the knowledge of Jesus Christ who is *the* truth.

Suppose that before I met my wife Pippa I had read a book about her. Then, after I had finished reading the book I thought, 'This sounds like a wonderful woman. This is the person I want to marry.' There would be a big difference in my state of mind then –

intellectually convinced that she was a wonderful person – and my state of mind now after the experience of many years of marriage from which I can say, 'I know she is a wonderful person.' When a Christian says, in relation to his faith, 'I know Jesus is the truth,' he does not mean only that he knows intellectually that he is the truth, but that he has experienced Jesus as the truth. As we come into relationship with the One who is the truth, our perceptions change, and we begin to understand the truth about the world around us.

LIFE IN A DARK WORLD

Jesus said, 'I am . . . the life.' In Jesus we find life where previously there has been guilt, addiction, fear and the prospect of death. It is true that all of us were created in the image of God and there is, therefore, something noble about all human beings. However, we are all also fallen – we are born with a propensity to do evil. In every human being the image of God has been to a greater or lesser extent tarnished, and in some cases almost eradicated, by sin. Good and bad, strength and weakness coexist in all human beings. Alexander Solzhenitsyn, the Russian writer, said, 'The line separating good and evil passes, not through states, nor through classes, nor between political parties . . . but right through every human heart and through all human hearts.'

I used to think I was a 'nice' person – because I didn't rob banks or commit other serious crimes. Only when I began to see my life alongside the life of Jesus Christ did I realise how much there was wrong. Many others have had this same experience. C. S. Lewis wrote: 'For the first time I examined myself with a seriously practical purpose. And there I found what appalled me; a zoo of lusts, a bedlam of ambitions, a nursery of fears, a harem of fondled hatreds. My name was Legion.'[5]

We all need forgiveness and only in Christ can it be found. Marghanita Laski, the humanist, debating on television with a Christian, made an amazing confession. She said, 'What I envy most about you Christians is your forgiveness.' Then she added, rather pathetically, 'I have no one to forgive me.'

What Jesus did when he was crucified for us was to pay the penalty for all the things that we have done wrong. We will look at this subject in Chapter 4 in more detail. We will see that he died to remove our guilt, to set us free from addiction, fear and ultimately death. He died instead of us.

If you or I had been the only person in the world, Jesus Christ would have died instead of us to remove our guilt. When our guilt is removed we have a new life.

Jesus not only died for us, he also rose again from the dead for us. In this act he defeated death. Most rational people are aware of the inevitability of death, although today some people make bizarre attempts to avoid it. *The Church of England Newspaper* described one such attempt:

In 1960 Californian millionaire James McGill died. He left detailed instructions that his body should be preserved and frozen in the hope that one day scientists might discover a cure for the disease that killed him. There are hundreds of people in Southern California who have put hopes of one day living again in this process which freezes and preserves human bodies. The latest development in Cryonics technology is called neuro-suspension which preserves just the human head. One reason why it is becoming popular is that it is much cheaper than preserving and maintaining a whole body. It reminds me of Woody Allen in *Sleeper*, where he preserved his nose.[6]

Such attempts to avoid the inevitability of death are plainly absurd and, indeed, unnecessary. Jesus came to bring us 'eternal life'. Eternal life is a quality of life which comes from living in a relationship with God and Jesus Christ (John 17:3). Jesus never promised anyone an easy life, but he promised fullness of life (John 10:10). This new quality of life starts now and goes on into eternity. Our time on earth is relatively short, but eternity is vast. Through Jesus, who said, 'I am . . . the life' we can not only enjoy fullness of life here, but we can be sure that it will never end.

Christianity is not boring; it is about living life to the full. It is not untrue; it is *the* truth. It is not irrelevant; it transforms the whole of our lives. The theologian and philosopher Paul Tillich described the human condition as one that always involves three fears: fear about meaninglessness, fear about death and fear about guilt. Jesus Christ meets each of these fears head on. He is vital to every one of us because he is 'the way, and the truth, and the life'.

2

Who Is Jesus?

A missionary working among children in the Middle East was driving her jeep down a road when she ran out of petrol. She had no jerrycan in her car. All she could find was a potty. She walked a mile down the road to the nearest petrol station and filled the potty with petrol. As she was pouring the petrol into the tank, a very large Cadillac drew up occupied by wealthy oil sheikhs. They were absolutely fascinated at seeing her pouring the contents of the potty into the jeep. One of them opened the window and said, 'Excuse me! My friend and I, although we do not share your religion, greatly admire your faith!'

Some people see becoming a Christian as a blind leap of faith – the type of faith that would be needed to expect a car to run on the usual contents of a potty. There is indeed a step of faith required. However, it is not a blind leap of faith, but a step of faith based on firm historical evidence. In this chapter I want to examine some of that historical evidence.

I am told that in a communist Russian dictionary Jesus is described as 'a mythical figure who never existed'. No serious historian could maintain that position today. There is a great deal of evidence for Jesus' existence. This comes not only from the

Gospels and other Christian writings, but also from non-Christian sources. For example, the Roman historians Tacitus (directly) and Suetonius (indirectly) both write about him. The Jewish historian Josephus, born in AD 37, describes Jesus and his followers thus:

> Now there was about this time, Jesus, a wise man, if it be lawful to call him a man, for he was a doer of wonderful works – a teacher of such men as receive the truth with pleasure. He drew over to him both many of the Jews, and many of the Gentiles. He was [the] Christ; and when Pilate, at the suggestion of the principal men amongst us, had condemned him to the cross, those that loved him at first did not forsake him, for he appeared to them alive again the third day, as the divine prophets had foretold these and ten thousand other wonderful things concerning him; and the tribe of Christians so named after him, are not extinct at this day.[7]

So there is evidence outside the New Testament for the existence of Jesus. Furthermore, the evidence in the New Testament is very strong. Sometimes people say, 'The New Testament was written a long time ago. How do we know that what they wrote down has not been changed over the years?'

The answer is that we do know, very accurately through the science of textual criticism, what the New Testament writers wrote. Essentially the more texts we have, the less doubt there is about the original. The late Professor F. F. Bruce (who was Rylands professor of biblical criticism and exegesis at the University of Manchester) shows in his book *Are the New Testament Documents Reliable?* how wealthy the New Testament is in manuscript attestation by comparing its texts with other historical works.

The table below summarises the facts and shows the extent of the New Testament evidence.

Work	When written	Earliest copy	Time span (yrs)	No. of copies
Herodotus	488-428 BC	AD 900	1,300	8
Thucydides	c. 460-400 BC	C. AD 900	1,300	8
Tacitus	AD 100	1100	1,000	20
Caesar's *Gallic War*	58-50 BC	AD 900	950	9-10
Livy's *Roman History*	59 BC-AD 17	AD 900	900	20
New Testament	AD 40-100	AD 130 (full manuscripts AD 350)	300	5,000+ Greek 10,000 Latin 9,300 others

F. F. Bruce points out that for Caesar's *Gallic War* we have nine or ten copies and the oldest was written some 900 years later than Caesar's day. For Livy's *Roman History* we have not more than twenty copies, the earliest of which comes from around AD 900. Of the fourteen books of the histories of Tacitus only twenty copies survive; of the sixteen books of his *Annals*, ten portions of his two great historical works depend entirely on two manuscripts, one of the ninth century and one of the eleventh century. The history of Thucydides is known almost entirely from eight manuscripts belonging to c. AD 900. The same is true of the history of Herodotus. Yet no classical scholar doubts the authenticity of these works, in spite of the large time gap and the relatively small number of manuscripts.

As regards the New Testament we have a great wealth of material. The New Testament was probably written between AD 40 and AD 100. We have excellent full manuscripts of the whole New Testament dating from as early as AD 350 (a time span of only 300 years), papyri containing most of the New Testament writings dating from the third century and even a fragment of John's Gospel dating from about AD 130. There are over 5,000 Greek manuscripts, over 10,000 Latin manuscripts and 9,300 other manuscripts, as well as over 36,000 citings in the writings of the early church fathers. As one of the greatest ever textual critics, F. J. A. Hort, said, 'In the variety and fullness of the evidence on which it rests, the text of the New Testament stands absolutely and unapproachably alone among ancient prose writings.'[8]

F. F. Bruce summarises the evidence by quoting Sir Frederic Kenyon, a leading scholar in this area:

> The interval then between the dates of original composition and the earliest extant evidence becomes so small as to be in fact negligible, and the last foundation for any doubt that the Scriptures have come down to us substantially as they were written has now been removed. Both the *authenticity* and the *general integrity* of the books of the New Testament may be regarded as finally established.[9]

We know from evidence outside and inside the New Testament that Jesus existed.[10] But who is he? I heard Martin Scorsese say on television that he made the film *The Last Temptation of Christ* in order to show that Jesus was a real human being. Yet that is not the issue at the moment. Few people today would doubt that Jesus was fully human. He had a human body; he was sometimes tired (John 4:6) and hungry (Matthew 4:2). He had human emotions; he was angry (Mark 11:15-17), he loved (Mark 10:21) and he was sad (John 11:35). He had human experiences; he was tempted (Mark 1:13), he learned (Luke 2:52), he worked (Mark 6:3) and he obeyed his parents (Luke 2:51).

What many say today is that Jesus was *only* a human being – albeit a great religious teacher. The comedian Billy Connolly spoke for many when he said, 'I can't believe in Christianity, but I think Jesus was a wonderful man.'

What evidence is there to suggest that Jesus was more than just a wonderful man or a great moral teacher? The answer, as we shall see, is that there is a great deal of evidence. This evidence supports the Christian contention that Jesus was and is the unique Son of God. Indeed, he is God the Son, the second Person of the Trinity.

WHAT DID HE SAY ABOUT HIMSELF?

Some people say, 'Jesus never claimed to be God.' Indeed, it is true that Jesus did not go round saying the words, 'I am God.' Yet when one looks at all he taught and claimed, there is little doubt that he was conscious of being a person whose identity was God.

Teaching centred on himself

One of the fascinating things about Jesus is that so much of his teaching was centred on himself. He said to people, in effect, 'If you want to have a relationship with God you need to come to me' (see John 14:6). It is through a relationship with him that we encounter God.

There is a hunger deep within the human heart. The leading psychologists of the twentieth century have all recognised this. Freud said, 'People are hungry for love.' Jung said, 'People are hungry for security.' Adler said, 'People are hungry for significance.' Jesus said, 'I am the bread of life' (John 6:35). In other words, 'If you want your hunger satisfied, come to me.'

Many people are walking in darkness, depression, disillusionment and despair. They are looking for direction. Jesus said, 'I am the light of the world. Whoever follows me will never walk in darkness, but will have the light of life' (John 8:12). Someone said to me after they had become a Christian, 'It was as if

25

the light had suddenly been turned on and I could see things for the first time.'

Many are fearful of death. One woman said to me that sometimes she couldn't sleep and that she would wake up in a cold sweat, frightened about death, because she didn't know what was going to happen when she died. Jesus said, 'I am the resurrection and the life. Those who believe in me will live, even though they die; and whoever lives and believes in me will never die' (John 11:25-26).

So many are burdened by worries, anxieties, fears and guilt. Jesus said, 'Come to me, all you who are weary and burdened, and I will give you rest' (Matthew 11:28). They are not sure how to run their lives or who they should follow. I can remember, before I was a Christian, that I would be impressed by someone and want to be like them, and then by a different person and follow them. Jesus said, 'Follow *me*' (Mark 1:17).

He said to receive him was to receive God (Matthew 10:40), to welcome him was to welcome God (Mark 9:37) and to have seen him was to have seen God (John 14:9). A child once drew a picture and her mother asked what she was doing. The child said, 'I am drawing a picture of God.' The mother said, 'Don't be silly. You can't draw a picture of God. No one knows what God looks like.' The child replied, 'Well, they will do by the time I have finished!'

Jesus said in effect, 'If you want to know what God looks like, look at me.'

Indirect claims

Jesus said a number of things which, although not direct claims to be God, show that he regarded himself as being in the same position as God, as we will see in the examples which follow.

Jesus' claim to be able to forgive sins is well known. For example, on one occasion he said to a man who was paralysed, 'Son, your sins are forgiven' (Mark 2:5). The reaction of the religious leaders was, 'Why does this fellow talk like that? He's blaspheming! Who can forgive sins but God alone?' Jesus went on to prove that he did have the authority to forgive sins by healing the paralysed man. This claim to be able to forgive sins is indeed an astonishing claim.

C. S. Lewis puts it well when he says in his book *Mere Christianity*:

One part of the claim tends to slip past us unnoticed because we have heard it so often that we no longer see what it amounts to. I mean the claim to forgive sins: any sins. Now unless the speaker is God, this is really so preposterous as to be comic. We can all understand how a man forgives offences against himself. You tread on my toes and I forgive you, you steal my money and I forgive you. But what should we make of a man, himself unrobbed and untrodden on, who announced that he forgave you for treading on other men's toes and stealing other men's money? Asinine fatuity is the kindest description we should give of his conduct. Yet this is what Jesus did. He told people that their sins were forgiven, and never waited to consult all the other people whom their sins had undoubtedly injured. He unhesitatingly behaved as if He was the party chiefly concerned, the person chiefly offended in all offences. This makes sense only if He really was the God whose laws are broken and whose love is wounded in every sin. In the mouth of any speaker who is not God, these words would imply what I can only

27

regard as a silliness and conceit unrivalled by any other character in history.[11]

Another extraordinary claim that Jesus made was that one day he would judge the world (Matthew 25:31-32). He said he would return and 'sit on his throne in heavenly glory' (v. 31). All the nations would be gathered before him. He would pass judgement on them. Some would receive an inheritance prepared for them since the creation of the world and eternal life, but others would suffer the punishment of being separated from him for ever.

Jesus said he would decide what happens to every one of us at the end of time. Not only would he be the Judge, he would also be the criterion of judgement. What happens to us on the Day of Judgement depends on how we respond to Jesus in this life (Matthew 25:40, 45). Suppose the vicar of your local church were to get up in the pulpit and say, 'On the Day of Judgement you will all appear before me and I will decide your eternal destiny. What happens to you will depend on how you've treated me and my followers.' For a mere human being to make such a claim would be preposterous. Here we have another indirect claim to have the identity of Almighty God.

Direct claims

When the question was put to him, 'Are you the Christ, the Son of the Blessed One?' Jesus said, 'I am . . . and you will see the Son of Man sitting at the right hand of the Mighty One and coming on the clouds of heaven.' The high priest tore his clothes. 'Why do we need any more witnesses?' he asked. 'You have heard the blasphemy. What do you think?' (Mark 14:61-64). In this account it appears Jesus was condemned to death for the assertion he made about himself. A claim tantamount to a claim to be God was blasphemy in Jewish eyes, worthy of death.

On one occasion, when the Jews started to stone Jesus, he asked, 'Why are you stoning me?' They replied that they were stoning him for blasphemy 'because you, a mere man, *claim to be God*' (John 10:33, italics mine). His enemies clearly thought that this was exactly what he was declaring.

When Thomas, one of his disciples, knelt down before Jesus and said, 'My Lord and my God' (John 20:28), Jesus didn't turn to him and say, 'No, no, don't say that; I am not God.' He said, 'Because you have seen me, you have believed; blessed are those who have not seen and yet have believed' (John 20:29). He rebuked Thomas for being so slow to get the point.

If somebody makes claims like these they need to be tested. There are all sorts of people who make all kinds of claims. The mere fact that somebody claims to be someone does not mean that they are right. There are many people, some in psychiatric hospitals, who are deluded. They think they are Napoleon or the Pope, but they are not.

So how can we test people's claims? Jesus claimed to be the unique Son of God – God made flesh. There are three logical possibilities. If the claims were untrue, either he knew they were untrue – in which case he was an imposter, and an evil one at that. That is the first possibility. Or he did not know – in which case he was deluded; indeed, he was insane. That is the second possibility. The third possibility is that the claims were true.

C. S. Lewis pointed out that: 'A man who was merely a man and said the sort of things Jesus said would not be a great moral teacher.' He would either be insane or else he would be 'the Devil of Hell'. 'You must make your choice,' he writes. Either Jesus was, and is, the Son of God or else he was insane or evil but, C. S. Lewis goes on, 'let us not come up with any patronising nonsense about His being a great human teacher. He has not left that open to us. He did not intend to.'[12]

WHAT EVIDENCE IS THERE TO SUPPORT WHAT HE SAID?

In order to assess which of these three possibilities is right we need to examine the evidence we have about his life.

His teaching

The teaching of Jesus is widely acknowledged to be the greatest teaching that has ever fallen from human lips. Some who are not Christians say, 'I love the Sermon on the Mount; I live by it.' (If they were to read it they would realise that this is easier to say than to do, but they acknowledge that the Sermon on the Mount is great teaching.)

Bernard Ramm, an American professor of theology, said this about the teachings of Jesus:

> They are read more, quoted more, loved more, believed more, and translated more because they are the greatest words ever spoken . . . Their greatness lies in the pure lucid spirituality in dealing clearly, definitively, and authoritatively with the greatest problems that throb in the human breast . . . No other man's words have the appeal of Jesus' words because no other man can answer these fundamental human questions as Jesus answered them. They are the kind of words and the kind of answers we would expect God to give.[13]

His teaching is the foundation of our entire civilisation in the West. Many of the laws in this country were originally based on the teachings of Jesus. We are making progress in virtually every field of science and technology. We travel faster and know more, and yet in nearly 2,000 years no one has improved on the moral teaching of Jesus Christ. Could that teaching really have come from someone evil or insane?

30

His works

Jesus said that the miracles he performed were in themselves evidence that 'the Father is in me, and I in the Father' (John 10:38).

Jesus must have been the most extraordinary person to have around. Sometimes people say that Christianity is boring. Well, it was not boring being with Jesus.

When he went to a party, he turned water into wine (John 2:1-11). He received one man's picnic and multiplied it so that it could feed thousands (Mark 6:30-44). He had control over the elements and could speak to the wind and the waves and thereby stop a storm (Mark 4:35-41). He carried out the most remarkable healings: opening blind eyes, causing the deaf and dumb to hear and speak and enabling the paralysed to walk again. When he visited a hospital a man who had been an invalid for thirty-eight years was able to pick up his bed and walk (John 5:1-9). He set people free from evil forces which had dominated their lives. On occasions, he even brought those who had died back to life (John 11:38-44).

Yet it was not just his miracles that made his work so impressive. It was his love, especially for the loveless (such as the lepers and the prostitutes), which seemed to motivate all that he did. The supreme demonstration of his love for us was shown on the cross (which, as we shall see in the next chapter, was the chief reason for his coming to earth). When they tortured him and nailed him to the cross he said, 'Father, forgive them, for they do not know what they are doing' (Luke 22:34). Surely these are not the activities of an evil or deluded man?

His character

The character of Jesus has impressed millions who would not call themselves Christians. For example, Bernard Levin wrote of Jesus:

31

Is not the nature of Christ, in the words of the New Testament, enough to pierce to the soul anyone with a soul to be pierced? . . . he still looms over the world, his message still clear, his pity still infinite, his consolation still effective, his words still full of glory, wisdom and love.[14]

One of my favourite descriptions of the character of Jesus comes from the former Lord Chancellor, Lord Hailsham. In his autobiographical *The Door Wherein I Went* he describes how the person of Jesus came alive to him when he was at university:

The first thing we must learn about him is that we should have been absolutely entranced by his company. Jesus was irresistibly attractive as a man . . . What they crucified was a young man, vital, full of life and the joy of it, the Lord of life itself, and even more the Lord of laughter, someone so utterly attractive that people followed him for the sheer fun of it . . . the Twentieth Century needs to recapture the vision of this glorious and happy man whose mere presence filled his companions with delight. No pale Galilean he, but a veritable Pied Piper of Hamelin who would have the children laughing all round him and squealing with pleasure and joy as he picked them up.[15]

Here was someone who exemplified supreme unselfishness but never self-pity; humility but not weakness; joy but never at another's expense; kindness but not indulgence. He was a person in whom even his enemies could find no fault and where friends who knew him well said he was without sin. Surely no one could suggest that a man with a character like that was evil or unbalanced?

His fulfilment of Old Testament prophecy
Wilbur Smith, the American writer on theological topics, said:

The ancient world had many different devices for determining the future, known as divination, but not in the entire gamut of Greek and

Latin literature, even though they used the words prophet and prophecy, can we find any real specific prophecy of a great historic event to come in the distant future, nor any prophecy of a Saviour to arrive in the human race . . . Mohammedanism cannot point to any prophecies of the coming of Mohammed uttered hundreds of years before his birth. Neither can the founders of any cult in this country rightly identify any ancient text specifically foretelling their appearance.[16]

Yet in the case of Jesus, he fulfilled over 300 prophecies (spoken by different voices over 500 years), including twenty-nine major prophecies fulfilled in a single day – the day he died. Although some of these prophecies may have found fulfilment at one level in the prophet's own day, they found their ultimate fulfilment in Jesus Christ.

I suppose it could be suggested that Jesus was a clever con man who deliberately set out to fulfil these prophecies in order to show that he was the Messiah foretold in the Old Testament.

The problem with that suggestion is, first, the sheer number of them would have made it extremely difficult. Secondly, humanly speaking he had no control over many of the events. For example, the exact manner of his death was foretold in the Old Testament (Isaiah 53), the place of his burial and even the place of his birth (Micah 5:2). Suppose Jesus had been a con man wanting to fulfil all these prophecies. It would have been a bit late by the time he discovered the place in which he was supposed to have been born!

His resurrection

The physical resurrection from the dead of Jesus Christ is the cornerstone of Christianity. But what is the evidence that it really happened? I want to summarise the evidence under four main headings.

1. His absence from the tomb. Many theories have been put forward to explain the fact that Jesus' body was absent from the tomb on the first Easter Day, but none of them is very convincing.

First, it has been suggested that Jesus did not die on the cross. There was once a headline in a major UK newspaper: 'Jesus did not die on the cross'. Dr Trevor Lloyd Davies claimed that Jesus was still alive when he was taken from the cross and that he later recovered.

Jesus had undergone a Roman flogging, under which many died. He had been nailed to a cross for six hours. Could a man in this condition push away a stone weighing probably a ton and a half? The soldiers were clearly convinced that he was dead or they would not have taken his body down. If they had allowed a prisoner to escape, they would have been liable to the death penalty.

Furthermore, when the soldiers discovered that Jesus was already dead, 'one of the soldiers pierced Jesus' side with a spear, bringing a sudden flow of blood and water' (John 19:34). This appears to be the separation of clot and serum which we know today is strong medical evidence that Jesus was dead. John did not write it for that reason; he would not have possessed that knowledge, which makes it even more powerful evidence that Jesus was indeed dead.

Secondly, it has been argued that the disciples stole the body. Some have suggested that the disciples stole the body and began a rumour that Jesus had risen from the dead. Leaving aside the fact that the tomb was guarded, this theory is psychologically improbable. The disciples were depressed and disillusioned at the time of Jesus' death. It would have needed something extraordinary to transform the apostle Peter into the man who preached at Pentecost when 3,000 people were converted.

In addition, when one considers how much they had to suffer for what they believed (floggings, torture, and for some even death), it seems inconceivable that they would be prepared to endure all that for something they knew to be untrue. I have a friend who was a scientist at Cambridge University who became a Christian because, as he examined the evidence, he was convinced that the disciples would not have been willing to die for what they knew to be a lie.

Thirdly, some have said that the authorities stole the body. This seems the least probable theory of all. If the authorities had stolen the body, why did they not produce it when they were trying to quash the rumour that Jesus had risen from the dead?

Perhaps the most fascinating piece of evidence relating to Jesus' absence from the tomb is John's description of the grave-clothes. In a way, the 'empty tomb' is a misnomer. When Peter and John went to the tomb they saw the grave-clothes which were, as the Christian apologist Josh McDowell put it in *The Resurrection Factor*, 'like the empty chrysalis of a caterpillar's cocoon' – when the butterfly has emerged.[17] It was as if Jesus had simply passed through the grave-clothes. Not surprisingly, John 'saw and believed' (John 20:8).

2. His appearances to the disciples. Were these hallucinations? The Concise Oxford Dictionary describes a hallucination as an 'apparent perception of an external object not actually present'. Hallucinations normally occur in highly strung, highly imaginative and very nervous people, or in people who are sick or on drugs. The disciples do not fit into any of these categories. Burly fishermen, tax collectors and sceptics like Thomas are unlikely to hallucinate. People who hallucinate would be unlikely suddenly to stop doing so. Jesus appeared to his disciples on eleven different occasions over a period of six weeks. The number of occasions and the sudden cessation make the hallucination theory highly improbable.

Furthermore, over 500 people saw the risen Jesus. It is possible for one person to hallucinate. Maybe it is possible for two or three people to share the same hallucination. But is it likely that 500 people would all share the same hallucination?

Finally, hallucinations are subjective. There is no objective reality – it is like seeing a ghost. Jesus could be touched, he ate a piece of broiled fish (Luke 24:42-43) and on one occasion he cooked breakfast for the disciples (John 21:1-14). Peter says, '[They] ate and drank with him after he rose from the dead' (Acts 10:41). He held long conversations with them, teaching them many things about the kingdom of God (Acts 1:3).

3. The immediate effect. The fact of Jesus rising from the dead, as one would expect, had a dramatic impact on the world. The church was born and grew at a tremendous rate. As Michael Green, writer of many popular and scholarly works, puts it:

> [The] church . . . beginning from a handful of uneducated fishermen and tax gatherers, swept across the whole known world in the next three hundred years. It is a perfectly amazing story of peaceful revolution that has no parallel in the history of the world. It came about because Christians were able to say to inquirers: 'Jesus did not only die for you. He is alive! You can meet him and discover for yourself the reality we are talking about!' They did, and joined the church and the church, born from that Easter grave, spread everywhere.[18]

4. Christian experience. Countless millions of people down the ages have experienced the risen Jesus Christ. They consist of people of every colour, race, tribe, continent and nationality. They come from different economic, social and intellectual backgrounds. Yet they all unite in a common experience of the risen Jesus Christ. Wilson Carlile, who was head of the Church Army in this country, was preaching at Hyde Park Corner. He was saying, 'Jesus Christ is alive today.' One of the hecklers shouted out to him, 'How do you know?' Wilson Carlile replied, 'Because I was speaking to him for half an hour this morning!'

Millions of Christians all over the world today are experiencing a relationship with the risen Jesus Christ. Over the last eighteen years I too have found in my experience that Jesus Christ is alive today. I have experienced his love, his power and the reality of a relationship which convinces me that he really is alive.

The evidence that Jesus rose from the dead is very extensive. A former Chief Justice of England, Lord Darling, said, 'In its favour as living truth there exists such overwhelming evidence, positive and negative, factual and circumstantial, that no intelligent jury in the world could fail to bring in a verdict that the resurrection story is true.'[19]

We saw when we looked earlier in the chapter at what Jesus said about himself that there were only three realistic possibilities – either he was and is the Son of God, or else deluded or something more sinister. When one looks at the evidence it does not make sense to say that he was insane or evil. The whole weight of his teaching, his works, his character, his fulfilment of Old Testament prophecy and his conquest of death make those suggestions absurd, illogical and unbelievable. On the other hand, they lend the strongest possible support to Jesus' own consciousness of being a man whose identity was God.

In conclusion, as C. S. Lewis pointed out: 'We are faced then with a frightening alternative.' Either Jesus was (and is) exactly what he said, or else he was insane or something worse. To C. S. Lewis it seemed clear that he could have been neither insane nor evil and thus he concludes, 'However strange or terrifying or unlikely it may seem, I have to accept the view that he was and is God.'[20]

3

Why Did Jesus Die?

Many people today go around with a cross on their earrings, bracelet or necklace. We are so used to seeing this that we are not shocked by it. We might be if we saw someone wearing a gallows or an electric chair on a chain; but the cross was just as much a form of execution. Indeed, it was one of the cruellest forms of execution known to humankind. It was abolished in AD 315 because even the Romans considered it too inhumane.

Yet the cross has always been regarded as the symbol of the Christian faith. A high proportion of the Gospels is about the death of Jesus. Much of the rest of the New Testament is concerned with explaining what happened on the cross. The central service of the church, the Communion service, centres on the broken body and shed blood of Jesus. Churches are often built in the shape of a cross. When the apostle Paul went to Corinth he said, 'I resolved to know nothing while I was with you except Jesus Christ and him crucified' (1 Corinthians 2:2). Most leaders who have influenced nations or even changed the world, are remembered for the impact of their lives. Jesus, who more than any other person changed the face of world history, is remembered not so much for his life but for his death.

Why is there such concentration on the death of Jesus? What is the difference between his death and the death of Socrates, or one of the martyrs, or war heroes? What did it achieve? What does it mean when the New Testament says he died 'for our sins'? Why did he die? The answer in a nutshell is 'because God loves you'. 'The whole Bible,' St Augustine observed, 'does nothing but tell of God's love.'[21] Raniero Cantalamessa, preacher to the Pope, said, 'The love of God is the answer to all the "whys" in the Bible.' It is because 'God so loved the world' that he sent his one and only Son to die for us so that 'whoever believes in him shall not perish but have eternal life' (John 3:16).

THE PROBLEM

Sometimes people say, 'I have no need for Christianity.' They say something along the lines of, 'I am quite happy, my life is full and I try to be nice to other people and lead a good life.' In order to understand why Jesus died we have to go back and look at the greatest problem which confronts every person.

If we are honest, we would all have to admit that we do things which we know are wrong. Paul wrote: 'All have sinned and fall short of the glory of God' (Romans 3:23). In other words, relative to God's standards we all fall a long way short. If we compare ourselves to armed robbers or child molesters or even our neighbours, we may think we come off quite well. But when we compare ourselves to Jesus Christ, we see how far short we fall. Somerset Maugham once said, 'If I wrote down every thought I have ever thought and every deed I have ever done, men would call me a monster of depravity.'

The essence of sin is a rebellion against God – our ignoring God in the sense of behaving as if he doesn't exist (Genesis 3) with the result that we are cut off from him. Like the Prodigal Son (Luke 15), we find ourselves far from our Father's home and with our lives in a mess. Sometimes people say, 'If we are all in the same boat, does it really matter?' The answer is that it does matter because of the consequences of sin in our lives, which can be summarised under four headings.

The pollution of sin

Jesus said, 'What comes out of you is what makes you "unclean". For from within, out of your hearts, come evil thoughts, sexual immorality, theft, murder, adultery, greed, malice, deceit, lewdness, envy, slander, arrogance and folly. All these evils come from inside and make you "unclean"' (Mark 7:20-23). These things pollute our lives.

You may say, 'I do not do most of these things.' But one of them alone is enough to mess up our lives. We might wish the Ten Commandments were like an examination paper in which we only have to 'attempt any three' of them. The New Testament says that if we break *any* part of the Law we are guilty of breaking all of it (James 2:10). It is not possible, for example, to have a 'reasonably clean' driving licence. Either it is clean or it is not. One driving offence stops it from being a clean licence. So it is with us. One offence makes our lives unclean.

The power of sin

The things we do wrong have an addictive power. Jesus said, 'Everyone who sins is a slave to sin' (John 8:34). It is easier to see this in some areas of our wrong-doing than with others. For example, it is well-known that if someone takes a hard drug like heroin, it soon becomes an addiction.

It is also possible to be addicted to bad temper, envy, arrogance, pride, selfishness, slander or sexual immorality. We can become addicted to patterns of thought or behaviour which, on our own, we cannot break. This is the slavery which Jesus spoke about and which has a destructive power in our lives.

Bishop J. C. Ryle, a former bishop of Liverpool, once wrote:

> Each and all [sins] have crowds of unhappy prisoners bound hand and foot in their chains . . . The wretched prisoners . . . boast sometimes that they are eminently free . . . There is no slavery like this. Sin is indeed the hardest of all task-masters. Misery and disappointment by the way, despair and hell in the end – these are the only wages that sin pays to its servants.[22]

The penalty for sin

There is something in human nature which cries out for justice. When we see children molested, old people attacked in their homes or babies battered, we long for the people who have done these things to be caught and punished. Often our motives may be mixed: there may be an element of revenge. But there is such a thing as justifiable anger. We are right to feel that sins should be punished; that people who do such things should not get away with it.

It is not just other people's sins that deserve punishment; it is our own as well. One day we will all be subject to the judgement of God. St Paul tells us that 'the wages of sin is death' (Romans 6:23).

The partition of sin

The death Paul speaks of is not only physical. It is a spiritual death which results in eternal isolation from God. This cutting off from God begins now. The prophet Isaiah proclaimed, 'Surely the arm of the Lord is not too short to save, nor his ear too dull to hear. But your iniquities have separated you from your God; your sins have hidden his face from you, so that he will not hear' (Isaiah 59:1-2). The things we do wrong cause this barrier.

THE SOLUTION

We all have a need to deal with the problem of sin in our lives. The greater our understanding of our need the more we will appreciate what God has done. The Lord Chancellor, Lord Mackay of Clashfern, wrote: 'The central theme of our faith is the sacrifice of himself by our Lord Jesus Christ on the cross for our sins. . . . The deeper our appreciation of our own need the greater will be our love for the Lord Jesus and, therefore, the more fervent our desire to serve him.'[23] The good news of Christianity is that God loves us and he did not leave us in the mess that we make of our own lives. He came to earth, in the person of his Son Jesus, to die instead of us (2 Corinthians 5:21; Galatians 3:13). This has been called the 'self-substitution of God'.[24] In the words of the apostle Peter, '*He* himself bore *our* sins in *his* body on the tree . . . by *his* wounds you have been healed' (1 Peter 2:24, italics mine).

On 31 July 1991 a remarkable event was celebrated. On the last day of July 1941 the Auschwitz sirens announced the escape of a prisoner. As a reprisal, ten of his fellow prisoners would die – a long, slow starvation, buried alive in a specially constructed, concrete bunker.

So all day, tortured by sun, hunger and fear, the men waited as the German commandant and his Gestapo assistant walked between the ranks to select, quite arbitrarily, the chosen ten. As the commandant pointed to one man, Francis Gajowniczek, he cried out in despair, 'My poor wife and children.' At that moment the unimpressive figure of a man with sunken eyes and round glasses in wire frames stepped out of line and took off his cap. 'What does this Polish pig want?' asked the commandant.

'I am a Catholic priest; I want to die for that man. I am old, he has a wife and children . . . I have no one,' said Father Maximilian Kolbe.

'Accepted,' retorted the commandant, and moved on.

That night, nine men and one priest went to the starvation bunker. Normally they would tear each other apart like cannibals. Not so this time. While they had strength, lying naked on the floor, the men prayed and sang hymns. After two weeks, three of the men and Father Maximilian were still alive. The bunker was required for others, so on 14 August, the remaining four were disposed of. At 12.50 pm, after two weeks in the starvation bunker and still conscious, the Polish priest was finally given an injection of phenol and died at the age of forty-seven.

On 10 October 1982 in St Peter's Square, Rome, Father Maximilian's death was put in its proper perspective. Present in the crowd of 150,000 was Francis Gajowniczek, his wife, his children, and his children's children – for indeed, many had been saved by that one man. The Pope describing Father Maximilian's death said, 'This was victory won over all the systems of contempt and hate in man – a victory like that won by our Lord Jesus Christ.'[25]

Jesus' death was, indeed, even more amazing because Jesus died, not just for one man, but for every single individual in the world.

Jesus came as our substitute. He endured crucifixion for us. Cicero described crucifixion as 'the most cruel and hideous of tortures'. Jesus was stripped and tied to a whipping post. He was flogged with four or five thongs of leather interwoven with sharp jagged bone and lead. Eusebius, the third-century church historian, described Roman flogging in these terms: the sufferer's 'veins were laid bare, and . . . the very muscles, sinews and bowels of the victim were open to exposure'. He was then taken to the Praetorium where a crown of thorns was thrust onto his head. He was mocked by a battalion of about 600 men and hit about the face and head. He was then forced to carry a heavy cross bar on his bleeding shoulders until he collapsed, and Simon of Cyrene was press-ganged into carrying it for him.

When they reached the site of crucifixion, he was again stripped naked. He was laid on the cross, and six-inch nails were driven into his forearms, just above the wrist. His knees were twisted sideways so that the ankles could be nailed between the tibia and the Achilles' tendon. He was lifted up on the cross which was then dropped into a socket in the ground. There he was left to hang in intense heat and unbearable thirst, exposed to the ridicule of the crowd. He hung there in unthinkable pain for six hours while his life slowly drained away.

Yet the worst part of his suffering was not the physical trauma of torture and crucifixion nor even the emotional pain of being rejected by the world and deserted by his friends, but the spiritual agony of being cut off from his Father for us – as he carried our sins.

Jesus' victory was total – he died not just for one person but for all of us – and it was also costly. In all four Gospels, we hear of Jesus' agony in the Garden of Gethsemane, alone, crying out to his Father, 'Abba, Father . . . take this cup from me. Yet not what I will, but what you will' (Mark 14:36).

Raniero Cantalamessa writes:

In the Bible the image of the cup almost always evokes the idea of God's wrath against sin. . . Wherever sin exists, God's judgment cannot but be focussed on it, otherwise God would reach a compromise with sin and the very distinction itself between good and evil would no longer exist. Now, Jesus in Gethsemane is. . . man 'made sin'. Christ, it is written, died 'for sinners'; he died in their place and not only in their favour. . . he is, therefore, 'responsible' for all, the guilty one before God! It is against him that God's wrath is 'revealed' and that is what 'drinking the cup' means.[26]

THE RESULT

Like a beautiful diamond the cross has many facets. On the cross, the powers of evil were disarmed (Colossians 2:15). Death and demonic powers were defeated. On the cross, God revealed his love for us. He showed that he is not a God who is aloof from suffering. He is 'the crucified God' (as the title of the book by the German theologian Jürgen Moltmann puts it). He has entered our world and knows and understands all about suffering. On the cross Jesus sets us an example of self-sacrificial love (1 Peter 2:21). Each of these aspects deserves a chapter of its own, which space does not allow. I want to concentrate here on four images that the New Testament uses to describe what Jesus did on the cross for us.[27] As John Stott, well-known author and Rector Emeritus of All Souls Langham Place, points out, each of them is taken from a different area of day-to-day life.

The first image comes from the *temple*. In the Old Testament, very careful laws were laid down as to how sins should be dealt with. There was a whole system of sacrifices which demonstrated the seriousness of sin and the need for cleansing from it.

In a typical case the sinner would take an animal. The animal was to be as near perfection as possible. The sinner would lay his hands on the animal and confess his sins. Thus the sins were seen to pass from the sinner to the animal which was then killed.

The writer of Hebrews points out that it is 'impossible for the blood of bulls and goats to take away sins' (Hebrews 10:4). It was only a picture or a 'shadow' (Hebrews 10:1). The reality came with the sacrifice of Jesus. Only the blood of Christ, our substitute, can take away our sin, because he alone was the perfect sacrifice since he alone lived a perfect life. His blood purifies us from all sin (1 John 1:7) and removes *the pollution of sin*.

The second image comes from *the market-place*. Debt is not a problem confined to the present day; it was a problem in the ancient world as well. If someone had serious debts, he might be forced to sell himself into slavery in order to pay them off. Suppose a man was standing in the market-place, offering himself as a slave. Someone might have pity on him and ask, 'How much do you owe?' The debtor might say, '10,000.' Suppose the customer offers to pay the 10,000 and then lets him go free. In doing so, he would be 'redeeming him' by paying a 'ransom price'.

In a similar way for us 'redemption . . . came by Jesus Christ' (Romans 3:24). Jesus by his death on the cross paid the ransom price (Mark 10:45). In this way, we are set free from the power of sin. This is true freedom. Jesus said, 'If the Son sets you free, you will be free indeed' (John 8:36). It is not that we never sin again, but that sin's hold over us is broken.

Billy Nolan was an alcoholic for thirty-five years. For twenty years he sat outside Holy Trinity Brompton drinking alcohol, begging for money. On 13 May 1990, he looked in the mirror and said, 'You're not the Billy Nolan I once knew.' To use his own expression, he asked the Lord Jesus Christ into his life and made a covenant with him that he would never drink alcohol again. He has not touched a drop since. His life is transformed. He radiates the love and joy of Christ. I once said to him, 'Billy, you look happy.' He replied, 'I am happy because I am free. Life is like a maze and at last I have found a way out through Jesus Christ.' Jesus' death on the cross made this freedom from *the power of sin* possible.

The third image comes from *the law court*. Paul says that through Christ's death 'we have been justified' (Romans 5:1). Justification is a legal term. If you went to court and were acquitted, you were justified. There is one illustration that particularly helped me to understand what this means.

Two people went through school and university together and developed a close friendship. Life went on and they went their different ways and lost contact. One went on to become a judge, while the other one went down and down and ended up a criminal. One day the criminal appeared before the judge. He had committed a crime to which he pleaded guilty. The judge recognised his old friend, and faced a dilemma. He was a judge so he had to be just; he couldn't let the man off. On the other hand, he didn't want to punish the man, because he loved him. So he told his friend that he would fine him the correct penalty for the offence. That is justice. Then he came down from his position as judge and he wrote a cheque for the amount of the fine. He gave it to his friend, saying that he would pay the penalty for him. That is love.

This is an illustration of what God has done for us. In his justice, he judges us because we are guilty, but then, in his love, he came down in the person of his Son Jesus Christ and paid the penalty for us. In this way he is both 'just' (in that he does not allow the guilty to go unpunished) and 'the one who justifies' – Romans 3:26 (in that by taking the penalty himself, in the person of his Son, he enables us to go free). He is both our Judge and our Saviour. It is not an innocent third party but God himself who saves us. In effect, he gives us a cheque and says we have a choice: do we want him to pay it for us or are we going to face the judgement of God for our own wrong-doing?

The illustration I have used is not an exact one for three reasons.

First, our plight is worse. The penalty we are facing is not just a fine, but death. Secondly, the relationship is closer. This is not just two friends: it is our Father in heaven who loves us more than any earthly parent loves their own child. Thirdly, the cost was greater: it cost God not money, but his one and only Son – who paid *the penalty of sin.*

The fourth image comes from *the home.* We saw that both the root and the result of sin were a broken relationship with God. The result of the cross is the possibility of a restored relationship with God. Paul says that '*God was* reconciling the world to himself *in Christ*' (2 Corinthians 5:19, italics mine). Some people caricature the New Testament teaching and suggest that God is unjust because he punished Jesus, an innocent party, instead of us. This is not what the New Testament says. Rather, Paul says, 'God was . . . in Christ.' He was himself the substitute in the person of his Son. He made it possible for us to be restored to a relationship with him. The *partition of sin* has been destroyed. What happened to the Prodigal Son can happen to us. We can come back to the Father and experience his love and blessing. The relationship is not only for this life: it is eternal. One day we will be with the Father in heaven – there we will be free, not only from the penalty of sin, the power of sin, the pollution of sin and the partition of sin, but also from the presence of sin. That is what God has made possible through his self-substitution on the cross.

God loves each one of us so much and longs to be in a relationship with us as a human parent longs to be in a relationship with each of their children. It is not just that Jesus died for everyone. He died for you and for me; it is very personal. Paul writes of 'the Son of God, who loved me and gave himself for me' (Galatians 2:20). If you had been the only person in the world, Jesus would have died for you. Once we see the cross in these personal terms, our lives will be transformed.

John Wimber, an American pastor and church leader, described how the cross became a personal reality to him:

After I had studied the Bible . . . for about three months I could have passed an elementary exam on the cross. I understood there is one God who could be known in three Persons. I understood Jesus is fully God and fully man and he died on the cross for the sins of the world. But I didn't understand that I was a sinner. I thought I was a good guy. I knew I messed up here and there but I didn't realise how serious my condition was.

But one evening around this time Carol [his wife] said, 'I think it's time to do something about all that we've been learning.' Then, as I looked on in utter amazement, she knelt down on the floor and started praying to what seemed to me to be the ceiling plaster. 'Oh God,' she said, 'I am sorry for my sin.'

I couldn't believe it. Carol was a better person than I, yet she thought she was a sinner. I could feel her pain and the depth of her prayers. Soon she was weeping and repeating, 'I am sorry for my sin.' There were six or seven people in the room, all with their eyes closed. I looked at them and then it hit me: *They've all prayed this prayer too!* I started sweating bullets. I thought I was going to die. The perspiration ran down my face and I thought, 'I'm not going to do this. This is dumb. I'm a good guy.' Then it struck me. Carol wasn't praying to the plaster; she was praying to a person, to a God who could hear her. In comparison to him she knew she was a sinner in need of forgiveness.

In a flash the cross made personal sense to me. Suddenly I knew something that I had never known before; I had hurt God's feelings. He loved me and in his love for me he sent Jesus. But I had turned away from that love; I had shunned it all of my life. I was a sinner, desperately in need of the cross.

Then I too was kneeling on the floor, sobbing, nose running, eyes watering, every square inch of my flesh perspiring profusely. I had this overwhelming sense that I was talking with someone who had been with me all of my life, but whom I failed to recognise. Like Carol, I began talking to the living God, telling him that I was a sinner but the only words I could say aloud were, 'Oh God, Oh God.'

I knew something revolutionary was going on inside of me. I thought, 'I hope this works, because I'm making a complete fool of myself.' Then the Lord brought to mind a man I had seen in Pershing Square in Los Angeles a number of years before. He was wearing a sign that said, 'I'm a fool for Christ. Whose fool are you?' I thought at the time, 'That's the most stupid thing I've ever seen.' But as I kneeled on the floor I realised the truth of the odd sign: the cross is foolishness 'to those who are perishing' (1 Corinthians 1:18). That night I knelt at the cross and believed in Jesus. I've been a fool for Christ ever since.[28]

4

How Can We Have Faith?

At the age of eighteen in many ways life could not have been better. I was halfway through my first year at university. I was having fun and every opportunity of life seemed open to me. Christianity had no appeal for me; indeed the reverse. I felt that if I became a Christian, life would become very boring. I imagined God wanted to stop all the fun and make me do all sorts of tedious religious things.

On the other hand, as I looked at the evidence for Christianity, I became convinced it was true. I thought the answer was to delay the decision, enjoy life now and become a Christian on my death-bed. Yet I knew I could not do that with integrity. Very reluctantly I gave my life to Christ.

What I had failed to realise is that Christianity is about a relationship with God – a God who loves us and wants the very best for us. I was, to use the title of C. S. Lewis' book about his own experience of Christ, 'surprised by joy'. Becoming a Christian was the start of the most exciting relationship. Indeed, it was the start of a new life. As Paul wrote, 'those who become Christians become new persons. They are not the same any more for the old is gone. A new life has begun' (2 Corinthians 5:17, *The New Living Bible*). I sometimes keep a note of what people say or write after they have just started the new life that Paul is speaking about. Here are two examples:

> I now have hope where previously there was only despair. I can forgive now, where before there was only coldness . . . God is so alive for me. I can feel him guiding me and the complete and utter loneliness which I have been feeling is gone. God is filling a deep, deep void.

> I felt like hugging everybody in the street . . . I cannot stop praying, I even missed my bus stop today because I was so busy praying on the top deck.

Experiences vary greatly. Some immediately know a difference. For others it is more gradual. What matters is not so much the experience as the fact that when we receive Christ, we become a child of God. It is the start of a new relationship. As the Apostle John writes, 'Yet to all who received him, to those who believed in his name, he gave the right to become children of God' (John 1:12).

Good parents want their children to be sure about their

relationship with them. In the same way, God wants us to be sure about our relationship with him. Many people are uncertain about whether they are Christians or not. I ask people at the end of Alpha courses to fill in questionnaires. One of the questions I ask is, 'Would you have described yourself as a Christian at the beginning of the course?' Here is a list of some of the answers:

'Yes, but without any real experience of a relationship with God.'

'Sort of.'

'Possibly yes/think so.'

'Not sure.'

'Probably.'

'Ish.'

'Yes – though looking back possibly no.'

'No, a semi-Christian.'

The New Testament makes it clear that it is possible for us to be sure that we are Christians and that we have eternal life. The Apostle John writes, 'I write these things to you who believe in the name of the Son of God so that you may *know* that you have eternal life' (1 John 5:13, italics mine).

Just as three legs support a camera tripod, our assurance of our relationship with God stands firmly based on the activity of all three members of the Trinity: the promises which the Father gives us in his word, the sacrifice of the Son for us on the cross and the assurance of the Spirit in our hearts. These can be summarised under three headings: the word of God, the work of Jesus and the witness of the Holy Spirit.

THE WORD OF GOD

If we were to rely only on our feelings we could never be sure about anything. Our feelings go up and down depending on all sorts of factors, such as the weather or what we have had for breakfast.

They can be changeable and even deceptive. The promises in the Bible, which is the word of God, do not change and are totally reliable.

There are many great promises in the Bible. A verse which I found helpful, especially at the beginning of my Christian life, is one which comes in the last book of the Bible. In a vision John sees Jesus speaking to seven different churches. To the church in Laodicea Jesus says: 'Here I am! I stand at the door and knock. If anyone hears my voice and opens the door, I will come in and eat with them, and they with me' (Revelation 3:20).

There are many ways of speaking about starting the new life of the Christian faith – 'becoming a Christian', 'giving our lives to Christ', 'receiving Christ', 'inviting Jesus into our lives', 'believing in him' and 'opening the door to Jesus' are some of the variations. All of them describe the same reality; that Jesus enters our lives by the Holy Spirit, as is pictured in this verse.

The Pre-Raphaelite artist, Holman Hunt (1827-1910), inspired by this verse painted *The Light of the World*. He painted three versions in all. One hangs in Keble College, Oxford; another version is in the Manchester City Art Gallery; the most famous toured the colonies in 1905-7 and was presented to St Paul's Cathedral in June 1908, where it still hangs. When the first version was shown it received generally poor reviews. Then, on 5 May 1854, John Ruskin, the artist and critic, wrote to *The Times* and explained the symbolism at length and brilliantly defended it as 'one of the very noblest works of sacred art ever produced in this or any other age'.

Jesus, the Light of the World, stands at a door, which is overgrown with ivy and weeds. The door clearly represents the door of someone's life. This person has never invited Jesus to come into his or her life. Jesus is standing at the door and knocking. He is awaiting a response. He wants to come in and be part of that person's life. Apparently, someone said to Holman Hunt that he had made a mistake. They told him, 'You have forgotten to paint a handle on the door.'

'Oh no,' replied Hunt, 'that is deliberate. There is only one handle and that is on the inside.'

In other words, we have to open the door to let Jesus into our lives. Jesus will never force his way in. He gives us the freedom to choose. It is up to us whether or not we open the door to him. If we do, he promises, 'I will come in and eat with them and they with me.' Eating together is a sign of the friendship which Jesus offers to all those who open the door of their lives to him.

Once we have invited Jesus to come in, he promises that he will never leave us. He says to his disciples, 'I am with you always' (Matthew 28:20). We may not always be in direct conversation with him, but he will always be there. If you are working in a room with a friend, you may not be talking to each other all the time, but you are nevertheless aware of each other's presence. This is how it is with the presence of Jesus. He is with us always.

This promise of the presence of Jesus with us is closely related to another marvellous promise which comes in the New Testament. Jesus promises to give his followers eternal life (John 10:28). As we have seen, 'eternal life' in the New Testament is a quality of life which comes from living in a relationship with God through Jesus Christ (John 17:3). It starts now, when we experience the fullness of life which Jesus came to bring (John 10:10). Yet it is not just in this life; it goes on into eternity.

The resurrection of Jesus from the dead has many implications. First, it assures us about the past, that what Jesus achieved on the cross was effective. 'The resurrection is not the reversal of a defeat, but the proclamation of a victory.'[29] Secondly, it assures us about the present. Jesus is alive. His power is with us, bringing us life in all its fullness. Thirdly, it assures us about the future. This life is not the end; there is life beyond the grave. History is not meaningless or cyclical; it is moving towards a glorious climax.

One day Jesus will return to earth to establish a new heaven and a new earth (Revelation 21:1). Then those who are in Christ will go to 'be with the Lord for ever' (1 Thessalonians 4:17). There will be no more crying, for there will be no more pain. There will be no more temptation, for there will be no more sin. There will be no more suffering and no more separation from loved ones. Then we will see Jesus face to face (1 Corinthians 13:12). We will be given glorious and painless resurrection bodies (1 Corinthians 15). We will be transformed into the moral likeness of Jesus Christ (1 John 3:2). Heaven will be a place of intense joy and delight which goes on for ever. Some have ridiculed this by suggesting it would be monotonous or boring. But: 'No eye has seen, no ear has heard, no mind has conceived what God has prepared for those who love him' (1 Corinthians 2:9 quoting Isaiah 64:4).

As C. S. Lewis put it in one of his Narnia books:

The term is over: the holidays have begun. The dream is ended: this is the morning . . . all their life in this world . . . had only been the cover and the title page: now at last they were beginning Chapter One of the Great Story which no one on earth has read: which goes on forever: in which every chapter is better than the one before.[30]

THE WORK OF JESUS

When I was at university, I came across a book called *Heaven, Here I Come.* At first I, like many today, thought this was an arrogant claim. It *would* be arrogant to be so confident if it depended on us. If my entry into heaven depended on how good a life I'd led I would not have any hope of getting in at all.

The wonderful news is that it does not depend on me. It

depends on what Jesus has done for me. It depends not on what I do or achieve, but on his work on the cross. What he did on the cross enables him to give us eternal life as a gift (John 10:28; Romans 6:23b). We do not earn a gift. We accept it with gratitude.

Although eternal life is free, it is not cheap. It cost Jesus his life. We receive the gift by repentance and faith. The word for 'repentance' means changing our minds. If we want to receive this gift, we have to be willing to turn our backs on everything we know to be wrong. These are the things which do us harm and lead to 'death' (Romans 6:23a). Turning away from them is what the Bible calls repentance (literally changing our minds). C. S. Lewis describes it like this: 'Laying down your arms, surrendering, saying you are sorry, realising that you have been on the wrong track and being ready to start life over again from the ground floor – that is the only way out of this hole.'

What is faith? John Patton (1824-1907), a Scot from Dumfriesshire, travelled to the New Hebrides (a group of islands in the South-West Pacific) to tell the tribal people about Jesus. The islanders were cannibals and his life was in constant danger. Patton decided to work on a translation of John's Gospel, but found that there was no word in their language for 'belief' or 'trust'. Nobody trusted anybody else. Eventually, Patton hit upon a way to find the word he was looking for. One day, when his native servant came in, Patton raised both feet off the floor, sat back in his chair and asked, 'What am I doing now?' In reply, the servant used a word which means 'to lean your whole weight upon'. This was the expression Patton used. Faith is leaning our whole weight upon Jesus and what he has done for us on the cross.

Jean-Francois Gravelet (1824-1897), better known as Blondin, was a famous tightrope walker and acrobat. He was perhaps best known for his many crossings of a tightrope 1,100 feet (335 m) in length suspended 160 feet (50 m) above the Niagara Falls. His act would be watched by large crowds and began with a relatively simple crossing using a balancing pole. Then he would throw the pole away and begin to amaze the onlookers. On one occasion in 1860, a Royal party from Britain went to watch Blondin perform. He crossed the tightrope on stilts, then blindfolded; next he stopped halfway to cook and eat an omelette. He then wheeled a wheelbarrow from one side to the other as the crowd cheered. He put a sack of potatoes into the wheelbarrow and wheeled that across. The crowd cheered louder. Then he approached the Royal party and asked the Duke of Newcastle, 'Do you believe that I could take a man across the tightrope in this wheelbarrow?'

'Yes, I do,' said the Duke.

'Hop in!' replied Blondin. The crowd fell silent, but the Duke of Newcastle would not accept Blondin's challenge.

'Is there anyone else here who believes I could do it?' asked Blondin. No one was willing to volunteer. Eventually, an old woman stepped out of the crowd and climbed into the wheelbarrow. Blondin wheeled her all the way across and all the way back. The old woman was Blondin's mother, the only person willing to put her life in his hands. Faith is not merely intellectual, it involves an active step of putting our trust in Jesus.

If we accept God's gift, we cannot be secretive about it. We have to be ready to be known as Christians (Romans 10:9-10) and to identify with the people of God (Hebrews 11:25). It is not that we earn our salvation by our repentance, faith and public acceptance, but these are the means by which we accept the free gift. It was earned not by us, but by Jesus.

It all starts with God's love for us: 'For God so loved the world that he gave his one and only Son, that whoever believes in him shall not perish but have eternal life' (John 3:16). We all deserve to 'perish'. God, in his love for us, saw the mess we were in and gave his only Son, Jesus, to die for us. As a result of his death, everlasting life is offered to all who believe.

On the cross, Jesus took all our wrong-doing upon himself. This had been clearly prophesied in the Old Testament. In the Book of Isaiah, written hundreds of years beforehand, the prophet foresaw what 'the suffering servant' would do for us and said: 'We all, like sheep, have gone astray, each of us has turned to our own way; and the Lord has laid on him [ie, Jesus] the iniquity of us all' (Isaiah 53:6).

What the prophet is saying is that we have all done wrong – we have all gone astray. He says elsewhere that the things which we do wrong cause a separation between us and God (Isaiah 59:1-2). This is one of the reasons why God can seem remote. There is a barrier between us and him which prevents us from experiencing his love.

On the other hand, Jesus never did anything wrong. He lived a perfect life. There was no barrier between him and his Father. On the cross, God transferred our wrong-doings ('our iniquity') onto Jesus ('the Lord has laid on him the iniquity of us all'). That is why Jesus cried out on the cross, 'My God, my God, why have you forsaken me?' (Mark 15:34). At that moment he was cut off from God – not because of his own wrong-doing, but because of ours.

This made it possible for the barrier between us and God to be removed – for all who accept for themselves what Jesus has done for them. As a result, we can be sure of God's forgiveness. Our guilt has been taken away. We can be sure that we will never be condemned. As Paul puts it, 'Therefore, there is now no condemnation for those who are in Christ Jesus' (Romans 8:1). This, then, is the second reason we can be sure that we have eternal life – because of what Jesus achieved for us on the cross by dying for us.

THE WITNESS OF THE SPIRIT

When someone becomes a Christian, God's Holy Spirit comes to live within them. There are two aspects in particular of the many activities of the Holy Spirit which help us to be sure of our faith in Christ.

First, he transforms us from within. He produces the character of Jesus in our lives. This is called 'the fruit of the Spirit' – 'love, joy, peace, patience, kindness, goodness, faithfulness, gentleness and self-control' (Galatians 5:22-23). When the Holy Spirit comes to live within us this 'fruit' begins to grow.

There will be changes in our character which should be observable by other people, but obviously these changes do not occur overnight. We have just planted a pear tree in our garden and almost every day I look to see if it has any fruit. One day a friend of mine (the illustrator of this book) played a practical joke on me. He hung a large Granny Smith apple on the tree with cotton. Even I was not fooled by this. My limited knowledge of gardening tells me that fruit takes time to grow (and pear trees do not produce apples). We hope that over a period of time other people will notice that we are more loving, more joyful, more peaceful, more patient, more kind and more self-controlled.

As well as changes in our character there should be changes in our relationships – both with God and with other people. We develop a new love for God – Father, Son and Holy Spirit. For example, hearing the word 'Jesus' has a different emotional impact. Before I was a Christian, if I was listening to the radio or watching television and heard the subject change to Jesus Christ, I would probably have turned it off. After I became a Christian, I would turn it up, because my attitude to him had totally changed. This was a little sign of my new love for him.

Our attitude to others also changes. Often new Christians say to me that they are suddenly noticing the faces of people in the street and on the bus. Before they had little interest; now they feel a concern for people who often look sad and lost. I found that one of the biggest differences was in my attitude to other Christians. I am afraid that beforehand I had tended to avoid anyone who had a Christian faith. Afterwards, I found they weren't as bad as I had expected! Indeed, I soon started to experience a depth of friendship with other Christians which I had never known in my life before.

Secondly, as well as these changes which can be observed in our lives, the Holy Spirit also brings an inner experience of God. He creates a deep, personal conviction that we are children of God (Romans 8:15-16). This experience is different for everyone.

I have three children. To my mind, so many children are over-worked during their schooldays! The main advice I give them is, 'Don't work so hard!' Whatever is said in my children's school reports, I think they are fantastic. I remember looking at my thirteen-year-old daughter's report, which I (of course) thought was wonderful. She, however, was pointing out areas in which she was disappointed, and was saying that she should have done better in French, and so on. I kept responding, 'I don't really care how you did in French. I think you're fantastic. In fact, I wouldn't really care if your whole report was bad, I love you because I love you.'

As I was saying this, I suddenly sensed God saying, 'This is how I feel about you.' The love of God for each one of us is far greater than the love of human parents for their children. I am always feeling that I could do better, that I am not good at one thing or another, that I fail again and again. Yet God accepts us and loves us simply because he loves us. That is an example of the witness of the Spirit, the third way in which we are assured of our relationship with God, and that we are forgiven and have eternal life. We know it because the Spirit of God witnesses to us – both objectively through an ongoing change in our character and in our relationships, and subjectively through a deep inner conviction that we are children of God.

In these ways (the word of God, the work of Jesus and the witness of the Spirit), those who believe in Jesus can be sure that they are children of God and that they have eternal life.

It is not arrogant to be sure. It is based on what God has promised, on what Jesus died to achieve, and on the work of the Holy Spirit in our lives. It is one of the privileges of being a child of God that we can be absolutely confident about our relationship with our Father, that we can know his forgiveness and be sure that we are Christians and that we have eternal life.

If you are unsure about whether you have ever really believed in Jesus, here is a prayer which you can pray as a way of starting the Christian life and receiving all the benefits which Christ died to make possible.

Heavenly Father, I am sorry for the things I have done wrong in my life. [Take a few moments to ask his forgiveness for anything particular that is on your conscience.] Please forgive me. I now turn from everything which I know is wrong.

Thank you that you sent your Son, Jesus, to die on the cross for me so that I could be forgiven and set free. From now on I will follow and obey him as my Lord.

Thank you that you now offer me this gift of forgiveness and your Spirit. I now receive that gift.

Please come into my life by your Holy Spirit to be with me for ever. Through Jesus Christ, our Lord. Amen.

5

Why and How Do I Pray?

Surveys have shown that three-quarters of the population of sceptical, secular Britain admit to praying at least once a week. Before I became a Christian I prayed two different types of prayers. First, I prayed a prayer taught me as a child by my grandmother (who was not herself a churchgoer), 'God bless Mummy and Daddy . . . and everybody and make me a good boy. Amen.' There was nothing wrong with the prayer, but for me it was only a formula which I prayed every night before I went to sleep, with superstitious fears about what might go wrong if I didn't.

Secondly, I prayed in times of crisis. For example, at the age of seventeen I was travelling by myself in the USA. The bus company managed to lose my rucksack which contained my clothes, money and address book. I was left with virtually nothing. I spent ten days living on a hippie colony in Key West, sharing a tent with an alcoholic. After that, with a feeling of mounting loneliness and desperation, I spent the days wandering around various American cities and the nights on the bus. One day as I walked along the street, I cried out to God (in whom I did not believe) and prayed that I would meet someone I knew. Not long afterwards, I got on the bus at 6 am in Phoenix, Arizona, and there I saw an old school friend. He lent me some money and we travelled together for a few days. It made all the difference. I did not see it as an answer to prayer; only as a coincidence. Since becoming a Christian I have found that it is remarkable how many coincidences happen when we pray.

What is prayer?

Prayer is the most important activity of our lives. It is the main way in which we develop a relationship with our Father in heaven. Jesus said, 'When you pray, go into your room, close the door and pray to your Father, who is unseen' (Matthew 6:6). It is a relationship rather than a ritual. It is not a torrent of mechanical and mindless words. Jesus said, 'Do not keep on babbling like pagans' (Matthew 6:7). It is a conversation with our Father in heaven; a vertical conversation, not a horizontal one. A little boy once yelled, 'Please, God, bring me a big box of chocolates for my birthday.' To which his mother answered, 'There is no need to shout, dear! God isn't deaf.' Back came the reply, 'No, but Grandpa is, and he is in the next room!' When we pray, it is not to others, or to ourselves, but to God. So prayer is a matter of relationships and when we pray the whole Trinity is involved.

Christian prayer is prayer 'to your Father'
Jesus taught us to pray, 'Our Father in heaven' (Matthew 6:9). God is personal. Of course he is 'beyond personality' as C. S. Lewis put it, but he is nevertheless personal. All human beings are made in the image of God. Personhood is a reflection of something within the nature of God. He is our loving Father and we have the extraordinary privilege of being able to come into his presence and call him 'Abba' – the Aramaic word for which the nearest translation is 'Daddy' or 'Dear Father'. There is a remarkable

intimacy about our relationship with God and about praying to our Father in heaven.

He is not only 'our Father'; he is 'our Father in heaven'. He has heavenly power. When we pray we are speaking to the Creator of the universe. On 20 August 1977, Voyager II, the inter-planetary probe launched to observe and transmit to earth data about the outer planetary system, set off from earth travelling faster than the speed of a bullet (90,000 miles per hour). On 28 August 1989 it reached planet Neptune, 2,700 million miles from the earth. Voyager II then left the solar system. It will not come within one light year of any star for 958,000 years. In our galaxy there are 100,000 million stars, like our sun. Our galaxy is one of 100,000 million galaxies. In a throwaway line in Genesis, the writer tells us, 'He also made the stars' (Genesis 1:16). Such is his power. Andrew Murray, the Christian writer, once said, 'The power of prayer depends almost entirely upon our apprehension of who it is with whom we speak.'

When we pray, we are speaking to a God who is both transcendent and immanent. He is far greater and more powerful than the universe which he created and yet he is there with us when we pray.

Christian prayer is through the 'Son'
Paul says that 'through him [Jesus] we both [Jews and Gentiles] have access to the Father by one Spirit' (Ephesians 2:18). Jesus said that his Father would give 'whatever you ask in my name' (John 15:16). We have no right in ourselves to come to God but we are able to do so 'through Jesus' and 'in his name'. That is why it is customary to end prayers with 'through Jesus Christ our Lord' or 'in the name of Jesus'. This is not just a formula; it is our acknowledgement of the fact that we can only come to God through Jesus.

It is Jesus, through his death on the cross, who removed the barrier between us and God. He is our great High Priest. That is why there is such power in the name of Jesus.

The value of a cheque depends not only on the amount, but also on the name that appears at the bottom. If I wrote out a cheque for ten million pounds it would be worthless; but if Bill Gates, reputed to be the richest man in the world, were to write a cheque for ten million pounds it would be worth exactly that. When we go to the bank of heaven, we have nothing deposited there. If I go in my own name I can achieve nothing; but Jesus Christ has unlimited credit in heaven. He has given us the privilege of using his name.

Christian prayer is prayer 'by one Spirit' (Ephesians 2:18)

We find it hard to pray, but God has not left us alone. He has given us his Spirit to live within us and help us to pray. Paul writes, 'In the same way, the Spirit helps us in our weakness. We do not know what we ought to pray, but the Spirit himself intercedes for us with groans that words cannot express. And he who searches our hearts knows the mind of the Spirit, because the Spirit intercedes for the saints in accordance with God's will' (Romans 8:26-27). In a later chapter we shall look in more detail at the work of the Spirit. Here, it is sufficient to note that when we pray, God is praying through us by his Spirit who lives in us as Christians.

WHY PRAY?

Prayer is a vital activity. There are many reasons for praying. In the first place it is the way in which we develop a relationship with our Father in heaven. Sometimes people say, 'God knows our needs, so why do we have to ask?' Well, it would not be much of a relationship if there was no communication. Of course, asking is not the only way in which we communicate with God. There are other forms of prayer: thanksgiving, praise, adoration, confession, listening, etc. But asking is an important part. As we ask God for things and see our prayers answered, our relationship with him grows.

Next, Jesus prayed and taught us to do the same. Jesus had an uninterrupted relationship with his Father. His life was one of constant prayer. There are numerous references to his praying (eg, Mark 1:35; Luke 6:12). He assumed his disciples would pray. He said, 'When you pray' (Matthew 6:7) not, 'If you pray.'

Then again, if we need any further incentive, Jesus taught us that there are rewards for prayer (Matthew 6:6).

> The hidden rewards of prayer are too many to enumerate. In the words of the apostle Paul, when we cry, 'Abba, Father,' the Holy Spirit witnesses with our spirit that we are indeed God's children, and we are granted a strong assurance of his fatherhood and love. He lifts the light of his face upon us and gives us his peace. He refreshes our soul, satisfies our hunger, quenches our thirst. We know we are no longer orphans for the Father has adopted us; no longer prodigals for we have been forgiven; no longer alienated, for we have come home.[31]

Finally, prayer not only changes us but it also changes situations. Many people can accept that prayer will have a beneficial effect on themselves, but some have philosophical objections to the concept that prayer can change events and third parties. Rabbi Daniel Cohn-Sherbok of Kent University once wrote an article arguing that as God already knows the future it therefore must be fixed. To this Clifford Longley, the Religious Affairs correspondent of *The Times*, correctly replied, 'If God lives in the eternal present, he hears all prayers simultaneously. Therefore he can appropriate a prayer from next week, and attach it to an event a month ago. Prayers said after the event can be heard before they are spoken and taken into account before the event.' Or, to put it another way, God has all eternity to answer the split-second prayer of a driver who is about to crash.

On numerous occasions Jesus encouraged us to ask. He said, 'Ask and it will be given to you; seek and you will find; knock and the door will be opened to you. For everyone who asks receives; everyone who seeks finds; and to everyone who knocks, the door will be opened' (Matthew 7:7-8).

Every Christian knows, through experience, that God answers prayer. It is not possible to prove Christianity on the basis of answers to prayer because they can always be explained away by cynics as coincidences. But the cumulative effective of answered prayer reinforces our faith in God. I keep a prayer diary and it is fascinating to me to see how day after day, week after week, year after year, God has answered my prayers.

DOES GOD ALWAYS ANSWER PRAYER?

In the passage I have cited from Matthew 7:7-8 and in many other New Testament passages the promises appear to be absolute. However, when we look at the whole of Scripture, we see there are good reasons why we may not always get what we ask for.

Unconfessed sin causes a barrier between us and God: 'Surely the arm of the Lord is not too short to save, nor his ear too dull to hear. But your iniquities have separated you from your God; your sins have hidden his face from you, so that he will not hear' (Isaiah 59:1-2). God never promises to answer the prayer of a person who is not living in a relationship with him. Sometimes, he may graciously answer the prayer of an unbeliever (as he did in the example I gave at the beginning of the chapter), but we have no right to expect it. When people say, 'I don't feel I am getting through to God. I don't feel there is anyone there,' the first question to ask them is whether they have ever received God's forgiveness through Christ on the cross. The barrier must be removed before we can expect God to hear and answer our prayers.

Even as Christians our friendship with God can be marred by sin or disobedience. John writes, 'Dear friends, if our hearts do not condemn us, we have confidence before God and receive from him anything we ask, because we obey his commands and do what pleases him' (1 John 3:21-22). If we are conscious of any sin or disobedience towards God, we need to confess it and turn from it so that our friendship with God can be restored and we can approach him again with confidence.

Our motivation can also be a hindrance to getting what we ask for. Not every request for a new Porsche gets answered! James, the brother of Jesus, writes:

> You want something but don't get it. You kill and covet, but you cannot have what you want. You quarrel and fight. You do not have, because you do not ask God. When you ask, you do not receive, because you ask with wrong motives, that you may spend what you get on your pleasures (James 4:2-3).

A famous example of a prayer riddled with wrong motives is that of John Ward of Hackney, written in the eighteenth century:

> O Lord, thou knowest that I have nine estates in the City of London, and likewise that I have lately purchased one estate in fee simple in the county of Essex; I beseech thee to preserve the two counties of Essex and Middlesex from fire and earthquake; and as I have a mortgage in Hertfordshire, I beg of thee likewise to have an eye of compassion on that county; and for the rest of the counties thou mayest deal with them as thou art pleased.
>
> O Lord, enable the bank to answer their bills, and make all my debtors good men. Give a prosperous voyage and return to the Mermaid ship, because I have insured it; and as thou hast said that the days of the wicked are but short, I trust in thee, that thou wilt not forget thy promise, as I have purchased an estate in reversion which will be mine on the death of that profligate young man, Sir J. L.
>
> Keep my friends from sinking, and preserve me from thieves and house breakers, and make all my servants so honest and faithful that they may attend to my interests, and never cheat me out of my property, night or day.

We see here why the promises in the Bible that prayers will be answered are sometimes qualified. For example, John writes, 'If we ask anything *according to his will*, he hears us' (1 John 5:14, italics mine). The more we get to know God, the better we will know his will and the more our prayers will be answered.

Sometimes prayers are not answered because what we are requesting is not good for us. God only promises to give us 'good gifts' (Matthew 7:11). He loves us and knows what is best for us. Good parents do not always give their children what they ask for. If a five-year-old wants to play with a carving knife, hopefully a good parent will say 'no'! God will answer 'no' if the things we ask for are 'either not good in themselves, or not good for us or for others, directly or indirectly, immediately or ultimately', as John Stott has written.

The answer to our prayer will either be 'yes', 'no' or sometimes 'wait', and for this we should be extremely grateful. If we were given carte blanche we would never dare pray again. As the preacher Martyn Lloyd-Jones put it, 'I thank God that he is not prepared to do anything that I may chance to ask him . . . I am profoundly grateful to God that he did not grant me certain things for which I asked, and that he shut certain doors in my face.'[32] Any Christian who has been a Christian for some time will appreciate this sentiment. Ruth Graham (married to Billy Graham) told an audience in Minneapolis, 'God has not always answered my prayers. If he had, I would have married the wrong man – several times.' Sometimes we will not know during this life why the answer was 'no'. I can think of an occasion in 1996 when I was playing squash with one of my closest friends, Mick Hawkins, a man of forty-two with six children. In the middle of the game he dropped dead from a heart attack. I have never cried out to God more than I did on that occasion; asking him to heal him, restore him, praying that the heart attack would not be fatal. I do not know why he died.

I remember early the following morning – obviously I could not sleep – I went out for a walk and said to the Lord, 'I don't understand why Mick died. He was such an amazing person, such a wonderful husband and father. I don't understand . . .' Then I realised I had a choice. I could say, 'I am going to stop believing.' The alternative was to say, 'I am going to go on believing in spite of the fact that I don't understand and I am going to trust you, Lord, even though I don't think I will ever understand – in this life – why it happened.'

There may be times when we will have to wait until we meet God face to face to understand what his will was and why our prayer did not get the answer we hoped for.

HOW SHOULD WE PRAY?

There is no set way to pray. Prayer is an integral part of our relationship with God and therefore we are free to talk to him as we wish. God does not want us to repeat meaningless words; he wants to hear what is on our hearts. Having said that, many people find it helpful to have a pattern for prayer. For some years I used the mnemonic ACTS.

A – adoration – praising God for who he is and what he has done.

C – confession – asking God's forgiveness for anything that we have done wrong.

T – thanksgiving – for health, family, friends, and so on.

S – supplication – praying for ourselves, for our friends, and for others.

More recently I have found that I often follow the pattern from the Lord's Prayer (Matthew 6:9-13):

'Our Father in heaven' (v. 9)
We have already looked earlier in the chapter at what this phrase means. Under this heading, I spend time thanking God for who he is and for my relationship with him and for the ways in which he has answered prayers.

'Hallowed be your name' (v. 9)
In Hebrew someone's name signified a revelation of that person's character. To pray that God's name be hallowed is to pray that he will be honoured. So often we look around our society and see that God's name is dishonoured – many people pay no attention to him or his laws. We should start by praying that God's name is honoured in our own lives, in our church and in the society around us.

'Your kingdom come' (v. 10)

God's kingdom is his rule and reign. That will be complete when Jesus comes again. But this kingdom broke into history when Jesus came for the first time. Jesus demonstrated this presence of God's kingdom in his own ministry. When we pray, 'Your kingdom come,' we are praying for God's rule and reign to come both in the future and in the present. It includes praying for people to be converted, healed, set free from evil, filled with the Spirit and given the gifts of the Spirit, in order that we may together serve and obey the King.

I am told that D. L. Moody wrote down a list of 100 people and prayed for them to be converted in his lifetime. Ninety-six of them were converted by the time he died and the other four were converted at his funeral.

One Christian mother was having problems with her rebellious teenage son. He was lazy, bad-tempered, a cheat, a liar and a thief. Later on, though outwardly respected as a lawyer, his life was dominated by worldly ambition and a desire to make money. His morals were loose. He lived with several different women and had a son by one of them. At one stage he joined a weird religious sect and adopted all kinds of strange practices. Throughout this time his mother continued to pray for him. One day, the Lord gave her a vision and she wept as she prayed, because she saw the light of Jesus Christ in him, and his face transformed. She had to wait another nine years before her son gave his life to Jesus Christ at the age of thirty-two. That man's name was Augustine. He went on to become one of the greatest theologians in the church. He always attributed his conversion to the prayers of his mother.

We are praying not simply for God's rule and reign in individuals' lives but ultimately for the transformation of society. We are praying for God's peace, justice and compassion. We are praying for those often marginalised by society but for whom God cares especially, such as widows, orphans, the lonely and prisoners (Psalm 68:4-6a).

'Your will be done on earth as it is in heaven' (v. 10)

This is not resignation, it is a releasing of the burdens that we so often carry. Many people are worried about decisions they are facing. The decisions may be about major or minor issues but if we want to be sure that we don't make a mistake we need to pray, 'Your will be done.' The psalmist says, 'Commit your way to the Lord; trust in him and he will act' (Psalm 37:5, RSV). For example, if you are praying about whether a relationship is right, you might pray, 'If this relationship is wrong, I pray that you stop it. If it is right I pray that nothing will stop it.' Then, having committed it to the Lord, you can trust him and wait for him to act. (We will look at this subject in more detail in Chapter 7 – and the principles in that chapter need to be taken into account.)

'Give us today our daily bread' (v. 11)

Some have suggested that Jesus meant the spiritual bread of Holy Communion or the Bible. This is possible, but I believe the reformers were right to say that Jesus is referring here to our basic needs. Luther said it indicated 'everything necessary for the preservation of this life, like food, a healthy body, good weather, house, home, wife, children, good government and peace'. God is concerned about everything that you and I are concerned about. Just as I want my children to talk about anything they are worried about, so God wants to hear about the things we are concerned about.

A friend of mine asked a new Christian how her small business was going. She replied that it was not going very well. So my friend offered to pray for it. The new Christian replied, 'I didn't know that was allowed.' My friend explained that it was. They prayed and the following week the business improved considerably. The Lord's Prayer teaches us that it is not wrong to pray about our own concerns, provided that God's name, God's kingdom and God's will are our first priority.

'Forgive us our debts, as we also have forgiven our debtors' (v. 12)
Jesus taught us to pray that God would forgive us our debts (ie, the things which we do wrong). Some say, 'Why do we need to pray for forgiveness? Surely when we come to the cross we are already forgiven for everything, past, present and future?' It is true, as we have seen in the chapter on why Jesus died, that we are totally forgiven for everything, past, present and future because Jesus took all our sins on himself on the cross. Yet Jesus still tells us to pray, 'Forgive us our debts.' I find the most helpful analogy is the one given by Jesus in John 13 when Jesus moves to wash Peter's feet. Peter said, 'No, you shall never wash my feet.' Jesus answered, 'Unless I wash you, you have no part of me.' Peter replied, in effect, 'Well, in that case wash my whole body.' Jesus said, 'A person who has had a bath needs only to wash his feet; his whole body is clean.' This is a picture of forgiveness. When we come to the cross we are made totally clean and we are forgiven – everything is dealt with. But as we go through the world we do things which tarnish our friendship with God. Our relationship is always secure but our friendship is sullied with the dirt that we pick up on our feet. Each day we need to pray, 'Lord forgive us, cleanse us from the dirt.' We don't need to have a bath again, Jesus has done that for us, but a measure of cleansing may be necessary every day.

Jesus went on to say, 'If you forgive others when they sin against you, your heavenly Father will also forgive you. But if you do not forgive others their sins, your Father will not forgive your sins' (Matthew 6:14-15). This does not mean that by forgiving people we can earn forgiveness. We can never earn forgiveness. Jesus achieved that for us on the cross. But the sign that we are forgiven is that we are willing to forgive other people. If we are not willing to forgive other people that is evidence that we do not know forgiveness ourselves. If we really know God's forgiveness, we cannot refuse forgiveness to someone else.

'Lead us not into temptation, but deliver us from the evil one' (v. 13)
God does not tempt us (James 1:13), but he is in control of how much we are exposed to the devil (eg, Job 1 –2). Every Christian has a weak area – be it fear, selfish ambition, greed, pride, lust, gossiping, cynicism or something else. If we know our weakness, we can pray for protection against it, as well, of course, as taking action to avoid unnecessary temptation. We will consider this whole issue in Chapter 11.

WHEN SHOULD WE PRAY?

The New Testament exhorts us to pray 'always' (1 Thessalonians 5:17; Ephesians 6:18). We do not have to be in a special building in order to pray. We can pray on the tube, on the bus, in the car, on our bike, walking along the road, as we lie in bed, in the middle of the night, whenever and wherever we are. As in any close relationship, we can continue an ongoing conversation. Nevertheless, it is helpful to have time together when you know that you are meeting simply to talk. Jesus said, 'When you pray, go into your room, close the door and pray to your Father, who is unseen' (Matthew 6:6). He himself went off to a solitary place in order to pray (Mark 1:35). I find it helpful to combine Bible reading and prayer at the beginning of the day, when my mind is most active. It is good to have a regular pattern. What time of day we choose will depend on our circumstances and our own particular make-up.

As well as praying alone, it is important to pray with other people. This could be in a small group of two or three for example. Jesus said, 'I tell you that if two of you on earth agree about anything you ask for, it will be done for you by my Father in heaven' (Matthew 18:19). It can be very hard praying aloud in front of other people. I remember the first time I did this, about two months after I had come to Christ. I was with two of my closest friends and we decided that we would spend some time praying together. We only prayed for about ten minutes, but when I took my shirt off afterwards it was wringing wet! Nevertheless, it is worth persevering since there is great power in praying together (Acts 12:5).

Prayer is at the heart of Christianity, because at the heart of Christianity is a relationship with God. That is why it is the most important activity of our lives. As the saying goes:

> Satan laughs at our words.
> Mocks at our toil.
> But trembles when we pray.

6

Why and How Should I Read the Bible?

It was Valentine's night 1974. I had been to a party and was sitting in my room at college when my greatest friend came back with his girlfriend (now his wife) and told me that they had become Christians. I was immediately alarmed about them, thinking that the Moonies had got them and they needed my help.

I was at times an atheist and at times an agnostic, unsure of what I believed. I had been baptised and confirmed, but it had not meant much to me. At school I had been to chapel regularly and studied the Bible in RE lessons. But I had ended up rejecting it all and, indeed, arguing powerfully (or so I thought) against Christianity.

Now I wanted to help my friends, so I thought I would embark on a thorough research of the subject. I made a plan to read the Koran, Karl Marx, Jean-Paul Sartre (the existentialist philosopher) and the Bible. I happened to have a rather dusty copy of the Bible on my shelves, so that night I picked it up and started reading. I read all the way through Matthew, Mark and Luke, and halfway through John's Gospel. Then I fell asleep. When I woke up, I finished John's Gospel and carried on through Acts, Romans, and

1 and 2 Corinthians. I was completely gripped by what I read. I had read it before and it had meant virtually nothing to me. This time it came alive and I could not put it down. It had a ring of truth about it. I knew as I read it that I had to respond because it spoke so powerfully to me. Very shortly afterwards I came to put my faith in Jesus Christ.

Since then the Bible has become a 'delight' to me. The psalmist says:

> Blessed are those who do not walk in the counsel of the wicked or stand in the way of sinners or sit in the seat of mockers. But their delight is in the law of the Lord, and on his law they meditate day and night. They are like trees planted by streams of water, which yield their fruit in season and whose leaves do not wither. Whatever they do prospers (Psalm 1:1-3).

I love that phrase, 'their delight is in the law of the Lord.' All the psalmist had at that stage was the first five books of the Bible. They were his delight. In this chapter I want to look at why and how the Bible can become a 'delight' for each of us, looking, by way of introduction, at its uniqueness.

First, it is uniquely popular. It is estimated that 44 million Bibles are sold a year and that there is an average of 6.8 Bibles in every American household. An article in *The Times* recently was subheaded 'Forget the modern British novelists and TV tie-ins; the Bible is the biggest-selling book every year'. The writer remarked:

> As usual the top seller by several miles was the . . . Bible. If cumulative sales of the Bible were frankly reflected in bestseller lists, it would be a rare week when anything else would achieve a look in. It is wonderful, weird, or just plain baffling in this increasingly godless age – when the range of books available grows wider with each passing year – that this one book should go on selling hand over fist, month in, month out. . . .

It is estimated that nearly 1,250,000 Bibles and Testaments are sold in the UK each year.

The writer ends by saying, '*All* versions of the Bible sell well *all* the time. Can the Bible Society offer an explanation? "Well," I am told disarmingly, "it is such a good book."'

Secondly, it is uniquely powerful. In May 1928, the Prime Minister Stanley Baldwin said, 'The Bible is a high explosive. But it works in strange ways and no living man can tell or know how

that book, in its journey through the world, has startled the individual soul in ten thousand different places into a new life, a new world, a new belief, a new conception, a new faith.'

In recent times there has been a rising interest in the occult. People play with ouija boards, see occult films, have their fortunes told and read horoscopes. They want to get in touch with the supernatural. The tragedy is that they are seeking to communicate with supernatural evil forces, whereas what God offers us in the Bible is an opportunity to meet with the supernatural powers of good. To meet with the living God is so much more thrilling, more satisfying and a great deal wiser.

Thirdly, it is uniquely precious. About sixteen years ago I was on holiday with my family in central Asia, part of the USSR as it then was. At that time Bibles were strictly illegal there, but I took some Christian literature, including some Russian Bibles. While I was there I went to churches and looked for people who seemed from their faces to be genuine Christians. (At that time the meetings were usually infiltrated by the KGB.) On one occasion I followed a man, who was probably in his sixties, down the street after a service. I went up to him and tapped him on the shoulder. There was nobody about. I took out one of my Bibles and handed it to him. For a moment he had an expression of almost disbelief. Then he took from his pocket a New Testament which was probably 100 years old. The pages were so threadbare they were virtually transparent. When he realised that he had received a whole Bible, he was elated. He didn't speak any English and I didn't speak any Russian. We hugged each other and he started to run down the street jumping for joy, because he knew that the Bible was the most precious thing in the world.

Why is it so popular, so powerful and so precious? Jesus said: 'People do not live on bread alone, but on every word that comes from the mouth of God' (Matthew 4:4). The word is in the present tense, and means 'is continually coming out of the mouth of God'; it is like a stream pouring forth and, like the stream of a fountain, is never static. God is continually wanting to communicate with his people. He does so, primarily, through the Bible.

A MANUAL FOR LIFE – GOD HAS SPOKEN

God has spoken to us through his Son, Jesus Christ (Hebrews 1:2). Christianity is a revealed faith. We cannot find out about God unless God reveals himself. God has revealed himself in a person, Jesus Christ. He is God's ultimate revelation.

The main way we know about Jesus is through God's revelation recorded in the Bible. Biblical theology should be the study of God's revelation in the Bible. God has also revealed himself through creation (Romans 1:19-20; Psalm 19). Science is an exploration of God's revelation in creation. (There should be no conflict between science and the Christian faith; rather they complement one another.) God also speaks to people directly by his Spirit: through prophecy, dreams, visions, and through other people. We will look at all these in more detail later – especially in the chapter on guidance. In this chapter we will look at the way in which God speaks through the Bible.

Paul wrote of the inspiration of the Scriptures that were available to him: 'All Scripture is God-breathed and is useful for teaching, rebuking, correcting and training in righteousness, so that God's servant may be thoroughly equipped for every good work' (2 Timothy 3:16-17).

The word for 'God-breathed' is *theopneustos*. It is often translated as 'inspired by God'; but transliterated it is 'God-breathed'. The writer is saying that Scripture is God speaking. Of course he used human agents. It is 100 per cent the work of human beings. But it is also 100 per cent inspired by God (just as Jesus is fully human and fully God).

This is the way in which Jesus himself treated the Scriptures of his day. For him, what the Scriptures said, God said (Mark 7:5-13). If Jesus is our Lord, our attitude to the Scriptures should be the same as his. 'Belief in Christ as the supreme revelation of God leads to belief in scriptural inspiration – of the Old Testament by the direct testimony of Jesus and of the New Testament by inference from his testimony.'[33]

This high view of the inspiration of the Bible has been held almost universally by the worldwide church down the ages. The early theologians of the church had this view. Irenaeus (c. AD 130-200) said, 'The Scriptures are perfect.' Likewise, the reformers, for example Martin Luther, spoke of 'Scripture which has never erred'. Today, the Roman Catholic official view is enshrined in Vatican II. The Scriptures 'written under the inspiration of the Holy Spirit ... have God as their author . . .'. Therefore they must be acknowledged as being 'without error'. This also, until the last century, was the view of all Protestant churches throughout the world, and although today it is questioned and even ridiculed at a school level, it continues to be held by many fine scholars.

This does not mean that there are no difficulties in the Bible. Even Peter found some of Paul's letters 'hard to understand' (2 Peter 3:16). There are moral and historical difficulties and some apparent contradictions. Some of the difficulties can be explained by the different contexts in which the authors were writing. It is important to remember that the Bible was written over a period of 1,500 years by at least forty authors, including kings, scholars, philosophers, fishermen, poets, statesmen, historians and doctors.

There is a whole range of genres: historical, narrative, poetry, prophecy, letters and apocalyptic literature.

Although some of the apparent contradictions can be explained by differing contexts, others are harder to resolve. This does not mean, however, that it is impossible and that we should abandon our belief in the inspiration of Scripture. Every great doctrine of the Christian faith has its difficulties. For example, it is hard to reconcile the love of God and the suffering in the world. Yet every Christian believes in the love of God and seeks an understanding of the problem of suffering within that framework. In a similar way we need to hold on to the belief in the inspiration of the Bible and try to understand the difficult passages within that context. It is important not to run away from the difficulties but to seek, so far as we can, to resolve them to our own satisfaction.

It is very important to hold on to the fact that *all* Scripture is inspired by God, even if we cannot immediately resolve all the difficulties. If we do, it should transform the way in which we live our lives. When Billy Graham was a young man several people (among them, one was called Chuck) started to say to him, 'You can't believe everything in the Bible.' He began to worry about it and started to become very muddled. John Pollock, in his biography of the evangelist, records what happened:

> So I went back and I got my Bible, and I went out in the moonlight. And I got to a stump and put the Bible on the stump, and I knelt down, and I said, 'Oh, God; I cannot prove certain things. I cannot answer some of the questions Chuck is raising and some of the other people are raising, but I accept this Book by faith as the Word of God.' I stayed by the stump praying wordlessly, my eyes moist . . . I had a tremendous sense of God's presence. I had a great peace that the decision I had made was right.[34]

If we accept that the Bible is inspired by God, then its authority must follow from that. If it is God's word then it must be our supreme authority for what we believe and how we act. For Jesus, it was his supreme authority – above what the church leaders of his time said (eg, Mark 7:1-20) and above the opinions of others, however clever they were (eg, Mark 12:18-27). Having said that, we must of course give due weight to what church leaders and others say.

The Bible should be our authority in all matters of 'creed and conduct'. As we have seen, 'All Scripture is God-breathed and is useful for teaching, rebuking, correcting and training in righteousness' (2 Timothy 3:16). First, it is our authority for what we believe (our creed) – and therefore for 'teaching' and 'rebuking'. It is in the Bible that we find what God says (and what we should, therefore, believe) about suffering, about Jesus, about the cross, and so on.

Secondly, it is our authority for how we act (our conduct) – for 'correcting' and for 'training in righteousness'. It is here that we find out what is wrong in God's eyes and how we can live a righteous life. For instance, 'The ten commandments . . . are a brilliant analysis of the minimum conditions on which a society, a people, a nation can live a sober, righteous and civilised life.'[35]

There are some things that are very clear in the Bible. It tells us how to conduct our day-to-day lives, for example, when we're at work or under pressure. We know from the Bible that the single state can be a high calling (1 Corinthians 7:7), but it is the exception rather than the rule; marriage is the norm (Genesis 2:24; 1 Corinthians 7:2). We know that sexual intercourse outside marriage is wrong. We know that it is right to try to get a job if we can. We know it is right to give and to forgive. We are also given, among other things, guidelines on how to bring up our children and to care for elderly relatives.

Some people say, 'I don't want this rule book. It is too restrictive – all those rules and regulations. I want to be free. If you live by the Bible, you are not free to enjoy life.' But is that really right? Does the Bible take away our freedom? Or does it in fact give us freedom? Rules and regulations can in fact create freedom and increase enjoyment.

A few years ago, a football match had been arranged involving twenty-two small boys, including one of my sons, aged eight at the time. A friend of mine called Andy (who had been training the boys all year) was going to referee. Unfortunately, by 2.30 pm he had not turned up. The boys could wait no longer. I was press-ganged into being the substitute referee. There were a number of difficulties with this: I had no whistle; there were no markings for the boundaries of the pitch; I didn't know any of the other boys' names; they did not have colours to distinguish which sides they were on; and I did not know the rules nearly as well as some of the boys.

The game soon descended into complete chaos. Some shouted that the ball was in. Others said that it was out. I wasn't at all sure, so I let things run. Then the fouls started. Some cried, 'Foul!' Others said, 'No foul!' I didn't know who was right. So I let them play on. Then people began to get hurt. By the time Andy arrived, there were three boys lying injured on the ground and all the rest were shouting, mainly at me! But the moment Andy arrived, he blew his whistle, arranged the teams, told them where the boundaries were and had them under complete control. Then the boys had the game of their lives.

Were the boys more free without the rules or were they in fact less free? Without any effective authority they were free to do exactly what they wanted. The result was that people were confused and hurt. They much preferred it when they knew where the boundaries were. Then within those boundaries they were free to enjoy the game.

In some ways the Bible is like that. It is God's rule book. He tells us what is 'in' and what is 'out'. He tells us what we can do and what we must not do. If we play within the rules there is freedom and joy. When we break the rules, people get hurt. God did not say, 'Do not murder,' in order to ruin our enjoyment of life. He did not say, 'Do not commit adultery,' because he is a spoilsport. He did not want people to get hurt. When people leave their wives or husbands and children to commit adultery, lives get messed up.

The Bible is God's revelation of his will for his people. The more we discover his will and put it into practice, the freer we shall be. God has spoken. We need to hear what he has said.

A LOVE LETTER FROM GOD – GOD SPEAKS

For some people the Bible is never more than a well-thumbed manual for life. They believe God has spoken and they may study the Bible for hours. They analyse it, read commentaries on it (and there is nothing wrong with that), but they do not seem to realise that not only has God spoken, but he still speaks today through what he has said in the Bible. God's desire is that we should live in a relationship with him. He wants to speak to us daily through his word. So as well as being a manual for life, it is also a love letter.

The main point of the Bible is to show us how to enter into a relationship with God through Jesus Christ. Jesus said, 'You diligently study the Scriptures because you think that by them you possess eternal life. These are the Scriptures that testify about me, yet you refuse to come to me to have life' (John 5:39–40).

Dr Christopher Chavasse, formerly Bishop of Rochester, said:

The Bible is the portrait of our Lord Jesus Christ. The Gospels are the figure itself in the portrait. The Old Testament is the background leading up to the divine figure, pointing towards it and absolutely necessary to the composition as a whole. The Epistles serve as the dress and accoutrements of the figure, explaining and describing it. Then, while by our Bible reading we study the portrait as a great whole, the miracle happens, the figure comes to life and stepping down from the canvas of the written word, the everlasting Christ of the Emmaus story becomes himself our Bible teacher, to interpret to us in all the Scriptures the things concerning himself.

It is no good studying the Bible if we never come to Jesus Christ; if we never meet with him as we read it. Martin Luther said, 'Scripture is the manger or "cradle" in which the infant Jesus lies. Don't let us inspect the cradle and forget to worship the baby.'

Our relationship with God is two-way. We speak to him in prayer and he speaks to us in many ways, but especially through the Bible. God speaks through what he has spoken. The writer of the epistle to the Hebrews says, when he quotes the Old Testament, 'As the Holy Spirit says' (Hebrews 3:7). It is not just that the Holy Spirit spoke in the past. He speaks afresh through what he spoke. This is what makes the Bible so alive. Again, as Martin Luther put it, 'The Bible is alive, it speaks to me; it has feet, it runs after me; it has hands, it lays hold on me.'

What happens when God speaks? *First, he brings faith to those who are not yet Christians.* Paul says, 'Faith comes from hearing the message, and the message is heard through the word of Christ' (Romans 10:17). It is often as people read the Bible that they come to faith in Jesus Christ. That was certainly my experience.

David Suchet, a leading Shakespearean actor and well-known for his title role in *Poirot*, tells how a few years ago he was lying in his bath in a hotel in America, when he had a sudden and impulsive desire to read the Bible. He managed to find a Gideon Bible and he started to read the New Testament. As he read, he came to put his faith in Jesus Christ. He said:

From somewhere I got this desire to read the Bible again. That's the most important part of my conversion. I started with the Acts of the

93

Apostles and then moved to Paul's Letters – Romans and Corinthians. And it was only after that I came to the gospels. In the New Testament I suddenly discovered the way that life should be followed.[36]

Secondly, he speaks to Christians. As we read the Bible we experience a transforming relationship with God through Jesus Christ. Paul says, 'We, who with unveiled faces all reflect the Lord's glory, are being transformed into his likeness with ever-increasing glory, which comes from the Lord, who is the Spirit' (2 Corinthians 3:18). As we study the Bible, we come into contact with Jesus Christ. It has always struck me as the most extraordinarily wonderful fact that we can speak to and hear from the person whom we read about in the pages of the New Testament – the same Jesus Christ. He will speak to us (not audibly, on the whole, but in our heart) as we read the Bible. We will hear his message for us. As we spend time with him, our characters will become more like his.

Spending time in his presence, listening to his voice, brings many blessings. He often brings joy and peace, even in the middle of a crisis in our lives (Psalm 23:5). When we are not sure which direction we should be going in, God often guides us through his word (Psalm 119:105). The Book of Proverbs even tells us that God's words bring healing to our bodies (Proverbs 4:22).

The Bible also provides us with a defence against spiritual attack. We only have one detailed example of Jesus facing temptation. Jesus faced intense attack by the devil at the start of his ministry (Matthew 4:1-11). Jesus met every temptation with a verse from the Scriptures. I find it fascinating that every one of his replies came from Deuteronomy 6–8. It seems plausible to infer that Jesus had been studying this portion of Scripture and that it was fresh in his mind.

The word of God has great power. The writer of the Book of Hebrews says, 'The word of God is living and active. Sharper than any double-edged sword, it penetrates even to dividing soul and spirit, joints and marrow; it judges the thoughts and attitudes of the heart' (Hebrews 4:12). It has power to pierce all our defences and get through to our hearts. I remember once reading Philippians 2:4, 'Each of you should look not only to your own interests, but also to the interests of others.' It was like an arrow going straight into me as I realised how selfish I was being. In these and many other ways, God's word speaks to us.

Sometimes God speaks to us in a very specific way. God spoke to me very clearly about my father after he died on 21 January 1981. I had become a Christian seven years earlier and my parents' initial reaction was one of complete horror. Gradually, over the years, they began to see a change in me. My mother became a committed Christian long before she died. My father was a man of few words. Initially, he was very unsure about my involvement in the Christian faith. By degrees, he started to become warmer about it. His death was quite sudden. What I found hardest about his death was that I wasn't sure whether he was a Christian or not.

Exactly ten days after his death, I was reading the Bible. I had asked God to speak to me about my father that day because I was still worrying about him. I happened to be reading Romans and I came across the verse, 'Everyone who calls on the name of the Lord will be saved' (Romans 10:13). I sensed at that moment God was saying to me that this verse was for my father; that he had called on the name of the Lord and been 'saved'. About five minutes later my wife, Pippa, came in and said to me, 'I have been reading a verse in Acts 2:21 and I think this verse is for your father. It says, ". . . and everyone who calls on the name of the Lord will be saved."' It was quite extraordinary because that verse only appears twice in the New Testament and God had spoken to both of us through the same words at the same time in different parts of the Bible.

Three days later, we went to a Bible study in a friend's home and the Bible study was on Romans 10:13, that same passage. So three times during those three days God spoke to me about my father through the same words. Nevertheless, on my way to work I was still thinking about my father and worrying about him. As I came out of the underground, I looked up and there was a huge poster saying, 'Whoever calls upon the name of the Lord will be saved' (Romans 10:13). I remember talking to a friend about it and telling him what had happened and he said, 'Do you think the Lord may be trying to speak to you?'!

As God speaks to us and we learn to hear his voice, our relationship with him grows, and our love for him deepens.

HOW IN PRACTICE DO WE HEAR GOD SPEAK THROUGH THE BIBLE?

Time is our most valuable possession. The pressure on time tends to increase as life goes on and we become busier and busier. There is a saying that 'money is power, but time is life'. If we are going to set aside time to read the Bible, we have to plan ahead. If we don't plan it, we will never do it. Don't be depressed if you only keep to 80 per cent of your plan. Sometimes we oversleep!

It is wise to start with a realistic goal. Don't be over-ambitious. It is better to spend a few minutes every day than to spend an hour-and-a-half the first day and then to give up. If you have never studied the Bible before, you might like to set aside seven minutes every day. I am sure that if you do that regularly you will steadily increase it. The more you hear God's word, the more you will want to hear it.

Mark tells us that Jesus got up early and went off to a *solitary place* to pray (Mark 1:35). It is important to try to find somewhere where we can be on our own. I love to go outside if I am in the country. In London it is harder to find 'a solitary place'. I have a corner of a room where I go to read the Bible and pray. I find that first thing in the morning is the best time – before the children are up and the telephone starts ringing. I take a cup of hot chocolate (to wake me up), the Bible, my diary and a notebook. I use the notebook to write down prayers and also things I think God may be saying to me. I use the diary as an aid to praying about each stage of my day, and also for jotting things down that come to my mind. This prevents them acting as a distracting thought.

Start by asking God to speak to you through the passage you are reading. Then read the passage. If you are a beginner I suggest reading a few verses of one of the Gospels each day. You might find it a help to use Bible reading notes which are available at most Christian bookshops.

As you read ask yourself three questions:

1. What does it say? Read it at least once and, if necessary, compare different translations.

2. What does it mean? What did it mean to the person who first wrote it and those who first read it? (This is where the notes may be helpful.)

3. How does it apply to me, my family, my work, my neighbours, the society around me? (This is the most important stage. It is when we see the relevance to our own lives that Bible reading becomes so exciting and we become conscious that we are hearing God's voice.)

Finally, we must put into practice what we hear from God. Jesus said, 'Therefore everyone who hears these words of mine and puts them into practice is like a wise man who built his house on the rock' (Matthew 7:24). As the nineteenth-century preacher D. L. Moody pointed out, 'The Bible was not given to increase our knowledge. It was given to change lives.'

I want to end by looking again at Psalm 1, with which we began this chapter. The psalmist encourages us to 'delight' in the word of God. If we do so, then he says that certain things will happen in our lives.

First, we shall *produce fruit*. The psalmist says, 'They are like trees planted by streams of water, which yield their fruit in season' (v. 3). This promise is that our life will produce fruit; the fruit of the Spirit (as we have seen in Chapter 4). And it will produce fruit in terms of other people's lives being changed as a result. It is not only for our benefit that we read the Bible, but so that we can be a blessing to other people – to our friends, colleagues, neighbours and the society in which we live. This is fruit that will last into eternity (John 15:16).

Secondly, we shall have the strength to *persevere* in our walk with the Lord. God's promise to those of us whose delight is in the law of the Lord is that we will be like trees whose 'leaves do not wither' (v. 3).

If we stay close to Jesus Christ through his word, we will not dry up or lose our spiritual vitality. It is not enough to have great spiritual experiences, although they are very important and very wonderful. Unless we are deeply rooted in Jesus Christ, in his word and in that relationship with him, we won't be able to withstand the storms of life. If we *are* rooted in that relationship, if we *are* delighting in his word, then when the storms come we shall stand.

Thirdly, the psalmist says that the person who delights in the word of God will *prosper* in 'whatever they do' (v. 3). Our lives may not be ones of material prosperity, but we shall prosper in ways that really matter in life – in our relationship with God, in our relationships with other people and in the transforming of our characters into the likeness of Jesus Christ. These things are far more valuable than material wealth.

I hope that you, with the psalmist and with millions of other Christians, will determine to make the Bible your 'delight'.

7

How Does God Guide Us?

We all have to make decisions in life. We are faced with decisions about relationships, marriage, children, use of time, jobs, homes, money, holidays, possessions, giving and so on. Some of these are very big decisions; some smaller. In many cases, it is of the utmost importance that we make the right decisions – for instance in our choice of a marriage partner. We need God's help.

Guidance springs out of our relationship with God. He promises to guide those who are walking with him. He says: 'I will instruct you and teach you in the way you should go' (Psalm 32:8). Jesus promises to lead and guide his followers: 'He calls his own sheep by name and leads them out . . . His sheep follow him because they know his voice' (John 10:3-4). He longs for us to discover his will (Colossians 1:9; Ephesians 5:17). He is concerned about each of us as individuals. He loves us and wants to speak to us about what we should be doing with our lives – about little things as well as big things.

God has a plan for our lives (Ephesians 2:10). Sometimes people are worried by this. They think, 'I'm not sure that I want God's plan for my life. Will his plans be good?' We need not fear. God loves us and wants the very best for our lives. Paul tells us that

God's will for our lives is 'good, pleasing and perfect' (Romans 12:2). He said to his people through the prophet Jeremiah: '"For I know the plans I have for you," declares the Lord, "plans to prosper you and not to harm you, plans to give you hope and a future"' (Jeremiah 29:11).

He is saying, 'Don't you realise that I have a really good plan for your life? I have prepared something wonderful.' This cry from the Lord's heart came because he saw the mess his people had got themselves into when they didn't follow his plans. All around us we see people whose lives are in a muddle. Often people say to me after they have come to Christ, 'I wish I had become a Christian five or ten years earlier. Look at my life now. It is such a mess.'

If we are to find out about God's plans for us, we need to ask him about them. God warned his people about embarking on plans without consulting him: '"Woe to the obstinate children," declares the Lord, "to those who carry out plans that are not mine . . . who go down to Egypt *without consulting me*"' (Isaiah 30:1-2, italics mine). Of course, Jesus is the supreme example of doing the will of his Father. He was consistently 'led by the Spirit' (Luke 4:1) and only did what he saw his Father doing (John 5:19).

We make mistakes because we fail to consult the Lord. We make some plan and think, 'I want to do that but I am not quite sure whether God wants me to do it. I think I'd better not ask him, just in case it's not his will for me!'

God guides us when we are prepared to do his will rather than insisting that our own way is right. The psalmist says, 'He guides the humble' (Psalm 25:9) and 'confides in those who fear [respect] him' (v. 14). God guides those whose attitude is like Mary's: 'I am the Lord's servant and I am willing to do whatever he wants' (Luke 1:38, The Living Bible). The moment we are prepared to do his will, he begins to reveal his plans for our lives.

There is a verse in the Psalms which I go back to time and time again: 'Commit your way to the Lord; trust in him, and he will act' (Psalm 37:5, RSV). Our part is to commit the decision to the Lord and then to trust him. When we have done that, we can wait expectantly for him to act.

Towards the end of our time at university, one of my friends called Nicky, who had become a Christian about the same time that I did, began to get to know very well a girl who was not a Christian. He felt it was not right to marry her unless she shared his faith in Christ. He did not want to put her under any pressure. So he did what the psalmist said and committed it to the Lord. He said, in effect, 'Lord, if this relationship is not right, I pray that you will stop it. If it is right, then I pray she will become a Christian by the last day of the Spring term.' He did not tell her or anyone else about this date. He put his 'trust in him' and waited for him to act. The final day of the Spring term arrived and they happened to be going to a party together that night. Just before midnight she told him she wanted to go for a drive. So they got into the car and she gave him a whole string of directions off the top of her head, just for fun: 'Three turnings left, three turnings right, drive straight for three miles and stop.' He played along and followed them. They ended up in the American cemetery which has one enormous cross in the centre surrounded by hundreds of little crosses. She was shocked and deeply moved by the symbol of the cross, and also by the fact that God had used her instructions to get her attention. She burst into tears. Moments later, she came to faith in Christ. They have now been happily married for many years and still look back and remember how God's hand was on them at that moment.

Given that we are willing to do what God wants us to do, in what ways should we expect God to speak to us and guide us? There are various ways in which he guides us. Sometimes God speaks through one of the ways set out below; sometimes it is a combination. If it is a major decision he may speak through all of them. They are sometimes called the five 'CSs'.

COMMANDING SCRIPTURE

As we have seen, God's general will for all people in all places in all circumstances is revealed in Scripture. He has told us what he thinks about a whole range of issues. From the Bible we know that certain things are wrong. Therefore, we can be quite sure that God will not guide us to do these things. Sometimes a married person says, 'I have fallen in love with this man/woman. We love each other so much. I feel God is leading me to leave my husband/wife and to start this new relationship.' But God has already made his will clear. He has said, 'You shall not commit adultery' (Exodus 20:14). We can be quite sure that God will not guide us to commit adultery.

Sometimes people feel led to save money by not paying their income tax! But God has made it clear that we are to pay any taxes which are due (Romans 13:7). In these and many other areas God has revealed his general will. We do not need to ask his guidance; he has already given it. If we are not sure, we may need to ask someone who knows the Bible better than we do whether there is anything on that issue. Once we have discovered what the Bible says, we need search no further.

Although God's general will is revealed in the Bible, we cannot always find his particular will for our lives there. As we have seen, the Bible tells us that it is his general will for people to get married. Although singleness is a high calling, it is the exception rather than the rule (eg, 1 Corinthians 7:2). We know that Christians are only free to marry other Christians (2 Corinthians 6:14). But the Bible does not tell us whom we should marry!

As we saw in the chapter on the Bible, God still speaks today through the Scriptures. He may speak to us as we read. The psalmist says, 'Your statutes . . . are my counsellors' (Psalm 119:24). That is not to say that we find God's will by opening the Bible anywhere at random and seeing what it says. Rather, as we develop the habit of regular, methodical Bible study we begin to find it quite extraordinary how appropriate each day's reading seems to be for our own particular circumstances.

Sometimes a verse seems almost to leap out of the page at us and we sense God speaking through it. This was certainly my experience, for example, when I sensed God calling me to change jobs. Each time I felt God speaking to me as I read the Bible, I wrote it down. I noted at least fifteen different occasions when I believe God spoke to me through the Bible about his call to me to leave my work as a lawyer and train for ordination in the Church of England.

COMPELLING SPIRIT

Guidance is very personal. When we become Christians, the Spirit of God comes to live within us. When he does so, he begins to communicate with us. We need to learn to hear his voice. Jesus said that his sheep (his followers) would recognise his voice (John 10:4-5). We recognise a good friend's voice immediately on the telephone. If we do not know the person so well, it may be harder and take more time. The more we get to know Jesus, the easier we will find it to recognise his voice.

We find Paul and his companions, for example, planning to enter Bithynia, 'but the Spirit of Jesus would not allow them to' (Acts 16:7). So they went a different way. We do not know how exactly the Spirit spoke to them, but it may have been in one of a number of ways.

Here are three examples of the way in which God speaks by his Spirit.

1. Often he speaks to us as we pray

Prayer is a two-way conversation. Suppose I go to the doctor and say, 'Doctor, I have a number of problems: I have a problem of fungus growing under my toenails, I have piles, my eyes itch, I need a flu jab; I have very bad backaches and I have tennis elbow.' Then, having got through my list of complaints, I look at my watch and say, 'Goodness me, time is getting on. Well, I must be off. Thanks very much for listening.' The doctor might want to say, 'Hang on a second. Why don't you listen to me?' If whenever we pray we only speak to God and never take time to listen, we make the same mistake. In the Bible we find God speaking to his people. For example, on one occasion as the Christians were worshipping the Lord and fasting, the Holy Spirit said, '"Set apart for me Barnabas and Saul for the work to which I have called them." So after they had fasted and prayed, they placed their hands on them and sent them off' (Acts 13:2-3).

Again, we don't know exactly how the Holy Spirit spoke. It may be that as they were praying the thought came into their minds. That is a common way in which God speaks. People sometimes describe it as 'impressions' or feeling it 'in their bones'. It is possible for the Holy Spirit to speak in all these ways.

Obviously such thoughts and feelings need to be tested (1 John 4:1). Is the impression in line with the Bible? Does it promote love? If it does not, it cannot come from a God who is love (1 John 4:16). Is it strengthening, encouraging and comforting (1 Corinthians 14:3)? When we have made the decision, do we know God's peace (Colossians 3:15)?

2. God sometimes speaks to us by giving us a strong desire to do something

'God . . . works in you to *will* and to act according to his good purpose' (Philippians 2:13, italics mine). As we surrender our wills

104

to God, he works in us and often changes our desires. Again, speaking from my own experience, before I became a Christian the last thing in the world I would have wanted to be was an ordained clergyman in the Church of England. Yet when I came to Christ and said I was willing to do what he wanted, I found my desires changed. Now I cannot imagine a greater privilege or a more fulfilling job for me than the one I am doing at the moment.

Sometimes people try to imagine the thing that they would least like to do and then assume that God will ask them to do exactly that. I do not believe God is like that. So don't be frightened and say, 'If I become a Christian, God will make me be a missionary.' If that is what he wants you to do, and your will is surrendered, he will give you a strong desire to do that.

3. God sometimes guides in more unusual ways

There are many examples in the Bible of God guiding individuals in dramatic ways. He spoke to Samuel as a small boy in a way in which he could hear with his physical ears (1 Samuel 3:4-14). He guided Abraham (Genesis 18), Joseph (Matthew 2:19) and Peter (Acts 12:7) through angels. He often spoke through prophets both in the Old Testament and in the New Testament (eg, Agabus – Acts 11:27-28; 21:10-11). He guided through visions (sometimes referred to today as 'pictures'). For example, one night God spoke to Paul in a vision. He saw a man in Macedonia standing and begging him, 'Come over to Macedonia and help us.' Not surprisingly, Paul and his companions took this as guidance that God had called them to preach the gospel in Macedonia (Acts 16:10).

We also find examples of God guiding through dreams (eg, Matthew 1:20; 2:12-13, 22). I was praying for a couple who were good friends of ours. The husband had recently come to faith in Christ. The wife was highly intelligent, but strongly against what had happened to her husband. She became a little hostile towards us. One night I had a dream in which I saw her face quite changed, her eyes full of the joy of the Lord. This encouraged us to continue praying and keeping close to them. A few months later she came to faith in Christ. I remember looking at her and seeing the face I had seen in the dream a few months earlier.

All these are ways in which God guided people in the past and he still does today.

COMMON SENSE

When we become Christians we are not called to abandon common sense. The psalmist warns: 'Do not be like the horse or mule, which have no understanding but must be controlled by bit and bridle or they will not come to you' (Psalm 32:9).

The New Testament writers often encourage us to think and never discourage us from using our minds (eg, 2 Timothy 2:7).

If we abandon common sense, then we get ourselves into absurd situations. In his book *Knowing God*, J. I. Packer quotes an example of a woman who each morning, having consecrated the day to the Lord as soon as she woke, 'would then ask him whether she was to get up or not', and would not stir till 'the voice' told her to dress.

As she put on each article she asked the Lord whether she was to put it on and very often the Lord would tell her to put on the right shoe and leave off the other; sometimes she was to put on both stockings and no shoes; and sometimes both shoes and no stockings. It was the same with all the articles of dress . . .[37]

It is true to say that God's promises of guidance were not given so that we could avoid the strain of thinking. Indeed, John Wesley, the father of Methodism, said that God *usually* guided him by presenting reasons to his mind for acting in a certain way. This is important in every area – especially in the areas of marriage and jobs.

Common sense is one of the factors to be taken into account in the whole area of choosing a partner for life. It is common sense to look at at least three very important areas.

First, *are we spiritually compatible?* Paul warns of the danger of marrying someone who is not a Christian (2 Corinthians 6:14). In practice, if one of the parties is not a Christian, it nearly always leads to a great tension in the marriage. The Christian feels torn between the desire to serve his or her partner and the desire to serve the Lord. But spiritual compatibility means more than the fact that both are Christians. It means that each party respects the other's spirituality, rather than simply being able to say, 'At least they pass the test of being a Christian.'

Secondly, *are we personally compatible?* Obviously, our marriage partner should be a very good friend and someone with whom we have a great deal in common. One of the many advantages of not sleeping together before getting married is that it is easier to concentrate on this area and discover whether or not there is personal compatibility. Often the sexual side can dominate the early stages of a relationship. If the foundations have not been built on friendship then when the initial sexual excitement wears off it can leave the relationship with a very fragile basis.

Thirdly, *are we physically compatible?* By this I mean that we should be attracted to each other. It is not enough to be spiritually and emotionally compatible; the chemistry must work as well. Often the secular world puts it first, but this comes last in the order of priorities. The world often says that it is necessary to sleep together in order to see whether there is sexual compatibility. This is quite wrong. In the biological sense, any incompatibility that can be tested by sexual intercourse is so rare that it can be discounted.

Again, common sense is vital when considering God's guidance about our jobs and careers. The general rule is that we should stay in our current job (if we are in employment) until God calls us to do something else (1 Corinthians 7:17-24). Having said that, in seeking God's will for one's career, it is common sense to take a long-term view of life. It is wise to look ahead ten, fifteen, twenty years and ask the questions: 'Where is my present job taking me? Is that where I want to go in the long term? Or is my long-term vision for something quite different? In which case, where should I be now in order to get there?'

COUNSEL OF THE SAINTS[38]

The Book of Proverbs is full of injunctions to seek wise advice. The writer asserts that 'the wise listen to advice' (Proverbs 12:15). He warns that 'plans fail for lack of counsel', but on the other hand, 'with many advisers they succeed' (Proverbs 15:22). Therefore, he urges, 'Make plans by seeking advice' (Proverbs 20:18).

While seeking advice is very important, we need to remember that ultimately our decisions are between us and God. They are our responsibility. We cannot shift that responsibility onto others or seek to blame them if things go wrong. The 'counsel of the saints' (ie other Christians) is part of guidance – but it is not the only part. Sometimes it may be right to go ahead in spite of the advice of others.

If we are faced with a decision where we need advice, whom should we consult? To the writer of Proverbs, 'fear of the Lord is the beginning of wisdom'. Presumably, therefore, he is thinking of advice from those who 'fear the Lord'. The best advisors are usually godly Christian people with wisdom and experience whom we respect. (It is also wise to seek the advice of parents whom we are to honour, even if we are past the age of being under their authority. Even if they are not Christians, they know us very well and can often have important insights into situations.)

I have found it a real help throughout my Christian life to have someone who is a mature Christian whom I respect and to whom I can go for advice on a whole range of issues. At different times this has been different people. I am so grateful to God for their wisdom and help in many areas. Often God's insight has come as we talked through the issues together.

When it comes to bigger decisions I have found it helpful to seek a range of advice. Over the question of ordination I sought the advice of two such men and my two closest friends, my vicar and those who were involved in the official process of selection.

The people whom we ask for advice should not be chosen on the basis that they will agree with what we have already planned to do! Sometimes one sees a person consulting countless people in the hope that they will eventually find somebody who will endorse their plans. Such advice has little weight and simply enables the person to say, 'And I consulted x and he or she agreed.'

We should consult people on the basis of their spiritual authority or their relationship to us, regardless of what we may anticipate their views to be. When my friends, Nicky and Sila Lee, who now run a church in central London, became Christians, they wondered whether it was right to continue their relationship, because although they were very much in love they were still so young and had no immediate prospects of marriage.

There was a very wise Christian man for whom Nicky had great respect. Nicky knew he had firm views on the subject of relationships and knew he felt it was unwise to be too deeply involved in a relationship while still at university. Nevertheless, Nicky decided to consult him.

The man asked Nicky, 'Have you committed your relationship with Sila to the Lord?' Nicky replied with some hesitation and great honesty, 'I think I have, but sometimes I am not sure,' to which this wise man replied, 'I can see that you love her. I think you should continue in your relationship with her.' Because this advice came from a surprising source it carried additional weight. The advice was very good and they have now had many years of happy married life to prove it.

CIRCUMSTANTIAL SIGNS

God is in ultimate control of all events. The writer of Proverbs points out: 'In your heart you may plan your course, but the Lord determines your steps' (Proverbs 16:9). Sometimes God opens doors (1 Corinthians 16:9) and sometimes he closes them (Acts 16:7). There have been two occasions in my life when God has closed the door on something which I very much wanted, and which I believed at the time was God's will. I tried to force the doors open. I prayed and I struggled and I fought, but they would not open. On both occasions I was bitterly disappointed. But I understand now, years later, why he closed those doors. Indeed I am grateful that he did. However, I am not sure we will ever know this side of heaven why God has closed certain doors in our lives.

Sometimes he opens doors in a remarkable way. The circumstances and the timing point clearly to the hand of God (eg, Genesis 24). Michael Bourdeaux is head of Keston College, a research unit devoted to helping believers in what were communist lands. His work and research are respected by governments all over the world. He studied Russian at Oxford and his Russian teacher, Dr Zernov, sent him a letter which he had received because he thought it would interest him. It detailed how monks were being beaten up by the KGB and subjected to inhuman medical examinations; how they were being rounded up in lorries and dumped many hundreds of miles away. The letter was written very simply, with no adornment, and as he read it Michael Bourdeaux felt he was hearing the true voice of the persecuted church. The letter was signed Varavva and Pronina.

In August 1964, he went on a trip to Moscow, and on his first evening there met up with old friends who explained that the persecutions were getting worse; in particular the old church of St Peter and St Paul had been demolished. They suggested that he go and see it for himself.

So he took a taxi, arriving at dusk. When he came to the square where he had remembered a very beautiful church, he found nothing except a twelve-foot-high fence which hid the rubble where the church had been. Over on the other side of the square, climbing the fence to try to see what was inside, were two women. He watched them, and when they finally left the square he followed them for a hundred yards and eventually caught them up. They asked, 'Who are you?' He replied, 'I am a foreigner. I have come to find out what is happening here in the Soviet Union.'

They took him back to the house of another woman who asked him why he had come. Whereupon he said he had received a letter from the Ukraine via Paris. When she asked who it was from, he replied, 'Varavva and Pronina.' There was silence. He wondered if he had said something wrong. There followed a flood of uncontrolled sobbing. The woman pointed and said, 'This is Varavva, and this is Pronina.'

The population of Russia is over 140 million. The Ukraine,

from where the letter was written, is 1,300 kilometres from Moscow. Michael Bourdeaux had flown from England six months after the letter had been written. They would not have met had either party arrived at the demolished church an hour earlier or an hour later. That was one of the ways God called Michael Bourdeaux to set up his life's work.[39]

Don't be in a hurry

Sometimes God's guidance seems to come immediately it is asked for (eg, Genesis 24), but often it takes much longer: sometimes months or even years. We may have a sense that God is going to do something in our lives, but have to wait a long time for it to happen. On these occasions we need patience like that of Abraham who 'after waiting patiently . . . received what was promised' (Hebrews 6:15). While waiting, he was tempted at one point to try to fulfil God's promises by his own means – with disastrous results (see Genesis 16 and 21).

Sometimes we hear God correctly, but we get the timing wrong. God spoke to Joseph in a dream about what would happen to him and his family. He probably expected immediate fulfilment, but he had to wait years. Indeed, while he was in prison it must have been hard for him to believe that his dreams would ever be fulfilled. But thirteen years after the original dream, he saw God's fulfilment. The waiting was part of the preparation (see Genesis 37–50).

In this area of guidance, we all make mistakes. Sometimes, like Abraham, we try to fulfil God's plans by our own wrong methods. Like Joseph we get the timing wrong. Sometimes we feel that we have made too much of a mess of our lives by the time we come to Christ for God to do anything with us. But God is greater than that. He is able to 'restore to you the years which the swarming locust has eaten' (Joel 2:25, RSV). He is able to make something good out of whatever is left of our lives – whether it is a short time or a long time – if we will offer what we have to him and co-operate with his Spirit.

Lord Radstock was staying in a hotel in Norway in the mid-nineteenth century. He heard a little girl playing the piano down in the hallway. She was making a terrible noise: 'Plink . . . plonk . . . plink. . . .' It was driving him mad! A man came and sat beside her and began playing alongside her, filling in the gaps. The result was the most beautiful music. He later discovered that the man playing alongside was the girl's father, Alexander Borodin, composer of the opera *Prince Igor*.

Paul writes that 'in all things God works for the good of those who love him, who have been called according to his purpose' (Romans 8:28). As we falteringly play our part – seeking his will for our lives by reading (commanding Scripture), listening (controlling Spirit), thinking (common sense), talking (counsel of the saints), watching (circumstantial signs) and waiting – God comes and sits alongside us 'and in all things . . . works for the good'. He takes our 'plink . . . plonk . . . plonk . . .' and makes something beautiful out of our lives.

8

Who Is the Holy Spirit?

I had a group of friends at university, five of whom were called Nicky! We used to meet for lunch most days. In February 1974 most of us came to faith in Jesus Christ. We immediately became very enthusiastic about our new-found faith. One of the Nickys, however, was slow to get going. He didn't seem excited about his relationship with God, with reading the Bible or with praying.

One day, someone prayed for him to be filled with the Spirit. He was; and it transformed his life. A great big smile came across his face. He became well-known for his radiance – he still is years later. Thereafter, if there was a Bible study or a prayer meeting or a church in reach, Nicky was there. He loved to be with other Christians. He became the most magnetic personality. People were drawn to him and he helped many others to believe and to be filled with the Spirit in the way that he had been.

What was it that made such a difference to Nicky? I think that he would answer that it was the experience of the Holy Spirit. Many people know a certain amount about God the Father and Jesus the Son. But there is a great deal of ignorance about the Holy Spirit. Hence, three chapters of this book are devoted to the third person of the Trinity.

Some old translations speak of the 'Holy Ghost' and this can make him seem a little frightening. The Holy Spirit is not a ghost but a Person. He has all the characteristics of personhood. He thinks (Acts 15:28), speaks (Acts 1:16), leads (Romans 8:14) and can be grieved (Ephesians 4:30). He is sometimes described as the Spirit of Christ (Romans 8:9) or the Spirit of Jesus (Acts 16:7). He is the way in which Jesus is present with his people. The schoolchild's definition is 'Jesus' other self'.

What is he like? He is sometimes described in the original Greek as the *parakletos* (John 14:16). This is a difficult word to translate. It means 'one called alongside' – a counsellor, a comforter and an encourager. Jesus said the Father will give you 'another' counsellor. The word for 'another' means 'of the same kind'. In other words, the Holy Spirit is just like Jesus.

In this chapter I want to look at the person of the Holy Spirit: who he is and what we can learn about him as we trace his activity through the Bible from Genesis 1 right through to the Day of Pentecost. Because the Pentecostal movement began at the beginning of this century it might be tempting to think that the Holy Spirit is a twentieth-century phenomenon. This is, of course, far from the truth.

He was involved in creation

We see evidence of the activity of the Holy Spirit in the opening

116

verses of the Bible: 'In the beginning God created the heavens and the earth. Now the earth was formless and empty, darkness was over the surface of the deep, and the Spirit of God was hovering over the waters' (Genesis 1:1-2).

We see in the account of the creation how the Spirit of God caused new things to come into being and brought order out of chaos. He is the same Spirit today. He often brings new things into people's lives and into churches. He brings order and peace into chaotic lives, freeing people from harmful habits and addictions and from the confusion and mess of broken relationships.

When God created humankind, he 'formed a man from the dust of the ground and breathed into his nostrils the breath of life, and the man became a living being' (Genesis 2:7). The Hebrew word implied here for breath is *ruach*, which is also the word for 'Spirit'. The *ruach* of God brings physical life to humanity formed from dust. Likewise, he brings spiritual life to people and churches, both of which can be as dry as dust!

Some years ago I was speaking to a clergyman who was telling me that his life and his church had been like that – a bit dusty. One day he and his wife were filled with the Spirit of God, they found a new enthusiasm for the Bible and their lives were transformed. His church became a centre of life. The youth group, started by his son who had also been filled with the Spirit, experienced explosive growth and became one of the largest in the area.

Many are hungry for life and are attracted to people and churches where they see the life of the Spirit of God.

HE CAME UPON PARTICULAR PEOPLE AT PARTICULAR TIMES FOR PARTICULAR TASKS

When the Spirit of God comes upon people something happens. He does not just bring a nice warm feeling! He comes for a purpose and we see examples of this in the Old Testament.

He filled people for artistic work. The Spirit of God filled Bezalel 'with skill, ability and knowledge in all kinds of crafts – to make artistic designs for work in gold, silver and bronze, to cut and set stones, to work in wood, and to engage in all kinds of craftsmanship' (Exodus 31:3-5).

It is possible to be a talented musician, writer or artist without being filled with the Spirit. But when the Spirit of God fills people for these tasks their work often takes on a new dimension. It has a different effect on others. It has a far greater spiritual impact. This can be true even where the natural ability of the musician or artist is not particularly outstanding. Hearts can be touched and lives changed. No doubt something like this happened through Bezalel.

He also filled individuals for the task of leadership. During the time of the Judges, the people of Israel were often overrun by various foreign nations. At one time it was the Midianites. God called Gideon to lead Israel. Gideon was very conscious of his own weakness and asked, 'How can I save Israel? My clan is the weakest in Manasseh, and I am the least in my family' (Judges 6:15). Yet when the Spirit of God came upon Gideon (v. 34), he became one of the remarkable leaders of the Old Testament.

In leadership, God often uses those who feel weak, inadequate and ill-equipped. When they are filled with the Spirit, they become outstanding leaders in the church. A notable example of this was the Revd E. J. H. 'Bash' Nash. As a nineteen-year-old clerk in an insurance office he had come to faith in Christ and was a man who was full of the Spirit of God. It has been written about him that 'there was nothing particularly impressive about him . . . He was neither athletic nor adventurous. He claimed no academic prowess or artistic talent.'[40] Yet John Stott (whom he led to Christ) said of him: 'Nondescript in outward appearance, his heart was ablaze with Christ.' The obituary in the national and the church press summed up his life like this:

> Bash . . . was a quiet, unassuming clergyman who never made the limelight, hit the headlines or wanted preferment, and yet whose influence within the Church of England during the last 50 years was probably greater than almost any of his contemporaries, for there must be hundreds of men today, many in positions of responsibility, who thank God for him for it was through his ministry that they were led to a Christian commitment.
>
> Those who knew him well, and those who worked with him, never expect to see his like again; for rarely can anyone have meant so much to so many as this quietly spoken, modest and deeply spiritual man.[41]

Elsewhere we see the Holy Spirit filling people with strength and power. The story of Samson is well-known. On one occasion, the Philistines tied him up by binding him with ropes. Then, 'The Holy Spirit of the Lord came upon him in power. The ropes on his arms became like charred flax, and the bindings dropped from his hands' (Judges 15:14).

What is true in the Old Testament physically is often true in the New Testament spiritually. It is not that we are physically bound by ropes, but that we are tied down by fears, habits or addictions which take a grip on our lives. We are controlled by bad temper or by patterns of thought such as envy, jealousy or lust. We know that we are bound when we cannot stop something, even when we want to. When the Spirit of God came upon Samson, the ropes became like charred flax and he was free. The Spirit of God is able to set people free today from anything that binds them.

Later on we see how the Spirit of God came upon the prophet Isaiah to enable him 'to preach good news to the poor . . . to bind up the broken-hearted, to proclaim freedom for the captives and release for the prisoners' and 'to comfort all who mourn' (Isaiah 61:1-3).

We sometimes feel a sense of helplessness when confronted with the problems of the world. I often felt this before I was a Christian. I knew I had little or nothing to offer those whose lives were in a mess. I still feel like that sometimes. But I know that with the help of the Spirit of God, we do indeed have something to give. The Spirit of God enables us to bring the good news of Jesus Christ to bind up those with broken hearts; to proclaim freedom to those who are in captivity to things in their lives which deep down they hate; to release those who are imprisoned by their own wrong-doing; and to bring the comfort of the Holy Spirit (who is after all the comforter) to those who are sad, grieving or mourning. If we are going to help people in a way which lasts eternally, we cannot do so without the Spirit of God.

HE WAS PROMISED BY THE FATHER

We have seen examples of the work of the Spirit of God in the Old Testament. But his activity was limited to particular people at particular times for particular tasks. As we go through the Old Testament we find that God promises that he is going to do something new. The New Testament calls this 'the promise of the Father'. There is an increasing sense of anticipation. *What was going to happen?*

In the Old Testament God made a covenant with his people. He said that he would be their God and that they would be his people. He required that they should keep his laws. Sadly, the people found that they were unable to keep his commands. The Old Covenant was consistently broken.

God promised that one day he would make a *new* covenant with his people. This covenant would be different from the first covenant: 'I will put my law in their minds and write it on their hearts' (Jeremiah 31:33). In other words, under the New Covenant the law would be internal rather than external. If you go on a long hike, you start off by carrying your provisions on your back. They weigh you down and slow you up. But when you have eaten them, not only has the weight gone but you also have a new energy coming from inside. What God promised through Jeremiah was a time when the law would no longer be a weight on the outside but would become a source of energy from inside. *How was this going to happen?*

Ezekiel gives us the answer. He was a prophet, and God spoke through him, elaborating on the earlier promise. 'I will give you a new heart and put a new spirit in you,' he said. 'I will remove from you your heart of stone and give you a heart of flesh. And I will put my Spirit in you and move you to follow my decrees and be careful to keep my laws' (Ezekiel 36:26-27).

God was saying through the prophet Ezekiel that this is what will happen when God puts his Spirit within us. This is how he will change our hearts and make them soft ('hearts of flesh') rather than hard ('hearts of stone'). The Spirit of God will move us to follow his decrees and keep his laws.

Jackie Pullinger has spent the last thirty years working in what was the lawless walled city of Kowloon in Hong Kong. She has given her life to working with prostitutes, heroin addicts and gang members. She began a memorable talk by saying, 'God wants us to have soft hearts and hard feet. The trouble with many of us is that we have hard hearts and soft feet.' Christians should have hard feet in that we should be tough rather than morally weak or 'wet'. Jackie is a glowing example of this in her willingness to go without sleep, food and comfort in order to serve others. Yet she also has a soft heart: a heart filled with compassion. The toughness is in her feet, not her heart.

We have seen what 'the promise of the Father' involves and how it is going to happen. The prophet Joel tells us *to whom it is going to happen*. God says through Joel:

> I will pour out my Spirit on all people.
> Your sons and daughters will prophesy,
> your old men will dream dreams,
> your young men will see visions.
> Even on my servants, both men and women,
> I will pour out my Spirit in those days.
>
> (Joel 2:28-29)

Joel is foretelling that the promise will no longer be reserved for particular people at particular times for particular tasks, but it will be for all. God will pour out his Spirit regardless of sex ('sons and daughters . . . men and women'); regardless of age ('old men . . . young men'); regardless of background, race, colour or rank ('even on my servants'). There will be a new ability to hear God ('prophesy . . . dream . . . see visions'). Joel prophesied that the Spirit would be poured out with great generosity on all God's people.

Yet all these promises remained unfulfilled for at least 300 years. The people waited and waited for the 'promise of the Father' to be fulfilled until at the coming of Jesus there was a burst of activity of the Spirit of God.

With the birth of Jesus, the trumpet sounds. Almost everyone connected with the birth of Jesus was filled with the Spirit of God. John the Baptist, who was to prepare the way, was filled with the

Spirit even before his birth (Luke 1:15). Mary, his mother, was promised: 'The Holy Spirit will come upon you, and the power of the Most High will overshadow you' (Luke 1:35). When Elizabeth her cousin came into the presence of Jesus, who was still in his mother's womb, she too was 'filled with the Holy Spirit' (v. 41) and even John the Baptist's father Zechariah was 'filled with the Holy Spirit' (v. 67). In almost every case there is an outburst of praise or prophecy.

JOHN THE BAPTIST LINKS HIM WITH JESUS

When John was asked whether he was the Christ he replied: 'I baptise you with water. But one more powerful than I will come, the thongs of whose sandals I am not worthy to untie. He will baptise you with the Holy Spirit and with fire' (Luke 3:16). Baptism with water is very important, but it is not enough. Jesus is the Spirit baptiser. The Greek word means 'to overwhelm', 'to immerse' or 'to plunge'. This is what should happen when we are baptised in the Spirit. We should be completely overwhelmed by, immersed in and plunged into the Spirit of God.

Sometimes this experience is like a hard, dry sponge being dropped into water. There can be a hardness in our lives which stops us absorbing the Spirit of God. It may take a little time for the initial hardness to wear off and for the sponge to be filled. So it is one thing for the sponge to be in the water ('baptised'), but it is another for the water to be in the sponge ('filled'). When the sponge is filled with water, the water literally pours out of it.

Jesus was a man completely filled with the Spirit of God. The Spirit of God descended on him in bodily form at his baptism (Luke 3:22). He returned to the Jordan 'full of the Holy Spirit' and was 'led by the Spirit in the desert' (Luke 4:1). He returned to Galilee 'in the power of the Spirit' (v. 14). In a synagogue in Nazareth he read the lesson from Isaiah 61:1, 'The Spirit of the Lord is on me . . .' and said, 'Today this scripture is fulfilled in your hearing' (v. 21).

JESUS PREDICTED HIS PRESENCE

On one occasion Jesus went to a Jewish feast called the Feast of Tabernacles. Thousands of Jews would go to Jerusalem to celebrate the feast, looking back to the time when Moses brought water from a rock. They thanked God for providing water in the past year and prayed that he would do the same in the coming year. They looked forward to a time when water would pour out of the temple (as prophesied by Ezekiel), becoming deeper and deeper and bringing life, fruitfulness and healing wherever it went (Ezekiel 47).

This passage was read at the Feast of Tabernacles and enacted visually. The High Priest would go down to the pool of Siloam and fill a golden pitcher with water. He would then lead the people to the temple where he would pour water through a funnel in the west side of the altar, and into the ground, in anticipation of the great river that would flow from the temple. According to Rabbinic tradition, Jerusalem was the navel of the earth and the temple of Mount Zion was the centre of the navel (its 'belly' or 'innermost being').

On the last day of the feast . . . Jesus stood up and proclaimed, 'If anyone thirst, let him come to me and drink. He who believes in me, as the scripture has said, "Out of his heart [the original word means 'belly' or 'innermost being'] shall flow rivers of living water"' (John 7:38, RSV). He was saying that the promises of Ezekiel and others would not be fulfilled in a place, but in a Person. It is out of the innermost being of Jesus that the river of life will flow. Also, in a derivative sense, the streams of living water will flow from every Christian! ('Whoever believes in me', v. 38). From us, Jesus says, this river will flow, bringing life, fruitfulness and healing to others promised by God through Ezekiel.

John went on to explain that Jesus was speaking about the Holy Spirit 'whom those who believed in him were later to receive' (v. 39). He added that 'up to that time the Spirit had not been given' (v. 39). The promise of the Father had still not been fulfilled. Even after the crucifixion and resurrection of Jesus, the Spirit was not poured out. Later, Jesus told his disciples, 'I am going to send you what my Father has promised; but stay in the city until you have been clothed with power from on high' (Luke 24:49).

Just before he ascended to heaven Jesus again promised, 'You will receive power when the Holy Spirit comes on you' (Acts 1:8). But still they had to wait and pray for another ten days. Then at last on the Day of Pentecost: 'Suddenly a sound like the blowing of a violent wind came from heaven and filled the whole house where they were sitting. They saw what seemed to be tongues of fire that separated and came to rest on each of them. All of them were filled with the Holy Spirit and began to speak in other tongues as the Spirit enabled them' (Acts 2:2-4).

It had happened. The promise of the Father had been fulfilled. The crowd was amazed and mystified.

Peter stood up and explained what had occurred. He looked back to the promises of God in the Old Testament and explained how all their hopes and aspirations were now being fulfilled before their eyes. He explained that Jesus had 'received from the Father the promised Holy Spirit' and had 'poured out what you now see and hear' (Acts 2:33).

When the crowd asked what they needed to do, Peter told them to repent and be baptised in the name of Jesus so that they could receive forgiveness. Then he promised that they would receive the gift of the Holy Spirit. For, he said: 'The promise is for you and your children and for *all* who are far off – for all whom the Lord our God will call' (v. 39, italics mine).

We now live in the age of the Spirit. The promise of the Father has been fulfilled. Every single Christian receives the promise of the Father. It is no longer just for particular people, at particular times for particular tasks. It is for *all* Christians, including you and me.

9

What Does the Holy Spirit Do?

Jesus answered, 'I tell you the truth, no-one can enter the kingdom of God without being born of water and the Spirit. Flesh gives birth to flesh, but the Spirit gives birth to spirit. You should not be surprised at my saying, "You must be born again." The wind blows wherever it pleases. You hear its sound, but you cannot tell where it comes from or where it is going. So it is with everyone born of the Spirit' (John 3:5-8).

A couple of years ago I was in a church in Brighton. One of the Sunday school teachers was telling us about her Sunday school class the previous week. She had been telling the children about Jesus' teaching on being born again in John 3:5-8. She was trying to explain to the children about the difference between physical birth and spiritual birth. In trying to draw them out on the subject she asked, 'Are you born a Christian?' One little boy replied, 'No, Miss. You are born normal!'

The expression 'born again' has become a cliché. It was popularised in America and has been used even to advertise cars. Actually, Jesus was the first person to use the expression of people who were 'born of the Spirit' (John 3:8).

A new baby is born as a result of a man and a woman coming

together in sexual intercourse. In the spiritual realm, when the Spirit of God and the spirit of a man or woman come together, a new spiritual being is created. There is a new birth, spiritually. This is what Jesus is speaking about when he says, 'You must be born again.'

Jesus was saying that physical birth is not enough. We need to be born again by the Spirit. This is what happens when we become Christians. Every single Christian is born again. We may not be able to put our finger on the exact moment it occurred, but just as we know whether or not we are alive physically, so we should know that we are alive spiritually.

When we are born physically, we are born into a family. When we are born again spiritually, we are born into a Christian family. Much of the work of the Spirit can be seen in terms of a family. He assures us of our relationship with our Father and helps us to develop that relationship. He produces in us a family likeness. He unites us with our brothers and sisters, giving each member of the family different gifts and abilities. And he enables the family to grow in size.

In this chapter we will look at each of these aspects of his work in us as Christians. Until we become Christians the Spirit's work is primarily to convict us of our sin and our need for Jesus Christ, to convince us of the truth and to enable us to put our faith in him (John 16:7-15).

Sons and daughters of God

The moment we come to Christ we receive complete forgiveness. The barrier between us and God has been removed. Paul says, 'There is now no condemnation for those who are in Christ Jesus' (Romans 8:1). Jesus took all our sins – past, present and future. God takes all our sins and buries them in the depths of the sea

(Micah 7:19), and as the Dutch author Corrie Ten Boom used to say, 'He puts up a sign saying "No fishing".'

Not only does he wipe the slate clean, but he also brings us into a relationship with God as sons and daughters. Not all men and women are children of God in this sense, although all of us were created by God. It is only to those who receive Jesus, to those who believe in his name, that he gives the 'right to become children of God' (John 1:12). Sonship in the New Testament (which is used in the generic sense to include sons and daughters) is not a natural status, but a spiritual one. We become sons and daughters of God not by being born, but by being born again by the Spirit.

The Book of Romans has been described as the Himalayas of the New Testament. Chapter 8 is Mount Everest and verses 14-17 could well be described as the peak of Everest.

Because those who are led by the Spirit of God are children of God. For you did not receive a spirit that makes you a slave again to fear, but you received the Spirit of adoption. And by him we cry, 'Abba, Father.' The Spirit himself testifies with our spirit that we are God's children. Now if we are children, then we are heirs – heirs of God and co-heirs with Christ, if indeed we share in his sufferings in order that we may also share in his glory (Romans 8:14-17).

First of all, there is no higher privilege than to be a child of God. Under Roman law if an adult wanted an heir he could either choose one of his own sons or adopt a son. God has only one begotten Son – Jesus, but he has many adopted sons. There is a fairy story in which a reigning monarch adopts waifs and strays and makes them princes. In Christ, the fairy story has become solid fact. We have been adopted into God's family. There could be no higher honour.

Billy Bray was a drunken and loose-living miner from Cornwall, born in 1794. He was always getting involved in fights and domestic quarrels. At the age of twenty-nine he became a Christian. He went home and told his wife, 'You will never see me drunk again, by the help of the Lord.' She never did. His words, his tones and his looks had magnetic power. He was charged with divine electricity. Crowds of miners would come and hear him preach. Many were converted and there were some remarkable healings. He was always praising God and saying that he had abundant reason to rejoice. He described himself as 'a young prince'. He was the adopted son of God, the King of kings and therefore he was a prince, already possessing royal rights and privileges. His favourite expression was, 'I am the son of a King.'[42]

Once we know our status as adopted sons and daughters of God, we realise that there is no status in the world that even compares with the privilege of being a child of the Creator of the universe.

Secondly, as children we have the closest possible intimacy with God. Paul says that by the Spirit we cry, '*Abba*, Father!' This Aramaic word, *Abba* (that we looked at in Chapter 5), is not found in the Old Testament. The use of this word in addressing God was distinctive of Jesus. It is impossible to translate it, but the nearest equivalent translation is probably 'dear Father' or 'Daddy'. The English word 'Daddy' tends to suggest a Western pally relationship to a parent, whereas in Jesus' day the father was an authority figure, and 'Abba', although a term of great intimacy, is not a juvenile word. It was the term Jesus used in addressing God. Jesus allows us to share in that intimate relationship with God when we receive his Spirit. 'For you did not receive a spirit that makes you a slave again to fear, but you received the Spirit of adoption' (v. 15).

Prince Charles has many titles. He is the Heir Apparent to the Crown, his Royal Highness, the Prince of Wales, Duke of Cornwall, Knight of the Garter, Colonel in Chief of the Royal Regiment of Wales, Duke of Rothesay, Knight of the Thistle, Rear Admiral,

Great Master of the Order of Bath, Earl of Chester, Earl of Carrick, Baron of Renfrew, Lord of the Isles and Great Steward of Scotland. We would address him as 'Your Royal Highness', but I suspect to William and Harry he is 'Daddy'. When we become children of God we have an intimacy with our heavenly King. John Wesley, who had been very religious before his conversion, said about his conversion, 'I exchanged the faith of a servant for the faith of a son.'

Thirdly, the Spirit gives us the deepest possible experience of God. 'The Spirit himself testifies with our spirit that we are God's children' (v. 16). He wants us to know, deep within, that we are children of God. In the same way that I want my children to know and experience my love for them and my relationship with them, so God wants his children to be assured of that love and of that relationship.

One man who only experienced this quite late in his life is the South African Bishop Bill Burnett, who was at one time Archbishop of Capetown. I heard him say, 'When I became a bishop I believed in theology [the truth about God], but not in God. I was a practical atheist. I sought righteousness by doing good.' One day, after he had been a bishop for fifteen years, he went to speak at a confirmation service on the text in Romans, 'God has poured out his love [that is, his love for us] into our hearts by the Holy Spirit, whom he has given us' (Romans 5:5). After he had preached, he came home, poured himself a strong drink and was reading the paper when he felt the Lord saying, 'Go and pray.' He went into his chapel, knelt down in silence and sensed the Lord saying to him, 'I want your body.' He could not quite understand why (he is tall and thin and says, 'I'm not exactly Mr Universe'). However, he gave every part of himself to the Lord. 'Then,' he said, 'what I preached about happened. I experienced electric shocks of love.' He found himself flat on the floor and heard the Lord saying,

'You are my son.' When he got up, he knew indeed that something had happened. It proved a turning point in his life and ministry. Since then, through his ministry, many others have come to experience sonship through the witness of the Spirit.

Fourthly, Paul tells us that to be a son or daughter of God is the greatest security. For if we are children of God we are also 'heirs of God and co-heirs with Christ' (Romans 8:17). Under Roman law an adopted son would take his father's name and inherit his estate. As children of God we are heirs. The only difference is that we inherit, not on the death of our father, but on our own death. This is why Billy Bray was thrilled to think that 'his heavenly Father had reserved everlasting glory and blessedness' for him. We will enjoy an eternity of love with Jesus.

Paul adds, 'If indeed we share in his sufferings in order that we may also share in his glory' (v. 17). This is not a condition but an observation. Christians identify with Jesus Christ. This may mean some rejection and opposition here and now, but that is nothing compared to our inheritance as children of God.

DEVELOPING THE RELATIONSHIP

Birth is not just the climax of a period of gestation; it is the beginning of a new life and new relationships. Our relationship with our parents grows and deepens over a long period. This happens as we spend time with them; it does not happen overnight.

Our relationship with God, as we have seen in the early chapters, grows and deepens as we spend time with him. The Spirit of God helps us to develop our relationship with God. He brings us into the presence of the Father. 'For through him [Jesus] we both [Jews and Gentiles alike] have access to the Father by one Spirit' (Ephesians 2:18). Through Jesus, by the Spirit, we have access to the presence of God.

Jesus, through his death on the cross, removed the barrier between us and God. That is why we are able to come into God's presence. Often we don't appreciate that when we are praying.

When I was at university I had a room above Barclays Bank in the High Street. We used to have regular lunch parties in this room, and one day we were discussing whether or not the noise we made could be heard in the bank below. In order to find out, we decided to conduct an experiment. A girl called Kay went down into the bank. As it was lunchtime, it was packed with customers. The arrangement was that we would gradually build up the noise. First, one would jump on the floor, then two, three, four and eventually five. Next we would jump off chairs and then off the table. We wanted to see at which point we could be heard downstairs in the bank.

It turned out that the ceiling was rather thinner than we had thought. The first jump could definitely be heard. The second made a loud noise. After about the fifth, which sounded like a thunderstorm, there was total silence in the bank. Everyone had stopped cashing cheques and was looking at the ceiling, wondering what was going on. Kay was right in the middle of the bank and thought, 'What do I do? If I go out it's going to look very odd, but if I stay it is going to get worse!' She stayed. The noise built up and up. Eventually bits of polystyrene started to fall from the ceiling. At that moment, fearing the ceiling would cave in, she rushed up to tell us that we could indeed be heard in the bank!

Since, through Jesus, the barrier has been removed, God hears us when we pray. We have immmediate access to his presence, by the Spirit. We don't need to jump up and down to get his attention!

Not only does the Spirit bring us into the presence of God, he also helps us to pray (Romans 8:26). What matters is not the place in which we pray, the position in which we pray or whether or not we use set forms of prayer; what matters is whether or not we are praying in the Spirit. All prayer should be led by the Spirit. Without his help prayer can easily become lifeless and dull. In the Spirit we are caught up in the Godhead and it becomes the most important activity of our lives.

Another part of developing our relationship with God is understanding what he is saying to us. Again the Spirit of God enables us to do this. Paul says, 'I keep asking that the God of our Lord Jesus Christ, the glorious Father, may give you the Spirit of wisdom and revelation, so that you may know him better. I pray also that the eyes of your heart may be enlightened . . .' (Ephesians 1:17-18). The Spirit of God is a Spirit of wisdom and revelation. He enlightens our eyes so that, for example, we can understand what God is saying through the Bible.

Before I became a Christian I read and heard the Bible endlessly, but I did not understand it. It meant nothing to me. The reason it did not make sense to me was that I did not have the Spirit of God to interpret it. The Spirit of God is the best interpreter of what God has said.

Ultimately we will never understand Christianity without the Holy Spirit enlightening our eyes. We can see enough to make a step of faith, which is not a blind leap of faith; but real understanding often only follows faith. Anselm of Canterbury said, 'I believe in order that I might understand.'[43] Only when we believe and receive the Holy Spirit can we really understand God's revelation.

The Spirit of God helps us to develop our relationship with God and he enables us to sustain that relationship. People are often worried that they will not be able to keep going in the Christian life. They are right to worry. We can't keep going by ourselves, but God by his Spirit keeps us going. It is the Spirit who brings us into a relationship with God and it is the Spirit who maintains that relationship. We are utterly dependent on him.

THE FAMILY LIKENESS

I always find it fascinating to observe how children can look like both parents at the same time when the parents themselves may look so different. Even husbands and wives sometimes grow to look like each other as they spend time together over the years!

As we spend time in the presence of God, the Spirit of God transforms us. As Paul writes, 'And we, who with unveiled faces all reflect the Lord's glory, are being transformed into his likeness with ever-increasing glory, which comes from the Lord, who is the Spirit' (2 Corinthians 3:18). We are transformed into the moral likeness of Jesus Christ. The fruit of the Spirit is developed in our lives. Paul tells us that 'the fruit of the Spirit is love, joy, peace, patience, kindness, goodness, faithfulness, gentleness and self-control' (Galatians 5:22). These are the characteristics that the Spirit of God develops in our lives. It is not that we become perfect immediately, but over a period of time there should be a change.

The first and most important fruit of the Spirit is love. Love lies at the heart of the Christian faith. The Bible is the story of God's love for us. His desire is that we should respond by loving him and loving our neighbour. The evidence of the work of the Spirit in our lives will be an increasing love for God and an increasing love for others. Without this love everything else counts for nothing.

Second in Paul's list is joy. The journalist, Malcolm Muggeridge, wrote: 'The most characteristic and uplifting of the manifestations of conversion is rapture – an inexpressible joy which suffuses our whole being, making our fears dissolve into nothing, and our expectations all move heavenwards.'[44] This joy is not dependent on our outward circumstances; it comes from the Spirit within. Richard Wurmbrand, who was imprisoned for many years and frequently tortured on account of his faith, wrote of this joy: 'Alone in my cell, cold, hungry and in rags, I danced for joy every night

135

QUESTIONS OF LIFE

... sometimes I was so filled with joy that I felt I would burst if I did not give it expression.'[45]

The third fruit listed is peace. Detached from Christ, inner peace is a kind of spiritual marshmallow full of softness and sweetness but without much actual substance. The Greek word and Hebrew equivalent *shalom* means 'wholeness', 'soundness', 'well-being' and 'oneness with God'. There is a longing within every human heart for peace like that. Epictetus, the first-century pagan thinker, said, 'While the Emperor may give peace from war on land and sea, he is unable to give peace from passion, grief and envy. He cannot give peace of heart, for which man yearns more than ever for outward peace.'

It is wonderful to see those whose characters have been transformed into the likeness of Jesus Christ as these and the other fruit of the Spirit have grown in their lives. A woman in her eighties in our congregation said of a former vicar, 'He gets more and more like our Lord.' I cannot think of a higher compliment than that. It is the work of the Spirit of God to make us more and more like Jesus so that we carry the fragrance of the knowledge of him wherever we go (2 Corinthians 2:14).

UNITY IN THE FAMILY

When we come to Christ and become sons and daughters of God we become part of a huge family. God's desire, like that of every normal parent, is that there should be unity in his family. Jesus prayed for unity among his followers (John 17). Paul pleaded with the Ephesian Christians to 'make every effort to keep *the unity of the Spirit* through the bond of peace' (Ephesians 4:3, italics mine).

The same Holy Spirit lives in every Christian wherever they are; whatever the denomination, background, colour or race. The same Spirit is in every child of God and his desire is that we should be united. Indeed, it is a nonsense for the church to be divided because there is '*one* body and *one* Spirit . . . *one* hope . . . *one* Lord, *one* faith, *one* baptism; *one* God and Father of *all*, who is over *all* and through *all* and in *all*' (Ephesians 4:4-6, italics mine).

The same Spirit indwells Christians in Russia, China, Africa, America, the UK or wherever. In one sense it is not so important what denomination we are – Roman Catholic or Protestant; Lutheran, Methodist, Baptist, Pentecostal, Anglican or House Church. What is more important is whether or not we have the Spirit of God. If people have the Spirit of God living within them, they are Christians, and our brothers and sisters. It is a tremendous privilege to be part of this huge family; one of the great joys of coming to Christ is to experience this unity. There is a closeness and depth of relationship in the Christian church which I have never found outside of it. We must make every effort to keep the unity of the Spirit at every level: in our small groups, congregations, local church and the worldwide church.

GIFTS FOR ALL THE CHILDREN

Although there is often a family likeness and, hopefully, unity in the family, there is also great variety. No two children are identical – not even 'identical' twins are exactly alike. So it is in the body of Christ. Every Christian is different; each has a different contribution to make, each has a different gift. In the New Testament there are lists of some of the gifts of the Spirit. In 1 Corinthians Paul lists nine gifts:

> Now to each one the manifestation of the Spirit is given for the common good. To one there is given through the Spirit the message of wisdom, to another the message of knowledge by means of the same Spirit, to another faith by the same Spirit, to another gifts of healing by

that one Spirit, to another miraculous powers, to another prophecy, to another the distinguishing between spirits, to another speaking in different kinds of tongues, and to still another the interpretation of tongues. All these are the work of one and the same Spirit, and he gives them to each one, just as he determines (1 Corinthians 12:7-11).

Elsewhere he mentions other gifts: those given to apostles, teachers, helpers, administrators (1 Corinthians 12:28-30), evangelists and pastors (Ephesians 4), gifts of serving, encouraging, giving, leadership, showing mercy (Romans 12:7), hospitality and speaking (1 Peter 4). No doubt these lists were not intended to be exhaustive.

All good gifts are from God, even if some, such as miracles, more obviously demonstrate the unusual acts of God in his world. Spiritual gifts include natural talents which have been transformed by the Holy Spirit. As the German theologian Jurgen Moltmann points out, 'In principle every human potentiality and capacity can become charismatic [ie, a gift of the Spirit] through a person's call, if only they are used in Christ.'

These gifts are given to all Christians. The expression 'to each one' runs like a thread through 1 Corinthians 12. Every Christian is part of the body of Christ. There are many different parts, but one body (v. 12). We are baptised by (or in) one Spirit (v. 13). We are all given the one Spirit to drink (v. 13). There are no first- and second-class Christians. All Christians receive the Spirit. All Christians have spiritual gifts.

There is an urgent need for the gifts to be exercised. One of the major problems in the church at large is that so few are exercising their gifts. The church growth expert Eddie Gibbs once said, 'The level of unemployment in the nation pales into insignificance in comparison with that which prevails in the church.'[46] As a result, a few people are left doing everything and are totally exhausted, while the rest are under-utilised. The church has been likened to a football match, in which thousands of people desperately in need of exercise watch twenty-two people desperately in need of a rest!

The church cannot operate in maximum effectiveness until each person is playing his or her part. As David Watson, the writer and church leader, pointed out, 'In different traditions, the church for years has been either pulpit-centred or altar-centred. In both situations the dominant role has been played by the minister or priest.'[47] The church will only operate with maximum effectiveness when every person is using his or her gifts.

The Spirit of God gives each of us gifts. God does not require us to have many gifts, but he does require us to use what we have and to desire more (1 Corinthians 12:31; 14:1).

THE GROWING FAMILY

It is natural for families to grow. God said to Adam and Eve, 'Be fruitful and multiply.' It should be natural for the family of God to grow. Again, this is the work of the Spirit. Jesus said, 'You will receive power when the Holy Spirit comes on you; and you will be my witnesses in Jerusalem, and in all Judea and Samaria, and to the ends of the earth' (Acts 1:8).

The Spirit of God gives us both a desire and the ability to tell others. The playwright Murray Watts tells the story of a young man who was convinced of the truth of Christianity, but was paralysed with fear at the very thought of having to admit to being 'a Christian'. The idea of telling anyone about his new-found faith, with all the dangers of being dubbed a religious nutcase, appalled him.

For many weeks he tried to banish the thought of religion from his mind, but it was no use. It was as if he heard a whisper in his conscience, repeating over and over again, 'Follow me.'

At last he could stand it no longer and he went to a very old man, who had been a Christian for the best part of a century. He told him of his nightmare, this terrible burden of 'witnessing to the light', and how it stopped him from becoming a Christian. The man sighed and shook his head. 'This is a matter between you and Christ,' he said. 'Why bring all these other people into it?' The young man nodded slowly.

'Go home,' said the old man. 'Go into your bedroom alone. Forget the world. Forget your family, and make it a secret between you and God.'

The young man felt a weight fall from him as the old man spoke. 'You mean, I don't have to tell anyone?'

'No,' said the old man.

'No one at all?'

'Not if you don't want to.' Never had anyone dared to give him this advice before.

'Are you *sure*?' asked the young man, beginning to tremble with anticipation. 'Can this be right?'

'It is right for you,' said the old man.

So the young man went home, knelt down in prayer and was converted to Christ. Immediately, he ran down the stairs and into the kitchen, where his wife, father and three friends were sitting. 'Do you realise,' he said, breathless with excitement, 'that it's possible to be a Christian without telling anyone?'[48]

When we experience the Spirit of God we want to tell others. As we do, the family grows. The Christian family should never be static. It should be continually growing and drawing in new people, who themselves receive the power of the Holy Spirit and go out and tell others about Jesus.

I have stressed throughout this chapter that every Christian is indwelt by the Holy Spirit. Paul says, 'And if anyone does not have the Spirit of Christ, that person does not belong to Christ'

(Romans 8:9). Yet not every Christian is filled with the Spirit. Paul writes to the Christians at Ephesus and says, 'Be filled with the Spirit' (Ephesians 5:18). In the next chapter we will look at how we can be filled with the Spirit.

We started the previous chapter with Genesis 1:1-2 (the first verses in the Bible) and I want to end this chapter by looking at Revelation 22:17 (one of the last verses in the Bible). The Spirit of God is active throughout the Bible from Genesis to Revelation.

'The Spirit and the bride say, "Come!" And let those who hear say, "Come!" Let those who are thirsty come; and let all who wish take the free gift of the water of life' (Revelation 22:17).

God wants to fill every one of us with his Spirit. Some people are longing for this. Some are not so sure that they want it – in which case they do not really have a thirst. If you do not have a thirst for more of the Spirit's fullness why not pray for such a thirst? God takes us as we are. When we thirst and ask, God will give us 'the free gift of the water of life'.

10

How Can I Be Filled with the Spirit?

The evangelist J. John once addressed a conference on the subject of preaching. One of the points he made was that so often preachers exhort their hearers to do something, but they never tell them *how* to do it. They say, 'Read your Bible.' He wants to ask, 'Yes, but how?' They say, 'Pray more.' He asks, 'Yes, but how?' They say, 'Tell people about Jesus.' He asks, 'Yes, but how?' In this chapter I want to look at the question of *how* we can be filled with the Spirit.[49]

We have an old gas boiler in our house. The pilot light is on all the time. But the boiler is not always giving out heat and power. Some people have only got the pilot light of the Holy Spirit in their lives, whereas when people are filled with the Holy Spirit, they begin to fire on all cylinders (if you will forgive my mixing metaphors!). When you look at them you can almost see and feel the difference.

The Book of Acts has been described as Volume I of the history of the church. In it we see several examples of people experiencing the Holy Spirit. In an ideal world every Christian would be filled with the Holy Spirit from the moment of conversion. Sometimes it happens like that (both in the New Testament and now), but not always – even in the New Testament. We have already looked at the first occasion of the outpouring of the Holy Spirit at Pentecost in Acts 2. As we go through Acts we will see other examples.

When Peter and John prayed for the Samaritan believers and the Holy Spirit came upon them, Simon the Magician was so impressed that he offered money in order to be able to do the same thing (Acts 8:14-18). Peter warned him that it was a terrible thing to try and buy God's gift for money. But the account shows that something very wonderful must have happened.

In the next chapter (Acts 9) we see one of the most remarkable conversions of all times. When Stephen the first Christian martyr was stoned, Saul approved his death (Acts 8:1) and afterwards began to destroy the church. Going from house to house, he dragged men and women off to prison (v. 3). At the beginning of chapter 9 we find him still 'breathing out murderous threats against the Lord's disciples'.

Within the space of a few days, Saul was preaching in synagogues that 'Jesus is the Son of God' (v. 20). He caused total astonishment, with people asking, 'Isn't he the man who caused havoc in Jerusalem among those who call on this name [of Jesus]?'

What had happened in those few days to change him so completely? First, he had encountered Jesus on the road to Damascus. Secondly, he had been filled with the Spirit (v. 17). That moment, 'something like scales fell from Saul's eyes, and he could see again' (v. 18). It sometimes happens that people who were not Christians, or who were even strongly anti-Christian, have a complete turnabout in their lives when they come to Christ and are filled with the Spirit. They can become powerful advocates of the Christian faith.

At Ephesus, Paul came across a group who 'believed', but who had not even heard of the Holy Spirit. He placed his hands on them, the Holy Spirit came on them and they spoke in tongues and prophesied (Acts 19:1-7). There are people today who are in a similar position. They may have 'believed' for some time or even all their lives. They may have been baptised, confirmed and gone to church from time to time or even regularly. Yet they may know little or nothing about the Holy Spirit.

Another incident occurs early in the Book of Acts and I want to look at it in a little more detail. It is the first occasion when Gentiles were filled with the Spirit. God did something extraordinary which started with a vision given to a man called Cornelius (who had been prepared by the first vision). God also spoke to Peter through a vision and told him he wanted him to go and speak to the Gentiles at the house of this man Cornelius. Halfway through Peter's talk something remarkable happened: 'The Holy Spirit came on all who heard the message. The circumcised believers [ie, the Jews] who had come with Peter were astonished that the gift of the Holy Spirit had been poured out even on the Gentiles. For they heard them speaking in tongues and praising God' (Acts 10:44-46). In the rest of the chapter I want to examine three aspects of what happened.

THEY EXPERIENCED THE POWER OF THE HOLY SPIRIT

Peter had to stop his talk because it was obvious that something was happening. The filling of the Spirit rarely happens imperceptibly, although the experience is different for everyone.

In the description of the Day of Pentecost (Acts 2), Luke uses the language of a heavy tropical rainstorm. It is a picture of the power of the Spirit flooding their beings. There were physical manifestations. They heard a gale (v. 2) which was not a real gale, but it resembled one. It was the mighty invisible power of the ruach of God; the same word as we have seen for wind, breath and spirit in the Old Testament. Sometimes, when people are filled, they shake like a leaf in the wind. Others find themselves breathing deeply as if almost physically breathing in the Spirit.

They also saw something that resembled fire (v. 3). Physical heat sometimes accompanies the filling of the Spirit and people experience it in their hands or some other part of their bodies. One person described a feeling of 'glowing all over'. Another said she experienced 'liquid heat'. Still another described 'burning in my arms when I was not hot'. Fire perhaps symbolises the power, passion and purity which the Spirit of God brings to our lives.

For many, the experience of the Spirit may be an overwhelming experience of the love of God. Paul prays for the Christians at Ephesus that they might have 'power, together with all the saints, to grasp how wide and long and high and deep is the love of Christ' (Ephesians 3:18). The love of Christ is wide enough to reach every person in the world. It reaches across every continent to people of every race, colour, tribe and background. It is long enough to last throughout a lifetime and into eternity. It is deep enough to reach us however far we have fallen. It is high enough to lift us into the heavenly places. We see this love supremely in the cross of Christ. We know Christ's love for us because he was willing to die for us. Paul prayed that we would 'grasp' the extent of this love.

Yet he does not stop there. He goes on to pray that we would '*know* this love that *surpasses knowledge*' – that you would 'be filled to the measure of all the fulness of God' (v. 19). It is not enough to understand his love; we need to experience his love that 'surpasses knowledge'. It is often as people are filled with the Spirit – 'filled to the measure of all the fulness of God' (v. 19) that they experience in their heart this transforming love of Christ.

Thomas Goodwin, one of the Puritans of 300 years ago, illustrated this experience. He pictured a man walking along a road hand in hand with his little boy. The little boy knows that this man is his father, and that his father loves him. But suddenly the father stops, picks up the boy, lifts him into his arms, embraces him, kisses him and hugs him. Then he puts him down again, and they continue walking. It is a wonderful thing to be walking along holding your father's hand; but it is an incomparably greater thing to have his arms enfolded around you.

'He has embraced us,' says Spurgeon and he pours his love upon us and he 'hugs' us. Martyn Lloyd-Jones quotes these examples among many others in his book on Romans, and comments on the experience of the Spirit:

> Let us realize then the profound character of the experience. This is not light and superficial and ordinary; it is not something of which you can say, 'Don't worry about your feelings.' Worry about your feelings? You will have such a depth of feeling that for a moment you may well imagine that you have never 'felt' anything in your life before. It is the profoundest experience that a man can ever know.[50]

THEY WERE RELEASED IN PRAISE

When these Gentiles were filled with the Spirit they started 'praising God'. Spontaneous praise is the language of people who are excited and thrilled about their experience of God. It should involve our whole personality, including our emotions. I am asked, 'Is it right to express emotions in church? Isn't there a danger of emotionalism?'

The danger for most of us in our relationship with God is not emotionalism, but a lack of emotion – a lack of feeling. Our relationship with God can be rather cold. Every relationship of love involves our emotions. Of course, there must be more than emotions. There must be friendship, communication, understanding and service. But if I never showed any emotion towards my wife, there would be something lacking in my love for her. If we do not experience any emotion in our relationship with

God, then our whole personality is not involved. We are called to love, praise and worship God with *all* of our beings.

It could be argued that emotions are all right in private, but what about the public demonstration of emotion? After a conference at Brighton attended by the Archbishop of Canterbury there was a correspondence in *The Times* about the place of emotions in church. Under the title 'Carey's charisms' one man wrote:

> Why is it that if a cinema comedy produces laughter, the film is regarded as successful; if a theatre tragedy brings tears to the audience the production is regarded as touching; if a football match thrills the spectators, the game is reviewed as exciting; but if the congregation are moved by the glory of God in worship, the audience are accused of emotionalism?

Of course, there is such a thing as emotionalism, where emotions take precedence over the solid foundation of teaching from the Bible. But as the former Bishop of Coventry Cuthbert Bardsley once said, 'The chief danger of the Anglican church is not delirious emotionalism.' One might add, 'Nor in many other churches.' Our worship of God should involve our whole personality, mind, heart, will and emotions.

THEY RECEIVED A NEW LANGUAGE

As on the Day of Pentecost and with the Ephesian Christians (Acts 19), when the Gentiles were filled with the Spirit they received the gift of tongues. The word for 'tongues' is the same word as that for 'languages' and it means the ability to speak in a language you have never learned. It may be an angelic language (1 Corinthians 13:1) which presumably is not recognisable or it may be a recognisable human language (as at Pentecost). A young woman called Penny, in our congregation, was praying with another girl. She ran out of words in English and started praying in tongues. The girl smiled and then opened her eyes and started laughing. She said, 'You have just spoken to me in Russian.' The girl, although English, spoke fluent Russian and had a great love for the language. Penny asked, 'What have I been saying?' The girl told her that she had been saying, 'My dear child,' over and over again. Penny does not speak a single word of Russian. For that young woman those three words were of great significance. She was assured that she was important to God.

The gift of tongues has brought great blessing to many people. It is, as we have seen, one of the gifts of the Spirit. It is not the only gift or even the most important gift. Not all Christians speak in tongues nor is it necessarily a sign of being filled with the Spirit. It is possible to be filled with the Spirit and not speak in tongues. Nevertheless, for many, both in the New Testament and in Christian experience, it accompanies an experience of the Holy Spirit and may be the first experience of the more obviously supernatural activity of the Spirit. Many today are puzzled by the gift. Hence, I have devoted quite a lot of space in this chapter to the subject. In 1 Corinthians 14 Paul deals with a number of questions which are often raised.

What exactly is speaking in tongues?

It is a form of prayer (one of the many different forms of prayer found in the New Testament), according to Paul, 'for those who speak in a tongue do not speak to people but *to God*' (1 Corinthians 14:2, italics mine). It is a form of prayer which builds up the individual Christian (v. 4). Obviously, the gifts which directly edify the church are even more important, but this does not make tongues unimportant. The benefit of tongues is that it is a form of prayer which transcends the limitation of human language. This seems to be what Paul means when he says 'For if I

QUESTIONS OF LIFE

pray in a tongue, my spirit prays, but my mind is unfruitful'
(1 Corinthians 14:14).

Everybody, to a greater or lesser extent, is limited by language. I
am told that the average Englishman knows 5,000 English words.
Winston Churchill apparently used 50,000 words. But even he was
limited to that extent. Often people experience frustration that
they cannot express what they really feel, even in a human
relationship. They feel things in their spirits, but they do not know
how to put them into words. This is often true also in our
relationship with God.

This is where the gift of tongues can be a great help. It enables us
to express to God what we really feel in our spirits without going
through the process of translating it into English. (Hence Paul says,
'My mind is unfruitful.') It is not mindless; it is unfruitful because
it is not going through the process of translation into an intelligible
language.

In what areas does it help?
There are three areas in which many people have found this gift
especially helpful.

First, in the area of *praise and worship*. We are particularly
limited in our language. When children (or even adults) write
thank-you letters it is not long before they run out of language, and
we find that words such as 'lovely', 'wonderful' or 'brilliant' are
repeated over and over again. In our praise and worship of God we
can often find language limiting.

We long to express our love, worship and praise of God,
particularly when we are filled with the Spirit. The gift of tongues
enables us to do this without the limitation of human language.

Secondly, it can be a great help when *praying under pressure*.
There are times in our lives when it is hard to know exactly how to
pray. It can be because we are burdened by many pressures,

anxieties or griefs. Not long ago I prayed for a man aged twenty-six whose wife had died of cancer after only one year of married life. He asked for and instantly received the gift of tongues and all the things that he had pushed down in his life seemed to pour out. He told me afterwards what a relief it had been to be able to unburden all those things.

I too have found this in my own experience. In 1987 during a staff meeting at our church, I received a message to say that my mother had had a heart attack and was in hospital. As I dashed up to the main road and caught a taxi to the hospital, I have never been more grateful for the gift of tongues. I desperately wanted to pray, but felt too shocked to form any sentences in English. The gift of tongues enabled me to pray all the way to the hospital and to bring the situation to God in a time of crisis.

Thirdly, many people have found the gift a help in *praying for other people*. It is hard to pray for others – especially if you have not seen them or heard from them for some time. After a while, 'Lord, bless them' might be our most elaborate prayer. It can be a real help to start praying in tongues for them. Often, as we do that, God gives us the words to pray in English.

It is not selfish to want to pray in tongues. Although, 'Those who speak in a tongue edify themselves' (1 Corinthians 14:4), the indirect effects of this can be very great. Jackie Pullinger describes the transformation in her ministry when she began to use the gift:

By the clock I prayed 15 minutes a day in the language of the Spirit and still felt nothing as I asked the Spirit to help me intercede for those he wanted to reach. After about six weeks of this I began to lead people to Jesus without trying. Gangsters fell to their knees sobbing in the streets, women were healed, heroin addicts were miraculously set free. And I knew it all had nothing to do with me.

It was also the gateway for her to receive other gifts of the Spirit:

> With my friends I began to learn about the other gifts of the Spirit and
> we experienced a remarkable few years of ministry. Scores of gangsters
> and well-to-do people, students and churchmen, were converted and
> all received a new language to pray in private and other gifts to use when
> meeting together. We opened several homes to house heroin addicts
> and all were delivered from drugs painlessly because of the power of the
> Holy Spirit.[51]

Does Paul approve of speaking in tongues?

The context of 1 Corinthians 14 is excessive public use in church of
the gift of tongues. Paul says, '*In the church* I would rather speak
five intelligible words to instruct others than ten thousand words in
a tongue' (v. 19, italics mine). There would be little point in Paul
arriving at Corinth and giving his sermon in tongues. They would
not be able to understand unless there was someone to interpret. So
he lays down guidelines for the public use of tongues (v. 27).

Nevertheless, Paul makes it clear that speaking in tongues should
not be forbidden (v. 39). With regard to the private use of this gift
(on our own with God), he strongly encourages it. He says, 'I
would like every one of you to speak in tongues' (v. 5) and, 'I thank
God that I speak in tongues more than all of you' (v. 18). This does
not mean that every Christian has to speak in tongues or that we
are second-class Christians if we do not speak in tongues. There is
no such thing as first- and second-class Christians. Nor does it
mean that God loves us any less if we don't yet speak in tongues.
Nevertheless, the gift of tongues is a blessing from God.

How do we receive the gift of tongues?

Some say, 'I don't want the gift of tongues.' God will never force
you to receive a gift. Tongues is just one of the wonderful gifts of
the Spirit, and not the only one by any means, as we saw in the last

chapter. Like every gift, it has to be received by faith.

Not every Christian speaks in tongues, but there is no reason why anyone who wants this gift should not receive it. Paul is not saying that speaking in tongues is the be-all and end-all of the Christian life; he is saying that it is a very helpful gift. If you would like to receive it, there is no reason why you should not.

Like all the gifts of God, we have to co-operate with his Spirit. God does not force his gifts on us. When I first became a Christian I read somewhere that the gifts of the Spirit went out in the apostolic age (ie, the first century). They were not for today. When I heard about speaking in tongues I decided to confirm that they were not for today, so I prayed for the gift and then kept my mouth firmly shut! I didn't start praying in tongues and felt that this proved that the gifts had gone out with the apostles.

One day two friends of mine, who had just been filled with the Spirit and received the gift of tongues, came round to see me. I told them quite firmly that the gifts of the Spirit had gone out with the apostolic age, but I could see the difference it had made to them. There was a new radiance about them, and there still is years later. I decided to ask the people who had prayed for them to pray for me to be filled with the Spirit and to receive the gift of tongues. As they did, I experienced the power of the Holy Spirit. They explained to me that if I wanted to receive the gift of tongues, I had to co-operate with the Spirit of God and open my mouth and start to speak to God in any language but English or another known to me. As I did, I received the gift of tongues also.

WHAT ARE THE COMMON HINDRANCES TO BEING FILLED WITH THE SPIRIT?

On one occasion Jesus was speaking to his disciples on the subject of prayer and the Holy Spirit (Luke 11:9-13). In that passage he deals with some of the principal difficulties we may have in receiving from God.

Doubt

There are many doubts people have in this whole area, the principal one being, 'If I ask will I receive?'

Jesus says simply: 'I say to you: Ask and it will be given to you.'

Jesus must have seen that they were a little sceptical because he repeats it in a different way: 'Seek and you will find.'

And again he says a third time: 'Knock and the door will be opened to you.'

He knows human nature so he goes on a fourth time: 'For everyone who asks receives.'

They are not convinced so he says it a fifth time: 'He who seeks finds.'

Again a sixth time: 'To him who knocks, the door will be opened.'

Why does he say it six times? Because he knows what we are like. We find it very difficult to believe that God would give us anything – let alone something as unusual and wonderful as his Holy Spirit and the gifts that come with the Spirit.

Fear

Even if we have cleared the first hurdle of doubt, some of us trip up on the next hurdle of fear. The fear is about what we will receive. Will it be something good?

Jesus uses the analogy of a human father. If a child asks for a fish, no father would give him a snake. If a child asks for an egg, no father would give him a scorpion (Luke 11:11-12). It is unthinkable that we would treat our children like that. Jesus goes on to say that in comparison with God we are evil! If we would not treat our children like that, it is inconceivable that God would treat us like that. He is not going to let us down. If we ask for the Holy Spirit and all the wonderful gifts he brings, that is exactly what we will receive (Luke 11:13).

Inadequacy

Of course it is important that there is no unforgiveness or other sin in our lives, and that we have turned our back on all that we know is wrong. However, even after we have done that, we often have a vague feeling of unworthiness and inadequacy. We cannot believe that God would give us anything. We can believe that he would give gifts to very advanced Christians, but not to us. But Jesus does not say, 'How much more will your Father in heaven give the Holy Spirit to all very advanced Christians.' He says, 'How much more will your Father in heaven give the Holy Spirit to *those who ask him*' (Luke 11:13, italics mine).

If you would like to be filled with the Spirit you might like to find someone who would pray for you. If you don't have anyone who would be able to pray for you, there is nothing to stop you from praying on your own. Some are filled with the Spirit without receiving the gift of tongues. The two do not necessarily go together. Yet in the New Testament and in experience they often do go together. There is no reason why we should not pray for both.

If you are praying on your own:

1. Ask God to forgive you for anything that could be a barrier to receiving.

2. Turn from any area of your life that you know is wrong.

3. Ask God to fill you with his Spirit. Go on seeking him until you find. Go on knocking until the door opens. Seek God with all your heart.

4. If you would like to receive the gift of tongues, ask. Then open your mouth and start to praise God in any language but English or any other language known to you.

5. Believe that what you receive is from God. Don't let anyone tell you that you made it up. (It is most unlikely that you have.)

6. Persevere. Languages take time to develop. Most of us start with a very limited vocabulary. Gradually it develops. Tongues is like that. It takes time to develop the gift. But don't give up.

7. If you have prayed for any other gift, seek opportunities to use it. Remember that all gifts have to be developed by use.

Being filled with the Spirit is not a one-off experience. Peter was filled with the Spirit three times in the space of chapters 2-4 in the Book of Acts (Acts 2:4; 4:8, 31). When Paul says, 'Be filled with the Spirit' (Ephesians 5:18), he uses the present continuous tense, urging them and us to go on and on being filled with the Spirit.

11

How Can I Resist Evil?

There is a close connection between good and God and between evil and the devil. Indeed, in each case the difference is only one letter! Behind the power of good lies Goodness himself. Directly or indirectly behind our own evil desires and the temptations of the world lies evil personified – the devil.

Because there is so much evil in the world some find it easier to believe in the devil than in God. 'As far as God goes, I am a non-believer . . . but when it comes to the devil – well that's something else . . . the devil keeps advertising . . . the devil does lots of commercials,' said William Peter Blatty who wrote and produced *The Exorcist.*[52]

On the other hand, many Westerners find belief in the devil more difficult than belief in God. This may be partly because of a false image of what the devil is like. If the image of God as a white bearded old man sitting on a cloud is absurd and incredible, so also is the image of a horned devil trudging through Dante's inferno. We are not dealing with an alien from outer space but with a real personal force of evil who is active in the world today.

Once we have come to believe in a transcendent God, in some ways it is only logical to accept belief in a devil.

Belief in a great transcendent power of evil adds nothing whatever to the difficulties imposed by belief in a transcendent power of good. Indeed, it eases them somewhat. For if there were no Satan, it would be hard to resist the conclusion that God is a fiend both because of what he does, in nature, and what he allows, in human wickedness.[53]

According to the biblical worldview behind the evil in the world there lies the devil. The Greek word for the devil, *diabolos*, translates the Hebrew word *satan*. We are not told very much about the origins of Satan in the Bible. There is a hint that he may have been a fallen angel (Isaiah 14:12-23). He appears on a few occasions in the books of the Old Testament (Job 1; 1 Chronicles 21:1). He is not merely a force but is personal.

We are given a clearer picture of his activities in the New Testament. The devil is a personal spiritual being who is in active rebellion against God and has the leadership of many demons like himself. Paul tells us to take our 'stand against the devil's schemes. For our struggle is not against flesh and blood, but against the rulers, against the authorities . . . against the spiritual forces of evil in the heavenly realms' (Ephesians 6:11-12).

The devil and his angels, according to Paul, are not to be underestimated. They are cunning ('the devil's schemes' v. 11). They are powerful ('rulers', 'authorities' and 'forces' v. 12). They are evil ('forces of evil' v. 12). Therefore, we should not be surprised when we come under a powerful assault from the enemy.

WHY SHOULD WE BELIEVE IN THE DEVIL?

Why should we believe in the existence of the devil? Some say, 'Nowadays you can't believe in the devil.' However, there are very good reasons to believe in his existence.

First, it is biblical. That is not to say that the Bible concentrates on the devil. Satan is not mentioned very often in the Old Testament and it is only when we come to the New Testament that the doctrine is developed more fully. Jesus clearly believed in the existence of Satan and was tempted by him. He frequently cast out demons, freeing people from the forces of evil and sin in their lives, and gave his disciples authority to do the same. In the rest of the New Testament there are many references to the work of the devil (1 Peter 5:8-11; Ephesians 6:1-12).

Secondly, Christians down the ages have almost invariably believed in the existence of the devil. The early church theologians, the Reformers, the great evangelists like Wesley and Whitefield, and the overwhelming majority of men and women of God, knew that there were very real spiritual forces of evil around. As soon as we start to serve the Lord, his interest is aroused. 'The devil only tempts those souls that wish to abandon sin . . . the others belong to him: he has no need to tempt them.'[54]

Thirdly, common sense confirms the existence of the devil. Any kind of theology which ignores the existence of a personal devil has a great deal to explain: evil regimes, institutional torture and violence, mass murders, brutal rapes, large scale drug trafficking, terrorist atrocities, sexual and physical abuse of children, occult activity and satanic rituals. Who is behind all of this? There is a ditty which goes like this:

> Some say the devil's been,
> Some say the devil's gone,
> But simple people,
> like you and me,
> Would like to know,
> who carries the business on?

So Scripture, tradition and reason all point to the existence of the devil. This does not mean that we should become obsessed by him. As C. S. Lewis points out, 'There are two equal and opposite errors into which our race can fall about the devils. One is to disbelieve in their existence. The other is to believe, and to feel an excessive and unhealthy interest in them. They themselves are equally pleased by both errors and hail a materialist or a magician with the same delight.'[55]

As Michael Green has put it:

> Like any general who can persuade the opposition to underestimate him, Satan . . . must be enchanted at the present state of affairs which leaves him free to operate with the maximum of ease and efficiency, confident that nobody takes him seriously. The more he can do to encourage this doubt of his existence, the better. The more he can blind people's minds to the true state of affairs, the better his aims are furthered.[56]

Many fall into the opposite danger of having an excessive and unhealthy interest in him. There is a whole new interest in spiritualism, palm-reading, ouija boards, 'channelling' (consulting the dead), astrology, horoscopes, witchcraft and occult powers. Involvement in these things is expressly forbidden in Scripture (Deuteronomy 18:10; Leviticus 19:20ff; Galatians 5:19ff; Revelation 21:8; 22:15). If we have meddled in any of these things, we can be forgiven. We need to repent and destroy anything associated with that activity such as books, charms, videos and magazines (Acts 19:19).

Christians too can have an unhealthy interest in these things. A new Christian recently showed me a couple of supposedly Christian books where the whole emphasis was on the work of the enemy – with a lot of space devoted to speculation concerning the number of the beast in Revelation, and tying this in with credit cards! The intention was good, I am sure, but the focus on the work of the enemy seemed to me to be unhealthy. The Bible never has this kind of focus. The spotlight is always on God.

WHAT ARE THE DEVIL'S TACTICS?

The ultimate aim of Satan is to destroy every human being (John 10:10). He wants us to follow a path that leads to destruction. To that end, he tries to prevent anyone coming to faith in Jesus Christ. Paul tells us: 'The god of this age [the devil] has blinded the minds of unbelievers, so that they cannot see the light of the gospel of the glory of Christ, who is the image of God' (2 Corinthians 4:4).

So long as we are going along Satan's path and our eyes are blinded, we will probably be almost totally unaware of his tactics. Once we start walking along the path that leads to life and our eyes are opened to the truth, we become aware that we are under attack.

The initial line of attack is often in the area of doubt. We see this in the opening chapters of Genesis where the enemy, in the form of a serpent, says to Eve, 'Did God *really* say . . . ?' His opening move is to raise a doubt in her mind.

We see the same tactic in the temptation of Jesus. The devil comes to him and says, '*If* you are the Son of God . . .' (Matthew 4:3, italics mine). First, he raises doubts, then come the temptations. His tactics have not changed. He still raises doubts in our mind: 'Did God *really* say that such and such a course of action is wrong?' or, '*If* you are a Christian. . . .' He tries to undermine our confidence in what God has said and in our relationship with him. We need to recognise this source of many of our doubts.

Raising doubts was the precursor to the main attack on both Eve in the Garden of Eden and Jesus in the wilderness. In Genesis 3, we see an exposé of the way in which Satan, who is described as 'the tempter' (Matthew 4:2), so often works.

In Genesis 2:16-17, God gave Adam and Eve a far-reaching permission ('You are free to eat from any tree in the garden'), one prohibition ('But you must not eat from the tree of the knowledge of good and evil') and then warned them of the penalty if they disobeyed ('For when you eat of it you will surely die').

Satan ignores the wide scope of the permission and concentrates on the one prohibition – which he then exaggerates (Genesis 3:1). His tactics have not changed. He still ignores the permission. He ignores the fact that God has given us all things richly to enjoy (1 Timothy 6:17). He ignores the great blessing of walking in a relationship with God. He ignores the riches of Christian marriages and families, the security of a Christian home, the level of friendship that we can enjoy as Christians, and countless other things which God offers to those who know and love him. He does not tell us about these things. Instead he concentrates on a tiny unimaginative list of prohibitions of what Christians are not allowed to do – reminding us again and again that we can't get drunk, swear or be promiscuous. There are relatively few things that God does not allow us to do and there are very good reasons why he prohibits them.

Finally, he denies the penalty. He says, 'You will not surely die' (Genesis 3:4). He says, in effect, that it will not do you any harm to disobey God. He suggests to us that God is really a spoilsport, that God does not want the best for our lives and that we will miss out if we don't disobey. In fact the opposite is the case, as Adam and Eve found out. It is disobedience which causes us to miss out on so much of what God intended for us.

In the verses that follow, we see the consequences of disobeying God. First, there is shame and embarrassment. Adam and Eve felt exposed and began a cover-up operation (v. 7). How quickly would we want to leave the room if every action we had ever done was displayed on a screen, followed by a written list of every thought we had ever entertained? Deep down, we all feel ashamed and embarrassed by our sin. We don't want people to find us out. Sir Arthur Conan Doyle once played a practical joke on twelve men. They were all very well-known, respected and respectable men, regarded as pillars of the establishment. He sent each of them a telegram, with the same message in each: 'Flee at once. All is discovered.' Within twenty-four hours, they had all fled the country! Virtually all of us have something in our lives of which we are ashamed; something we would not want everyone to know about. We often put up barriers around us to avoid the possibility of being found out.

Next, Adam and Eve's friendship with God was broken. When they heard God coming, they hid (v. 8). Many people today shy away from God. They don't want to face up to the fact of the possibility of his existence. Like Adam they are afraid (v. 10). Some have a real fear of going to church or mixing with Christians. A couple in our congregation told me about a sixteen-stone rugby player from Australia whom they had invited to church. He got as far as the drive, then he started shaking in the car. He said, 'I can't go. I'm too frightened to go into the church.' He could not look God in the face. There was a separation between him and God, just as there was with Adam and Eve. God immediately started to try to draw them back into a relationship. He called out, 'Where are you?' (v. 9). He still does.

Then, there is a separation between Adam and Eve themselves. Adam blames Eve. Eve blames the devil. But they and we are responsible for our own sin. We cannot blame God or others or even the devil (James 1:13-15). We see this in our society today. When people turn away from God, they start fighting one another. We see the breakdown of relationships wherever we look: broken marriages, broken homes, broken relationships at work, civil war and war between nations.

Finally, we see in God's punishment of Adam and Eve (v. 14 onwards) that they were deceived by Satan. We see how his deception led Adam and Eve away from God into a path which, as Satan knew from the beginning, led to destruction.

We see that Satan is a deceiver, a destroyer, a tempter and one who raises doubts. He is also an accuser. The Hebrew word for Satan means 'accuser' or 'slanderer'. He accuses God before people. God gets the blame for everything. God, he says, is not to be trusted. Secondly, he accuses Christians before God (Revelation 12:10). He denies the power of the death of Jesus. He condemns us and makes us feel guilty – not for any particular sin, but with a general and vague feeling of guilt. In contrast, when the Holy Spirit draws attention to a sin, he identifies it so that we can turn from it.

Temptation is not the same thing as sin. Sometimes the devil puts a thought into our mind which we know is wrong. At that moment we have a choice whether to accept it or reject it. If we accept it, we are on the way towards sin. If we reject it, we do what Jesus did. He was 'tempted in every way, just as we are – yet was without sin' (Hebrews 4:15). When Satan put evil thoughts in his mind, he rejected them. But often before we have the chance to decide one way or the other, Satan accuses us. Within a split second he says, 'Look at you! Call yourself a Christian? What was that you were thinking about? You can't be a Christian. What a terrible thing to think!' He wants us to agree and say, 'Oh no! I can't be a Christian,' or, 'Oh no! I've blown it now, so it doesn't matter if I blow it a bit more!' We are on the way down, and this is his aim. The tactics are those of condemnation and accusation. If he can provoke guilt in us he knows the thought is: 'It doesn't really make any difference now if I do it or not. I have already failed.' So we do it and temptation becomes sin.

He wants failure to become a pattern in our lives. He knows that the more we fall into sin, the more sin will start to control our lives.

The first injection of heroin may not be enough to get a grip, but if you inject it day after day, month after month, year after year, it gets a grip and you become an addict. It has taken hold of you. If we fall into a pattern of doing things which we know to be wrong, these things grip our lives. We become addicted and we are on the path that Satan desires – the one that leads to destruction (Matthew 7:13).

What is Our Position?

As Christians, God has rescued us from 'the dominion of darkness and brought us into the kingdom of the Son he loves' (Colossians 1:13). Before we were Christians, Paul says, we were in the dominion of darkness. Satan rules us and we were subject to sin, slavery, death and destruction. That is what the dominion of darkness is like.

Now, Paul says, we have been transferred from the kingdom of darkness to the kingdom of light. The moment we come to Christ we are transferred from darkness to light, and in the kingdom of light, Jesus is King. There is forgiveness, freedom, life and salvation. Once we have been transferred, we belong to someone else: to Jesus Christ and his kingdom.

In 1992 the Italian club Lazio paid £5.5 million for Paul Gascoigne to be transferred from Tottenham Hotspur to Lazio. Imagine that Gazza, while playing for Lazio, one day gets a phone-call from Terry Venables, his previous manager at Tottenham Hotspur, saying, 'Why weren't you at the practice this morning?' He would reply, 'I don't work for you any more. I have been transferred. I am working for another club' (or at least that is the gist of what he would say!).

In a far more wonderful way, we have been transferred from the kingdom of darkness where Satan is in charge, to the kingdom of God where Jesus is in charge. When Satan asks us to do his work our reply is, 'I don't belong to you any more.'

Satan is a conquered foe (Luke 10:17-20). On the cross Jesus 'disarmed the powers and authorities' and 'made a public spectacle of them, triumphing over them by the cross' (Colossians 2:15). Satan and all his minions were defeated at the cross, and that is why Satan and his demons are so frightened of the name of Jesus (Acts 16:18). They know they are defeated.

Jesus has freed us from guilt, so we don't need to be condemned. He has set us free from addictions. Jesus broke the power of these things and set us free. He broke the fear of death when he defeated death. With that, he set us free, potentially, from every fear. All these things – guilt, addiction and fear – belong to the kingdom of darkness. Jesus has transferred us to a new kingdom.

The cross was a great victory over Satan and his minions, and we now live in the time of the mopping-up operations. Although the enemy is not yet destroyed and is still capable of inflicting casualties, he is disarmed, defeated and demoralised. This is our position, and it is vital to realise the strength of the position we are in, due to the victory of Jesus on the cross for us.

HOW DO WE DEFEND OURSELVES?

Since the war is not over and Satan is not yet destroyed, we need to make sure that our defences are in order. Paul tells us to 'put on the full armour of God so that you can take your stand against the devil's schemes' (Ephesians 6:11). He then mentions six pieces of equipment which we need. Sometimes it is said, 'The secret of the Christian life is. . . .' But there is no one secret; we need *all* the armour.

First, we need the 'belt of truth' (v. 14). This probably means the foundation of Christian doctrine and truth. It means getting the whole Christian truth (or as much of it as one can) into one's system. We do this by reading the Bible, listening to sermons and talks, reading Christian books and listening to tapes. This will enable us to distinguish what is true and what are Satan's lies, for Satan is 'a liar and the father of lies' (John 8:44).

Next, we need the breastplate of righteousness (v. 14). This is the righteousness that comes from God through what Jesus has done for us on the cross. It enables us to be in a relationship with God and to live a righteous life. We need to resist the devil. The apostle James says, 'Resist the devil, and he will flee from you. Come near to God and he will come near to you' (James 4:7-8). We all fall from time to time. When we do, we need to get up quickly. We do this by telling God how sorry we are for what we have done, being as specific as possible (1 John 1:9). He then promises to restore his friendship with us.

Then, we also need the boots of the gospel of peace (v. 15). I understand this to mean a readiness to speak about the gospel of Jesus Christ. As John Wimber often said, 'It is hard to sit still and be good.' If we are constantly seeking opportunities to pass on the good news, we have an effective defence against the enemy. Once we declare our Christian faith to our families and at work, we strengthen our defence. It is hard, because we know that we are being watched to see if we live up to our faith. But it is a great incentive to do so.

The fourth piece of armour is the shield of faith (v. 16). With this, we 'can extinguish all the flaming arrows of the evil one'. Faith is the opposite of cynicism and scepticism which wreak havoc in many lives. One aspect of faith has been defined as 'taking a promise of God and daring to believe it'. Satan will throw his arrows of doubt to undermine us – but with the shield of faith we resist him.

Fifthly, Paul tells us to take the helmet of salvation (v. 17). As Bishop Westcott, Regius Professor of Divinity at Cambridge, once pointed out, there are three tenses of salvation. We have been saved from the penalty of sin. We are being saved from the power of sin. We shall be saved from the presence of sin. We need to grasp these great concepts in our mind; to know them so that we can answer the enemy's doubts and accusations.

Finally, we are to take 'the sword of the Spirit, which is the word of God' (v. 17). Probably here Paul is thinking of the Scriptures. Jesus used the Scriptures when Satan attacked. Each time Jesus replied with the word of God and in the end Satan had to leave. It is well worth learning verses from the Bible which we can use to see off the enemy and remind ourselves of the promises of God.

HOW DO WE ATTACK?

As we have already seen, Satan and his minions were defeated on the cross, and we are now involved in the final mopping-up operations before the return of Jesus. As Christians, we need not be afraid of Satan; he has a great deal to fear from the activity of Christians.

We are called to pray. We are involved in spiritual warfare, though 'the weapons we fight with are not the weapons of the world. On the contrary, they have divine power to demolish strongholds' (2 Corinthians 10:4). Prayer was a very high priority for Jesus, and it should be for us. In the words of the hymn, 'Satan trembles when he sees the weakest Christian on his knees.'

We are also called to action. Again, in the life of Jesus, prayer and action go hand in hand. Jesus proclaimed the kingdom of God, healed the sick and cast out demons. He commissioned his disciples to do the same. Later on we will look in more detail at what this means.

It is important to stress the greatness of God and the relative powerlessness of the enemy. We do not believe that there are two equal and opposite powers – God and Satan. That is not the biblical picture. God is the Creator of the universe. Satan is a part of his creation – a fallen part. He is a small part. Further, he is a defeated enemy and is about to be utterly wiped out when Jesus returns (Revelation 12:12).

In a superb picture in C. S. Lewis' book *The Great Divorce*, where he speaks about hell as the place where Satan and his demons operate, a man has arrived in heaven and is being shown round by his 'teacher'. He goes down on hands and knees, takes a blade of grass and, using the thin end as a pointer, he eventually finds a tiny crack in the soil in which is concealed the whole of hell:

> 'Do you mean then that Hell – all that infinite empty town – is down in some little crack like this?'
>
> 'Yes. All Hell is smaller than one pebble of your earthly world: but it is smaller than one atom of *this* world, the Real World. Look at yon butterfly. If it swallowed all Hell, Hell would not be big enough to do it any harm or to have any taste.'
>
> 'It seems big enough when you are in it, Sir.'
>
> 'And yet all loneliness, angers, hatreds, envies and itchings that it contains, if rolled into one single experience and put into the scale against the least moment of the joy that is felt by the least in Heaven, would have no weight that could be registered at all. Bad cannot succeed even in being bad as truly as good is good. If all Hell's miseries

together entered the consciousness of yon wee yellow bird on the bough there, they would be swallowed up without trace, as if one drop of ink had been dropped into that Great Ocean to which your terrestrial Pacific itself is only a molecule.'[57]

12

Why and How Should I Tell Others?

Why should we talk about our Christian faith? Isn't it a private matter? Isn't the best sort of Christian the one who just lives the Christian life? Sometimes people say to me, 'I know someone [usually their mother or their aunt] who is a Christian. They have a really strong faith – but they do not talk about it. Isn't that the highest form of Christianity?'

The short answer is that someone must have told them about the Christian faith. The slightly longer answer is that there are good reasons for telling others about Jesus. First, it is a command of Jesus himself. Tom Forrest, the Roman Catholic priest who first suggested to the Pope the idea of calling the 1990s 'The Decade of Evangelism', points out that the word 'go' appears 1,514 times in the Bible (RSV), 233 times in the New Testament and 54 times in Matthew's Gospel. Jesus tells us to 'go':

'Go to the lost sheep . . .'
'Go and tell John . . .'
'Go and invite all you meet . . .'
'Go and make disciples . . .'

171

Indeed, these are the last recorded words of Jesus in Matthew's Gospel:

> Then Jesus came to them and said, 'All authority in heaven and on earth has been given to me. Therefore go and make disciples of all nations, baptising them in the name of the Father and of the Son and of the Holy Spirit, and teaching them to obey everything I have commanded you. And surely I will be with you always, to the very end of the age' (Matthew 28:18-20).

Secondly, we tell people because there is a desperate need for people to hear the good news of Jesus Christ. If we were in the Sahara Desert and had discovered an oasis, it would be extremely selfish not to tell the people around us who were thirsty where their thirst could be satisfied. Jesus is the only One who can satisfy the thirsty hearts of men and women. Often the recognition of this thirst comes from surprising sources. The singer, Sinead O'Connor, said in an interview: 'As a race we feel empty. This is because our spirituality has been wiped out and we don't know how to express ourselves. As a result we're encouraged to fill that gap with alcohol, drugs, sex or money. People out there are screaming for the truth.'

Thirdly, we tell others because, having discovered the good news ourselves, we feel an urgent desire to pass it on. If we have received good news we want to tell others. When our first child was born, my wife Pippa gave me a list of about ten people to ring. The first person I rang was her mother. I told her that we had a son and that he and Pippa were well. I then tried ringing my mother, but the phone was engaged. The third person on the list was Pippa's sister. By the time I had telephoned her she had already heard the news from Pippa's mother and so had all the others on the list. My mother's phone had been engaged because Pippa's mother was ringing her with the news. Good news travels fast. I did not need to implore Pippa's mother to pass on the message. She was bursting to tell them all. When we appreciate what good news the gospel is, we shall be bursting to tell others.

But how do we go about telling others? It seems to me that there are two opposite dangers. First, there is the danger of insensitivity. When I first became a Christian I fell into this. I was so excited about what had happened that I longed for everyone else to follow suit. After I had been a Christian for a few days I went to a party, determined to tell everyone. I saw a friend dancing and decided the first step was to make her realise her need. So I went up to her and said, 'You look awful. You really need Jesus.' She thought that I had gone mad. It was not the most effective way of telling someone the good news! (However, she did later become a Christian – quite independently of me, and she is now my wife!)

The next party I went to I decided to go well equipped. So I got hold of a number of booklets, Christian books on various issues and a New Testament. I stuffed them into every pocket I could find. Somehow I managed to find a girl who was willing to dance with me. It was hard going with so many books in my pocket, so I asked if we could sit down. I soon brought the subject round to Christianity. For every question she asked, I was able to produce a book from my pocket on exactly that subject. Eventually she went away with an armful of books. The next day she was going to France and was reading one of the books I had given her on the boat. Suddenly she understood the truth of what Jesus had done for her and, turning to her neighbour, she said, 'I have just become a Christian.' She died in a riding accident at the age of twenty-one. It was wonderful that she had come to Christ before she died – even though I don't think I went about it in quite the right way.

If we charge around like a bull in a china shop, sooner or later we get hurt. Even if we approach the subject sensitively, we may still get hurt. When we do, we tend to withdraw. Certainly this was my experience. After a few years, I moved from the danger of insensitivity and fell into the opposite danger of fear. There was a time (ironically it was when I was at theological college) when I became fearful of even talking about Jesus to those who were not Christians. On one occasion, a group of us went from the college to a parish mission on the outskirts of Liverpool, to tell people the good news. Each night we had supper with different people from the parish. One night a friend of mine called Rupert and I were sent to supper with a couple who were on the fringe of the church (or, to be more accurate, the wife was on the fringe and the husband was not a churchgoer). Halfway through the main course the husband asked me what we were doing up there. I stumbled, stammered, hesitated and prevaricated. He kept on repeating the question. Eventually Rupert said straight out, 'We have come here to tell people about Jesus.' I felt deeply embarrassed and hoped the ground would swallow us all up! I realised how frozen with fear I had become and that I was afraid even to take the name of Jesus on my lips.

In order to avoid these dangers of insensitivity and fear, we need to realise that telling others about Jesus arises out of our own relationship with God. It is a natural part of that relationship. As we walk with God, it should be quite natural for us to talk to people about that relationship in co-operation with the Spirit of God.

I find it helpful to think of this subject under five headings – all beginning with the letter 'p' – presence, persuasion, proclamation, power and prayer.

PRESENCE

Jesus said to his disciples:

> You are the salt of the earth. But if the salt loses its saltiness, how can it be made salty again? It is no longer good for anything, except to be thrown out and trampled under foot. You are the light of the world. A city on a hill cannot be hidden. Neither do people light a lamp and put it under a bowl. Instead they put it on its stand, and it gives light to everyone in the house. In the same way, let your light shine before others, that they may see your good deeds and praise your Father in heaven (Matthew 5:13-16).

Jesus calls us to have a wide-ranging influence ('salt of the *earth*' and 'the light of the *world*'). In order to exercise this influence, we need to be 'in the world' (at work, in our neighbourhood and among our family and friends) and not to withdraw into what John Stott calls our 'elegant little ecclesiastical salt cellars'. Yet we are called to be different – to live a radically different lifestyle from the world, so that we may be effective as salt and light in it.

We are called first to be salt. In centuries before refrigeration was invented salt was used to keep meat wholesome and to prevent decay. We are called as Christians to stop society going bad. We do this by our words, as we speak out about moral standards and moral issues, and as we use our influence to bring about God's standards in society around us. We do it by our deeds as we play our part as citizens, aiming to create better social structures, working for justice, freedom and dignity for the individual, and by helping to abolish discrimination. We do it also by our social action to help those who are casualties of our society. To this end, some Christians are called to get involved in local or national politics. Others are called to spend their lives like Mother Teresa and Jackie Pullinger 'ministering *with* the poor' (to use Jackie Pullinger's expression). All of us are called to play a part in this to a greater or lesser extent.

Secondly, Jesus calls us to be light – to allow the light of Christ to shine through us. We do this by what Jesus calls 'your good deeds' – everything that we do or say because we are Christians. They can be summarised as 'loving our neighbour as ourselves'.

Living out the Christian life is the most appropriate way of passing on the good news to those who live in very close proximity to us. This certainly applies to our family, colleagues at work and flatmates. If they know we are Christians, that fact alone puts them under a degree of pressure. To be continually speaking about our faith may backfire. They are more likely to be affected by genuine love and concern. At work people should notice our consistency, honesty, truthfulness, hard work, reliability, avoidance of gossip and desire to encourage other people. At home, parents, family and flatmates will be influenced by our service to others, our patience and our kindness, far more than by our words.

This is of great importance if one's husband or wife is not a Christian. Peter encouraged Christian wives that if any of them have husbands who 'do not believe the word, they may be won over *without talk* by the behaviour of their wives, when they see the purity and reverence of your lives' (1 Peter 3:1, italics mine).

Bruce and Geraldine Streather were married in December 1973. When Geraldine came to Christ in 1981, Bruce was not remotely interested. Bruce was a busy lawyer and a very keen golfer: he used to play most weekends. He never came to church.

For ten years Geraldine prayed for him and lived out the Christian life in front of him. She did not put any pressure on him and did not engage in any arguments about it. Over the years, Bruce was struck by her extraordinary kindness and consideration, especially to his mother whose cancer and related illnesses made her increasingly difficult. Eventually, in 1991, she invited him to come to an Alpha supper. Bruce came, and decided to come on the following Alpha course.

Geraldine wrote to me afterwards saying, 'I cried all the way home and prayed, telling God that as I had got Bruce to Alpha, he must do the rest. When Bruce returned from the first night of the course, I only asked him if he had enjoyed himself.'

On week seven of the course, Bruce gave his life to Christ and by the end he was the most enthusiastic Christian one could ever meet. I asked Geraldine what it was like living with him now. She replied, 'It's a bit like living with Billy Graham!'

Her letter continued: 'He tells everyone about Jesus. Instead of trying not to mention Christianity in front of friends when Bruce was there, in case it harmed our marriage, at every dinner party he talks to people about God and I am left at the other end listening to what he is saying. It seems that all my prayers have been answered. Last March I told God that I was fed up with Bruce not being a Christian. I told him I didn't care what happened to our house or money as long as Bruce became a Christian. Life will never be the same again – thank God for that.'

Nevertheless, being 'lights in the world' does not just involve our lifestyle. It also involves our lips. Our family, our flatmates and our colleagues will eventually ask questions about our faith. It is often better to wait until they do. If we are asked, we should always be prepared to give an answer. Peter writes: 'Always be prepared to give an answer to everyone who asks you to give the reason for the hope that you have. But do this with gentleness and respect' (1 Peter 3:15).

When we do get opportunities to speak, how do we go about it?

PERSUASION

Many people today have objections to the Christian faith or, at least, questions which they want answered before they are ready to come to faith in Christ. They need to be persuaded about the truth. Paul was willing to try to persuade people. He regarded it as his duty out of love for them: 'Since, then, we know what it is to fear the Lord, we try to *persuade* people' (2 Corinthians 5:11, italics mine).

When he went to Thessalonica he 'reasoned', 'explained' and 'proved' from the Scriptures that the Christ had to suffer and rise from the dead: '. . . some of the Jews were persuaded . . .' (Acts 17:4). In Corinth, while working on tents during the week, 'every Sabbath he reasoned in the synagogue, trying to persuade Jews and Greeks' (Acts 18:4).

During the course of conversations about the Christian faith, objections will often be raised and we need to be equipped to deal with these. On one occasion, Jesus was talking to a woman about the mess her life was in (John 4). Then he offered her eternal life. At that moment she raised a theological question about places of worship. He answered it, but quickly brought the conversation back to the essential issue. This is a good example for us to follow.

Usually when people raise theological questions and objections, they are genuinely looking for the answers. The most common questions which I get asked are, 'Why does God allow suffering?' and, 'What about other religions?' But there are a whole range of other questions. These may be serious, and may require a serious answer. Sometimes, however, these questions can be a smokescreen to avoid the real issue. Such people are put off becoming Christians, not by the theological objections, but by the moral ones. They are not willing to give their lives to Christ for fear of the change of lifestyle that Christianity will involve.

On the mission which I mentioned earlier in the chapter, Rupert and I went to speak at a meeting about our Christian faith. After we had spoken, a university lecturer raised a large number of questions and objections. I didn't know where to begin to answer them all. Rupert simply asked, 'If we could answer all your questions satisfactorily, would you become a Christian?' He replied, very honestly, 'No.' So there didn't seem a great deal of point in answering what for him were purely academic enquiries. But when the questions are genuine, reasoning, explaining and proving form an important part of telling others about Jesus.

PROCLAMATION

The heart of telling others is the proclamation of the good news of Jesus Christ. It is announcing, communicating and proclaiming the Christian faith to those outside the faith. There are many ways in which this can be done. One of the most effective ways is bringing people to hear the gospel explained by someone else. This can often be more advisable, especially in the early stages of our Christian lives, than trying to explain the gospel ourselves.

Many who come to faith in Christ have lots of friends who have little or no connection with the church. This provides an excellent opportunity to say to these friends, as Jesus did on one occasion, 'Come . . . and you will see' (John 1:39). A woman in her twenties recently became a Christian and started coming to church in London. At weekends, however, she would stay with her parents in Wiltshire, and she then insisted on leaving them at 3 pm on Sunday afternoon in order to be in time for church. One Sunday evening she got stuck in a bad traffic jam on the Hammersmith flyover and could not get to the evening service. She was so upset that she burst into tears. She went round to see some friends, who did not even know she had become a Christian. They asked her what was wrong. She answered through the tears, 'I've missed church.' They were totally mystified. The next Sunday they all came to see what they were missing! One of them came to Christ very shortly afterwards.

There is no greater privilege and no greater joy than enabling someone to find out about Jesus Christ. The former Archbishop of Canterbury, William Temple, wrote his commentary on John's Gospel while on his knees, asking God to speak to his heart. When he came to the words, 'And he [Andrew] brought Simon to Jesus' (John 1:42), he wrote a short but momentous sentence: 'The greatest service that one man can render another.'

We don't hear much more about Andrew except that he was always bringing people to Jesus (John 6:8; 12:22). But Simon Peter his brother went on to be one of the greatest influences in the history of Christianity. We cannot all be Simon Peters, but we can all do what Andrew did – we can bring someone to Jesus.

Albert McMakin was a twenty-four-year-old farmer who had recently come to faith in Christ. He was so full of enthusiasm that he filled a truck with people and took them to a meeting to hear about Jesus. There was a good-looking farmer's son whom he was especially keen to get to a meeting, but this young man was hard to persuade – he was busy falling in and out of love with different girls, and did not seem to be attracted to Christianity. Eventually, Albert McMakin managed to persuade him to come by asking him to drive the truck. When they arrived, Albert's guest decided to go in and was 'spellbound' and began to have thoughts he had never known before. He went back again and again until one night, he went forward and gave his life to Jesus Christ. That man, the driver of the truck, was Billy Graham. The year was 1934. Since then Billy Graham has led thousands to faith in Jesus Christ. We cannot all be like Billy Graham, but we can all be like Albert McMakin – we can all bring our friends to Jesus.

Sometimes we are given the opportunity to explain the gospel ourselves. One good way of doing this is to tell the story of what has happened to us. We see a biblical model in Paul's testimony in Acts 26:9-23. It falls into three parts: he speaks about what he was like before (vv. 9-11), what it meant to meet Jesus (vv. 12-15) and what it has meant for him since (vv. 19-23). When explaining what someone has to do to become a Christian, a framework can be helpful. There are many different ways of presenting the gospel. I have set out the method I use in a booklet called *Why Jesus?*. I then lead people in the prayer which you will find at the end of Chapter 4 of *this* book.

One man in our church told me recently about how he had come to Christ. He was going through difficulties in his business and had to go to the United States on a business trip. He was not feeling very happy as he rode in a taxi to the airport. On the dashboard of the taxi he noticed pictures of the taxi driver's children. He could not see the face of the driver, but he asked him about his family. He felt great love coming from the man. As the conversation went on, the taxi driver said to him, 'I sense that you are not happy. If you believe in Christ it makes all the difference.'

The businessman said to me, 'Here was a man speaking with authority. I thought I was the one in authority. After all, I was paying.' The taxi driver said to him eventually, 'Don't you think it's time you settled all this by accepting Christ?' They arrived at the airport. For the first time the taxi driver turned round and the businessman saw his face – it was full of kindness. He said to him, 'Why don't we pray? If you want Christ in your life, ask him.' They prayed together and the driver gave him a booklet about the Christian faith. The taxi driver was a modest unassuming person who was there one moment and gone the next, but he had taken the opportunity to proclaim the good news of Jesus Christ. This changed the whole course of a man's life.

POWER

In the New Testament the proclamation of the gospel is often accompanied by a demonstration of the power of God. Jesus came proclaiming: 'The kingdom of God is near. Repent and believe the good news!' (Mark 1:15). Jesus went on to demonstrate the power of the gospel by the expulsion of evil (Mark 1:21-28) and by healing the sick (Mark 1:29-34, 40-45).

Jesus told his disciples to do what he had been doing. He told them to do the works of the kingdom – 'to heal the sick who are there' and to proclaim the good news – and to tell them, 'The kingdom of God is near you' (Luke 10:9). As we read on in the Gospels and Acts we see that that is what they did. Paul wrote to the Thessalonians: 'Our gospel came to you not simply with words, but also with power' (1 Thessalonians 1:5).

Proclamation and demonstration go hand in hand. Often one leads to the other. On one occasion Peter and John were on their way to church. Outside was a man crippled from birth. He had been sitting there for years. He asked for money. Peter said, in effect, 'I am sorry. I haven't got any money, but I will give you what I have. In the name of Jesus Christ of Nazareth, walk.' He took his hand and helped him up. Instantly, he jumped to his feet and began to walk. When he realised he was healed, he leapt and jumped and praised God (Acts 3:1-10).

Everyone knew that this man had been crippled for years, and a huge crowd gathered around. After the demonstration of the power of God came the proclamation of the gospel. People were asking, 'How did this happen?' Peter was able to tell them all about Jesus: 'It is Jesus' name and the faith that comes through him that has given this complete healing to him, as you can all see' (Acts 3:16). In the next chapter we shall examine this area in more detail by looking at the nature of the kingdom of God and the place of healing in it.

PRAYER

We have already seen the importance that prayer had in the life of Jesus. While he was proclaiming and demonstrating the gospel he was also praying (Mark 1:35-37). Prayer is essential in the area of telling others the good news.

We need to pray for blind eyes to be opened. Many people are blinded to the gospel (2 Corinthians 4:4). They can see physically, but they cannot see the spiritual world. We need to pray that the Spirit of God will open the eyes of the blind so that they can understand the truth about Jesus.

Most of us find, when we come to faith in Christ, that there has been somebody praying for us. It may be a member of the family, a godparent or a friend. There will be somebody, I suspect, in nearly every case who has been praying that our eyes will be opened to see the truth. James Hudson Taylor, who founded the China Inland Mission, influenced millions for Jesus Christ. He was brought up in Yorkshire and became a rebellious teenager. One day, when his mother was away and his sister was out, he picked up a Christian book, intending to read the story and skip the moral. He curled up in the barn behind the house and began to read.

As he read, he was struck by the phrase 'the finished work of Christ'. He thought Christianity to be a dreary struggle to pay off bad debts with good. He had long since abandoned the struggle. He owed too much. He sought simply to have a good time. This phrase broke open his mind to a sudden certainty that Christ, by his death on the cross, had already discharged this debt of sins: 'And with this dawned the joyful conviction, as light was flashed into my soul by the Holy Spirit, that there was nothing in the world to be done but to fall down on one's knees and accepting this Saviour and His Salvation, to praise Him for evermore.' No Luther, Bunyan or Wesley had a more complete sense of the rolling away of his burden, of light dismissing darkness, of rebirth and the close friendship of Christ, than did Hudson Taylor on that June afternoon in 1849 at the age of seventeen.

Ten days later his mother came home. He ran to the door 'to tell her I had such glad news to give'. She replied as she hugged him, 'I know, my boy. I have been rejoicing for a fortnight in the glad tidings you have to tell me.' Hudson was amazed. She had been eighty miles away, and on the very day of the incident in the barn she had felt such an overwhelming desire to pray for Hudson that she had spent hours on her knees, and had arisen with the unshakeable conviction that her prayers had been answered. He never forgot the importance of prayer.[58]

When a friend of mine, Ric, became a Christian he rang a friend whom he knew to be a Christian as well, and told him what had happened. The friend replied, 'I have been praying for you for four years.' Ric then started to pray for one of his own friends, and within ten weeks he too became a Christian.

We need to pray for our friends. We also need to pray for ourselves. When we talk to people about Jesus, we may sometimes get a negative reaction. The temptation at that moment is to give up. When Peter and John healed the crippled man and proclaimed the gospel, they were arrested and threatened with dire consequences should they continue. At times, they got a decidedly negative reaction; but they did not give up. Rather, they prayed – not for protection, but for boldness in preaching the gospel and for God to perform more signs and wonders through the name of Jesus (Acts 4:29-31).

It is vital for all of us as Christians to persevere in telling others about Jesus – by our presence, persuasion, proclamation, power and prayer. If we do, over the course of a lifetime we shall see many lives changed.

During the war a man was shot and lay dying in the trenches. A friend leaned over to him and said, 'Is there anything I can do for you?'

He replied, 'No, I am dying.'

'Is there anyone I can send a message to for you?'

'Yes, you can send a message to this man at this address. Tell him that in my last minutes what he taught me as a child is helping me to die.'

The man was his old Sunday school teacher. When the message got back to him, he said, 'God forgive me. I gave up Sunday school teaching years ago because I thought I was getting nowhere. I thought it was no use.'

When we tell people about Jesus, it is never 'no use'. For the gospel 'is the power of God for the salvation of everyone who believes' (Romans 1:16).

13

Does God Heal Today?

A few years ago, a Japanese girl asked myself and my wife to pray for her back problem to be healed. We placed our hands on her and asked God to heal her. Thereafter, I tried to avoid bumping into her because I was not sure how to explain to her why she had not been healed. One day she came round the corner and I could not avoid her. I thought it only polite to ask the dreaded question, 'How is your back?'

'Oh,' she replied, 'it was completely healed after you prayed for it.'

I don't know why I was so surprised, but I was.

When John Wimber came to our church with a team from his church (the Vineyard Christian Fellowship), he preached one Sunday on the subject of healing. On Monday he came to a gathering of leaders. There were about sixty or seventy of us in the room and he spoke again about healing. We had heard talks on healing before, and felt quite happy about what he said on the subject. That was until he said that we were going to break for coffee and then have a 'workshop'. We were now on unfamiliar ground. John Wimber said that his team had had some twelve 'words of knowledge' about the people in the room. He told us that by a 'word of knowledge' (1 Corinthians 12:8) he meant a supernatural revelation of facts concerning a person or a situation, which is not learned by the efforts of the natural mind, but is made known by the Spirit of God. This may be in the form of a picture, a word seen or heard in the mind, or a feeling experienced physically. He then gave a whole list of them and said that he was going to invite people to come forward to be prayed for. I, for one, was most sceptical about the whole event.

However, as one by one the people responded to some of the quite detailed descriptions (my recollection is that one of them was for 'a man who had injured his back chopping wood when he was fourteen'), the level of faith in the room began to rise. Every word of knowledge was responded to. One of them concerned sterility. We all knew each other well and felt sure that this was not applicable to anyone in the group. However, a girl who had been unable to conceive, bravely went forward. She was prayed for and had her first of five children exactly nine months later!

My attitude during that evening reflects the fear and scepticism many of us in the twenty-first century bring to the subject of healing. I decided to reread the Bible to try to understand what it said about healing. Of course, God heals with the co-operation of doctors, nurses and the whole medical profession. But the more I have looked, the more convinced I am that we should also expect God to heal miraculously today.

HEALING IN THE BIBLE

In the Old Testament we find God's promises to bring healing and health to his people if they obey him (eg, Exodus 23:25-26; Deuteronomy 28; Psalm 41). Indeed, it is in his character to heal, for he says, 'I am the Lord who heals you' (Exodus 15:26). We also find several examples of miraculous healing (eg, 1 Kings 13:6;

2 Kings 4:8-37; Isaiah 38).

One of the most striking examples is the healing of Naaman, the commander of the army of the King of Aram, who had leprosy. God healed him after he had reluctantly dipped himself seven times in the River Jordan. 'His flesh was restored and became clean like that of a young boy' (2 Kings 5:14), and he recognised the God of Israel to be the only true God. Elisha, who had instructed him, refused the payment which Naaman offered (although his servant Gehazi made the fatal mistake of trying, deceitfully, to get money for himself as a result of the healing). We see, first, from this story that healing can have a remarkable effect on a person's life – not just physically, but also in their relationship with God. Healing and faith can go hand in hand. Secondly, if God acted in this way in the Old Testament, when there were only glimpses of the kingdom of God and the outpouring of the Spirit, we can confidently expect that he will do so, even more, now that Jesus has inaugurated the kingdom of God and the age of the Spirit.

The first recorded words of Jesus in Mark's Gospel are, 'The time has come . . . The kingdom of God is near. Repent and believe the good news!' (Mark 1:15). The theme of the kingdom of God is central to the ministry of Jesus. The expressions 'the kingdom of God' and 'the kingdom of heaven' are used more than eighty-two times, although the latter is confined to Matthew's Gospel. The two terms are synonymous. 'Heaven' was a common Jewish expression for referring to God without mentioning the divine name. The Jewish background to Matthew's Gospel, as opposed to the Gentile orientation of Luke and Mark, probably explains the different use.

The Greek word for 'kingdom', *basileia*, is a translation of the Aramaic *malkuth*, which was in all probability the expression that Jesus used. It means not only 'kingdom' in the sense of a political or geographical realm, but also carries the notion of activity – the activity of ruling or reigning. Thus 'the kingdom of God' means 'the rule and reign of God'.

In the teaching of Jesus, the kingdom of God has a future aspect which will only be fulfilled with a decisive event at 'the end of the age' (Matthew 13:49). For example, in one of the parables of the kingdom, he speaks of a coming harvest at the end of the age when 'the Son of Man . . . will weed out of his kingdom everything that causes sin and all who do evil . . . Then the righteous will shine like the sun in the kingdom of their Father' (Matthew 13:24-43). The end of the age will come when Jesus returns. When he came the first time, he came in weakness; when he returns, he will come 'with power and great glory' (Matthew 24:30).

History is moving towards this climax with the glorious coming of Jesus Christ (Matthew 25:31). In all, there are over 300 references in the New Testament to the second coming of Christ. When he returns it will be obvious to all. History, as we know it, will end. There will be a universal resurrection and a Day of Judgement. For some (those who reject Christ), it will be a day of destruction (2 Thessalonians 1:8-9); for others, it will be a day of receiving their inheritance in the kingdom of God (Matthew 25:34). There will be a new heaven and a new earth (2 Peter 3:13; Revelation 21:1). Jesus himself will be there (Revelation 21:22-23) and so will all who love and obey him. It will be a place of intense happiness which goes on for ever (1 Corinthians 2:9). We shall have new bodies which are imperishable and glorious (1 Corinthians 15:42-43). There will be no more death or mourning or crying or pain (Revelation 21:4). All who believe will be totally healed on that day.

On the other hand, there is a present aspect to the kingdom of God in the teaching and activity of Jesus. We see the signs, the dawning, the budding of the approaching kingdom. Jesus told the Pharisees, 'The kingdom of God is among you' (Luke 17:20-21).

In his parable of the hidden treasure and the pearl (Matthew 13:44-46), Jesus suggests that the kingdom is something which can be discovered and experienced in this age. Throughout the Gospels it is clear that Jesus saw his ministry as the fulfilment of the Old Testament promises in history. In the synagogue at Nazareth, Jesus read the prophecy from Isaiah 61:1-2 and asserted, 'Today this scripture is fulfilled in your hearing' (Luke 4:21). He went on to demonstrate this present reality of the kingdom by all that he did during his ministry, in the forgiveness of sins, the suppression of evil and the healing of the sick.

The kingdom is both 'now' and 'not yet'. The Jewish expectation was that the Messiah would immediately inaugurate a completed kingdom, as shown in the diagram below:

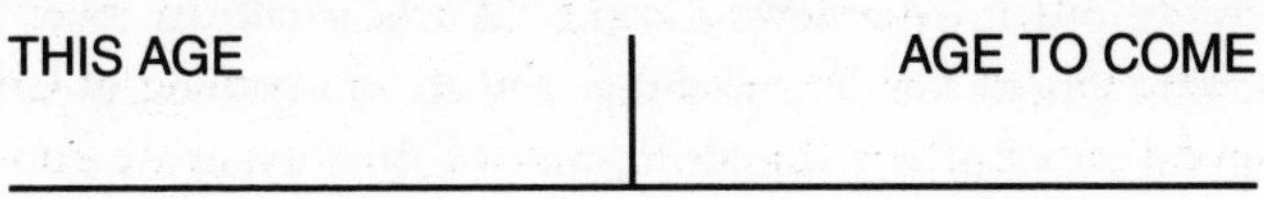

THIS AGE | **AGE TO COME**

Jesus' teaching was a modification of this and can be summarised in the diagram below:

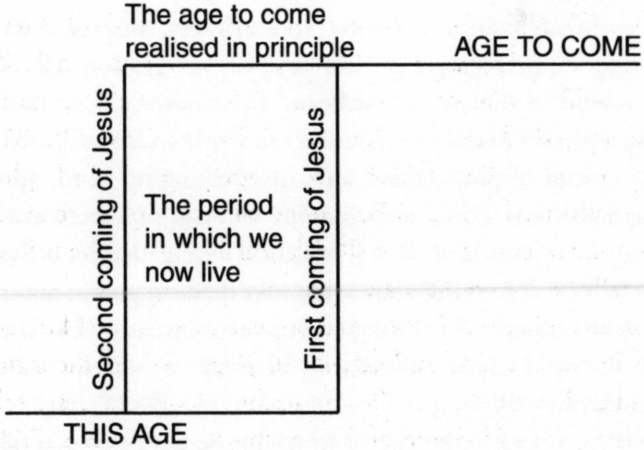

The age to come
realised in principle   **AGE TO COME**

Second coming of Jesus

The period
in which we
now live

First coming of Jesus

THIS AGE

191

We live between the times, when the age to come has broken into history. The old age goes on, but the powers of the new age have erupted into this age. The future kingdom has broken into history. Jesus preached the kingdom of God. He also demonstrated its breaking into history by healing the sick, raising the dead and driving out demons.

A quarter of the Gospels is concerned with healing. Although Jesus did not heal all in Judea who were sick, we often read of him healing either individuals or groups of people (eg, Matthew 4:23; 9:35; Mark 6:56; Luke 4:40; 6:19; 9:11). It was part of the normal activity of the kingdom.

Not only did he do this himself, but he commissioned his disciples to do the same. First, he commissioned the twelve. This is clearly set out in Matthew's Gospel. Matthew tells us that 'Jesus went throughout Galilee, teaching in their synagogues, preaching the good news of the kingdom, and healing every disease and sickness among the people' (Matthew 4:23). He then gives some of the teaching and preaching of Jesus in Matthew 5–7 (the Sermon on the Mount), then nine miracles (mainly of healing) and he concludes with an almost exact repetition of Matthew 4:23: 'Jesus went through all the towns and villages, teaching in their synagogues, preaching the good news of the kingdom and healing every kind of disease and sickness' (Matthew 9:35). Matthew is using a literary device of repetition known as an *inclusio*, which was used instead of punctuation and the breaking up of the text with paragraphs to indicate the beginning and end of a section. Having shown what Jesus himself did, Matthew tells us that Jesus then sent the twelve out to do the same. He told them to go out and preach the same message: '"The kingdom of heaven is near." Heal the sick, raise the dead, cleanse those who have leprosy, drive out demons . . .' (Matthew 10:8).

Nor was it only the twelve to whom he gave this commission.

There was also a further group of seventy-two whom he appointed. He told them to go out and 'heal the sick . . . and tell them, "The kingdom of God is near you"' (Luke 10:9). They returned with joy and said, 'Lord, even the demons submit to us in your name' (v. 17).

Nor were his commissions confined to the twelve and the seventy-two. Jesus expected *all* his disciples to do the same. He told his disciples to 'go and make disciples of all nations . . . teaching them to obey *everything* I have commanded you' (Matthew 28:18-20, italics mine). He did not say, 'Everything except, of course, the healing bit.'

We find the same in the longer ending of Mark's Gospel (which is, at least, very good evidence of what the early church understood Jesus' commission to be). Jesus said, '"Go into all the world and preach the good news to all creation . . . and these signs will accompany *those who believe*: In my name they will drive out demons . . . they will place their hands on sick people, and they will get well" . . . Then the disciples went out and preached everywhere, and the Lord worked with them and confirmed his word by the signs that accompanied it' (Mark 16:15-20, italics mine). Jesus says, 'These signs will accompany *those who believe*' – that is to say those 'who believe' in Jesus Christ, which means all Christians.

We find the same in John's Gospel. Jesus said, in the context of miracles, 'Anyone who has faith in me will do what I have been doing. He will do even greater things than these, because I am going to the Father' (John 14:12). Clearly no one has performed miracles of greater quality than Jesus, but there has been a greater quantity since Jesus returned to the Father. He has not ceased to perform miracles, but he now uses weak and imperfect human beings. Again it is 'anyone who has faith in me'. That is you and me. These commands and promises are not restricted anywhere to a special category of Christians.

Jesus healed; he told his disciples to do the same and they did so.

In the Book of Acts we see the working out of this commission. The disciples continued to preach and teach, but also to heal the sick, raise the dead and cast out demons (Acts 3:1-10; 4:12; 5:12-16; 8:5-13; 9:32-43; 14:3, 8-10; 19:11-12; 20:9-12; 28:8-9). It is clear from 1 Corinthians 12–14 that Paul did not believe that such abilities were confined to the apostles. Likewise, the writer to the Hebrews says that God testified to his message by 'signs, wonders and various miracles, and gifts of the Holy Spirit' (Hebrews 2:4).

Nowhere in the Bible does it say that healing was confined to any particular period of history. On the contrary, healing is one of the signs of the kingdom which was inaugurated by Jesus Christ and continues to this day. We should expect God to continue to heal miraculously today as part of his kingdom activity.

HEALING IN CHURCH HISTORY

In her book *Christian Healing* Evelyn Frost examined in detail passages of early church writers, such as Quadratus, Justin Martyr, Theophilus of Antioch, Irenaeus, Tertullian and Origen, and concluded that healing formed a normal part of the activity of the early church.

Irenaeus (c. 130-c. 200) who was Bishop of Lyons and one of the theologians of the early church wrote:

Those who are in truth his disciples, receiving grace from him, do in his name perform [miracles], so as to promote the welfare of other men, according to the gift which each one has received from him. For some do certainly and truly drive out devils, so that those who have thus been cleansed from evil spirits frequently both believe [in Christ], and join themselves to the church. Others have foreknowledge of things to come: they see visions, and utter prophetic expressions.

194

Others still, heal the sick by laying their hands upon them and they are made whole. Yea, moreover, as I have said, the dead have been raised up, and remain among us for many years.[59]

Origen (c. 185-c. 254), another theologian, biblical scholar and writer of the early church, said of Christians: 'They expel evil spirits, and perform many cures, and foresee certain events . . . the name of Jesus . . . can take away diseases.'

Two hundred years later there was still an expectation that God would heal people directly. Augustine of Hippo (AD 354-430), whom many regard as the greatest theologian of the first four centuries, says in his book *The City of God* that '*even now* miracles are wrought in the name of Christ'. He cites the example of a blind man's sight restored in Milan, when he was there. He then describes the cure of a man he was staying with, called Innocentius. He was being treated by the doctors for fistulae, of which he had 'a large number intricately seated in the rectum'! He had undergone one very painful operation. It was not thought that he would survive another operation. While they were praying for him he was cast down to the ground as if someone had hurled him violently to the earth, groaning and sobbing, his whole body shaking so that he could not speak. The dreaded day for the next operation came. 'The surgeons arrived . . . the frightful instruments are produced . . . the part is bared; the surgeon . . . with knife in hand, eagerly looks for the sinus that is to be cut. He searches for it with his eyes; he feels for it with his finger; he applies every kind of scrutiny.' He found a perfectly healed wound. 'No words of mine can describe the joy, and praise, and thanksgiving to the merciful and almighty God which was poured from the lips of all, with tears and gladness. Let the scene be imagined rather than described!'

Next he described the healing of Innocentia – a devout woman of the highest rank in the state – who was healed of what the doctors described as incurable breast cancer. The doctor was curious to find out how she had been healed. When she told him that Jesus had healed her, he was furious and said, 'I thought you would make some great discovery to me.' She, shuddering at the indifference, quickly replied, 'What great thing was it for Christ to heal a cancer, who raised one who had been four days dead?'

He goes on to tell of a doctor with gout who was healed in the 'very act of baptism' and an old comedian who was also cured at baptism, not only of paralysis, but also of a hernia. Augustine says he knows of so many miraculous healings that he says at one point, 'What am I to do? I am so pressed by the promise of finishing this work, that I cannot record all the miracles I know . . . even now, therefore many miracles are wrought, the same God, who wrought those we read of, still performing them, by whom he will and as he will.'

All the way through church history God has continued to heal people directly. There has never been a time when healing has died out – right up to the present day.

Edward Gibbon, the English rationalist, historian and scholar, best known as the author of *The History of the Decline and Fall of the Roman Empire* (1776-1788), lists five causes for the remarkable and rapid growth of Christianity. One of these is 'the miraculous powers of the primitive Church'. He says, 'The Christian Church, from the time of the apostles and their first disciples has claimed an uninterrupted succession of miraculous powers, the gift of tongues, of vision and of prophecy, the power of expelling demons, of healing the sick and of raising the dead.' Gibbon goes on to point out the inconsistency of his own day when 'a latent, and even involuntary, scepticism adheres to the most pious dispositions'. By contrast to the early church, he writes that in the church of his day 'admission of supernatural truths is much less an active consent than a cold and placid acquiescence. Accustomed long since to observe and to respect the invariable order of Nature, our reason, or at least our imagination, is not sufficiently prepared to sustain the visible action of the Deity.' The same could be said even more so of our own day.

HEALING TODAY

God is still healing people today. There are so many wonderful stories of God healing that it is difficult to know which to give as an example. Ajay Gohill told his story at a recent baptism and confirmation service at our church. He was born in Kenya and came to England in 1971. He had been brought up as a Hindu and worked in his family business as a newsagent in Neasden. At the age of twenty-one he contracted erythrodermic psoriasis, a chronic skin disease. His weight dropped from 11.5 to 7.5 stone. He was treated all over the world – in the United States, Germany, Switzerland, Israel and all over England, including Harley Street. He said that he spent 80 per cent of his earnings on trying to find a cure. He took strong drugs which affected his liver. Eventually, he had to give up his job. The disease was all over his body from head to toe. He was so horrible to look at that he could not go swimming or even wear a T-shirt. He lost all his friends. His wife and son left him. He wanted to die. On 20 August 1987 he was in a wheelchair in the Elizabeth Ward of St Thomas' Hospital. He spent over seven weeks in hospital receiving various kinds of treatments. On 14 October he was lying in his bed and wanted to die. He cried out, 'God, if you are watching, let me die – I am sorry if I have done something wrong.' He said that as he prayed he 'felt a presence'. He looked in his locker and pulled out a Good News Bible. He opened it at random and read Psalm 38:

O Lord, don't punish me in your anger! You have wounded me with your arrows; you have struck me down. Because of your anger, I am in great pain; my whole body is diseased because of my sins. I am drowning in the flood of my sins; they are a burden too heavy to bear. Because I have been foolish, my sores stink and rot. I am bowed down, I am crushed; I mourn all day long. I am burning with fever and I am near to death. I am worn out and utterly crushed; my heart is troubled, and I groan with pain. O Lord, you know what I long for; you hear all my groans. My heart is pounding, my strength is gone, and my eyes have lost their brightness. My friends and neighbours will not come near me, because of my sores; even my family keeps away from me. . . . Do not abandon me, O Lord; do not stay away, my God! Help me now, O Lord my saviour! (Psalm 38:1-11, 21-22, GNB).

Each and every verse seemed relevant to him. He prayed for God to heal him and fell into a deep sleep. When he awoke the next morning 'everything looked new'. He went to the bathroom and relaxed in a bath. As he looked at the bathwater, he saw his skin had lifted off and was floating in the bath. He called the nurses in and told them that God was healing him. All his skin was new like a baby's. He had been totally healed. Since then he has been reunited with his son. He says that the inner healing that has taken place in his life is even greater than the physical healing. He says, 'Every day I live for Jesus. I am his servant today.'

God is a God who heals. The Greek word which means 'I save' also means 'I heal'. God is concerned not just about our spiritual salvation, but also about our whole being. One day we shall have a new perfect body but in this life we will never reach perfection. When God heals someone miraculously today we get a glimpse of the future when the final redemption of our bodies will take place (Romans 8:23). Of course not everyone we pray for will necessarily be healed and no human being can ultimately avoid death. Our bodies are decaying. At some point it may even be right to prepare a person for death rather than praying for their healing. Indeed, the

198

love and concern shown to people who are dying, for example, by the hospice movement, gives dignity to the terminally ill and is another outworking of Jesus' commission to care for the sick. So we need to be sensitive to the guidance of the Holy Spirit.

This should not discourage us from praying for people to be healed. The more people we pray for, the more we shall see healed. Those who are not healed usually speak of the blessing of being prayed for – provided they are prayed for with love and sensitivity. I remember a group of us at theological college praying for a man with a bad back. I don't think he was healed, but he said to me afterwards, 'This is the first time since I have been at theological college that I felt anyone cared.' Another man said to me recently that although he had not been healed when he was prayed for, he had had his greatest experience ever of the Spirit of God, and his life has been transformed.

Some are given special gifts of healing (1 Corinthians 12:9). Today, around the world, we find examples of those with an extraordinary gift of healing. This does not mean that we can leave it all to them. The commission to heal is for all of us. Just as we do not all have the gift of evangelism, but we are all called to tell others about Jesus, so we do not all have the gift of healing, but we are all called to pray for the sick.

How in practice do we go about praying for the sick? It is vital to remember that it is God who heals, not us. There is no technique involved. We pray with love and simplicity. The motivation of Jesus was his compassion for people (Mark 1:41; Matthew 9:36). If we love people we will always treat them with respect and dignity. If we believe it is Jesus who heals we will pray with simplicity, because it is not our prayer but the power of God that brings healing.

Here is a simple pattern:

Where does it hurt?
We ask the person who wants prayer for healing what is wrong and what they would like us to pray for.

Why does the person have this condition?
Of course, a leg broken in a car accident will be obvious, but at other times we may need to ask God to show us if there is a root cause to the problem. One woman in our congregation had developed backache with pain in her left hip, which interfered with sleep, movement and work. The doctor prescribed pills for arthritis. She asked for prayer one evening. The girl who was praying for her said that the word 'forgiveness' had come to her mind. After a struggle the woman was able to forgive somebody who had wronged her, and she was partially healed. She was totally healed at the moment she posted a forgiving letter to her friend.

How do I pray?
There are various models in the New Testament which we follow. They are all simple. Sometimes we pray for God to heal in the name of Jesus and we ask the Holy Spirit to come on the person. Prayer may be accompanied by anointing with oil (James 5:14). More often it is accompanied by the laying on of hands (Luke 4:40).

How are they feeling?
After we have prayed we usually ask the person what they are experiencing. Sometimes they feel nothing – in which case we continue to pray. At other times they feel that they are healed, although time alone will tell. On other occasions they feel better but are not totally healed, in which case we continue as Jesus did with the blind man (Mark 8:22-25). We continue praying until we feel it is right to stop.

What next?

After praying for healing it is important to reassure people of God's love for them regardless of whether they are healed or not, and to give them the liberty to come back and be prayed for again. We must avoid putting burdens on people, such as suggesting that it is their lack of faith that has prevented healing from taking place. We always encourage people to go on praying and to ensure that their lives are rooted in the healing community of the church – which is the place where long-term healing so often occurs.

Finally, it is important to persist in praying for people to be healed. It is easy to get discouraged, especially if we do not see immediate dramatic results. We continue because of our obedience to the calling and commission from Jesus Christ to preach the kingdom and to demonstrate its coming by, among other things, healing the sick. If we persist over the years we will see God healing people.

I was once asked to visit a woman in the Brompton Hospital. She was in her thirties, had three children and was pregnant with a fourth. Her common-law husband had left her and she was on her own. Her third child, who was a Down's syndrome child, had a hole in his heart which had been operated on. The operation had not been a success and, not unnaturally, the medical staff wanted to turn the machines off. Three times they asked her if they could turn the machines off and let the baby die. She said no, as she wanted to try one last thing. She wanted someone to pray for him. So I came, and she told me that she didn't believe in God, but she showed me her son. He had tubes all over him and his body was bruised and swollen. She said that the doctors had indicated that even if he recovered he would have brain damage because his heart had stopped for such a long time. She said, 'Will you pray?' So I prayed in the name of Jesus for God to heal him. Then I explained to her how she could give her life to Jesus Christ and she did that. I

201

left, but returned two days later. She came running out the moment she saw me. She said, 'I've been trying to get hold of you: something amazing has happened. The night after you prayed he completely turned the corner. He has recovered.' Within a few days he had gone home. I tried to keep in contact with her, but didn't know where she lived, although she kept leaving messages on the phone. About six months later I was in the lift in another hospital and saw a mother and child whom I did not recognise at once. The woman said, 'Are you Nicky?' I said, 'Yes.' She said, 'That is the little boy you prayed for. It is amazing. Not only has he recovered from the operation, but his hearing, which was bad beforehand, is better. He still has Down's syndrome, but he is much better than he was before.'

Since then I have taken two funerals for other members of that family. At each of them people have come up to me, none of them churchgoers, saying, 'You were the person who prayed for Craig to be healed and God healed him.' They all believe that God healed him, because they know that he was dying. The change in Vivienne, the child's mother, had also made a deep impression on them. She was so changed after coming to Christ that she decided to marry the person with whom she was living. He had come back to her after seeing the change in her life. They are now married and she is totally transformed. On the second occasion, Vivienne went round all the relatives and friends saying, 'I didn't believe, but now I do believe.' Not long afterwards, Craig's uncle and aunt came to church, sat in the front row and gave their lives to Jesus Christ. They did so because they knew they had seen God's power in healing.

14

What about the Church?

Abraham Lincoln once said, 'If all the people who fell asleep in church on Sunday morning were laid out end to end . . . they would be a great deal more comfortable.' Hard pews, unsingable tunes, enforced silence and excruciating boredom are just a few ingredients that make up the common image of church on Sunday. It is seen as an experience through which to grit one's teeth stoically until the aroma of gravy brightens up the prospects of the day. A vicar was taking a small boy around his church and showing him the memorials. 'These are the names of those who died in the Services.' The boy asked, 'Did they die at the morning service or at the evening service?'

Some associate the word 'church' with the clergy. Somebody who is entering the ordained ministry is said to be 'going into the church'. Those embarking on such a career are often viewed with suspicion, and the assumption is made that they are absolutely incapable of doing anything else. Hence a recent advert in the church press: 'Are you forty-five and getting nowhere? Why not consider the Christian ministry?' Clergy are sometimes perceived as: 'Six days invisible, one day incomprehensible!'

Others associate the word 'church' with a particular denomination. For example, Baptists or Methodists. Still others associate the word 'church' with church buildings. They assume that to be a minister you must be interested in church architecture, and when they go on holiday they send their vicar a picture of the local church building. I heard one clergyman imploring his congregation not to send him postcards of churches, telling them he had very little interest in church architecture!

Some tick off 'church' on their list of yearly duties, somewhere between visiting Great Aunt Edna in Hove and making a cake for the village fete. The attitude of others is summed up in a ditty:

> So when I've nothing else to do,
> I think I'll pay a visit,
> So when at last I'm carried in,
> The Lord won't say, 'Who is it?'

There may be an element of truth in some of these views. However, many Christians are seeking to bury this image of the church as it is wholly inadequate when compared to the picture of the church in the New Testament. Many churches are now creating a wonderfully warm and outward-going Christian family which is much closer to the biblical picture. In the New Testament there are over 100 images or analogies of the church, and in this chapter I want to look at five which are central to the understanding of the church.

THE PEOPLE OF GOD

The church is made up of people. The Greek word for church, *ekklesia*, means 'an assembly' or 'gathering of people'. Sometimes the New Testament refers to the universal church (eg, Ephesians 3:10, 21; 5:23, 25, 27, 29, 32). The universal church consists of all those worldwide and down the ages who profess or have professed the name of Christ.

Baptism is a visible mark of being a member of the church. It is also a visible sign of what it means to be a Christian. It signifies cleansing from sin (1 Corinthians 6:11), dying and rising with Christ to a new life (Romans 6:3-5; Colossians 2:12) and the living water which the Holy Spirit brings to our lives (1 Corinthians 12:13). Jesus himself commanded his followers to go and make disciples and to baptise them (Matthew 28:19).

The universal Christian church is vast. According to the *Encyclopaedia Britannica,* it has nearly 1,900,000,000 adherents in 270 countries, consisting of 34 per cent of the world population. In many parts of the world, where there are extreme and oppressive regimes, the church is persecuted. In these parts it is mainly underground but, by all accounts, very strong. In the Third World it is growing rapidly. In some countries, such as Kenya, it is estimated that 80 per cent of the population are now professed Christians. On the other hand, in the free world the church has largely been in decline. According to a survey carried out by *Christian Research,* in the course of the 1990s a million people stopped going to church on an average Sunday in Britain. At one time the West was sending missionaries to the Third World. However, I remember that when I was in Cambridge, three Ugandan missionaries came there to preach the gospel. It struck me then how much the world had changed in the last 150 years and that England needed missionaries as much as anywhere else.

In the New Testament, Paul speaks of local churches, for example the 'Galatian churches' (1 Corinthians 16:1), 'the churches in the province of Asia' (1 Corinthians 16:19) and 'all the churches of Christ' (Romans 16:16). Even those local churches seem at times to have broken down into smaller gatherings which met in homes (Romans 16:5; 1 Corinthians 16:19).

In effect, there seems to have been three types of gathering in the Bible: the large, the medium-sized and the small. These are practical levels at which we experience what the church is: the celebration, congregation and cell. All three are important and complement each other.

The celebration is a large gathering of Christians. This may take place every Sunday in big churches, or when a number of small churches come together for worship. In the Old Testament, the people of God came together for special celebrations with a festive atmosphere at Passover, Pentecost or at the New Year. Today, large gatherings of Christians provide inspiration. Through them many can recapture a vision of the greatness of God and a profound sense of worship. These gatherings of hundreds of Christians together can restore confidence to those who have felt isolated and provide a visible presence of the church in the community. However, on their own such gatherings are not enough. They are not places where Christian friendships can easily develop.

The congregation, in this sense, is a medium-sized gathering. The size makes it possible to know most people and be known by most. It is a place where lasting Christian friendships can be made. It is also a place where the gifts and ministries of the Spirit can be exercised in an atmosphere of love and acceptance, where people are free to risk making mistakes. It is a place where individuals can learn, for example, to give talks, lead worship, pray for the sick, develop the gift of prophecy and learn to pray out loud.

The third level of meeting is the 'cell', which we call the 'small group'. These groups consist of two to twelve people who gather to study the Bible and pray together. It is in these groups that the closest friendships in the church are made. They are characterised by confidentiality (that we can speak openly without fear of gossip), intimacy (that it is a group where we can speak about what really matters in our lives) and accountability (that we are willing to listen to and learn from one another).

THE FAMILY OF GOD

When we receive Jesus Christ into our lives, we become children of God (John 1:12). This is what gives the church its unity. We have God as our Father, Jesus Christ as our Saviour and the Holy Spirit as our indweller. We all belong to one family. Although brothers and sisters may squabble and fall out or not see each other for long periods of time, they still remain brothers and sisters. Nothing can end that relationship. So the church is one, even though it often appears to be divided.

This does not mean that we settle for disunity. Jesus prayed for his followers 'that they may be one' (John 17:11). Paul says, 'Make every effort to keep the unity of the Spirit' (Ephesians 4:3). Like a divided family we should always strive for reconciliation. The incarnation demands a visible expression of our invisible unity. Of course, this unity should not be achieved at the expense of truth but, as the Medieval writer Rupertus Meldenius put it, 'On the necessary points, unity; on the questionable points, liberty; in everything, love.'

At every level we should seek unity – in the small group,

congregation and celebration; within our denomination and between denominations. This unity is brought about as theologians and church leaders get together to debate and work through theological differences. But it is also achieved, often more effectively, by ordinary Christians getting together to worship and work together. The nearer we come to Christ, the nearer we come together. David Watson used a striking illustration. He said:

> When you travel by air and the plane lifts off the ground, the walls and hedges which may seem large and impressive at ground level, at once lose their significance. In the same way, when the power of the Holy Spirit lifts us up together into the conscious realisation of the presence of Jesus, the barriers between us become unimportant. Seated with Christ in the heavenly places, the differences between Christians can often seem petty and marginal.[60]

Since we have the same Father, we are brothers and sisters and are all called to love one another. John puts it very clearly:

> If we say we love God yet hate a brother or sister, we are liars. For any of us who do not love a brother or sister, whom we have seen, cannot love God, whom we have not seen. And he has given us this command: Those who love God must also love one another. Everyone who believes that Jesus is the Christ is born of God, and everyone who loves the father loves his child as well (1 John 4:20 – 5:1).

The Pope's personal preacher, Father Raniero Cantalamessa, addressing a gathering of thousands from many different denominations said, 'When Christians quarrel we say to God: "Choose between us and them." But the Father loves *all* his children. We should say, "We accept as our brothers all those whom you receive as your children."'

We are called to fellowship with one another. The Greek word *koinonia* means 'having in common' or 'sharing'. It is the word used for the marital relationship, the most intimate between human beings. Our fellowship is with God (Father, Son and Holy Spirit – 1 John 1:3; 2 Corinthians 13:14) and with one another (1 John 1:7). Christian fellowship cuts across race, colour, education, background and every other cultural barrier. There is a level of friendship in the church which I have certainly never experienced outside the church.

John Wesley said, 'The New Testament knows nothing of solitary religion.' We are called to fellowship with one another. It is not an optional extra. There are two things we simply cannot do alone. We cannot marry alone and we cannot be a Christian alone. Professor C.E.B. Cranfield put it like this: 'The freelance Christian, who would be a Christian but is too superior to belong to the visible Church upon earth in one of its forms, is simply a contradiction in terms.'

The writer of Hebrews urges his readers, 'Let us consider how we may spur one another on towards love and good deeds. Let us not give up meeting together, as some are in the habit of doing, but let us encourage one another – and all the more as you see the Day approaching' (Hebrews 10:24-25). Often Christians lose their love for the Lord and their enthusiasm for their faith because they neglect fellowship.

One man who found himself in this position was visited by a wise old Christian. They sat in front of the coal fire in the sitting room. The old man never spoke, but went to the coal fire and picked out a red-hot coal with some tongs and put it on the hearth. He still said nothing. In a few minutes the coal had lost its glow. Then he picked it up and put it back in the fire. After a short time it began to glow again. The old man still said nothing at all but, as he got up to leave, the other man knew exactly why he had lost his fervour – a Christian out of fellowship is like a coal out of the fire.

Martin Luther wrote in his diary, 'At home in my house there is no warmth or vigour in one, but in the church when the multitude is gathered together, a fire is kindled in my heart and it breaks its way through.'

THE BODY OF CHRIST

Paul had been persecuting the Christian church when he encountered Jesus Christ on the road to Damascus. Jesus said to him, 'Saul, Saul, why do you persecute *me?*' (Acts 9:4, italics mine). Paul had never met Jesus before so he must have realised that Jesus was saying that, in persecuting Christians, he was persecuting Jesus himself. It may well be that from his encounter Paul realised that the church was, in effect, the body of Christ. 'He calls the church Christ,' wrote the sixteenth-century reformer, Calvin. We Christians are Christ to the world. As the old hymn says:

> He has no hands but our hands
> To do His work today;
> He has no feet but our feet
> To lead men in His way;
> He has no voice but our voice
> To tell men how He died;
> He has no help but our help
> To lead them to His side.

Paul develops this analogy in 1 Corinthians 12. The body is a unit (v. 12), yet this unity does not mean uniformity. 'Those who are members of one another become as diverse as the hand and the ear. That is why the worldlings are so monotonously alike compared with the almost fantastic variety of the saints. Obedience is the road to freedom, humility the road to pleasure, unity the road to personality.'[61] There are 'many parts' and they are all different with

210

'different kinds of gifts' and 'different kinds of working' (vv. 4-6).

What then should our attitude be to other parts of the body of Christ?

Paul deals with two wrong attitudes. First, he speaks to those who feel inferior and who feel that they have nothing to offer. For example, Paul says the foot may feel inferior to the hand or the ear inferior to the eye (vv. 14-19). It is a human tendency to feel envious of others.

It is easy to look round the church and feel inferior and therefore not needed. As a result we do nothing. In fact we are *all* needed. God has given gifts 'to each one' (v. 7). The term 'to each one' runs through 1 Corinthians 12 as a common thread. Each person has at least one gift which is absolutely necessary for the proper functioning of the body. Unless each of us plays the part God has designed for us, the church will not be able to function as it should. In the following verses, Paul turns to those who feel superior (vv. 21-25) and are saying to others, 'I don't need you.' Again, Paul points out the folly of this position. A body without a foot is not as effective as it might be (see v. 21). Often the parts which are unseen are even more important than those with a higher profile.

The right attitude is one which recognises that we are all in it together. We are all part of a team – each part affects the whole. From Plato onwards, the 'I' has been the personality that gives unity to the body. We do not say, 'My head has an ache.' We say, 'I have a headache.' So it is with the body of Christ. 'If one part suffers, every part suffers with it; if one part is honoured, every part rejoices with it' (v. 26).

Every Christian is a part of the church. John Wimber was once approached by a member of his congregation who had met somebody in great need. After the Sunday service this man told John Wimber of his frustration in trying to get help. 'This man needed a place to stay, food and support while he gets on his feet and looks for a job,' he said. 'I am really frustrated. I tried telephoning the church office, but no one could see me and they couldn't help me. I finally ended up having to let him stay with *me* for the week! Don't you think the church should take care of people like this?' John Wimber says he thought for a moment and then said, 'It looks like *the church* did.'

As we saw in Chapter 8, the problem with the church is that for years it has either been pulpit-centred or altar-centred, according to our different traditions. In both situations the dominant role has been played by the minister or the priest. As Michael Green said, commenting on the spectacular spread of the Pentecostal churches in South America, 'It is . . . due to many causes, but not least to the fact that it is predominantly a lay church.'[62]

A HOLY TEMPLE

The only church building the New Testament speaks about is a building made of people. Paul says that the Christians are 'being built together to become a dwelling in which God lives by his Spirit' (Ephesians 2:22). Jesus is the chief cornerstone. He is the one who founded the church and around whom the church is built. The foundations are 'the apostles and prophets' and the result is a holy temple made of 'living stones'.

In the Old Testament the tabernacle (and later the temple) was central to Israel's worship. This was the place where people went to meet with God. At times his presence filled the temple (1 Kings 8:11) and especially the Holy of Holies. Access to his presence was strictly limited (see Hebrews 9).

Through his death on the cross for us, Jesus opened up access to the Father for all believers all the time. His presence is no longer confined to a physical temple; now he is present by his Spirit with all believers. His presence is especially sensed when Christians gather together (Matthew 18:20). His new temple is the church which is 'a dwelling in which God lives by his Spirit'.

Gordon Fee, Professor of NT at Regent's College, Canada, has written:

> Presence is a delicious word – because it points to one of our truly great gifts. Nothing else can take the place of presence, not gifts, not telephone calls, not pictures, not mementos, nothing. Ask the person who has lost a lifelong mate what they miss the most; the answer is invariably 'presence'. When we are ill, we don't need soothing words nearly as much as we need loved ones to be present. What makes a shared life – games, walks, concerts, outings, and a myriad of other things – so pleasurable? Presence.[63]

The presence of God was what Adam and Eve lost in the Garden of Eden. But God promised that he would restore his presence. In the Old Testament his presence came into the temple. His glory filled the temple. That is why the people of Israel longed to go there. 'How lovely is your dwelling-place, O Lord Almighty! My soul yearns, even faints, for the courts of the Lord; my heart and my flesh cry out for the living God' (Psalm 84:1). One of the reasons the exile was such a disaster is that the people of God were away from God's presence. Then God promised that one day he was going to make his presence more widely known. On the day of Pentecost when the Spirit of God was poured out, the presence of God came to live among his people.

Paul writes of individual Christians, 'Do you not know that your bodies are temples of the Holy Spirit, who is in you, whom you have received from God?' (1 Corinthians 6:19). But more often he writes that the church, the gathered community of Christians, is the temple of the Holy Spirit. That is where God lives by his Spirit.

Under the Old Covenant (before Jesus), access to the Father was through a priest (Hebrews 4:14), who made sacrifices on behalf of believers. Now Jesus, our great high priest, has made the supreme sacrifice of his own life on our behalf. Jesus 'appeared once for all at the end of the ages to do away with sin by the sacrifice of himself' (Hebrews 9:26). We do not need to make further sacrifices for our sins. Rather, we need to be constantly reminded of his sacrifice for us. At the service of Holy Communion, sometimes called the Lord's Supper or the Eucharist, we remember his sacrifice with thanksgiving and partake of its benefits.

As we receive the bread and wine we look in four directions:

We look back with thanks
The bread and wine remind us of the broken body and shed blood of Jesus Christ on the cross. As we receive Communion we look back to the cross with thankfulness that he died for us so that our sins could be forgiven and our guilt removed (Matthew 26:26-28).

We look forward with anticipation
Jesus could have left us some other way to remember his death, but he chose to leave us a meal. A meal is often a way in which we celebrate great occasions. One day in heaven we are going to celebrate for eternity at 'the wedding supper' of Jesus Christ (Revelation 19:9). The bread and wine are a foretaste of this (Luke 22:16; 1 Corinthians 11:26).

We look around at the Christian family
Drinking from one cup and eating the one loaf symbolises our unity in Christ. 'Because there is one loaf, we, who are many, are one body, for we all partake of the one loaf' (1 Corinthians 10:17). That is why we do not receive the bread and the wine on our own. Eating and drinking together in this way should not only remind us of our unity, it should strengthen that unity as we look around at

our brothers and sisters for whom Christ died.

We look up in expectation
The bread and wine represent the body and blood of Jesus. Jesus promised to be with us by his Spirit after his death, and especially wherever Christians meet together: 'Where two or three come together in my name, there am I with them' (Matthew 18:20). So as we receive Communion we look up to Jesus with expectancy. In our experience, we have found that on such occasions there are sometimes conversions, healing and powerful encounters with the presence of Christ.

THE BRIDE OF CHRIST

This is one of the most beautiful analogies of the church in the New Testament. Paul says when speaking of the husband and wife relationship: 'This is a profound mystery – but I am talking about Christ and the church' (Ephesians 5:32). As the Old Testament speaks about God being a husband to Israel (Isaiah 54:1-8), so in the New Testament Paul speaks about Christ being a husband to the church and the model of every human marriage relationship. So he tells husbands to love their wives 'just as Christ loved the church and gave himself up for her to make her holy, cleansing her by the washing with water through the word, and to present her to himself as a radiant church, without stain or wrinkle or any other blemish, but holy and blameless' (Ephesians 5:25-27).

This picture of the holy and radiant church may not accord entirely with the present condition of the church, but we get a glimpse here of what Jesus intends for his church. One day Jesus will return in glory. In the Book of Revelation, John has a vision of the church, 'the new Jerusalem, coming down out of heaven from God, prepared as a bride beautifully dressed for her husband' (Revelation 21:2). Today the church is small and weak. One day we shall see the

215

church as Jesus intends it to be. In the meantime, we must try to bring our experiences as close as possible to the vision of the New Testament.

Our response to Christ's love for us should be one of love for him. The way we show our love for him is by living in holiness and purity – being a bride fit for him and fulfilling his purpose for us. This is his intention for us. This is how his purposes for us will be fulfilled. We are to be changed and to be made beautiful until we are fit to be his bride.

Moreover, his purpose for his church is that we 'may declare the praises of him who called you out of darkness into his wonderful light' (1 Peter 2:9). Declaring his praises involves both worship and witness. Our worship is the expression of our love and reverence for God with our whole beings – heart, mind and bodies. This is the purpose for which we were made. As the Westminster catechism puts it, 'The chief end of man is to glorify God and enjoy him for ever.'

Our witness is our response of love towards other people. He has called us to tell others the good news and draw them into his church – to declare his wonderful deeds to the people around us. In both our worship and our witness we need to find a contemporary expression for eternal truths. God does not change; neither does the gospel. We cannot change our doctrine or our message just to suit passing fashions. But the way in which we worship and the way in which we communicate the gospel must resonate with modern men and women. For many this will mean contemporary music and contemporary language.

If the church was closer to the New Testament images, church services would be far from dull and boring. Indeed, they should be very exciting and sometimes are. The church is made up of the people belonging to God, who are bound together in love as a family with Christ in their midst. They represent Christ to the world, loving their Lord as a bride loves the bridegroom, and being loved by him as a bride is loved by the bridegroom. What a place to be – it should be near heaven on earth.

A young couple who have recently come to faith in Christ wrote:

We have been coming to church for a year now and it already feels like home. The atmosphere of love, friendship and excitement is impossible to find elsewhere. The joy of it far exceeds any evening at a pub, party or restaurant . . . I am shocked to say (although I continue to enjoy all three). Both of us find that Sunday's service and Wednesday's gathering are two high points of the week. At times, it feels like coming up for air, especially as by Wednesday it is easy to be drowning in the deep waters of working life! If we miss either, we feel somehow 'diluted'. Of course, we can keep talking to God together and alone, but I feel that the act of meeting together is the bellows that keep on fanning the flames of our faith.

15

How Can I Make the Most of the Rest of My Life?

We only get one life. We might wish for more. D. H. Lawrence said, 'If only one could have two lives. The first in which to make one's mistakes . . . and the second in which to profit by them.' But there are no dress rehearsals for life; we are on stage straightaway.

Even if we have made mistakes in the past, it is possible with God's help to make something of what is left. Paul tells us in Romans 12:1-2 how we can do this.

Therefore, I urge you, brothers and sisters, in view of God's mercy, to offer your bodies as living sacrifices, holy and pleasing to God – which is your spiritual worship. Do not conform any longer to the pattern of this world, but be transformed by the renewing of your mind. Then you will be able to test and approve what God's will is – his good, pleasing and perfect will.

WHAT SHOULD WE DO?

Break with the past
As Christians we are called to be different from the world around

us. Paul writes, 'Do not conform any longer to the pattern of this world' (by which he means the world that has shut God out). Or as J. B. Phillips translates this verse, 'Don't let the world around you squeeze you into its own mould'. This is not easy; there is a pressure to conform, to be like everybody else. It is very hard to be different.

A young police officer was taking his final exam at Hendon Police College in north London. Here is one of the questions:

You are on patrol in outer London when an explosion occurs in a gas main in a nearby street. On investigation you find that a large hole has been blown in the footpath and there is an overturned van lying nearby. Inside the van there is a strong smell of alcohol. Both occupants – a man and a woman – are injured. You recognise the woman as the wife of your Divisional Inspector, who is at present away in the USA. A passing motorist stops to offer you assistance and you realise that he is a man who is wanted for armed robbery. Suddenly a man runs out of a nearby house, shouting that his wife is expecting a baby and that the shock of the explosion has made the birth imminent.

Another man is crying for help, having been blown into an adjacent canal by the explosion, and he cannot swim.

Bearing in mind the provisions of the Mental Health Act, describe in a few words what actions you would take.

The officer thought for a moment, picked up his pen, and wrote: 'I would take off my uniform and mingle with the crowd.'

We can sympathise with his answer. As a Christian, it is often easier to take off our Christian uniform and 'mingle with the crowd'. But we are called to remain distinctive, to retain our Christian identity, wherever we are and whatever the circumstances.

A Christian is called to be a chrysalis rather than a chameleon. A chrysalis is a pupa which turns into a beautiful butterfly. A chameleon is a lizard with the power to change colour: many can assume shades of green, yellow, cream or dark brown. It is popularly thought to change colour to match its background. Similarly, chameleon Christians merge with their surroundings, happy to be Christians in the company of other Christians, but willing to change their standards in an environment which is not Christian. Legend has it that an experiment was carried out on a chameleon. It was put on a tartan background, could not take the tension, and exploded! The chameleon Christian experiences an almost unbearable tension in his or her life and, unlike the chrysalis Christian, does not reach his or her potential.

Christians are not called to fit in with their background, but to be different. Being different does not mean being odd. We are not called to wear weird clothes or to start speaking in a peculiar religious language. We can be normal! The abnormality that some people feel to be a necessary part of Christianity is complete nonsense. Indeed, a relationship with God through Jesus should bring integration to our personalities. The more like Jesus we become, the more 'normal' we become – in the sense that we become more fully human.

When we follow Christ, we are free to shed patterns and habits that bring us and others down. For example, it means that we should no longer indulge in character assassination behind people's backs. It means we do not need to spend our time grumbling and complaining (if that is what we were like before). It means that we are free not to conform to the world's standards of sexual morality. This might all sound very negative, but it should not be so. Rather than being backbiters, we should be encouragers, constantly looking to build others up out of love for them. Rather than grumbling and complaining, we should be full of thankfulness and joy. Rather than indulging in sexual immorality, we should be demonstrating the blessing of keeping God's standards.

This latter example is one area where Christians are called to be different, but which many find difficult. In my experience of speaking about the Christian faith there is one subject which arises time and time again – the whole question of sexual morality. Questions most frequently asked in this area are, 'What about sex outside marriage? Is it wrong? Where does it say so in the Bible? Why is it wrong?'

God's pattern here, as elsewhere, is far superior to any other. God invented marriage. He also invented sex. He is not, as some seem to think, looking down in astonishment and saying, 'Oh my goodness, whatever will they think of next?' C. S. Lewis pointed out that pleasure is God's idea, not the devil's. The Bible affirms our sexuality. God made us sexual beings and designed our sexual organs for our enjoyment. The Bible celebrates sexual intimacy. In the Song of Songs we see the delight, contentment and satisfaction it brings.

The inventor of sex also tells us how it can be enjoyed to the full. The biblical context of sexual intercourse is the lifelong commitment in marriage between one man and one woman. The

Christian doctrine is set out in Genesis 2:24 and quoted by Jesus in Mark 10:7 – 'For this reason a man will leave his father and mother and be united to his wife, and the two will become one flesh.' Marriage involves the public act of leaving parents and making a lifelong commitment. It involves being 'united' with one's partner – the Hebrew word meaning literally 'glued' together – not just physically and biologically, but emotionally, psychologically, spiritually and socially. This is the Christian context of the 'one flesh' union. The biblical doctrine of marriage is the most exciting, thrilling and positive view of marriage that exists. It sets before us God's perfect plan.

God warns of the danger of going outside the boundaries he has laid down. There is no such thing as 'casual sex'. Every act of sexual intercourse effects a 'one flesh' union (1 Corinthians 6:13-20). When this union is broken people get hurt. If you glue two pieces of card together and then pull them apart, you can hear the sound of ripping and see that bits of each are left behind on the other. Similarly, becoming one flesh and then being torn apart leaves scars. We leave broken bits of ourselves in broken relationships. All around us we see what happens when God's standards are ignored. We see broken marriages, broken hearts, hurt children, sexual disease and those whose lives are in a mess. On the other hand, in so many Christian marriages where God's standards are kept, we see the blessing that God intended to bestow on the whole area of sex and marriage. Of course, it is never too late. God's love through Jesus can bring forgiveness, heal scars and restore wholeness to lives that have been torn apart. But it is far better to avoid the necessity of such measures.

So, let us not allow the world to squeeze us into its mould. Let us show the world something far, far better.

Make a new start

Paul says we are to 'be transformed' (Romans 12:2). In other words, we are to be like the chrysalis which changes into a beautiful butterfly. Many are fearful of change in their life: two caterpillars sitting on a leaf saw a butterfly passing by. One turned to the other and said, 'You won't catch me going up in one of those!' Such is our fear of leaving behind what we know.

God does not ask us to leave behind anything that is good. But he does ask us to get rid of the rubbish. Until we leave the rubbish behind we cannot enjoy the wonderful things God has for us. There was a woman who lived on the streets and walked round our parish. She would ask for money and react aggressively to those who refused. She walked the streets for years, accompanied by a mass of plastic bags. When she died, I took the funeral. Although I didn't expect anyone to be there, there were in fact several well-dressed people at the service. I discovered afterwards that this woman had inherited a large fortune. She had acquired a luxurious flat and many valuable paintings, but she chose to live on the streets with her plastic bags full of rubbish. She could not bring herself to leave her lifestyle, and she never enjoyed her inheritance.

As Christians we have inherited far more – all the riches of Christ. In order to enjoy these treasures, we have to leave behind the rubbish in our lives. Paul tells us to 'hate what is evil' (v. 9). That is what must be left behind.

In the verses that follow (Romans 12:9-21) we get a glimpse of some of those treasures to be enjoyed:

> Love must be sincere. Hate what is evil; cling to what is good. Be devoted to one another with mutual affection. Honour one another above yourselves. Never be lacking in zeal, but keep your spiritual fervour, serving the Lord. Be joyful in hope, patient in affliction, faithful in prayer. Share with God's people who are in need. Practise hospitality.
>
> Bless those who persecute you; bless and do not curse. Rejoice with

those who rejoice; mourn with those who mourn. Live in harmony with one another. Do not be proud, but be willing to associate with people of low position. Do not be conceited.

Do not repay anyone evil for evil. Be careful to do what is right in the eyes of everybody. If it is possible, as far as it depends on you, live at peace with everyone. Do not take revenge, my friends, but leave room for God's wrath, for it is written: 'It is mine to avenge; I will repay,' says the Lord. On the contrary: 'If your enemies are hungry, feed them; if they are thirsty, give them something to drink. In doing this, you will heap burning coals on their heads.' Do not overcome by evil; but overcome evil with good.

The Greek word for 'sincere' means 'without hypocrisy', or literally 'without play acting' or 'without a mask'. Often, relationships in the world are quite superficial. We all put up fronts to protect ourselves. I certainly did before I was a Christian (and it carried on to some extent afterwards – though it shouldn't have). I said, in effect, 'I don't really like what I am inside, so I will pretend I am somebody different.'

If other people are doing the same then there are two 'fronts' or 'masks' meeting. The real people never meet. This is the opposite of 'sincere love'. Sincere love means taking off our masks and daring to reveal who we are. When we know that God loves us as we are, we are set free to take off our masks. This means that there is a completely new depth in our relationships.

Sometimes people are cynical about enthusiasm, but there is nothing wrong with it. There is a joy and excitement, a 'spiritual fervour' (v. 11) which comes from our relationship with God. This initial experience of Christ is meant to last, and not to peter out. Paul says, '*Never* be lacking in zeal,' but, '*keep* your spiritual fervour, serving the Lord.' The longer we have been Christians, the more enthusiastic we should be.

Paul urges Christians to live in harmony with one another and to be generous (v. 13), hospitable (v. 13), forgiving (v. 14), empathetic (v. 15), and to live at peace with everyone (v. 18). It is a glorious picture of the Christian family into which God calls us, beckoning us into an atmosphere of love, joy, patience, faithfulness, generosity, hospitality, blessing, rejoicing, harmony, humility and peace; where good is not overcome by evil, but evil is overcome by good. These are some of the treasures in store when we leave behind the rubbish.

HOW DO WE DO IT?

'Present your bodies . . .'

This requires an act of the will. Paul commands us, in view of everything that God has done for us, to offer our bodies as living sacrifices, holy and pleasing to God (Romans 12:1). God wants us to offer all of ourselves and all of our lives.

First, we offer our time. Our time is our most valuable possession and we need to give God all of it. This does not mean we spend all of it in prayer and Bible study, but that we allow his priorities to be established in our lives.

It is easy to get our priorities wrong. An advertisement appeared in a newspaper: 'Farmer seeks lady with tractor with view to companionship and possible marriage. Please send picture – of tractor.' I don't think the farmer had his priorities quite right. Our priorities must be our relationships, and our number one priority is our relationship with God. We need to set aside time to be alone with him. We also need to set aside time to be with other Christians – on Sundays and perhaps some mid-week meeting where we can encourage one another.

Secondly, we need to offer our ambitions to the Lord, saying to him, 'Lord, I trust you with my ambitions and hand them over to you.' He asks us to seek his kingdom and his righteousness as our foremost ambition and then he promises to meet all our other needs (Matthew 6:33). This does not necessarily mean that our former ambitions disappear; they may become secondary to Christ's ambitions for us. There is nothing wrong with wanting to be successful in our job, provided that our motivation in everything is seeking his kingdom and his righteousness, and that we use what we have for his glory.

Thirdly, we need to offer him our possessions and our money. In the New Testament there is no ban on private property or making money or saving or even enjoying the good things of life. What is forbidden is a selfish accumulation for ourselves, an unhealthy obsession with material things and putting our trust in riches. What promises security leads to perpetual insecurity and leads us away from God (Matthew 7:9-24). Generous giving is the appropriate response to the generosity of God and the needs of others around us. It is also the best way to break the hold of materialism in our lives.

Next, we need to give him our ears (that is, what we listen to) – to be prepared to stop listening to gossip and other things that drag us and others down. Instead we need to attune our ears to hearing what God is saying to us through the Bible, through prayer and through books and tapes and so on. We offer him our eyes and what we see. Again, some things we look at can harm us through jealousy, lust or some other sin. Other things can lead us closer to God. Rather than criticising the people we meet, we should see them through God's eyes and ask, 'How can I be a blessing to that person?'

Then we need to give him our mouths. The apostle James reminds us what a powerful instrument the tongue is (James 3:1-12). We can use our tongues to destroy, to deceive, to curse, to gossip or to draw attention to ourselves. Or we can use our tongues to worship God and to encourage others. Further, we offer him our hands. We can use our hands either to take for ourselves or to give to others in practical acts of service. Finally, we offer him our sexuality. We can either use our sexuality for our own self-gratification or we can reserve it for the good and pleasure of our marriage partner.

We cannot pick and choose. Paul says, 'Present your bodies' – that is every part of us. The extraordinary paradox is that as we give him everything, we find freedom. Living for ourselves is slavery; but 'his service is perfect freedom' (as the *Book of Common Prayer* puts it).

'. . . as living sacrifices'

There will be a cost to doing all this. It may involve some sacrifice. As the commentator William Barclay put it, 'Jesus came not to make life easy but to make men great.' We have to be prepared to go God's way and not ours. We have to be willing to give up anything in our lives which we know is wrong and put things right where restitution is required, and we need to be willing to fly his flag in a world that may be hostile to the Christian faith.

In many parts of the world, being a Christian involves physical persecution. More Christians have died for their faith in this century than in any other. Others are imprisoned and tortured. We, in the free world, are privileged to live in a society where Christians are not persecuted. The criticism and mocking we may receive are hardly worth mentioning compared to the suffering of the early church and the persecuted church today.

Nevertheless, our faith may involve making sacrifices. For example, I have a friend who was disinherited by his parents when he became a Christian. I know one couple who had to sell their home because they felt that as Christians they must let the Inland Revenue know that over the years they had not been entirely honest in their tax returns.

I had a great friend who was sleeping with his girlfriend before he became a Christian. When he began to look at the Christian faith, he realised that this would have to change if he put his faith in Christ. For many months he wrestled with it. Eventually both he and his girlfriend became Christians and decided that from that moment they would stop sleeping together. For various reasons they were not in a position to get married for another two-and-a-half years. There was a sacrifice involved for them, although they do not see it in that way. God has blessed them richly with a happy marriage and four wonderful children. But at the time there was a cost involved.

WHY SHOULD WE DO IT?

What God has planned for our future

God loves us and wants the very best for our lives. He wants us to entrust our lives to him so that we can 'test and approve what God's will is – his good, pleasing and perfect will' (Romans 12:2).

I sometimes think that the chief work of the devil is to give people a false view of God. The Hebrew word for 'Satan' means 'slanderer'. He slanders God, telling us that he is not to be trusted. He tells us God is a spoilsport and that he wants to ruin our lives.

Often we believe these lies. We think that if we trust our Father in heaven with our lives he will take away all our enjoyment in life. Imagine a human parent like that. Suppose one of my sons were to come to me and say, 'Daddy, I want to give you my day to spend it however you want.' Of course, I would not say, 'Right, that is what I have been waiting for. You can spend the day locked in the cupboard!'

It is absurd even to consider that God would treat us worse than a human parent. He loves us more than any human parent and wants the very best for our lives. His will for us is *good*. He wants the very best (as every good parent does). It is *pleasing* – it will please him and us in the long run. It is *perfect* – we will not be able to improve on it.

Sadly, people feel they can improve on it. They think, 'I can do a little better than God. God is a bit out of touch. He hasn't caught up with the modern world and the things that we enjoy. I think I will run my own life and keep God well out of it.' But we can never do a better job than God, and sometimes we end up making an awful mess.

One of my sons was given some homework that involved making an advertisement for a Roman slave market. It was a school project and he spent most of the weekend doing it. When he had finished the drawing and written all the inscriptions, he wanted to make it look 2,000 years old. The way to do that, he had been told, is to hold the paper over a flame until it goes brown, which gives it the appearance of age. It is quite a tricky job for a nine-year-old, so my wife Pippa offered to help – several times – but could not persuade him. He insisted on doing it himself. The result was that the advertisement was burned to a cinder, accompanied by many tears of frustration and hurt pride.

Some people insist on running their own lives. They do not want any help, they will not trust God, and often it ends in tears. But God gives us a second chance. My son did his poster again and this time he trusted Pippa to do the delicate singeing operation. If we will trust God with our lives, then he will show us what his will is – his good, pleasing and perfect will.

What God has done for us
The little sacrifices he asks us to make are nothing when we compare them with the sacrifice that God made for us. C. T. Studd, the nineteenth-century England cricket captain who gave up wealth and comfort (and cricket!) to serve God in inland China, once said, 'If Jesus Christ be God, and he died for me, nothing is too hard for me to do for him.' C. T. Studd was looking

to Jesus. The writer of Hebrews urges us, 'Let us run with perseverance the race that is set before us, looking to Jesus the pioneer and perfecter of our faith, who for the joy that was set before him endured the cross, despising the shame, and is seated at the right hand of the throne of God' (Hebrews 12:1-2, RSV).

As we look at Jesus, God's only Son who 'endured the cross', we see how much God loves us. It is absurd not to trust him. If God loves us so much we can be sure he will not deprive us of anything good. Paul wrote, 'He who did not spare his own Son, but gave him up for us all – how will he not also, along with him, graciously give us all things?' (Romans 8:32). Our motivation for living the Christian life is the love of the Father. Our model in life is the example of the Son. The means by which we can live this life is the power of the Holy Spirit.

How great God is and what a privilege it is to walk in a relationship with him, to be loved by him and to serve him all our lives. It is the best, most rewarding, fulfilling, meaningful, satisfying way to live. Indeed it is here we find the answers to the great questions of life.

Notes

1. Ronald Brown (ed), *Bishop's Brew* (Arthur James Ltd, 1989).
2. By kind permission of Bernard Levin.
3. *Ibid.*
4. C. S. Lewis, *Timeless at Heart*, Christian Apologetics (Fount).
5. C. S. Lewis, *Surprised by Joy* (Fontana, 1955).
6. John Martyn, *Church of England Newspaper*, 2nd November 1990.
7. Josephus, Antiquities, XVIII 63f. Even if, as some suggest, the text has been corrupted, none the less the evidence of Josephus confirms the historical existence of Jesus.
8. F. J. A. Hort, *The New Testament in the Original Greek*, Vol. I, page 561 (New York: Macmillan Co).
9. Sir Frederic Kenyon, *The Bible and Archaeology* (Harper and Row, 1940).
10. If you are interested in pursuing the subject of gospel historicity, I would recommend reading R. T. France, *The Evidence for Jesus* from *The Jesus Library* (Hodder & Stoughton, 1986) or N.T. Wright, *Jesus and the Victory of God* (SPCK, 1996).
11. C. S. Lewis, *Mere Christianity* (Fount, 1952).
12. *Ibid.*
13. Bernard Ramm, *Protestant Christian Evidence* (Moody Press).

14. By kind permission of Bernard Levin.

15. Lord Hailsham, *The Door Wherein I Went* (Fount/Collins, 1975).

16. Wilbur Smith, *The Incomparable Book* (Beacon Publications, 1961).

17. Josh McDowell, *The Resurrection Factor* (Here's Life Publishers).

18. Michael Green, *Evangelism through the Local Church* (Hodder & Stoughton, 1990).

19. Michael Green, *Man Alive* (InterVarsity Press, 1968).

20. C. S. Lewis, *Surprised by Joy* (Fontana, 1955).

21. Cat.rud.I, 8, 4; PL 40, 319.

22. Bishop J. C. Ryle, *Expository Thoughts on The Gospel*, Vol. III, John 1:1-John 10:30 (Evangelical Press, 1977).

23. *The Journal of the Lawyers' Christian Fellowship.*

24. John Stott, *The Cross of Christ* (IVP, 1996). See also *Catechism of the Catholic Church*, Chapter 2, line 444, paragraph 615, entitled: 'Jesus substitutes his obedience for our disobedience.' By his obedience unto death, Jesus accomplished the substitution of the suffering Servant, who 'makes himself an *offering for sin*', when 'he bore the sin of many', and who 'shall make many to be accounted righteous', for 'he shall bear their iniquities'.

25. Bishop Michael Marshall, *Church of England Newspaper*, 9th August 1991.

26. Father Raneiro Cantalamessa, *Life in the Lordship of Christ* (Sheed & Ward, 1989).

27. We (of course) need to deal with all religious concepts using metaphors and parables. For the atonement there is no one seminal metaphor, no one all-encompassing parable. All are approximations which, like the radii of a circle, converge on the same central point without ever quite touching it.

28. John Wimber, *Equipping the Saints* Vol. 2, No. 2, Spring 1988 (Vineyard Ministries Int.).
29. Lesslie Newbigin, *Foolishness to the Greeks* (SPCK, 1995).
30. C. S. Lewis, *The Last Battle* (HarperCollins, 1956).
31. John Stott, *Christian Counter-Culture* (InterVarsity Press, 1978).
32. Quoted in John Stott, *Christian Counter-Culture* (InterVarsity Press, 1978).
33. John W. Wenham, *Christ and the Bible* (Tyndale: USA, 1972).
34. John Pollock, *Billy Graham: the Authorised Biography* (Hodder & Stoughton, 1966).
35. Bishop Stephen Neill, *The Supremacy of Jesus* (Hodder & Stoughton, 1984).
36. *Family Magazine*.
37. J. I. Packer, *Knowing God* (Hodder & Stoughton, 1973).
38. 'Saints' is the New Testament way of describing all Christians (eg, Philippians 1:1).
39. Michael Bourdeaux, *Risen Indeed* (Darton, Longman & Todd, 1983).
40. John Eddison, *A Study in Spiritual Power* (Highland, 1982).
41. *Ibid.*
42. F. W. Bourne, *Billy Bray: The King's Son* (Epworth Press, 1937).
43. J. Hopkins & H. Richardson (eds.), *Anselm of Canterbury, Proslogion Vol I* (SCM Press, 1974).
44. Malcolm Muggeridge, *Conversion* (Collins, 1988).
45. Richard Wurmbrand, *In God's Underground* (Hodder & Stoughton).
46. Eddie Gibbs, *I Believe in Church Growth* (Hodder & Stoughton).
47. David Watson, *One in the Spirit* (Hodder & Stoughton).
48. Murray Watts, *Rolling in the Aisles* (Monarch Publications, 1987).

49. There has been a great deal of discussion in recent years about whether this experience of the Holy Spirit should be described as 'baptism', 'filling', 'releasing', 'empowering' or some other term. For all that has been said and written on the subject, I do not think it is entirely clear from the New Testament which is the right term. What is clear is that we need the experience of the power of the Holy Spirit in our lives. I myself think that the filling of the Holy Spirit is the most faithful to the New Testament and I have used that expression in this chapter.

50. Martyn Lloyd-Jones, *Romans,* Vol. VIII (Banner of Truth, 1974).

51. Wimber & Springer (eds), *Riding the Third Wave* (Marshall Pickering).

52. Alan MacDonald, *Films in Close Up* (Frameworks, 1991).

53. Michael Green, *I Believe in Satan's Downfall* (Hodder & Stoughton, 1981).

54. Jean-Baptiste Vianney.

55. C. S. Lewis, *The Screwtape Letters* (Fount, 1942).

56. Michael Green, *I Believe in Satan's Downfall* (Hodder & Stoughton, 1981).

57. C. S. Lewis, *The Great Divorce* (Fount, 1973).

58. J. C. Pollock, *Hudson Taylor and Maria* (Hodder & Stoughton, 1962).

59. Irenaeus, *Against Heresies,* II Ch XXXII.

60. David Watson, *I Believe in the Church* (Hodder & Stoughton, 1978).

61. C. S. Lewis, *Fern Seeds and Elephants* (Fontana, 1975).

62. Michael Green, *Called to Serve* (Hodder & Stoughton, 1964). With thanks to the Curtis Brown Agency.

63. Gordon Fee, *Paul, The Spirit and the People of God* (Hodder & Stoughton, 1997).

The Alpha Course

The Alpha course is a practical introduction to the Christian faith initiated by Holy Trinity Brompton in London, which is now being run by thousands of churches, of many denominations, throughout the world.

For more information about Alpha, and related ministries such as The Marriage Course and The Marriage Preparation Course, please see:

alphafriends.org

Or contact:

Alpha International
Holy Trinity Brompton
Brompton Road
London SW7 1JA
Tel: 0845 644 7544
Email: info@alpha.org

If you would like a copy of the Alpha Publications Brochure, outlining details of resources available for purchase, or to order course materials, please contact the **Alpha Publications Hotline** on:

Tel: 0845 758 1278

To order from overseas:
Tel: +44 1228 611749
Or visit: alphashop.org

Alpha

Alpha titles available

Why Jesus? A booklet – given to all participants at the start of the Alpha course. 'The clearest, best illustrated and most challenging short presentation of Jesus that I know.' – Michael Green

Why Christmas? The Christmas version of *Why Jesus?*

Searching Issues The seven issues most often raised by participants on the Alpha course: suffering, other religions, sex before marriage, the New Age, homosexuality, science and Christianity, and the Trinity. Also available as booklets.

A Life Worth Living What happens after Alpha? Based on the book of Philippians, this is an invaluable next step for those who have just completed the Alpha course, and for anyone eager to put their faith on a firm biblical footing.

Telling Others The theological principles and the practical details of how courses are run. Each alternate chapter consists of a testimony of someone whose life has been changed by God through an Alpha course.

Challenging Lifestyle Studies in the Sermon on the Mount showing how Jesus' teaching flies in the face of modern lifestyle and presents us with a radical alternative.

The Heart of Revival Ten Bible studies based on the book of Isaiah, drawing out important truths for today by interpreting some of the teaching of the Old Testament prophet Isaiah. The book seeks to understand what revival might mean and how we can prepare to be part of it.

30 Days Nicky Gumbel selects thirty passages from the Old and New Testament which can be read over thirty days. It is designed for those on an Alpha course and others who are interested in beginning to explore the Bible.

All titles are by Nicky Gumbel, who is Vicar of
Holy Trinity Brompton

—— ❖ ——

A False
Proposal

A False Proposal

Pamela Mingle

Entangled Publishing, LLC
2614 South Timberline Road
Suite 109
Fort Collins, CO 80525
Visit our website at www.entangledpublishing.com.

Select Historical is an imprint of Entangled Publishing, LLC.

Edited by Erin Molta
Cover design by Erin Dameron-Hill
Cover art by Period Images

ISBN 978-1-68281-162-7

Manufactured in the United States of America

First Edition June 2016

For Jim, my own true love.

Chapter One

Cass Linford stifled a yawn and tried to concentrate on her sister's French translation. "No, dearest, this should be *nous allons*, not *nous allez*." She sent Pippa a sympathetic look, fully expecting an outburst. It was late afternoon, and she knew well enough the child's limits. At this time of day, her own were sorely tested.

Pippa sighed and formed her mouth into a pout. "May I be done for today?"

Cass had to clamp her lips together to keep from laughing. "You may."

"Thank the lord," their Cousin Louisa said. "Philippa, please ring for tea."

Freed from the odious task of conjugating French verbs, the young girl spun over to the bell rope and tugged it. "*Sur le pont, d'Avignon, l'ony danse, l'ony danse…*"

Despite hating her French lessons, Pippa seemed to love

singing the old song about the bridge over the Rhone River. Cass had played and sung it for her, hoping to pique her interest in the language and culture, but it had only served to pique her own. Although she knew it was probably nothing more than a fool's dream, Cass nevertheless held close her hope of traveling to France, to Paris and Avignon. Anywhere in France would do. After the war was over, if it ever was.

But she knew it was only a dream. At age two and twenty, Cass was firmly anchored in Berkeley Square, seeing to Philippa's education. Well, there were worse places one could be.

Willis appeared in the doorway, and Cousin Louisa asked him to order tea. "Tea and some of those marvelous little raspberry pastries of Cook's. Sandwiches, too, if you please."

Cass sneaked a glance at her cousin and judged Louisa could do without quite so many pastries and sandwiches. Then, feeling guilty, she banished the thought. What her cousin ate was her own business, even if she was beginning to look a little portly.

After Willis departed, Cass heard the front door burst open, accompanied by voices. She identified one as belonging to her brother, Jack. But there was a second voice, one she didn't immediately recognize. *Botheration!* She was tired and not in the mood for company.

Philippa was still in motion when Jack stepped over the threshold, another gentleman in his wake. Taking no notice of where her whirling carried her, and still singing, she spun right into her older brother, who leaned down and hoisted her up into the air.

"Mind where you're going, scamp!" he said fondly, kissing her cheek before setting her down. She swayed, and the other man grabbed hold of her in time to prevent her from falling. At that moment, Cass had a clear view of him. With a sharp intake of breath, she recognized Adam Grey, a longtime friend of her brother. *Of her.* An older and more mature-looking Adam, to be sure, but it was unmistakably he. Suddenly, everything seemed out of balance.

She had not seen Adam in four years. Not since the evening of the Sheffield ball, during her first season. She would never forget it. Cass could, without any difficulty at all, conjure up a memory of how he'd looked that night, so handsome in black and white evening clothes. His slow, appreciative grin when he'd seen her in her finery, as if she'd made his heart beat a little faster. It was the first time he had looked at her in quite that way. She had idolized him since their childhood, when they'd spent summers together on their neighboring estates. But in the middle of the ball, she had wandered down a darkened hallway by mistake and came upon him in the act of seducing a young lady. Fondling her breasts, to be precise. Mortified, Cass had been rooted to the spot. Adam had harshly ordered her to go back from wherever she'd come and never speak of this to anyone. Sadly, she had concluded that he must be a rake. Not a man to admire. Her girlish dreams had died that night.

"Look who I found at White's!" Jack said, as if they should all be overcome with joy. "I insisted he come home with me." He turned to his guest. "You remember my cousin, Miss Ashman?"

Adam entered the room and walked directly to Louisa. "Your servant, ma'am." He bowed and took her proffered hand.

"Adam! Young man, you have kept yourself from our company for far too long. Are you in town to stay?"

Just like her cousin to scold him as though he were still a mischievous schoolboy. At times, Cass wished she could reach into heaven and have a little chat with her father. She'd ask what had possessed him to arrange for his humorless, pedantic relation to look after them.

"At least through the season. I have business in town."
His reply was somber, bordering on curt.

Cass had been standing when he'd entered the room,
and remained so. Now he stepped toward her and, as good
manners dictated, she held out her hand.

He grasped it and made a graceful bow, and she curtsied.

"Miss Linford," he said, his voice edged with...what?
Hesitancy? Unease?

"Mr. Grey. We did not know you were in London. How
nice to see you again." Her face felt as if it might crack and
shatter into little pieces, right there on the drawing room
floor. Although Cass couldn't do more than glance quickly at
him, she judged him to be as fashionably dressed as ever, in a
perfectly fitted coat of blue superfine and doeskin pantaloons.
His shoulders had broadened, probably from the rigors of
army life. His face no longer seemed as carefree as it once
had. Something around his eyes, and his mouth, too, gave it
away. But he was every bit as handsome as she remembered,
his unusual blue-gray eyes as striking as ever.

Cass blinked, recovering her poise before she was caught
staring. "Please, stay and drink tea with us, sir."

He nodded and flashed a brief smile. "Thank you. I will."

· · ·

Adam had spied Cassie as soon as he'd entered the room,
and with remarkable clarity, a memory of the last time he'd
seen her popped into his mind. A ball, and his tawdry liaison
in the passage. Cass had caught him in the middle of it.
Remembering the moment, the shock on her face, made him
cringe. He'd meant to apologize, but not long after that night
he'd purchased his commission and headed off to war. He
hadn't seen Cass and Jack again. So much time had passed;
he hadn't thought of what had happened at the ball in years.

Now he remembered, and all too vividly. Did she?

What an ass he'd been in his rebellious youth, acting out his hatred for his father in whatever way seemed the most outrageous. Now it was coming back to haunt him. He could only hope Cass had forgotten the incident. How he wished he had not agreed to stay for tea, but it was too late to change his mind. He would behave as a gentleman ought, make polite conversation, and hope to never see any of them again, except for Jack, of course.

"Please, do be seated," Miss Ashman said. "And tell us what you have been up to all these years." After a slight hesitation, she said, "You were in the Peninsula, I believe, were you not?"

"No, ma'am. I was at Walcheren, in the Netherlands." He never knew how to elaborate on that, what words best summed up such a horrific experience. The swamps, the mosquitoes, the raging fevers that had swept through the regiments. So he said nothing more. Most people had already forgotten about it, if they'd ever heard of it to begin with.

"Many died there from fevers, I believe," Cass said.

Taken aback, his eyes locked on hers and found compassion and understanding there. Cassie had always taken an interest in the world, far beyond the scope of other young girls, though she was no longer young.

The butler carried in the tea service, along with plates laden with sandwiches and pastries. "Thank you, Willis," Cass said. "Philippa will return to the nursery now."

"But I want to stay," the child protested. "I haven't had my tea."

"I know you do, dearest, but this is an adult conversation and you must leave. Willis will bring your tea. Say goodbye to our guest."

Philippa looked as though she might put up a fuss, but when Adam stood, bowed, and gallantly kissed her hand, she turned into a cooing ingénue.

"Good day, sir," she said, smiling and blushing.

Adam stared. For a moment, she looked exactly like Cass had at that age. "Good day, Miss Philippa. Lovely to make your acquaintance." Willis whisked her out of the room before she had time to reconsider her options.

"How do you take your tea, Mr. Grey?" Cass asked.

"Just milk, please." When she passed him the cup, the slight tremor in her hand was barely noticeable. Adam briefly studied her face, which had matured over the years, of course. Her features were delicate, and she still boasted creamy skin and luxuriant hair. When the light caught it a certain way, it was shot with coppery streaks. She averted her eyes and continued her serving duties, as if looking directly at him would be uncomfortable for her.

Miss Ashman's voice broke in. "What was it like there… at Walcheren? Did you know there was a play about it, performed for the Prince Regent? It was very popular with the public."

Lord, the woman was persistent. The play…when he'd first heard of it, he'd wanted to kill the insensitive ass responsible and be the first to drive a nail in his coffin. He couldn't say that to Jack's relation, but he had to say something to stop the questions. "Thousands of men died of fevers and dysentery. Chaos, confusion, fear, and more mosquitoes than you'll ever see in England. For some reason known only to God, I never caught the sickness. I was sent into battle and quickly wounded."

Miss Ashman blanched, and Adam felt a stab of guilt.

"You were wounded?" Cass said. "We didn't know."

"I did," Jack said. "I visited his mother on several occasions while Adam was fighting the French, and she told me."

Cass seemed flustered. "Why didn't you tell me? Too dreadful for a lady's delicate sensibilities?"

Jack shrugged. "Sorry. I thought it might upset you."

Their cousin rose, and the men got to their feet. "I must confer with Cook about dinner."

"It was a pleasure to meet you again, ma'am." Adam said.

"Will you be at the Mainwaring ball tomorrow night?"

Adam pictured the invitation propped on the mantel in his library. He hadn't responded. "Possibly." Non-committal. That was best.

After her cousin left the room, Cass said, "Have you made a successful recovery from your injuries, Mr. Grey?"

It irritated Adam that she was being so formal with him, so he made a point of staring until she dropped her eyes. "I have. I took some shrapnel in the leg—the calf muscle, to be precise—and I limp now and then. But no more pain. I was lucky."

"It hardly seems lucky to have sustained such an injury," she said, looking at him openly for the first time. Cassie's eyes— her best feature, without a doubt—shone with sympathy.

"If you'd been there and seen all the men who died from the fevers, you wouldn't say that. After I was shot, I sold my commission and got out. Neither the fever nor the metal in my leg killed me."

She nodded her understanding. "What have you been doing since Walcheren?"

"Traveling. On the continent, mostly. Continuing my education, if you will."

Jack chimed in. "What will you do now that you're home? Any plans?"

"I'm thinking about a seat in Commons," he said. From the stunned look on Cass's face, Adam wished he'd been evasive.

"You? Involved in politics?"

Adam couldn't help it. He bristled. "Why is that so unbelievable?"

"I didn't think your interests lay in that direction."

"No? You still think me the callow youth you knew when we were growing up?" *Damn it.* He couldn't keep the vexation from his voice.

"Oh, no," Cassie said. "I adored that boy. I was thinking more of the young man I remember from the year I made my come-out." Her look bordered on arch, and he was pretty sure he'd caught a flash of amusement in her eyes.

Adam's jaw dropped. She hadn't forgotten! He couldn't believe she had the cheek to mention it, and it made him defensive. "I'm not that man anymore," he said, noting the sparkle in her eye. "Did you think I would not have changed in four years?" The sparkle vanished. Nevertheless, he had the distinct feeling she was thrilled she'd stuck him with that particular barb. Instead of graciously ceding the moment to her, he answered the barb with one of his own.

"I'm shocked to find you as yet unmarried, Cass."

"Oh, I'm securely on the shelf, Mr. Grey."

She didn't seem ashamed or embarrassed, and Adam realized he was relieved. As soon as he'd spoken those words, he'd wanted to snatch them back. "And why is that? I can't believe you've had no offers."

Jack, who'd said little during the exchange between his friend and sister, now spoke up. "Cass was engaged at one time. I suppose you didn't hear."

He raised a brow, appealing to Jack. But Cass answered.

"My engagement is none of your affair, Ad—Mr. Grey." She glared at her brother, who bit back whatever he'd been about to say. *Damn.* Adam would have liked to know why, if she'd been engaged, she was not wed. It should be easy enough to find out. That kind of story made irresistible fodder for the gossips in the *ton*, including his own mother.

"You are not married, but were once engaged. Did he cry off?"

Cass's eyes darkened at the direct hit. "The reason I am not married is personal and private. Not to be discussed outside the family." She looked directly at Adam, her gaze frank and appraising. "Since women are subject to their husband's whims, why should I want one, anyway?"

"Apparently you did at one time. But indeed, marriage may not suit you. Most men don't want a wife who doesn't know her place and can't keep her tongue."

Cass's face turned ashen. She opened her mouth and started to speak, but then lowered her gaze and hastily rose, cutting off her own words. Dropping a curtsy, she smiled, and, all sweetness, said, "Good day, Mr. Grey. Do visit us again sometime." And then she rushed from the room.

Adam had gotten the last word. So why did he feel like the worst kind of rogue?

Chapter Two

Cass fled to her bedchamber, cursing herself for almost losing control. She'd rather be transported than allow Adam to know he'd reduced her to tears. But in truth, his words had stung, reopening a wound it seemed would never heal. She sat down at her dressing table and, chin propped in her hand, ruminated on their conversation.

First, the business about her fiancé crying off. Why had he assumed it wasn't she who'd cried off? Adam wouldn't have far to go for the truth. His mother, flamboyant and fashionable, had gained a reputation as a woman in the know. No doubt she remembered all the juicy details and would gleefully relate them to her son.

But it was the part about not being a suitable wife, not being able to hold her tongue… That truly hurt and seemed so unlike the old Adam, liaison-in-hallway notwithstanding. It bordered on cruel, and he had never been that. Perhaps he'd grown bitter because of his wartime experiences. She knew from Jack that Adam had been estranged from his father for some time; maybe that had made him jaded about everything.

Cass had always prided herself on her intelligence, her ability to hold her own in conversation. Her father, even though he'd been a viscount, was also a noted classics scholar. He had loved a good political debate and had been a close friend and supporter of Mr. Fox. From an early age, Cass had been encouraged to participate in family discussions by both her parents.

Apparently, Adam didn't approve of women who made their voices heard. That was a change. The year she'd made her come-out, before the disastrous ball, Adam had been a frequent guest at Linford House. Jack had enlisted his help, ostensibly to fine-tune her social skills—dancing, conversing, warding off overly aggressive suitors. But Cass knew her brother was more concerned about having a trusted friend upon whom he could rely, to help him watch over Cass and keep her safe. To make sure she never lacked for a dance partner or someone to go into supper with.

During his frequent visits to the house, she and Adam had discussed and debated all manner of topics—the war, the Catholic question, the Poor Laws. Never once had he made her feel he did not value her opinion.

Could he be on the hunt for a wife? Politicians needed one.

Cass had begun to wonder if she might yet want to marry, now that Philippa was no longer a little girl. She knew that was what her family wanted for her. After the disaster with Lord Bentley, her erstwhile fiancé, she'd pushed all thoughts of marriage from her mind. Looking after her sister had become her highest priority, especially after her mother's death. Although she'd maintained her equanimity when she told Adam she was securely on the shelf, in her deepest self, she didn't want to believe it. Which was why his last comment hurt so much. It was a bit too close to the truth. The things Cass liked to talk about: politics, history, travel, to name a few, marked her as a bluestocking, the kiss of death if she wanted a husband. Women were not meant to be interested in matters outside the home, unless they involved charitable work.

Cass rang for her maid, and while she waited for Agnes, studied herself in the glass. Could any man want her for a wife? Desire her? She used to think so, but now she wondered. Ordinary brown eyes and hair; a good, some might even say superior, complexion. A tiny mole on one side of her upper lip was the only flaw. Straight nose, unexceptional cheekbones, and a rounded chin. At least it was not pointed, or receding.

More to the point, perhaps, for Cass—was there any man who would do as a husband for her? She'd blundered so badly the first time, been wounded so deeply. The possibility of making the wrong choice a second time made her sick inside.

"Afternoon, Miss Cassandra." Cass's good-natured maid, Agnes, entered the room, with a ewer of hot water for washing. She helped Cass undress down to her chemise. When her ablutions were completed, she slipped into a dressing gown, as it was too early to dress for dinner. After asking Agnes to return in an hour, she grabbed a book and curled up in her window seat. For some reason, her attention kept straying from her reading, a lackluster account of a gentleman's travels in Italy and Greece. Was it because the man was a poor writer? More likely, the cause was her restless mind, which kept straying back to Adam. She wondered which countries he'd visited. Probably Italy and Greece, if he truly was, as he'd stated, continuing his education. One always heard that Mediterranean women were exotic, beautiful. Adam had probably romanced plenty of them.

It wasn't simply his cutting words that had upset her. It was his...presence. His handsome countenance, his confident air. And the way he seemed to fill up the room. It had always been thus with Adam, and Cass had always fallen prey to it. She couldn't allow herself to think about him as anything more than a longtime friend of her brother, a rather rude one at that. She must put him out of her head altogether. How hard could it be, when she hadn't seen him in years? If she desired a husband someday, he would be the last person she would consider, and she was convinced the feeling was mutual.

• • •

As they had no dinner guests, Cass dressed in a simple sprigged muslin, a pale green. Just because she felt like it, she asked Agnes to dress her hair in a more stylish way than the usual knot at the top of her head. Nothing fancy, only a few curls left loose to brush the nape of her neck. Cass had to admit she liked the feel of it. Her brother commented on it.

"You've changed your hair, Cass. It flatters you."

She blushed, aware of Cousin Louisa's quizzical brow.

Philippa, always on the alert for opportunities, said, "*OOO-oo*. I bet you were hoping that handsome Mr. Grey was staying for dinner. Do you fancy him?"

Refusing to succumb to a ten-year-old's teasing, Cass said, "Don't be nonsensical, Philippa."

"I wish *I* were old enough to dance with him at a ball, or accompany him to the theater," she said, sighing dramatically.

"Maybe your wish will come true," Jack said. "I don't believe Adam has any immediate plans to marry. If you ask nicely, he may wait for you."

"You're funning me, aren't you?" Philippa asked her brother, narrowing her eyes at him.

"Me? I would never do that, poppet."

Philippa's look was so scathing, Cass and Jack roared. Even Louisa chuckled. But afterward, she began instructing the child on the proper decorum at table.

"You had a rather extreme reaction to Adam today, Cass," Jack said, sipping his wine.

She immediately went into a coughing fit. "I beg your pardon?"

"You know what I mean."

"I would say I rather had the worst of it," Cass said. "He insulted me."

"But you goaded him into it by questioning his interest in politics. And calling him 'Mr. Grey.' What on earth were you referring to, something about the year you made your come-out? As I recall, Adam played the role of perfect gentleman."

"Nothing. Just some gossip I heard about him back then."

"To do with his being a rake, no doubt."

Cass glared at her brother. "Lower your voice. Pippa doesn't miss a thing."

"Well?"

"Yes, that's it exactly." She'd agree with anything to get him to hush up.

"He's much more serious now. The war changed him."

Cass paused with her spoon in midair. "I suppose it would." She recalled what Adam had said about Walcheren, how so many had died of disease rather than in battle. It seemed so unfair to go off to war, only to be struck down by an insidious enemy one had never anticipated. "It sounds as though what he experienced was horrifying."

"It was, and I'm sure he told us the cleansed version."

"It must be hard having to do that."

"Do what?"

"Never speak the complete truth about what you suffered, and what you witnessed." Cass was thoughtful for a moment. "Jack, is Adam still estranged from his father?"

"I'm not certain. He hasn't mentioned it. Why do you ask?"

"No reason, only that a man's father may be the only person who could listen and understand such a thing."

Jack looked thoughtful. "I've never known what caused

the break between them. Adam doesn't speak of it. Whatever happened, he and his mother have lived in town since." Jack paused long enough to drink some wine. "He rarely returns to Surrey, and she does only infrequently, though she owns a country home there. He's got an older brother who still lives with their father, you know."

"*Hmm*. I'd forgotten there was a brother."

"I say, are you going to eat that soup or not?"

Cass realized she was still holding her spoon cocked halfway to her mouth. Quickly she brought it to her lips and swallowed. She didn't taste a thing, though. Her thoughts, all her senses, were focused on Adam.

• • •

Cass hated balls. She blamed her former fiancé for it.

When she was younger, she'd enjoyed them well enough. Flirting with dance partners while keeping the complicated steps of a quadrille straight was a sort of competition for the younger set. After Adam had gone away for good, she relaxed and let herself be taken in by the excitement, fun-seeking crowds, and never-ending stream of *on-dits* spreading over town like the Thames overflowing its banks.

Somehow, she had managed to never become a target of the gossips. She'd conducted herself with dignity and some reserve, and although she loved to dance and flirt as much as anyone else, she had made certain her behavior was always above reproach. After all, she'd been schooled from an early age on ways of attracting a husband. Every girl was. She was also well schooled in French, Italian, the classics, music, and drawing, but somehow those didn't seem to count as much. Making a fool of oneself by becoming intoxicated, loud, or silly, well, those behaviors tended to repel a man.

Then, two years ago, Cass had met Oliver, Viscount

Bentley, and after a six-month courtship had become engaged to him. To her disillusionment, it was not a love match. She thought she might fall in love with him eventually, but realized it would be one sided. Handsome, sophisticated, and twelve years her senior, Bentley's choice of Cass as his bride had been a surprise to everyone, including herself. It seemed more a giving-in to his obligation to produce an heir than a true wish for her hand, in particular. She would be a suitable mate for him and mother to his children. After all, she was willing, the daughter of a peer, and passably attractive and intelligent.

To her chagrin, he had kept an emotional distance between them, never confiding anything personal, nor had he ever made a serious attempt to learn more about the lady who was to become his wife. She'd given up on drawing him out after her few attempts had been met with a raised brow, one-word answers, or complete silence. Since he'd been so disinterested during their betrothal, life with him in a marriage had hardly born thinking about. Cass had begun to worry that theirs would be one of those alliances for posterity's sake; that as soon as Bentley wed and sired an heir with her, she would see little of him. She had envisioned a lonely existence, spending her days with her children and other ladies who found themselves in the same situation, while her husband spent his at his club. And the evenings would have been even more depressing, Cass would have attended balls and musicales alone, while Bentley gambled and dallied with a mistress.

Cass had heard the rumors. She knew he'd kept a mistress. An honorable man would give up such a relationship before he wed, if only for a time. Perhaps her betrothed had not been an honorable man. She had considered talking to Jack about her concerns, but knew it would've been embarrassing for them both. And her mother, who had already been in the early stages of the illness that had taken her life, would have brushed her off and told her she was fortunate indeed to be marrying a man like Bentley.

After the horrifying event that had swiftly ended her engagement, she had stayed away from balls, indeed, from town; and when finally forced back by her family, she had situated herself squarely against the wall with the dowagers, chaperones, and the other women who were not yet married. Probably never would be married, most of them, herself included. She knew there were some in the *ton* who still regarded her with disdain; knew it, but was powerless to change it.

Tonight, though, for the first time, she felt a little flutter of anticipation in her belly. She tried to tell herself that it wasn't because Adam might be present, but she knew that was a lie. As she alighted from the carriage, she took a deep breath. *Calm down, Cass. He may not be here, and even if he is, he probably won't even look my way. And he insulted me! I should be furious with him.*

Dodging puddles and manure, she made her way to the sidewalk. The Mainwarings lived in a newly constructed home in Mayfair, and Cass paused to admire the elegant fanlights above the door and the lacy wrought iron work on the balconies above. They passed through a portico supported by fluted stone columns to join the receiving line. Since Jack had wished to escort his fiancée, Jenny, to the ball, Cass and Cousin Louisa were alone.

After greeting their hosts, she and her cousin entered the ballroom. Instead of making a beeline for the dowager's wall, though, she hovered at the door, hoping to spot Jack and Jenny.

"Come along, Cass," Louisa said. "Why are you dawdling?"

"Cousin, I believe I shall look for Jack. Do go on without me. I'll join you later."

Louisa cast her a suspicious look. Oh, for heaven's sake, was she that firmly entrenched with the dowagers, wallflowers, and women on the shelf? So much so that her own cousin couldn't believe she might want to do what other people did at balls?

"I-I need to speak with Jenny about something. Don't look at me that way."

After a brief nod, Louisa trooped off to find her friends. Cass looked about for Jack. And for Adam, too, although finding him would probably only cause her pain. The musicians had struck up a country dance tune, and partners were lining up. To her chagrin, Cass caught sight of Adam, partnered with this season's Incomparable, Elizabeth Morgan. His golden hair glinted in the candlelight; otherwise she probably wouldn't have seen him. A tall girl with a regal bearing, Miss Morgan looked quite at home parading with Adam.

"Cass!"

She tore her gaze away. It was Jack calling to her. She smiled and waved as she began to make her way through the crowd in her brother's direction. Elizabeth Morgan would make a superb political hostess someday. Maybe that's what Adam was thinking. A union with her would bring patronage, money, and influence. With a sudden shake of her head, she realized how foolish she was being. They were only dancing together, and she had them married.

Jenny, a sweet, naturally pretty girl, kissed Cass's cheek. "Hello, dearest. You look lovely tonight. Is that a new ball dress?"

Cass nodded, and Jenny, leaning close, said, "Adam Grey has been watching you since you stepped into the room."

Chapter Three

Hell and damnation. Adam had spotted Cassie and could barely wrest his gaze from her. She was wearing a pale yellow confection with a form-fitting bodice. Even with a lace trim, it was revealing. He'd been mulling over their conversation of the previous day and had concluded he should apologize to Cass for his thoughtless and needlessly cruel remarks.

Miss Morgan was speaking to him, and he pulled his gaze back to her. She really was quite enchanting, with her blond curls and winsome blue eyes.

"I just love balls!" she said.

But not a great conversationalist.

"Ah, well then, you must be enjoying your come-out."

"'Tis great fun." She cackled, spoiling her cool, stylish manner, and Adam had to stop himself from cringing. "My dance card is always full. What more could I desire?" Miss Morgan tilted her head up and smiled unabashedly at him. *Good God, she couldn't be more than eighteen.*

"What more indeed?"

The dance ended at last. Adam returned his partner to

her chaperone and bowed. Without wasting a minute, he went in search of Cassie. He wanted to ask her for a dance before they'd all been claimed. Madness, he was sure, but there it was. He hadn't taken five steps through the crush before he found himself surrounded, entrapped really, by a hoard of matrons and their daughters. Sweet Jesus, he should have been more careful! Now he was going to have to spend an hour, at least, in conversation with the matchmaking mamas and their progeny. There was no escaping it. He bowed politely to the woman on his left.

"Mr. Grey, so nice to see you back in town."

"How do you do? And this must be…?"

Before he knew what hit him, he was dancing the first waltz of the evening with…whoever she was. And the next dance with another ingénue. And the next, and the one after that. Fortune smiled on him, though, when he and his latest partner joined a quadrille with three other couples. Cass, dancing with Atherton, was among the ladies.

• • •

"May I have the honor, Miss Linford?"

Cass, who'd been hovering with her cousin against the wall for the last half hour, had groaned silently when Lord David Atherton, requested a dance. Although he was a close friend of Jack's, she felt a bit intimidated by him. But he'd always been kind to her, and she had no reason to spurn him. Truth be known, Jack had probably bribed him to dance with her.

She gave him her hand, and they walked toward a few other couples forming for a quadrille. Spotting Adam immediately, Cass felt her stomach tighten. He acknowledged her with the barest of nods. His partner looked no older than eighteen, and Cass didn't recognize her. Jack's fiancée, Jenny, and her brother-in-law were also part of the set.

They bowed and curtsied to each other, then began the figures. Cass had always loved the quadrille, and she knew she danced it well. She held herself erect and let her feet take flight. Atherton smiled at her and she smiled back. One time during the set when she was holding hands with Adam, he discreetly leaned in and whispered in her ear as they circled round. "Save me the next waltz?"

Cass, surprised and pleased, could only nod. He squeezed her fingers gently before passing her back to her partner, and she felt the heat from his hand surge through her body all the way to her toes. Earlier, she'd watched the predatory mothers and their daughters surround him, chuckling to herself. Then, as now, he hadn't seemed engaged, but had kept a rather bland, polite expression on his face. Could he actually have been hoping for a dance with her? Was he bored with the debutantes?

She thanked Atherton and asked him to return her not to her cousin, but to Jack, who was standing among a mixed crowd of his peers. Cass nearly turned on her heel when she saw that one of the group was Leonora Darling. She'd made her come-out the same year as Cass and had set a record in snagging herself an earl, albeit an elderly, creaky one. She was now Lady Leonora, Countess of Suttleworth, at least until her husband's heir took a wife. Her earl had turned up his toes more than a year ago, dead of a heart seizure, if the rumors were true. Marriage to Leonora had probably sent him to an early grave.

She was well out of mourning, gowned in purple satin with a deep décolletage. Plumes of exotic looking feathers adorned her black hair. The Earl of Suttleworth had been fabulously wealthy. Leonora must have inherited a fortune, since her husband had died childless. Cass had always disliked her, for the simple reason that she had brazenly flirted with

Adam at every opportunity during that fateful season. Cass had always suspected her of being the lady Adam was dallying with at the Sheffield ball, but the light had been too dim to be sure. And Adam had shielded the woman with his body. So gentlemanly of him.

"How was your dance?" Jack asked, turning toward her.

She blinked. "Lovely." Before she could say more, he'd turned away.

"Ah, here's Jenny," he said.

Cass marveled at the way Jack doted on his fiancée and warmed at the sight of him watching Jenny as she approached. And love shone from Jenny's eyes. How Cass envied what they shared. They seemed perfectly attuned to each other.

Jack and Jenny's brother-in-law struck up a conversation, so the two ladies did likewise.

"Mr. Grey can't seem to keep his eyes off you."

"Really?" Cass looked at her questioningly, as she was sometimes given to exaggeration. "I think he's a bit flummoxed by the marriage mart. Perhaps he's forgotten what it's like."

"Well, he was certainly bored with his partner. In fact, he's looked bored all evening." She paused a moment, then clutched Cass's hand and said *sotto voce*, "He's coming our way."

"He, uh, asked me for the next waltz," Cass said. She watched his approach, delayed by friends who wished to greet him, remembering how he always managed to be the handsomest man in the room. Tonight he wore black trousers and coat. As he drew closer, she saw that his waistcoat was of a pale gray silk, with a subtle diamond pattern. A small sapphire nestled in the folds of his cravat. He was restrained elegance.

Jenny was speaking. Cass tore her gaze from Adam to listen. "Really? Are you...glad?"

"It's nothing, Jenny. Don't imagine his asking me for a

dance has any hidden meaning."

"Oh, I would never be so foolish," Jenny said with a wink.

Cass sensed a rustling of skirts nearby. Lady Leonora stepped forward, practically shoving her aside.

"Mr. Grey," she cooed, thrusting out her bosom. "If you've come to request a dance, I believe I am — "

Adam cut her off. "Lady Leonora." He bowed and then immediately turned to Cass. "My dance, I believe, Miss Linford."

Glancing briefly at Leonora before allowing Adam to lead her out, Cass was gratified to see that she looked like she'd swallowed a frog. Cass could guess what was running through her mind: Why would Adam choose her, a girl who'd lived in virtual disgrace these past few years, over one such as herself?

. . .

Adam had noticed Leonora lingering in the group that included Cass, Jack, and his fiancée, but never dreamed she'd put herself forward so boldly. As he guided Cass to the dance floor, he hoped to hell she wouldn't mention it, since he'd gone out of his way to ignore the woman. He'd all but given her the cut direct.

While they waited for the music to begin, Adam placed his hand at the small of Cass's back, inching her closer to his body. Grasping her right hand in his left, he sensed her hesitation before she placed her other hand at his shoulder. The music began, and for a few moments, they were both caught up in the sounds, rhythm, and sweep of the dance. God, Cassie felt wonderful in his arms, and she was a fine dancer, too. He was enjoying the moment too much to spoil it by offering her his apology. He decided to wait until a more opportune time presented itself. If only he could get her to look up at him instead of staring directly at his cravat, maybe he could draw her out.

"Your brother seems very happy with his choice of a bride." Ah, success. She raised her head.

"He is, I believe. They both are."

"It is a love match, then?"

Now she looked up at him, her eyes softly glowing. "Yes."

"It seems a rarity. They are fortunate indeed."

"You believe love between husband and wife is rare?"

"From what I have observed, very few couples enjoy such felicity." The dance floor was crowded, and Adam had to do some fancy maneuvering to avoid smashing into other dancers. He steered Cass toward the fringes of the crowd where they might have more room.

"My parents had a very happy marriage," Cass said. "I see Jack gazing at Jenny in much the same way my father looked at my mother. I wish…" She cut herself off, and a pink flush spread over her cheeks.

God, she was adorable when she flushed that way. Some girls broke out in repulsive patches of crimson when they blushed, but not Cassie. She was rose petal pink. *What's the matter with me?* A few more spins around the floor and he'd be simpering at her feet. He needed to change the tone of the conversation, because he knew damn well what it was she wished.

"My father and mother detest each other," he said, and Cass's expression sobered immediately. But she needed to know that marriage was at best a dubious proposition. After growing up with the heartbreak that characterized his parents' union, he'd ruled it out for himself.

"I'm sorry," she murmured. Her footwork faltered, and Adam had to clasp her more tightly to steady her.

"He is a depraved man." *Christ, why did I say that?* He'd never told that to a living soul. And at a ball, no less. But something made him continue. "They've lived apart for ten years. I don't know if they've even seen each other during that time. They communicate through lawyers."

"I am sorry, Adam. I never knew—"

"Of course you didn't. How could you?" Their eyes met and held, and he felt her empathy and understanding deep in his chest, where something stirred and…and oh, hell, he had to stop this.

Just then, Leonora floated by in the arms of a dark stranger. His blood ran cold when, after a second look, he recognized the man's profile and the somber look on his face. Swiftly, he spun Cass so his back was to the other couple.

"Leonora still holds quite an allure for you, I see," Cassie said, obviously baiting him. "And she's exceedingly wealthy now."

She thought he'd been staring at Leonora! What a ridiculous notion. Adam steered her toward a column and off the dance floor. Releasing her, he took a step back into a sequestered nook, forcing her to follow. "Why do you think so poorly of me, Cassie?" he demanded, leaning in close. "Is it because of that incident so long ago?" Again she flushed, but this time he was too angry to notice how it made her skin glow.

She remained silent, although she continued to gaze steadily at him.

"Trust me. If you had experienced disease and death and war, you would not think a meaningless dalliance in a hallway so reprehensible. And, by the way, Leonora is the last woman in the world who could hold my interest." He noticed, for the first time ever, that Cassie's eyes were extraordinary. Not simply brown, but brown verging on amber.

They stared at each other, until Cass finally spoke. "Fair enough. But why were you going out of your way to ogle her just now, if that's the case?"

"I was not 'ogling' her." He couldn't hold back a knowing grin. "You're jealous!"

Cass bristled. "You flatter yourself, sir. I haven't seen you in years and have no claim on you. Why would I be jealous?"

"I don't know. Because you harbor a secret love for me?" Before she could protest, he took her in his arms and waltzed her back onto the dance floor. The dance was nearing its end, and he wanted somehow to fix things.

"Truly, Cassie, you've bewitched me tonight. You look splendid. Like a piece of Greek statuary."

"I gather you mean hard and unyielding?" She gave him a suspicious glance.

How could she think that? "No!" *Flowing and curvaceous and perfectly formed.* But he dared not say it out loud, so he continued his teasing. "I worship at the altar of your beauty," he added, widening his eyes at her and expecting a sharp retort.

But instead, the unexpected happened. She laughed. A joyous and sweet sound, not at all like the cackle of the Incomparable. So he laughed, too, and then he pulled her close, relishing the feel of her softness against him. He hadn't enjoyed flirting like this in years. He was probably holding her too close, beyond propriety, but he didn't care. She stiffened a little, but didn't pull away. After a moment, she relaxed in his arms and a tiny smile hovered at the corner of her lovely mouth. A mouth he would very much like to kiss.

Chapter Four

He'd made her laugh. That alone was worth the agony she suffered at balls.

And now, he held her so close she was stunned by the sheer intimacy of it. In truth, she was reveling in the feel of Adam's body pressed against hers, the way it made her tingle. Her skin felt on fire, every nerve-ending sensitive and receptive. She feared he would realize the impropriety of it and pull away. He was no doubt wondering why she allowed it. Bentley had never held her like this when they'd waltzed; if he had, she would have been shocked and embarrassed. They'd only kissed a few times after their engagement. Of course, she'd been younger then, and more naïve. She melted into Adam's embrace, and was vaguely aware of the smile on her lips. Cass didn't want the dance to end, ever.

And then suddenly, it did. They were across the room from her brother, and so she did not have to completely relinquish the thrill of having Adam near her. She set her hand on his sleeve and they began walking, skirting the dance floor to avoid the worst of the crush.

"All of town must be here," Adam said. "I expect Prinny to make an appearance at any moment. Do you think a man of his...proportion could navigate through this crowd?"

Cass ducked her head and laughed again. "You must know, a path opens before him when he arrives. Like a god or a...a—"

"King?" Adam said drily.

Cass smiled up at him, not the least bit self-consciously. She'd forgotten to be on her guard. Their eyes met, and for a brief moment, their gazes held. She felt a kind of yearning emanating from him, and she couldn't have looked away if she'd wanted to.

Without warning, Adam slowed their progress, and she nearly stumbled. When she glanced at him, he was staring straight ahead. She did likewise, and glimpsed a man striding toward them, boldly pushing his way forward with barely a care for who was in his way. He seemed vaguely familiar. In fact, he bore a distinct resemblance to Adam, who had now come to a dead stop, apparently waiting for the other gentleman to reach them. Cass sneaked a glance at Adam. His jaw was clenched, and she could have sworn his blue-gray eyes had darkened to black.

"Adam. Fancy meeting you here." The words seemed a challenge.

"Hugh," Adam said with a slight nod of his head. "What brings you to town?"

By now Cass had gathered her wits enough to know that this must be Adam's elder brother. She recalled meeting him only once or twice in her life, which was surprising since she had spent so many summer days with Adam when they were growing up.

"I am here for the marriage market, of course. Not that I wish to be leg-shackled, but Father is pushing, that is, encouraging me."

Cass felt Adam shudder slightly. Without a hint of humor, he said, "The eligible young ladies and their mamas should be put on their guard, in that case."

Anger registered, sharp but fleeting, on Hugh's face. He glanced at Cass and said, "May I be introduced to this lady?"

Adam said, "I believe you may already claim an acquaintance with her. Lady Cassandra Linford, may I present my brother, Hugh Grey?"

"How do you do?" Cass curtsied, but did not offer her hand. He really should have waited until she'd requested an introduction. Not that she usually stood on ceremony, but Adam's hostility toward his brother made her wary. Adam drew her arm through his in a protective gesture, pulling her closer to his side.

Hugh inclined his head. "Your servant, Miss Linford. I presume you are one in the same as the girl who used to ride horseback with Adam. Viscount Linford is your brother?"

"He is, sir. And I am that girl."

"All grown up now, I see. His eyes swept her body in frank appraisal, and then he glanced at Adam with a smirk. She had the impression Hugh had done it only to rankle his brother. Adam's face was tight and closed off. "I must return Miss Linford to the Viscount, if you'll excuse us."

"I wish to speak with you," Hugh said. "I'll wait here." He pointed to the column behind which Cass and Adam had so recently had their tête-à-tête. He strode away, giving Adam no chance to refuse.

Adam spun her around so fast she almost lost her footing in the middle of a quick curtsy. They moved at a brisk pace, the crowd having dispersed. Cass noticed that Adam, who'd danced gracefully and fluidly, was now limping. Although she very much wanted to say something to break the awkward silence that had descended since Hugh materialized out of the crowd, small talk didn't seem appropriate. Adam's manner had completely changed, from one of gaiety to unease, and she sensed a suppressed rage simmering beneath the surface. In a moment, they'd reached Jack, who was watching them with narrowed eyes.

"Thank you for the dance, Cass. May I get you a glass of lemonade or ratafia before I leave you?"

"No, thank you," she said hurriedly, acknowledging his need to rejoin his brother.

Jack grasped Adam's arm. "Was that Hugh I saw talking to you?"

"It was." After flicking an apologetic glance at Cass, he bowed and headed off to the meeting with his brother, she presumed.

"What happened?" Jack asked. "Hugh never comes to town."

"He said he was here to find a wife. It was an uncomfortable conversation. Adam was straining to maintain civility."

"Hugh is like their father, who's a loose fish if there ever was one. Use all caution around him."

Cass shrugged. "I don't expect to be in his company, so you've nothing to worry about. How do you know so much about him?"

"From Adam, of course. And one hears things." Jack paused. "What did he want?"

"He didn't say. Adam seemed so rattled, I didn't dare question him."

"I daresay that was the best course. He's very touchy about his family, you know." He paused briefly, as though to weigh his words. "His father and brother, I mean. Not his mother."

Cass nodded. She really would like that glass of lemonade, and sorely wished she could have drunk it with Adam. But she'd have to get it for herself. On the way to the refreshment table, she pondered Adam's strange behavior with his brother, and continued to do so as she sipped her drink. She was unable to make sense of it. Afterward, she made her way to her cousin and the dowagers, chaperones, and wallflowers. Oddly enough, for the first time since her return to society, Cass didn't feel as if she belonged to that group.

• • •

Whatever his despised brother wanted of him, the sooner Adam found out the better. Then he could dismiss the whole matter from his mind and get on with things. He hated deserting Cassie, but this couldn't wait. *The devil.* He realized he was limping as though he had recently been injured. Why was it always worse when he was upset or angry about something?

He found Hugh waiting near the column they'd designated as their meeting place, watching for him. "You're lame," he said. "From your war injury?"

"Yes, of course," Adam said gruffly. "What else?" He despised the word "lame," and Hugh using it rankled him no end.

Hugh took the hint and dropped the subject. "We need to find somewhere private to talk. Do you know the house?"

"I do not. But there must be a room off this hallway that would serve." Adam gestured toward the arched doorway leading to a corridor. He led the way toward a series of rooms, doors all closed. Which one to choose? He tapped lightly on the second door, pressed his ear against it to make sure he didn't hear any scampering about, giggling, or any other sounds of an assignation in progress, and cautiously cracked it open.

Windows at the far end of the room faced onto the back garden, which Adam could barely make out since there was no moonlight. He felt his way toward a table against one wall and fumbled for tinder and candles. Carrying a single lighted candle toward a small sitting area, he motioned his brother toward a chair and took the one opposite him. And waited.

In the weak glow of the flame, Hugh looked older than his years. Deep grooves defined his cheeks, and at the ripe old age of thirty, his forehead was creased and lined. Adam feared it was due to a life of dissipation. Perhaps that, combined with work out of doors. Impatiently he said, "Well?"

"My father wishes to see you at Longmere on a matter of some urgency."

Adam lifted a brow and waited for more information, but as it was not forthcoming, he finally spoke. "And what is this matter of such great urgency?"

"You probably won't believe me, but I was not privy to it. I think Father was afraid I would tell you, and for some reason he wants to do that himself."

"You must have some idea," Adam said, rising to pace about the room. "Father has made no attempt to see me in years, and now summons me without even telling me why?"

Adam paused mid-pace, long enough to see Hugh shrug. "Come, man, you know him better than anybody."

Hugh's jaw tightened. "I can only speculate that it has something to do with his...debts of honor. His *extensive* debts of honor."

Adam clicked his tongue in disgust. "What? Has he gone off the rails? Of what help could I possibly be in settling his debts?"

"See here, Adam, I told you I don't know! But if it comes down to losing what remains of the family fortune—and it's not much—you'd better go and find out."

"So that's what this is about? Since I'm to inherit nothing, I don't give a tinker's damn about the 'family fortune.' The family name is all I ever cared about, but you and my father have seen to it that whatever respect it once garnered no longer exists."

Hugh got to his feet and raised his voice a notch. "Think what you like, but you owe it to him to find out what he wants. He is your father, after all." He bit out the words.

Much to my everlasting regret. "I owe him nothing," Adam said, "nor you." He stepped closer to his brother and with satisfaction noted they were now of equal height. "The two of you make me sick. You can tell Father I won't be coming."

Hugh lowered his voice and seemed to be making an effort to rein in his temper. "Be reasonable, Adam. I know you have your differences, but he's getting on in years. What harm can it do you to pay him a visit and find out what he wants?"

Adam should insist the old man visit him in London. But, no, that would never do. The last thing he needed was his father here, carrying on with his usual antics, as Adam was about to launch a political career. And his mother would be furious. No, it was out of the question.

Adam quickly reviewed his calendar for the week. There was to be a dinner party at his mother's townhome a few days hence, where he intended to announce that he wished to stand for Commons. He'd arranged a private meeting with Jack Linford at White's tomorrow, to ask his friend to support him in his bid for one of the seats in the borough of Haslemere, in Surrey, where both families maintained country homes. Adam's father, in fact, lived there year round. It would do no harm for him to ride down and test the waters, see what his parent knew about the political climate, if anything. By all accounts, one of the current MPs was a drunk who rarely attended the sessions. He was sponsored by the other titled lord of the borough, Sir William Broxton, a baronet. Could be trouble there if Adam couldn't persuade him he needed a new man. Jack would know more, and so might his father.

"Haven't got all night, brother. What's your answer to

be?"

Reluctantly, Adam said, "I'll do it, but I have things to attend to here before I can leave."

"I'll get word to Father."

"No," Adam insisted. "I prefer you leave that to me, since I don't yet know when I can get away."

"As you wish."

"How long do you plan to remain in town?"

"A few weeks at a time, with trips home in between. No idea how long it will take to find a bit of muslin...er, bride."

"So I shall see you at Longmere?" Adam asked.

"Possibly."

Adam carried the candle back to the sideboard and snuffed it. He opened the door to the corridor and, after ensuring it was empty, said, "Until then."

Hugh strolled toward him. "Oh, you shall see me long before that. Deborah told me of your political aspirations. She invited me to the dinner she's giving in your honor. I wouldn't dream of missing it."

Adam cringed. If he weren't so fond of his mother...well, what he might do to her didn't bear thinking about.

Chapter Five

Adam's mother, Deborah Grey, waltzed into the breakfast room wearing a royal blue morning dress of merino wool. Although she had recently celebrated her fiftieth year, she was still beautiful. Adam threw down the copy of the *Times* he'd been perusing and rose.

"Good morning, dear," she said, kissing her son's cheek.

"Mother," he said, inclining his head. "Did you sleep well?" He poured her a cup of chocolate while a footman filled her plate with bacon, ham, eggs, and toast. Which she wouldn't eat one-quarter of.

"Oh, I was up half the night reading *Sense and Sensibility*, worrying about those Dashwood girls. And then when I knew I simply must get some rest, there was nothing for it but to drink a glass of sherry. That made me sleepy." She smiled charmingly at her son.

He broached the topic he knew would be awkward for them both. "I ran into Hugh at the Mainwaring ball last night. What a shock that was." He shot Deborah a sardonic glance.

Her finely arched brows knitted. "I am sorry, Adam. I

wanted to tell you he was in town, but I couldn't quite bring myself to do it."

"At least he's not staying here," Adam said. When his mother, innocently sipping her chocolate, didn't answer, he rattled his newspaper and said, "Mother?" using his most ominous tone of voice.

"What? Oh, no, dear. He's taken lodgings. You know I would never ask him to stay with us."

"But you did invite him to the dinner tomorrow night. Without checking with me first."

Deborah winced, sputtering a bit over her chocolate. "He is my son too, darling! And he wishes to be wed. I can't help feeling that a wife might help him to control some of his... baser impulses."

"Just so. On the other hand, he could quickly bring his wife to ruin by subjecting her to the sort of thing you ran away from."

Deborah hung her head, and Adam immediately felt guilty about throwing that in her face. He knelt by her chair and put his arms around her. "There, there, Mother. Forgive me. It's only that I cannot conceive of Hugh with a bride. I see only a life of misery for the poor girl."

Now his mother was crying, dash it all. Little sobs escaped her lips, and it was entirely his fault. "Don't cry, Mother. You're not to blame, after all."

"I should have stayed." *Gulp.* "I could have provided a stabilizing influence." *Gulp. Hiccup.* "But your father—"

"Do not reproach yourself, Mother. You couldn't have saved Hugh from taking up Father's ways. God knows, I'm grateful you had the wits—and money—to escape."

Gradually Deborah's sobs tapered off, and she dabbed at her eyes with a serviette. Adam returned to his chair and poured himself more coffee. "Father wants to see me. Did you know?"

"Certainly not!"

"Don't fuss, Mother. I didn't think you did." Adam related the gist of his conversation with Hugh. "Care to hazard a guess?"

"I haven't spoken with your father in ten years, Adam. I'm afraid I can provide no enlightenment. But a word to the wise. Don't be so foolish as to trust him. Whatever he wants will be in the guise of your best interests, but I've never known him to have anyone's best interests at heart other than his own."

"Does he have a heart, then?" Adam lifted a corner of his mouth. "I've never been sure."

Deborah's expression was pained. "A very black one, I'm afraid."

Adam took up his newspaper while his mother nibbled at her eggs and toast. "When is your meeting with Lord Linford?" Deborah asked between bites.

"This afternoon. You did send round the dinner party invitations?"

"Of course, dear. And we must decide whom to invite to the house party, as well."

Adam frowned. "House party?" *What is she up to now?*

"I know we discussed it. A house party in Surrey would be quite the thing to…to become better acquainted with certain ladies. And you will need to have a presence in Haslemere, in any case."

"'Better acquainted with certain ladies'? Really, Mother, even you can do better than that."

She raised a hand, placating him. "Never mind. We'll discuss it later. Allow me to tell you who will attend the dinner." When Adam nodded, she reeled off the list. "Viscount Linford, Cassandra, and their cousin, Miss Ashman. Linford's fiancée, Jenny, and her parents. Elizabeth Morgan and her mother. And Hugh, of course."

She cut him a sly look. "Hugh seeking a bride reminds

me, Adam, it would do you no harm to think about taking a wife. Political men need hostesses, you know."

He shrugged. "They do. But they don't have to be married to them."

"That's why I invited that lovely Elizabeth Morgan to the party. Now, there's a beauty for you!"

Somehow Adam had missed the name in his mother's recitation of the guests. "You invited that child? I danced with her last night at the Mainwaring's ball. She has little wit and less conversation."

"Well, she's being touted as this season's Incomparable. You should pay attention."

"She's eighteen! Maybe younger."

"I heard you danced with Lady Leonora, too, and so I took the liberty of inviting her as well."

"You heard wrong, Mother. I did not dance with her. I cannot abide that woman."

"Oh, come now, Adam. She's quite stunning and wealthy besides. Politics requires money, you know. And that's the other reason we need to carefully consider whom to invite to the house party."

Adam sighed. Perhaps his wish to stand for Parliament was misplaced. If he had to curry favors from the likes of Leonora, he didn't want any part of it. After he'd secured Jack's support, though, he was quite sure he could handle any unexpected expenses. He'd rather not have to ask his friend for money, but he'd no idea of what a campaign cost.

"My, my, the gossips have been busy, haven't they?" he said. "Since the ball was last night, how could you possibly know whom I danced with already?"

"Darling, you know the servants have their own network. Lucy told me everything while dressing me this morning."

"Did she neglect to mention Cass Linford? I *did* dance with her." Adam debated whether to ask his mother about

Cassie's broken engagement. He'd rather get the truth from Deborah than press Jack for it. Before broaching the subject, he sipped his coffee and cleared his throat.

"I wonder, Mother, if you're familiar…if you know why Cass never married? I believe she was once engaged."

"Why, yes, of course. Everyone knows."

Everyone but me. Adam waited, gritting his teeth but determined to remain silent until his mother decided to elaborate.

"I suppose you were out of the country when it all happened. Such a dreadful thing. Only think of the agonies that poor, dear girl suffered. Remember when you were children and—"

Adam's temper flared. "Mother!"

"Oh, sorry. Yes, well, her fiancé killed himself. Right in front of God and everybody. It was at Drury Lane. I believe *Othello* was on the bill. Cassandra and Lord Bentley, you knew him, didn't you? They were strolling during the interval, and he suddenly drew a pistol. I didn't see it, but those who did said he brandished the weapon at Cassandra, as though he meant to shoot her, then turned the gun on himself."

"So there were actual witnesses?"

"Well, now that you ask, I'm not certain, but that was part of the story that circulated."

Christ. "He might have killed her!" Adam moderated his voice before going on. It wouldn't do to have his mother thinking he was overly concerned about Cass. "When did this happen? And why did he do it, for God's sake?"

"Let me think. It happened during her second, maybe her third, season. A few years ago, now. I believe it was shortly before you sold your commission and began your sojourn on the Continent." She lifted a brow. "The Earl of Wilton, Bentley's father, gave it out that he'd changed his mind about marrying, that Cassandra was somehow to blame, but everyone knew the truth."

"Which was?" Why did he have to pry everything out of her?

"He had vowels out all over town. In Dun territory so deep, he could never get out. They say he was addicted to faro and hazard."

Adam tried to summon up an image of Lord Bentley, but they'd never really been friends, merely acquaintances. The other man had been titled and several years his senior, and they'd never done more than run into each other around town now and again. During his wild days, when he and Jack had frequented one gaming hell or another, he recalled seeing Bentley in some of those establishments. He couldn't imagine a union between him and Cass.

"I don't think Cassandra left Linford House for two years, except to travel to Haslemere. It was said she preferred rusticating there, but her brother finally forced her to return to town and to society. In hopes of a marriage for her, you see."

"I'd no idea," Adam said thoughtfully. He cringed when he thought about the cruel way he'd taunted her about her single state. Christ, if he'd only known. Had she loved the man? What pain she must have endured. And what a prize fool he was. He'd meant to apologize last night, but after Hugh made his appearance, he'd forgotten all about it.

He would beg her forgiveness the next time he saw her.

• • •

Adam drove his curricle to White's, on St. James Street, and found Jack seated at a table not far from the bay windows, personal domain of Beau Brummell. He wasn't present today; nevertheless, no one else dared sit there in case the man himself arrived. Adam found it annoying, rather than amusing, as some did.

The two men shook hands and Jack signaled a waiter.

After ordering wine, Adam said, "You must be wondering why I requested this meeting."

"I admit you've sparked my curiosity. Although after what you said when you drank tea with us, or maybe I should say, after what Cass pried out of you, I would wager it has something to do with a seat in Commons."

"You would be correct." Adam scrutinized his friend, trying to gauge his expression. He wanted to be taken seriously. If Jack felt the same as Cass, his bid would be finished before it began. "I want the other seat in Haslemere. I don't think I can manage it without a show of your support with the electors."

Jack gave him a wry grin. "What electors?"

Adam grimaced. "That bad, is it?"

"The freeholders exercise their franchise privilege, but as you well know, the Haslemere members are elected by the grace of Sir William Broxton and myself. They're influence seats. Have been since Queen Elizabeth's time."

Adam flung out his arms. "Which is precisely why we need reform!"

"Don't rip up at me," his friend said, showing Adam the palms of his hands. "I agree. I simply don't want to be bothered to bring it about. That's why we need men like you in Commons."

"You intend to support Halliwell again?" Adam asked. He thought this was the case, but needed to be certain.

"Afraid so, old man. He's smart, works hard, and pays attention to the good citizens of Haslemere. To the extent that he can." He paused a moment. "What do you know of Sir William's current man?"

Adam barked a caustic laugh. "Not much. I've heard he's doddering, in his cups much of the time, and an absentee Member for the most part. I think he is a relation of Sir William. It's my hope the old boy is ready for retirement, but of course I'll need to persuade Broxton to support me."

"Isn't he a friend of your father's? Speaking of whom… does he know of your plans yet?"

Adam took a long swallow of brandy before answering. "Their friendship is a longstanding one, but I don't know if that's still the case. And no, my father does not know anything about my plans."

"What do you think his reaction will be?"

"I've not seen him in many years. I imagine he has little or no interest in politics, and I'm quite sure he's badly neglected his tenants. That won't sit well with town folk. What little authority he may once have exercised can no longer be counted on."

"Well, somehow you'll have to convince the Baronet you're the man for the job."

"Your family wields the power and influence. If Broxton knows I have your support, that would be a strong inducement for him to let me be the one to replace his current man. Would you be willing to write to him on my behalf?"

"Of course. I'll do so immediately. By the way, did Hugh's sudden appearance at the ball have anything to do with your political ambitions?"

Confiding in his friend wouldn't matter, he supposed. "None at all. It seems my brother desires a leg shackle. My father's idea, apparently."

"Does that surprise you?"

"Worries me," Adam said. "As you know, he's very much the same man as my father. But there's more. He says Father wants to see me. Hugh claims he doesn't know why."

Jack nodded. "Before I lend you my support, I suppose I should ask where your politics lie. Here we sit in a stronghold of Tory ideals. You're a member here, as am I."

"In the spirit of honesty and truthfulness between us…I fall into the liberal Tory camp. Since the Tories hold the power at present, I thought it politic to put my name forward for White's. You and I both know the old place is more a gambling den than anything else." As Adam spoke, his gaze roved around the room. A few solitary men sat reading papers; others socialized in small groups. But it was no secret that the majority of those who frequented White's could usually be found in the rooms dedicated to hazard, whist, and faro.

Jack quizzed him. "We've already established you're for reform. What about Catholic emancipation?"

"I favor both, but they'll be a long time coming, in my opinion. First and foremost, I'd like to see an end to the damned war. It's been going on far too long, draining the Treasury and killing so many of our young men. We'll never get anything accomplished here at home until it's over."

"I'm with you on that," Jack said.

Adam carried on. "And we need to revise the Poor Laws, to make things a bit easier for people living at subsistence level."

"Good man. I agree with you on all those issues." Jack dropped his gaze momentarily, and when he looked up, Adam could tell that he was trying to prevent a smile from slipping out. "And what about women's rights? Cass will want to know your stand on that."

"Of course I support women in their bid for autonomy and education. You can tell your sister that."

"What's come between you two?" Jack asked, frowning. "I would haul you over the coals for being downright rude to her the other day, if she hadn't been the same to you."

"I didn't mean…I shouldn't have said what I did. It was ill-mannered of me. I've always been fond of Cassie. I still am. But sometimes she provokes me." He thought of how she'd provoked him at the ball. To the point he'd found her practically irresistible.

Jack guffawed. "As her brother, I quite understand. Say no more."

He didn't understand, in fact, but Adam wouldn't disabuse him of the notion. "We made our peace with each other at the ball last night," he said, not looking Jack in the eye.

"Indeed. I saw you dancing together. Be careful there, friend. I'd hate to have to call you out." Jack tossed back the rest of his drink and stood.

From Jack's expression, Adam could see he was only half kidding. A sister's reputation was a precious thing, especially in Cass's case. She'd barely weathered one scandal. Another would kill any chance of a decent marriage for her. Adam realized he'd better quash his attraction to the girl, before he got himself into trouble with the very person he needed to help him attain his goal.

"No worries there. I have the utmost respect for Cass." He pushed his chair back and got to his feet. "To be clear, I inherited money from my grandparents. I am not without resources. And Deborah has considerable funds of her own. I need your backing, which may entail a few trips to Surrey, but I don't anticipate needing your blunt unless something unanticipated arises."

Jack looked amused. "As you say. I'll get the letter off to Sir William this afternoon."

The two men claimed hats, gloves, and walking sticks and strolled toward the street to wait for their conveyances to be brought round. "Mother and I are hosting a house party at her country home," Adam said. "She's sending the invitations today."

"Ah," Jack said. "We shall look forward to it."

Adam noted the confusion on his friend's face, and the merest hint of hesitation in his voice. "We've invited Miss Farrington as well. No need to worry about that."

"Well, in that case, I can't think of anywhere I'd rather be. You have my support, Adam," Jack said, gripping his friend's hand. "I'll help in any way I can."

Adam gave a decisive nod. "Thank you. You won't regret it."

Chapter Six

Cass stood nervously looking around the Grey drawing room, secretly studying the other guests. Secretly studying Adam, to be perfectly honest. She, Jack, and Louisa had been escorted upstairs by a footman, where Adam and his family awaited them. Jenny and her mother and father entered the room shortly thereafter. Cass was shocked to find Hugh there, but politely offered her hand. Also present were the Incomparable, Elizabeth Morgan, and her mother. Cass had felt painfully drab and old when she was introduced to them. Elizabeth in her virginal pastel, she in her spinster colors.

What made her feel even worse was that, other than an obligatory greeting when he shook her hand, Adam had made no attempt to talk to her. She had to force herself not to stare at him, because from the moment she'd entered the room and clapped eyes on him, she realized with stunning clarity that he was the handsomest man she'd ever seen. He was wearing tight black pantaloons, which buttoned at the ankle, and a corbeau coat with covered buttons. His waistcoat was of pale green silk. Fortunately, her attention was diverted by Adam's mother, who had made her way unobtrusively to Cass's side.

"Cassandra, how good it is to see you out in society again," she said.

Cass considered the older woman, trying to judge the sincerity of the remark. In the years when they'd been summer neighbors, no one in Cass's family had seen much of Deborah, although Cass knew Adam had a great attachment to her. She hadn't attended the balls or assemblies, according to Lady Linford; nor had she made calls. As a result, the other families who might have been in a position to do so did not call upon her. To Cass's recollection, she'd only met Deborah once or twice during her childhood, and certainly hadn't seen her since.

"Thank you, ma'am. You have a lovely home."

"It belongs to Adam and Hugh's father. He has allowed me to live here these past ten years and decorate as I wish."

So she referred to Benjamin Grey as "Adam and Hugh's father," rather than as her husband. Well, Cass supposed that made sense. Especially if the man was the "devil incarnate," as Adam had confided to her at the ball.

"Tell me what occupies you these days, my dear."

Before answering, Cass studied Deborah's face. Adam resembled his mother. Although slightly faded and showing some gray, her hair had obviously once been the same rich gold as his. And her eyes were a brilliant blue. Cass couldn't find in their depths anything foreboding. "I spend most of my time tutoring my sister, Philippa. She is without a governess at present."

"Oh, quite a challenge for you, I'm sure," Deborah said merrily. "I'd nearly forgotten you had a younger sibling."

The entry of the remaining guests distracted them. "Pardon me, dear. I must perform my hostess duties," Deborah said with a chuckle and a roll of her bright eyes.

Cass's jaw dropped when she caught sight of Lady

Leonora entering the room. She took a step backward, and then another, hardly aware she was doing it.

"You're going to bump into me if you don't stop," Jenny said under her breath. "What is *she* doing here, I wonder?"

Cass stopped in her tracks and whispered over her shoulder. "Didn't you know? She's always fancied Adam." She couldn't express what she really thought, which was that Deborah, and possibly Adam, too, had singled Leonora out as the hostess-cum-wife every politician needed. At the ball, Adam had fervently denied any interest in her when she'd waltzed past. They may simply be courting her for her money. It all amounted to the same thing, didn't it? Surely Leonora wouldn't give of her money unless she got Adam, too.

Cass's spirits plummeted even further, if that was possible.

• • •

Lord, Adam wished he didn't have to play host. He wanted nothing more than to corner Cassie and spend the evening with her. Clearly, that was not going to happen. Nor would it be a good idea. If he repeated that to himself often enough, maybe he could quit thinking about her so damn much.

She was wearing an evening dress of apricot crepe cut low across her breasts. Tendrils of hair hung loose about her neck. Had they escaped from the knot at the top of her head, or had her hair been artfully arranged? Adam felt a stirring in his loins and was grateful for black evening pantaloons. Given the frequency with which they'd been in each other's company of late, he was spending a good deal of time feeling…stirred. And more alive than he'd felt in years.

Oh, God, here was Leonora. Wearing a gown of vermillion, with plenty of décolletage showing, she was a stunner, no doubt about it. With her raven hair, the deeper colors suited her best, and she knew it. All self-assurance and beauty, she dominated the room. He approached, and when she offered her hand, he brushed a kiss lightly across it, hating himself for doing it, especially with Cass watching.

"Lady Leonora. So happy you could join us."

"I wouldn't have missed it for the world."

Was he obligated to escort her into dinner, since she was the highest-ranking woman present? Or would Jack have the honor? He wanted to escort Cassie, if he could possibly maneuver his way over to her. By the expression on her face, he could see she'd been appalled when Leonora made her grand entrance. It might be wiser to avoid Cass right now, as he did not wish to be on the receiving end of one of her stinging remarks. *Coward*, his inner voice taunted.

Deborah, to his relief, was organizing the pairings. Jack was, indeed, escorting Leonora. His mother meant for him to pair with Jenny, but he decided instead to come to Jack's rescue. "Give your arm to your lovely fiancée," he said. "Lady Leonora, may I have the pleasure?" She smiled and immediately removed her hand from Jack's sleeve and placed it on his own. Before leading the procession downstairs, Adam risked a quick glance back. His mother's friend and admirer, Frederick Cochran, was walking alongside Deborah and the Morgan ladies, and Jenny's parents were arm and arm. Hugh, to Adam's dismay, was escorting Cassie. She met Adam's glance boldly but briefly, and then turned to his brother, who was leaning down to whisper something in her ear.

Damn him to hell!

• • •

Deborah had said Adam's father allowed her to decorate the townhome. Obviously, he hadn't worried about expense. Either that, or she was wealthy in her own right. The dining room was splendid. A gleaming mahogany table dominated the room, with chairs upholstered in striped silk at each place. One wall displayed landscapes, another, what Cass assumed were family portraits.

Adam, flanked by Miss Morgan and Leonora, held court at one end of the table; Deborah at the other. And there sat Cass, stranded in the middle, Hugh on one side and Jenny's father on the other. Good heavens, how was she to get through the lengthy meal trying to converse with those two? Not that she disliked Jenny's parent, but he never had much to say to her. She had no notion if this was because she was a female, and therefore he thought her unable to speak intelligently, or if he was simply a reserved gentleman.

At least Cass now comprehended her lack of consequence in Adam's eyes. It couldn't have been plainer if he'd had one of the footmen announce it as they entered the room: *The insignificant Miss Linford will be seated between a debauched rakehell and an insipid elderly man, whilst Lady Leonora and Miss Morgan will enjoy the company of their attractive, and most eligible, host.* A wrenching hurt settled somewhere in her chest, and she decided to make no effort at conversation. Let them try to engage her.

She cast a surreptitious glance at Hugh, the brother Adam so despised. On the way downstairs he'd been whispering some nonsensical joke in her ear, which she could barely hear, let alone comprehend.

Her contemplation of Hugh ended when Adam rose. "I have an announcement to make. A few of you already know what I'm about to say. I've decided to stand for Parliament, as one of the Members from Haslemere, down in Surrey. My good friend, Viscount Linford, has agreed to use his influence to help me achieve that goal. Jack, I'll try my best never to cause you to regret your decision." He paused until the laughter died down.

Cass was taken aback. When had this all been agreed

upon? Why hadn't Jack told her? The hurt in her chest notched up a level.

Frederick Cochran raised his glass. "To Viscount Linford." Obligingly, they all drank. "And to Adam for having the gumption to join the fray!"

Leonora said, "And which party do you ally yourself with, Mr. Grey?"

Adam took his seat. "To answer your question, Lady Leonora, I'm more inclined to be Tory, but of the liberal sort. I am hoping, perhaps naively, to remain an independent man."

When had Jack and Adam formed their little men's club? Cass wondered. Both of them knew she had a keen interest in politics, yet neither had bothered to tell her any of this, to seek her opinion or ideas. It proved what she'd feared. She was on the shelf in more ways than one. She'd become irrelevant. Of course, she hadn't exactly been encouraging when Adam first mentioned his interest in standing for Commons. Jack controlled one of the seats, but Cass knew he was well satisfied with Richard Halliwell, the current member. Sir William Broxton, a baronet who resided in the district, owned the other seat. If her recollection was accurate, his man had been serving a long time.

Cass was aware of her own voice, although she certainly hadn't intended to speak. "Tell us, Mr. Grey, do you favor female education? Or do you believe women must tend to home and hearth…oh, and keep their tongues?"

A few titters sprang up, and Jenny's father harrumphed beside her. "No need to educate our girls. Reading and writing, that's all they need to know." Though his own daughters had been well educated, tutored right alongside their brothers.

Adam looked nonplussed. "I have some thoughts on that, of course, but come, let's enjoy our meal and save politics for later." When his eyes remained fixed on her, Cass knew he could not have missed the obvious reference to the hurtful comments he'd made at Linford House. Although she tried to hold his gaze, she was first to drop her eyes.

The meal, served *a la russe*, proceeded. Cass remained determined to eat in self-imposed silence. She sipped distractedly at her turtle soup, because her mind was anything but silent. Straining to hear the conversation between Adam and Leonora, she nearly missed Hugh's question.

"May I ask, Miss Linford, why a lady so lovely and charming as yourself is as yet unmarried?"

You may ask, and I may choose not to answer. Was that forever to be the first question on the mind of any new acquaintance she formed? Fleetingly, it occurred to Cass that he might be having her on. He may well know what happened. On the other hand, Adam hadn't known. But he'd been at war and traveling, whereas Hugh had merely been living in the country. Oh, what difference did it make? It wasn't as if she was going to blurt out the whole sordid business right now.

"After my parents died, I took on the responsibility of educating my younger sister. Philippa is only ten."

"The child does not have a governess?"

"Not at present."

"Do you enjoy acting as a tutor? Does it not prevent you from doing other things young ladies take pleasure in? Shopping? Riding in the park, and the like?"

"You forget, sir, that I'm no longer a young lady. I have done my share of those things."

"Ah. So serious you are. And so elderly. We must find you a companion…or even a nurse."

Cass couldn't help smiling. "A very lowering thought. I may go into a decline at any moment." She didn't care to be the object of his attentions. It was time to cast the spotlight on him. "You live in Surrey most of the year, I collect. What do you do there?"

As Hugh began to speak, she glanced toward Adam.

Leonora was talking, Miss Morgan was giggling—actually, it sounded more like a cackle—but Adam was staring pointedly at her and Hugh, his expression one of barely concealed fury. She darted her eyes away, wishing she could get inside that head of his.

• • •

After an interminable dinner, Deborah rose, the signal that the men would now be left to their port while the ladies adjourned to the drawing room. Gratefully, Cass followed. Never had she been so happy to leave a table, although Hugh had turned out to be a better companion than she'd anticipated. Adam's attentions to his dining partners in full view of her were grating on her nerves by the end of the meal, though, and she had no idea what that furious glare had signified.

Too distracted when she first arrived, Cass had barely noticed the drawing room. It was lovely. Deep blue antique drapery, in the classical style that was fashionable among the *ton*, drew her eye. The color was stunning. A fire burned in the grate, and window embrasures opened up the room on both ends. Of course, the requisite pianoforte stood near the center of the room, and card tables were scattered about, as well as many chairs. Framed Etruscan engravings adorned one wall.

Jenny hurried to Cass's side and tugged on her arm, and she soon found herself huddling with the other girl near one of the windows. "Well?" Jenny demanded.

"Well what?"

"What's he like? Adam's mysterious, scary-looking brother?"

Cass laughed. "Oh, Jenny, he was quite pleasant and not at all scary."

"You have to admit he has a certain aura about him. What

did he talk about?"

"He told me about their home in Surrey. Sadly, it's falling to rack and ruin. It sounds pretty dire."

"But I thought they were wealthy."

Cass shrugged. "He did not elaborate on the reasons."

Just then, Deborah sought their attention. "Ladies, in a few days' time, you will all be receiving invitations to a house party at my country home in Surrey, hosted by Adam and me. We do hope you will be able to join us."

Cass and Jenny stared at each other. Were they being invited to the home that was falling apart, according to Hugh? And everyone knew Deborah and Benjamin Grey were estranged.

Their hostess laughed. "Don't everyone look so shocked. You are invited to my *personal* home, which I inherited from my parents some years ago. Do please say you will come, or I shall be quite blue-deviled!"

Talk and laughter broke out among all the ladies. Cass couldn't help wondering if Deborah meant to invite her. She hoped not. Now that Adam had made clear where she ranked in his affections, she couldn't see any reason that he would have asked his mother to include her. Apparently Cousin Louisa couldn't either, because she walked over to lecture Cass about it.

"I feel certain the invitation does not extend to us," the older woman began. "But even if it does, we shall politely decline. You cannot spare the time away from Philippa, Cassandra. But it should be delightful for you and Jack, dear Jenny."

Cass clamped her mouth shut on her anger, while Jenny looked embarrassed and could only manage a weak smile.

Someone was playing Mozart at the pianoforte. Cass's thoughts were in a muddle, and she fought against irritation with her cousin. Even though mere moments ago she'd convinced herself that she did not wish to be included, something about Louisa's high-handed dismissal of the whole idea rankled. What right did she have to assert that Cass could not spend any time away from her sister? She'd looked after Philippa on her own for a few years now, dutifully tutoring her in academic subjects, as well as teaching her embroidery and watercolors. Yes, she'd left instruction on the pianoforte to a master, but that was only because Cass herself had never been very proficient. Now that she was re-entering society, surely she had the right to make decisions for herself. On the other hand… she didn't particularly want to go. Not really. In all likelihood, the house party was planned by Deborah as a bride bazaar for Adam. She wouldn't fit in, and besides, it was simply easier to remain ensconced in the safe, protected environment she'd carved out for herself. She simply could not risk further heartbreak.

The butler carried the tea tray into the room, and the men followed in his wake. Instead of their usual high spirits, however, they were unnaturally quiet. The ladies, too, stopped talking, as if sensing something was wrong. Adam and Jack held a whispered conference, and then Adam stepped forward and said, "I bring you bad news. We've been informed that Prime Minister Perceval has been assassinated."

There was a stunned silence. Mrs. Morgan, the Incomparable's mother, swooned and had to be carried off to one of the couches. Cass trembled with the shock. Even though she didn't particularly admire the man, she knew he had a wife and several children. "How?" she asked, breaking the silence.

Adam met her eyes, but didn't speak immediately. His gaze conveyed sympathy, and after a long pause, he finally said, "Someone shot him."

Chapter Seven

Adam had dreaded telling Cass. She'd blanched when he said the Prime Minister had been shot, but remained standing and shook off her brother's hand when he grasped her arm. Jack hovered directly behind her, in case it was too much for her. But she showed remarkable poise, continuing to ask questions, even if they consisted of only one word.

"When? Where?"

"In the lobby of Commons, earlier today. I'm afraid I don't know specifics. I've sent someone out to see if any news sheets have been issued yet."

"How did you hear?"

"One of the footmen brought the news."

"I'll pour tea," Deborah said to Adam. "I think we could all use some." Cass's cousin walked over and offered her help.

"It's a damned shame!" Frederick Cochran said. "Just when we were on the verge of some stability." His already ruddy cheeks darkened. "Beg pardon, ladies."

"Who did it?" Cass asked. "Who...shot him?"

"We don't know that yet, Cass," Jack answered.

"Some lunatic, to be sure," Mrs. Morgan said, having sufficiently recovered herself enough to sit up and drink tea. "Oh, none of us is safe anymore, depend upon it! Mobs and riots at the slightest provocation, thieves prowling the streets, murderers—"

Good God, this kind of talk was the last thing they needed. Adam interrupted before things could get out of hand. "I beg you, ma'am, not to speculate. As yet the circumstances are unknown." His eyes scanned the room. "Who was playing the pianoforte?"

Elizabeth Morgan stepped forward.

"Please, Miss Morgan, continue. I think we would all find it soothing." He escorted her to the instrument and helped her find a suitable piece before returning to the others. Jack, he noticed, had convinced Cass to be seated. Adam considered whether to offer comfort, even though he had no idea if she would welcome it.

Deborah handed him a cup of tea. "I'm sorry, my dear. What a terrible turn of events."

Adam nodded, then moved toward the couch on which Cass was seated. He'd been hoping the talk would turn to other subjects, but as he crossed the room, he realized he'd been foolish. This was too big an event, too far reaching, to be pushed aside so easily. As he was about to claim the spot next to Cass, Leonora suddenly appeared and, stepping directly in front of him, took the place for herself. Bowing politely, he grinned at Cassie, and thought he detected the barest hint of amusement in her eyes. He moved to one side, but stayed close enough to overhear the conversation.

"*You* cannot help feeling particularly affected by this, Miss Linford," he heard Leonora say. "It must serve as a reminder of your own unfortunate ordeal."

Only Leonora could refer to the public suicide of someone's fiancé as an "unfortunate ordeal," Adam thought. He sipped his tea and waited to hear what Cass would say, or indeed if she would be able to say anything.

"The loss of those we love is always devastating, Lady Leonora, as I'm certain you know, since you lost your husband so recently."

Ah. Point to Cass.

"But your…unusual circumstance, so like this horrifying event." Leonora's voice dripped with false compassion. "Tell me, Miss Linford, what is it like to have a gun pointed at you? And to have your betrothed then turn the weapon and shoot himself, right there for all to see?"

Point to Leonora, the witch.

Cass got to her feet. "I never discuss the circumstances of Bentley's death with anyone I am not close to, Lady Leonora. You, thank heaven, in no way qualify."

Brava, Cassie.

She curtsied gracefully, with dignity, and walked right past him. Though she seemed unruffled, Adam could see the quiver of her pulse at her temple. She set her teacup down on a table and exited the room.

Leonora looked up at him. "I'm afraid I've upset her," she said. "But really, all of town will be talking about it again."

"Only those who are boorish and ill-mannered," Adam said. To his satisfaction, a look of surprise registered on her face and her lips flattened into a hard line. He smiled, bowed slightly, and removed himself from her presence, lest he say something else ungentlemanly. Miss Morgan was dutifully playing; the others were huddled in groups conversing softly. No one seemed to need him at present, and after a prudent amount of time, he left the room in search of Cass.

• • •

How dare that woman speak to me about Bentley? Cass wandered the corridor in search of an empty room in which to hide until she could regain her composure. In spite of the fact that there were no witnesses to Bentley's death besides herself, half the *ton* thought they'd seen it. In a moment, she saw light flickering from a partially open door. She stepped inside and inhaled the scent of old leather bindings, ink, and parchment. Adam's library, no doubt. Perhaps he would not mind if she sought refuge here.

The only light was from a fire burning in the grate, but she could see well enough. Her eyes wandered around the room, taking in the enormous mahogany desk, which occupied most of one wall, and the fireplace opposite. The two leather chairs before the hearth looked perfect for reading. At the far end of the room, a window seat beckoned. The windows overlooked the back garden, though not much of it was visible tonight. In a very unladylike fashion, Cass arranged herself on the cushioned seat, scooting around so that her back was leaning against one wall. She drew her knees up and wrapped her arms around them.

Clearly, it had been unrealistic to expect the *ton* to take her back, and Leonora's hurtful words proved it. There would always be the spiteful set, who found pleasure in hurting others. Why should she allow herself to be dragged through the muck again? She had a choice—no one was forcing her, except Jack, of course. If she were to tell him she preferred the life of a spinster, he would accept her decision. He wouldn't like it, but he would accept it.

Even if society did decide to welcome her back to the fold, there was still her enormous burden of guilt over Bentley's death. *Would it ever go away?* Her cousin was right—her place was at home with Philippa. Tears stung her eyes at the realization that her life would plod on as it was. She'd been a fool to think otherwise.

Cass sensed rather than heard the door opening and raised her head. *Blast!* Couldn't she be left alone for five minutes? It was probably Jack or Cousin Louisa coming to make sure she was all right. With the back of her hand, she brushed away the tears brimming over her eyelids and tracing a path down her cheeks.

"Well done, Cassie. Excellent set-down."

But no, it was Adam, making his way toward her.

Hastily, she swiveled and set her feet on the floor. "I imagine it flew right over her head."

She started to rise, but he reached out a hand and gently touched her shoulder. "Don't. Are you all right?" He looked down at her, his brow furrowed, and Cass's heart surged, knowing he was worried about her.

"Thank you, yes. The news was a shock, that is all."

"You're lying. I can see you've been weeping." His voice was soft, concerned.

Oh, no. His attentions were welcome, but she didn't want him to see her crying. It seemed so weak. "Only a little." She thought about the wisdom of confiding in Adam, drew a deep breath, and plunged in. She wanted to trust him. "For the first year, I thought about Bentley's death every day. I no longer do so. But with the news about Perceval…the memory of that awful night came roaring back. The fear. The chaos afterward…it was like Bedlam. For a moment, when you told us about Perceval, I felt as though I could hear the gunshot, see the blood, all over again."

"My dear Cass, don't torment yourself." He sat down next to her and reached for her hands, and she allowed him to take them. "I would never have said what I did upon meeting you again…seeing you for the first time after so long, had I known. It was unforgivable."

"Oh, don't speak of it. I was rude to you as well. Perhaps we both got what we deserved."

"You will not let this drive you back into hiding, will you?"

Smiling regretfully, she said, "It was easy enough to withdraw from society once, and I can surely do it again, if I must."

He tightened his grip on her hands. "No! You must not think of doing that."

She was shocked at the vehemence with which he spoke. "Whyever not?"

His eyes gleamed in the firelight. "Because I do not wish you to. Is that a good enough reason?"

And just like that, something changed. Cass wasn't sure what it was, but she felt a spark ignite in the air between them. Her senses heightened. Every breath felt charged. In the dim light, she couldn't read his expression. Was he saying that he cared for her? That he would feel the loss if she weren't present at balls and soirees and parties? Flustered, she stammered out a reply. "I—I suppose so. You are a future MP, and perhaps I will have to bend to your will."

He chuckled softly, certain she was unaware of the double entendre. "I like the sound of that."

"Wretch," she countered. "Just like a man."

He got to his feet, and still clutching onto one of her hands, he drew her slowly up. "And you, Cassie, are quite an irresistible woman."

She felt his breath skimming her face and knew he was going to kiss her. She should stop him. That is what a lady who observed the proprieties would do. But she simply could not, because she'd been longing for Adam's kiss her whole life. Instead, Cass lifted her face and closed her eyes, waiting. No one had ever called her irresistible before, after all. What if this was her only chance? The only time she would ever—

His lips touched hers, and she couldn't keep a moan from slipping out. With one strong hand, he cupped the back of her head, pulling her closer and skimming his tongue across the seam of her lips. She swayed against him, and he put his arms around her. Opening her mouth to him seemed natural. Cass had never been held or kissed like this before. It felt delicious. It felt wonderful. She wanted it to go on and on. Her body pressed against his, tingling and alive, her insides burning. If it had been possible to move closer to him, she would have. She wanted to feel every bit of his muscled body aligned with hers. She'd left her arms at her sides, but now moved them slowly up and around his neck.

His lips grazed her cheek, her jaw line, and moved down her neck, dropping sweet kisses as he went. Weaving one of her curls through his fingers, he whispered, "This hair. This beautiful hair," then brought it to his lips and kissed it. His mouth returned to her skin, moving downward, still feathering kisses. His hands lightly brushed her breasts through the thin fabric of her gown and chemise, but this time she stifled her moan. And then rational thought took over, and she reluctantly withdrew her arms.

Adam raised his head. More gently this time, he kissed her lips, stroking the side of her face with his thumb. As he drew away, he murmured, "Sweetest Cassie."

Suddenly, she felt embarrassed. What must he think of her, kissing him with such abandon? Offering herself to him? Not feeling capable of speech, she simply waited for him to say something.

Adam reached out and touched her hair. "Turn around and let me see your gown in back."

Not what she'd hoped he would say, but obediently, she spun round, and gasped when his hands smoothed away wrinkles, all of which seemed to be conveniently located on her derriere, and made a few other adjustments here and there. Obviously, he'd had practice at this.

"You look…perfect. I'll return to the drawing room first. Wait here for a few minutes."

Cass nodded, reaching out to make a minor alteration to his neck cloth. He captured her hand and kissed her palm, then strode toward the door. She could hardly bear the thought of his leaving her.

"Adam," she said softly, before he opened the door. "Thank you for watching over me."

"I'm at your service any time, Cassie. But I hardly think you needed me."

But I do need you. She felt intoxicated, bewildered by the overpowering attraction she felt for Adam. She'd experienced nothing like it before, although dancing with him had come close. Cass plunked back down onto the window seat. In an abrupt reversal of her earlier feelings, she decided she could take her place in society, provided Adam was there. Although she hadn't taken into account how he would feel about her if he knew the whole truth about the circumstances surrounding Bentley's horrific death. There were things even Jack did not know.

Shortly after Cass re-entered the drawing room, the party broke up, even though the hour was still early. Carriages were called for, and wraps retrieved. In a time of crisis, it was only natural for people to want to be at home, waiting for news and staying close to family. There was no further opportunity for Cass to speak privately with Adam, although he lightly kissed her fingers when they bid each other good night.

• • •

After Deborah retired, Adam sent his butler to bed, deciding to close up himself. He prowled from room to room, making sure candles were snuffed, and fires banked. Finally, he reached the library, where less than an hour ago he'd almost lost his head with Cass.

At the drinks trolley, he poured himself a finger of brandy and lowered his tall form onto one of the chairs in front of the fire, sipping slowly. He stretched his long legs out in front of him. What had possessed him to kiss her? It wasn't just the kiss, it was the undeniable fact that his desire to possess her had nearly consumed him. His need had been stirred by something else, though. She'd been so brave, speaking of her fiancé's death, then insisting she was prepared to become a pariah once again. But her tears revealed her underlying vulnerability, which was the one thing in Cassie he couldn't bear to see. Since their childhood, Adam had wanted to protect her from harm. The fact that Perceval's assassination could dredge up the old gossip about Cass infuriated him. Why couldn't people let it go?

It pleased him that he'd seen evidence of desire in her expressive eyes and felt it in her body as it hungered against his. Christ, it had been all he could do to stop himself. He hadn't expected Cass to respond so passionately. The extent of his need had been quite obvious, and she seemed more than willing to match it with her own.

But a gentleman couldn't trifle with a lady he did not intend to wed. Especially one who also happened to be the sister of his closest friend. That was the simple truth. There were plenty of other women around for that. Lord, he needed a mistress. He'd never kept one, because he'd either been at war or traveling. This did not seem the most opportune time, however, unless he could find himself a rich widow willing to play political hostess and pour money into his cause. That brought an image of Leonora to his mind and he shuddered with revulsion.

But Cassie. What was he to do about her? He wanted her, plain and simple. But she was Jack's sister, and still a virgin, he suspected. Though her enthusiasm was quite surprising and definitely arousing, it was apparent she had much to learn. Ah, but he'd love to teach her.

Abruptly, he sat up, pulling his feet in and setting them on the floor with a resounding thump. Out of the question. Adam had never seriously considered marriage. Was he not his father's son? He might end up like the man, a degenerate. So debauched, Deborah had had to leave him, taking her younger son with her. What if he'd somehow inherited a proclivity for the same kind of lewd and depraved behavior? Maybe it revealed itself as one grew older. He'd never subject any woman to what his mother had endured before making the final break with his father, and he probably didn't know the half of what Deborah had suffered.

And then there was the war. The horror of it had changed him. War in the abstract was most people's experience; the real thing was something else again. While it had hardened his body, it had also put lines in his face and a whole litany of surreal memories in his mind, of men moaning in death, crying out for their wives or mothers, and not a damn thing he could do except hold their hands and promise to write to their loved ones. The agonies the men had endured before death claimed them haunted his dreams. He didn't know if he could share his wartime experience with anyone, even Cass. Ending the war, if he gained a seat in Commons, was his most passionate cause.

Should he ask Deborah not to invite her to the house party? There was really no good reason for her to be included, other than the fact that she was Jack's sister. Being thrown together with her for a week would be bad. Very bad. But Jesus, he wanted her there.

He was definitely going to tell his mother that under no circumstances should she invite Leonora, even if she had already extended a verbal invitation. He would no longer receive that woman into his home. Her cruelty to Cass was unforgivable, and he didn't give a damn for her good opinion. Or her money.

Adam drained his glass and poured himself another, a short one this time. He drank and ruminated. What was Cassie thinking? Was she in her bed, dreaming about him? He snorted. For Christ's sake, these were the thoughts of a lovesick mooncalf. After a few more swallows, he reached for his candle and made his way to his bedchamber, trying to summon the strength to put all thoughts of her out of his mind.

• • •

At half eleven the following morning, Adam summoned Deborah to the library to confer about the house party. After a general discussion of pastimes and outings the group might undertake, Deborah said, "And a ball. We must host a ball at the end of the week!"

Adam groaned. "I suppose you won't hear any arguments against that idea?"

"My mind is quite made up, dear. The ladies will expect it. Talking about their gowns and jewelry and hair makes for lively discussion all week."

"And the men will tolerate it." Adam smiled. "Very well, have your ball." He hesitated before broaching a more difficult subject. "Mother, I don't want you to invite Lady Leonora."

She looked nonplussed. "Why not, dear? She has a certain mystique about her. One always runs the risk of boredom among the guests, and Leonora would spice things up a little." She paused a moment. "Quite comfortably circumstanced, too."

"So you've said."

"It doesn't hurt to have wealthy friends when one is seeking political office, Adam."

"I don't want her as a friend, and if I have to beg the likes of Leonora for money, I'll give up the whole scheme."

"What has riled you, Adam? What happened?"

"She said some cruel things to Cass last night and I happened to overhear. Then she made the mistake of repeating them to me privately after Cass had left the room."

"Perhaps a momentary lapse in good judgment?"

"No, Mother. That is her character, and I refuse to condone it. If other people in society wish to welcome her, I'm powerless to stop them. But I won't have her at any event we are hosting."

Deborah nodded. "Then we must not invite her."

Adam glanced at the ormolu clock on the mantel. Although it was currently only a few minutes past noon, it seemed their talk had been going on for at least a few hours already. He pushed on. "And I don't want you to invite Cass, either."

"I beg your pardon?"

"You heard me. I don't want Cass there."

"Adam, I really must protest! Her brother and his fiancée will be invited. It would be rude to exclude her."

"Nevertheless, that is my wish."

"Without both Cass and Leonora, the numbers will be off. Too many gentlemen and not enough ladies."

"I'm sure you'll work it out."

His mother stepped closer. "Whatever your reasons are, when weighed against the hurt you will cause Cass by excluding her, are you certain it's what you want? To be so heartless? Cassandra is still vulnerable. Mere moments ago you revealed you are sensitive to that."

That broke down his remaining resolve, and he held his arms up in surrender. "Oh, very well, invite Cass if you must."

"You still haven't explained why you don't wish her to be there."

"Nor will I, so don't push me. Send your invitations, and include Cass."

"Her existence is rather mundane, you know. She tutors her younger sister, no governess for some reason, so the child's education is on Cass's shoulders. And that relation of hers who trails her about—" Deborah shuddered dramatically.

"You've made your point, Mother. You may leave now. I have some work to do."

Uncharacteristically, she didn't utter another word. She simply dropped a kiss on his cheek and quietly left the room.

As much as it galled him to admit it, she was right. Excluding Cass would have been cruel. How could he have even considered it?

Chapter Eight

Cass sipped at her chocolate, more than a little preoccupied. She'd slept poorly last night. Over and over, she had re-lived the scene in the library, Adam's kiss, and her own wild urge to devour—and be devoured—by him. Lord above, what had come over her? An indefinable feeling had taken up residence in her belly. Excitement and a lightness that made her feel buoyant. Whatever it was, it was both driving her to distraction and irritating her. She was having a great deal of difficulty focusing on anything else, even though she was trying to concentrate on accounts of the prime minister's assassination in the morning papers.

Jack entered the room in high good humor, grating on Cass's already frayed nerves. "You might have told me about Adam's plans," she blurted out.

Jack, busy heaping his plate with kippers, eggs, and toast, barely spared her a glance. "Good morning to you, too, dear sister. Pour me some coffee, there's a good girl."

In an under voice, Cass applied some not very complimentary terms to her brother, but did as he asked.

"Did you say something?" he said.

She glared at him.

At last settled, coffee cup in hand, he deigned to answer her. "I'm sorry, Cass. I should have. It all happened so fast, you see. And I thought you would not be interested in Adam's affairs."

"But you know of my interest in politics! Enlighten me, please."

"The day after the Mainwaring's ball, which was only a few days after I'd first run into Adam, we had a meeting at White's. He asked for my backing for the Haslemere seat, and I agreed. That's all there was to it, Cass."

"It may not be as simple as you think."

"What do you mean?"

"The other seat—Sir William Broxton has it in his pocket. What do you intend to do about his man?"

Jack waved a hand through the air, showing his utter lack of concern. "Apparently, he hasn't attended the session in years."

Cass nibbled at a triangle of toast. "I see. I hadn't heard that. Sometimes those members are the most troublesome ones to dislodge. Their patrons are ridiculously loyal to them."

"True. Adam's riding down to see his father before joining the house party. He may know something. We talked about it last night. He's hoping to get the lay of the land while there."

"Mightn't his father oppose the scheme?"

"Why should he?"

She shrugged. "No real reason, except you said they'd been estranged for years. He might do it out of spite."

"Anything's possible, I suppose, but it shouldn't matter, in any case, unless Adam's father wields a great deal of influence over Broxton."

"From what Hugh told me during dinner, Benjamin Grey has allowed his estate to decline drastically, including the tenants' cottages. I cannot imagine he would be very well regarded any longer, if he ever was."

"Adam is not going to be pleased if things are as bad as all that. Of course, Hugh's assessment may not be truthful, or accurate either."

"Surely Adam must have an inkling."

"I rather think not. If he suspected, wouldn't he have mentioned it to me? By the way, in an attempt to be open and honest with you, I have posted a letter to Sir William about Adam, giving him my endorsement." He gave her a sardonic look, but Cass didn't rise to the bait. "He's the only man Adam needs to sway. I say, will you pass me the newspapers?"

Philippa and Cousin Louisa swept into the breakfast room as Cass was handing the papers over. The child ran straight for her brother, nearly spilling hot coffee down the front of his shirt. "Whoa, there, poppet," he said, pulling her up onto his lap. It wouldn't be much longer before she would be too mature to behave in such a way, Cass thought. In a year, maybe less, the youngest Linford wouldn't be caught dead sitting in her brother's lap.

"Your sister is eagerly awaiting her lessons," Louisa said, casting a sharp glance at Cass.

"Indeed? Is that true, Philippa?"

"No," the little girl said without a moment's pause. "Cousin Louisa is funning you."

A smothered laugh came from Jack. As well they knew, "funning" was not a part of their cousin's character. Cass stabbed a few raspberries, washing them down with the rest of her chocolate. "Cousin Louisa is right. It's time to get started."

"What are we doing today, Cassie?"

"I believe you have some French grammar and a translation to work on. Then penmanship, and if you work hard, we might read some myths before luncheon. This afternoon, your pianoforte tutor is coming. How does that sound?"

"Boring," Philippa proclaimed as Jack plopped her onto the floor.

Yes, I quite agree. Cass rose from her place and took her sister's hand. "Come along, dearest." As they left the room, she turned and smiled at Jack. "Thank you for explaining. About Adam."

"Of course. Please accept my apologies for not keeping you informed."

Cass could tell by the mocking look in his eyes that his sincerity was in question. At least she'd made her point, though. "What news of…?" Her voice tapered off as she realized she shouldn't speak of the Prime Minister's murder in front of Philippa.

Jack cast her a knowing glance. "We'll talk of it later," he said.

In the schoolroom, Cass reviewed irregular French verbs with Pippa and then got her started on a translation. "When you're done—and I don't expect you to be done for at least an hour—come and find me. We'll review your work together."

"All right," her sister said in her most tortured voice. "I wish I could paint with watercolors. Do something fun for a change."

"I'll tell you what. If you do a good job on your translation, tomorrow we shall paint in the morning and visit a museum in the afternoon. And maybe get an ice at Gunter's."

"Oh, could we, Cassie? Do you mean it? You're not teasing me?"

"No, I'm not." Impulsively, Cass reached out and drew the little girl into a tight hug. Sometimes—most of the time, lately—she hated being Philippa's governess instead of simply her sister. She stroked the length of her long blond locks, loving the silky feel. This hair would delight a very fortunate man someday, she thought. And that immediately sent her thoughts to Adam, and him kissing her hair and saying how beautiful it was.

"Cassie, let me go," Philippa squealed.

"I love you, little sister." Before releasing her, Cass plopped a kiss on her cheek. "Now, get to work. Pip-pip!"

"Hooray!" the little girl shouted. It was something they'd started long ago, and her sister still delighted in it. That would probably only last a few more years, too, until Pippa would view herself as much too sophisticated for such childish nonsense.

Instead of heading for the drawing room, where her cousin would be settled, Cass decided to work on mending some books in the library. It was a hobby she'd developed over the years, at first assisting her father. Then, under his tutelage, she had learned how to reinsert pages that had fallen out and how to repair broken bindings on her own.

It was here, as a small girl, she'd first heard the ancient tales of Zeus and the Olympians, and all her father's favorite myths. Demeter and Persephone, Apollo and Daphne, Athena and Poseidon, and Ajax, her brother's namesake, known for his strength and courage. And the story of her namesake, Cassandra, given the gift of prophecy by Apollo. When she hadn't returned his love, he'd put a curse on her, so that no one believed her prophecies. She had a great gift, but he had rendered her powerless. *Ha! It smacked of modern-day male-female relationships.* Men usually held all the power—as well as the purse strings.

She and her father had always been comfortable in each other's company, and from an adult perspective, Cass understood that learning the art of mending books had been a way to be close to him. He had been scholarly and somewhat reclusive. Now she found a measure of peace in the work and in remembering her father's resonant voice telling her the stories. She'd no sooner gotten her work table arranged, tools set out, glue pot ready, needle threaded, than her cousin whisked through the door.

"I thought I might find you here."

Botheration! After Cousin Louisa's comment last night, Cass was feeling excessively annoyed with her.

"Is Philippa working—?"

"On her French, yes, of course she is. I'll check it when she's finished."

"How you can bear to fuss with these ancient old tomes is beyond me. You should improve your skills with the needle or practice your music, like other young ladies."

"*Hmm.* I believe you've expressed that view before, Cousin. You know those things do not interest me, nor do I possess aptitude for them. And I am improving my skills with the needle. Just not the kind you're referring to."

Louisa plunked down on the sofa, and Cass realized with a sigh that she was there to stay. "I came to tell you that the invitations arrived for the house party. One for each of us, except for Philippa, of course."

"Ah." *What am I to say?*

"I am of the opinion that you should not attend, Cassandra. Depend upon it, Deborah Grey is using this as a way to look over prospective brides for Adam. It's nothing to do with you."

Thank you, Cousin, for dismissing me so readily from that select group. Cass chose her words carefully. "I have not made up my mind as to whether to attend. I must think about it."

"Philippa can hardly spare you for a whole day, never mind a week," the older woman argued. "She's such a poor student, I sometimes despair of her learning anything!"

At that, Cass turned and looked squarely at her cousin.

"Louisa, please refrain from describing her in that way. What if she overheard you? Philippa is not a poor student. Indeed, she possesses a keen mind. Left to her own devices, she would find hundreds of things to learn about. She's simply not very interested in the usual areas of study."

"Just so. It is up to you to develop her interest in things ladies need to know."

Cass couldn't help heaving an audible sigh. "I am doing my best to see to that." She busied herself preparing to reunite a book with a page that had fallen out. With great care, she laid the book open and placed a sheet of paraffin paper on top of the page. Then she opened the glue pot, found a fine brush, and began to apply glue to the edge of the page to be inserted.

"You are not setting your cap for Mr. Grey, are you, Cassandra? That would be very foolish indeed."

The brush slipped from Cass's hand and fell directly onto the open page of the volume she was working on, spreading glue onto its surface. She bit back the curse she wanted to utter and quickly grabbed the brush before it could do any further damage. Dipping a rag into some solvent, she dabbed lightly at the mess. In as calm a voice as she could muster, she said, "Why do you ask such a thing?" Then a horrible thought struck her. With relentless self-control, she managed to force her voice into the range of normality. "Did someone say that about me?" Deliberately, she neither looked at her cousin nor stopped her work.

"I noticed last night that the two of you were absent from the drawing room at the same time. No doubt others noticed as well."

"I was upset over the news about the Prime Minister, because it brought back a whole slew of unhappy memories. The room was close, and I needed some air, that is all." Should she deny that she'd had any contact with Adam? Probably best to stick with the truth, or partial truth. Her cousin had an uncanny way of ferreting out lies. "Adam was concerned, but when I told him I was fine, he returned to his guests."

"*Humph*. He knows about Bentley, then?"

"He does."

"That gossipy mother of his must have told him."

"What difference does it make how he knew? All of town knows! Only consider, Deborah was a very gracious hostess last evening. She made a point of telling me she was happy to see me back in society."

"That doesn't signify," Louisa said, her face pinched and obstinate. I am only concerned that you do not forget the promise you made to your dear mother on her deathbed, that you would look after Philippa until she makes her come-out."

Fury was building in Cass's chest, burning and seeking release, but she did not want to lose her temper with her cousin. That would make her look guilty, and would certainly give Louisa the upper hand. Now she turned and faced her unswervingly. "I assure you, Cousin, nothing could persuade me to renounce that commitment. Nothing."

Cass bent to her work, and after a few moments, when she heard the door click shut, her breathing eased. Louisa had succeeded in one thing. The buoyancy Cass experienced earlier had evaporated, replaced by a crushing weight pressing on her chest.

When the family sat down for a midday repast, Louisa unwisely raised the question again, with Jack present.

"I am of the opinion that Cassandra should not attend the Grey's house party. It is to be an opportunity for Mr. Grey and his mother to look over potential brides, a sort of marriage mart, albeit a private one. What do you think, Jack?"

"And you feel Cass is unworthy of consideration as a

bride for Adam?" Jack asked, raising one supercilious brow.

Cass gawped at her brother. Of course the idea was ridiculous, but nevertheless, she appreciated Jack's words.

"We all know the unfortunate incident with Bentley assured her spinsterhood. Why should she put herself forward like any other young girl seeking a husband? She's not like any other young girl—"

"I have never considered her to be 'like any other young girl,' Cousin. I have always thought Cass to be in the first stare of beauty, intelligence, and kindness, and I've been very gratified to see her begin to take her place in society once again." Jack looked at Cass, and she saw genuine emotion in his expression. If she was not mistaken, tears glossed his eyes. For the first time since Bentley's suicide, she understood the toll it had taken on her brother, as well as herself.

Did Jack really believe what he'd told Louisa, or was he simply warning her to back off? Cass felt tears of gratitude well in her eyes and blinked them away before anyone could notice.

"Cassandra has responsibilities here at home," Louisa continued, seemingly not sensing the bite behind Jack's words. "She must not sacrifice her sister to her own pleasure."

With deliberation, Jack set down his knife and fork. Trying to keep his temper in check, Cass realized.

"Indeed, Cousin, Cass has done precisely the opposite these last few years. Given up her own pleasures to the rearing and education of Pippa. She is a friend to Adam and his family as much as I, and if she wishes to, she will attend." Jack turned and pointedly looked at her.

"It's only for a week," Cass said. Suddenly and beyond all reason, she wanted to go. She wanted to be at that house party more than she'd wanted anything, ever. It was a chance, wasn't it? Possibly the last one she would have to shed her past and make a new life for herself. She was tired of being an observer of life's richest experiences. She longed to take part. Despite her insistence that she was on the shelf, she knew she was too young to give up on happiness.

Up until Louisa had begun badgering her about it, she'd been thinking of ways she could politely decline. Adam was too handsome, too charming, too…too impossible to resist. For one dizzying moment, she pictured herself in his embrace, the two of them alone in a sequestered woodland nook. Oh, she was vulnerable, and she knew it, but what was the point of living if she never again took a risk? So Cass said, "The Caldwells have offered many times to allow Philippa to take her lessons with their daughters if I have reason to be away. I shall send a note to Henrietta requesting that she stay with them for a week. Pippa will be thrilled."

"Excellent plan," Jack said. "And Cousin, you need not trouble yourself to come. There will be a sufficient number of ladies available to act as chaperones."

Louisa's mouth curved down in disapproval, but she maintained her composure, even though her face was rigid as a board, her words sharp as a razor. "It is my duty to chaperone Cassandra. If she insists on attending, I shall go as well."

"Suit yourself," Jack said. "But the matter is settled. Let's hear no more about it."

For a brief moment Cass had allowed herself to imagine an entire week without her cousin. But Louisa's presence wouldn't make a great deal of difference, actually. One could always elude her chaperone, with a little planning and ingenuity. She turned to the footman standing nearby. "Robert, would you tell Martin I shall need the carriage this afternoon?"

"Whatever for?" Louisa practically shouted.

Cass looked at her directly. "I am going to see the dressmaker. If I'm to be at a house party for an entire week, I need some new gowns. There's to be a ball; it said so right on the invitation." And then she smiled.

Louisa sputtered, choked, and was silent.

Chapter Nine

Since the weather was fine, Adam decided to drive his curricle down to Surrey. In his younger days, he'd had a reputation as a fine whip, and he still loved handling the ribbons. His matched pair of chestnuts needed a good outing, and so did he. Not healthy for horses to stand idle for too long. Humans, either. Deborah would be arriving tomorrow in her traveling coach, and they had no need of two such conveyances during their stay in the country.

Centuries old oak, beech, and ash grew in stately clusters in the thickly wooded countryside, reminding him how refreshing it was to be back in these environs. It had been too long since he'd been away from London, with its smog, filth, and jangle of competing noises every hour of the day. Not that he was looking forward to seeing his father. Though the upcoming visit had been on his mind since Hugh had told him about the summons, he still had no idea what the old man wanted. He was certain his brother had to be mistaken about it having something to do with debts of honor.

How would his father react to Adam's decision to seek

one of the Haslemere seats in Parliament? He couldn't imagine why he would oppose it, what possible objection he could have. Then again, since Adam had neither seen nor spoken with him in so many years, there was no way to predict his father's state of mind. He might thwart his son, out of spite, because of Adam's loyalty to Deborah. Since he and Deborah had left, Benjamin Grey had never cared for Adam the way he did Hugh. The old man had informed Adam years ago that Hugh would be his sole heir.

Adam would have the devil of a time convincing Sir William, a longtime friend of his father, to support him as the new Member if he knew of the acrimony between them. He'd have to set up a meeting with Sir William while he was down in Surrey, and he'd need to cultivate other prominent locals, what few there were. Adam hoped that this business with his father would be quickly concluded. He wanted it over with and settled, whatever it was, so he could get on with his plans. It galled him that he might need his father's intervention with the baronet.

Despite his vow to banish her from his thoughts, Adam's mind kept wandering to Cassie, and the fact that he'd be spending the week with her. Deuce take it, it was a damned sticky situation to be in. When he'd kissed her the night of the dinner party, her unhesitating enthusiasm had shocked him, so he suspected that she was interested and ready to explore that side of her nature. Which could lead down a path he most adamantly did not want to follow, the one that led directly to the altar. God knows, he wasn't in the habit of seducing virgins, but he didn't know if he was strong enough to keep his distance from her, his opposition to matrimony notwithstanding.

Late in the afternoon he passed through the village. He caught a few curious stares, but not many people were about. The half-timbered cottages and tiled roofs reminded him of his youth. When he and Hugh were boys, they would race to town on market days, buy themselves some sweets and cider, and make their way home with sticky hands and faces. Adam smiled, pleased that he could conjure up a few good memories of his boyhood with his brother.

Nothing could have prepared him for the sight that greeted him when he reached the boundaries of his childhood home. When Adam led his horses onto the approach road, he found it rutted and unfit for driving. The park, never well-tended at the best of times, appeared neglected and run down. His eyes roved over hedges, shrubs, and bushes, all needing to be trimmed or pruned. Leaves from last autumn lay in wet clumps under the trees, while droopy flowers poked up here and there as though at random.

The house itself was in a sorry state of disrepair. Built during Queen Elizabeth's reign, it was a manor house of solid construction, but even when Adam was growing up, it had needed constant patching up. Now it appeared to be falling into near ruin. When he dismounted, his boots crunched on shards of broken roofing tiles. One wing of the place seemed to be sinking. Shutters on some of the second story windows hung precariously, threatening to fall on some unsuspecting person at any moment.

Adam lifted the grimy brass knocker on the front door and waited for Wesley to let him in. And waited. He'd decided to try his luck at the kitchen entrance when the door slowly swung open, and poor old Wesley, looking as dingy as everything else, ushered him through.

"Mr. Adam," he said, his once strong voice now a bit shaky. "Good to see you again, sir."

"Thank you, Wesley." Adam swung around and looked at his curricle. "Is there anyone to see to the horses?"

"I shall tell Albert right away, sir." The old man turned, as if to bustle off.

"One moment, Wesley. Is my father at home?" He pulled his gloves off and handed them, along with his hat and whip, to the old fellow. A look of puzzlement crossed the man's face, as if he wasn't quite sure what he should do with them. After a moment, he set them on the hallway table.

"Follow me, Mr. Adam. Your father is in his library."

They climbed a flight of stairs lined with family portraits, Grey ancestors dating back to the Great Rebellion after which they'd acquired the house. Seized by Cromwell's men after the Protectorate ended, it was awarded to a Grey who'd been a loyal supporter of Charles II. It had remained in the family ever since.

At the top of the stairs, a narrow passage opened out into the Great Hall. Unfortunately, the term "great" no longer applied. A thick layer of dust covered everything, and no fire burned in the hearth. There wasn't a servant in sight; the place seemed as silent and drab as a poor man's tomb. They exited the hall and re-entered the passage leading to the billiard room, the gun room, and finally, the library.

"Mr. Adam Grey, sir," Wesley announced in sonorous tones, as if he were the major domo of some great house.

Adam stepped over the threshold. The room was dark and chill; no fire burning in here, either. Try though he might to recall the arrangement of the room, still he came up empty. Only the rustling of papers signaled Adam as to Benjamin Grey's location.

"Father?" Adam said, somewhat disoriented.

"Over here," his father said.

A bit of light seeped in through a crack in the heavy drapes. *Why are they drawn when it's so dark in here?* He made his way toward the voice, detouring around books and papers, and even a sleeping dog. His father sat behind his desk, steepling his fingers and not even rising to greet the son he hadn't seen in years.

"Hello, sir," Adam said.

"Well, well. You came. I wasn't sure if you would."

"Didn't you receive my message?"

"Yes, but I still doubted."

Adam's eyes were gradually growing accustomed to the dark, and what he saw before him shocked him even more than the condition of the grounds and house. His father looked haggard, and far older than his sixty-two years. Greasy hair hung in limp clumps, framing a face lined with the effects of debauchery and drink. Was he ill? Gout? Liver disease, to which heavy drinkers so often succumbed? Even worse, he might have the French pox.

"Don't just stand there, boy. Be seated." He waved at a chair, and Adam gratefully sank onto it.

"A brandy?"

Sighing with relief, Adam nodded. Brandy was the only thing that might get him through this. "Please."

His father rose, allowing his son to study him further. Slightly stooped, he moved slowly toward a table laid with all manner of decanters, bottles, and glasses and poured them both a drink. After handing Adam his glass, he remained standing and raised his own drink. "To your return," he said, reaching out to clink his glass with Adam's.

Adam rose for the toast, but made no response.

"Sit, sit," the old man growled. You must be wondering why I asked for this visit. How many years has it been?"

Adam slowly reclaimed his chair. "I don't know. Between the war and my European tour, at least four or five, maybe more."

"Since it will serve neither of us well to waste time, I'll get right to the point. It seems, due to some of my more egregious habits, I'm on the verge of ruin. Much as it galls me to ask you, I need your help."

"What's brought you to this pass, Father?"

A staccato laugh burst out. "Gambling debts. What else?"

Jesus. Hugh had been right. "How bad is it?"

The old man's eyes narrowed. "I told you I was facing

ruin! Are you blind? Haven't you taken it all in? There's no money left. I've let most of the servants go, except Wesley, Albert, and Mrs. Godwin. A man has to eat."

Mrs. Godwin, the cook, must be in dire straits if she'd stayed on after the other female servants had departed. And Albert, his father's valet, was doubling as a groom and God knew what else.

"What about Hugh?"

"Hugh does what he can, but he's as penniless as I."

"Yet you sent him to London for the season. To find a woman of means, I take it?"

"Precisely."

With a scowl, Adam said, "What are the chances of that? With your—and his—reputation, who would accept him, especially once word gets out about the state of your finances?"

"Chances are slim, but we had to try. There are desperate women out there. Desperate women with fortunes."

Adam shuddered. The idea of his brother preying on innocent young girls whose fathers simply wished to be rid of them sickened him. "I don't know how I can be of help, Father. I've little incentive to pay your debts."

The elder Grey tossed back the rest of his brandy and leaned forward, his piercing eyes pinning Adam to his chair. "I have a proposition for you."

Adam stared back at him for a long moment. "Let's hear it, then," he said, reasonably certain he would come to regret those words.

"The man who holds my vowels and mortgages, Sir William Broxton, has a daughter he wants to marry off. You're his choice. He'll forgive my debt if you marry the chit."

With a sinking feeling, Adam realized his father was speaking of the very man crucial to his chances of becoming an MP. But he wasn't about to agree to a marriage for a seat in Parliament. "Impossible." Adam considered a moment. "You want Hugh to marry. Let him have her."

"Sir William wants you, the military hero."

"I'm no hero, sir." Adam detested the label. "And I can't imagine why he would want his daughter to marry into this family."

"Her name's Eleanor. A pretty little piece."

A memory came rushing in. A yellow-haired little girl who had sometimes accompanied her father when he came to Longmere on business. "Ah, now I remember her," Adam said, rolling his eyes. "She's barely out of the school room. I must be a good ten years older than she."

"She's twenty, and marriages are arranged every day between people with far greater gaps in their ages than that. It's nothing."

"No. I won't do it."

His father went very quiet, and Adam recalled that this always occurred when he was at his most intimidating. The elder Grey made his way back to the drinks table and refilled his glass, not offering any to his son. "It is my understanding you wish to stand for election. I happen to know Sir William wants to get rid of that old fool he's been sponsoring for years. Through the baronet's auspices, you may succeed. However, without his help, you don't have a prayer. He owns the seat. Your marriage to his girl would assure your election."

Hugh must have informed him after the dinner party. Adam felt his political ambitions slipping away. Even so, he would not trade a seat in Commons for a wife he neither knew nor wanted. His refusal had to be irrevocable and beyond question. Before he could consider the consequences, he said, "I am recently betrothed, and under no circumstances would I consider breaking my engagement."

His father slammed the brandy glass onto the desk. The amber liquid splashed out and ran in lazy rivulets toward the papers scattered across the surface, enough of it that Adam could smell the rich, woody scent.

"You're lying! Hugh would have mentioned it in his missive—"

"It only just happened. In fact, I am en route to a house party at my mother's estate for a celebration. We have not even drawn up the marriage settlements yet."

The old man grunted. "Then there is still time to cry off, if you haven't put your signature to anything. You must think of your future!"

Adam struggled to keep his temper. "Don't pretend to care about my future. It's your own hide you're worried about."

If his words offended, there was no sign. His father went right on pressing his case. "You say you and your mother are having guests? Include Eleanor Broxton. You may change your mind when you've seen her. A prime article, they say."

Adam felt nothing but distaste at the thought of inviting Miss Broxton, but he needed time to think through this wrinkle in his plan. At least he'd be showing courtesy to the girl by including her. That might appease her father—his too.

"Very well. I shall ask Deborah to send round an invitation for her. But that will be the extent of it." He made his way to the library door, where he hesitated. "How much do you owe Sir William?"

"Over 50,000 pounds."

"Good God, Father!" Adam jerked open the door, his escape now seeming quite urgent.

"Not so fast, boy. You haven't said. Who's to be your bride?"

Without wavering, Adam named the woman who'd been haunting his dreams. "Cassandra Linford." He strode through to the corridor before the old man had time to react. Adam's lack of belief in ill omens notwithstanding, he felt a sharp sense of doom settle in his belly. How ironic that he'd thought his father might have a positive influence over Sir William. None of this boded well for his career as an MP, or for a future bond with Cass.

Chapter Ten

Cass sighed with relief when the Linford carriage drove down the long avenue with its canopy of tall trees overhead, the final approach to Deborah Grey's country home. Jack had ridden his spirited bay alongside them, so he had not been subjected to Cousin Louisa's ceaseless lecture on the unsuitability of Cass's attendance at the house party. When Cass had reached the end of her patience, she finally barked out, "It's done. We're nearly there. May we speak of something else?" Louisa had grimaced, but she said no more. When she'd dozed off at last, Cass had entertained herself by sticking her tongue out at her cousin and making some very rude and unfeminine gestures she'd learned from Jack and his friends when they were boys.

Deborah, Hugh, and some of the guests who had already arrived were stationed in front of the somewhat austere-looking house, awaiting them. Jenny, her mother, and Atherton. Adam, Cass noted, was conspicuously absent. Perhaps his arrival had been delayed for some reason.

"No introductions are needed, I think," Deborah said

when the stairs had been lowered and they'd stepped from the carriage. Atherton and Hugh bowed, and Jenny gave Cass a quick hug. And then Deborah took her arm and pulled her a little apart from the others.

"I am so pleased you accepted our invitation, my dear."

Cass smiled. "Thank you, ma'am. It was kind of you to include me."

"Not at all. My son was most adamant about it, and I agreed." She glanced quickly at a landau driving up. "Will you excuse me, Cassandra? I must greet the latest guests."

Who turned out to be Elizabeth Morgan and her mother. *Oh, no.* Cass had had the impression that Adam didn't care for Miss Morgan. The thought of competing with the younger girl, who had the advantages of youth, beauty, and a fresh face on her side, made her insides roil. Ridiculous, in any case. This was a house party, for pity's sake, not a competition.

After they'd all been shown to their bedchambers, and served tea and a light meal afterward, Cass decided fresh air and a walk would lift her spirits. If she left immediately, there would still be time to enjoy the spring sun before it dropped too low on the horizon. Jack was out walking with Jenny. She knew some of the others were in the drawing room, but there was no expectation for her to join them until dinner. After grabbing her bonnet by the strings, she hurried off down the corridor and ran smack into her cousin, outside her own chamber.

"Where are you going?" Louisa asked, managing to make her question sound like an interrogation.

"For a walk."

"Be so good as to wait a moment. I'll get my—"

"I've no need of a chaperone. I don't intend to be gone long or go far afield."

"Nevertheless, you should not be alone." She turned back toward her chamber to get her bonnet, and Cass tried a different approach.

"You look tired, Cousin. There's a group gathered in the drawing room. Wouldn't it be more restful to sit and have a comfortable chat with Jenny's mother and the other chaperones?"

Her cousin paused, thinking it over. Deciding if it would be proper for her charge to walk out alone, and if she was willing to relinquish this modicum of control over her. After giving Cass a suspicious look, she relented. "You may be right. I would enjoy that. See you are back in time to dress for dinner."

"Of course," Cass said, feeling like a child of Philippa's age instead of a grown woman. Sighing with frustration, she hurried away before Louisa changed her mind. If she wouldn't even allow Cass to explore the expansive—and perfectly safe—park by herself, what would the rest of the week be like? She'd be hovering every time Cass turned around.

Cass skipped down the front steps, her bonnet flapping against her legs. She paused a moment at the bottom to don her hat and admire the parterre gracing the front of the home. The intricate geometrical beds were planted with iris, lobelia, petunias, and gillyflowers. One section was filled with a profusion of blooming roses, white, damask, and deep red. Since rose was Cass's favorite scent, she thought they smelled enchanting. The parterre was beautifully designed and meticulously cared for, and the purples, pinks, and scarlets did much to relieve the stark façade of the Jacobean home.

Deborah owned a lovely piece of property, and Cass intended to explore it more fully another day. For now she'd make do with following the graveled path through the wood near the house. In the distance, she caught sight of Jack, Jenny on his arm, studying a temple that had been constructed near a pond. Since their betrothal, Jenny's mother had allowed the couple a greater degree of privacy. Oh, how she envied them that. The path would take Cass in a different direction, which was good, since she didn't feel like socializing, even with her brother and his fiancée.

No sooner had she stepped onto the path than she saw a man walking toward her. She couldn't see his face, but nevertheless recognized Adam immediately by his form and gait. Had he been out walking around since their arrival, deliberately avoiding his guests? He hesitated for a split second before approaching her, which made her suspect she was the last person he wanted to see.

"Miss Linford," he said formally. But his eyes were warm.

"Mr. Grey." Cass wondered how much longer they'd keep up this formality, though she was to blame for starting it in the first place, that day Jack had brought him home. Since their kiss the night of the dinner party, it hardly seemed necessary, except perhaps in public. Adam was wearing tight fitting riding britches with a blue, swallow-tailed coat. He seemed a bit disheveled, which didn't make him any less attractive. When he offered his arm, it was her turn to hesitate.

"You appear to be on your way to the house. I can go on by myself," she pointed out.

"Come, let me walk with you. It would give me pleasure."

• • •

When Cass wrapped her fingers around Adam's arm, a stab of that pleasure shot through him, and he barely registered it when she spoke.

"This is quite a spacious park," she commented. And then, "Adam?"

She was staring at him, and he wondered how many seconds had passed since she'd spoken. He gave his head a shake. *Pay attention, fool.* At least he'd caught the question. "Indeed. I'm very pleased this property belongs to my mother outright."

"It was in her family, I think?"

Adam nodded. "When Deborah and my father married, it was placed in trust for her. After she left him, she applied to the trustee for occupation of the house and grounds." He gazed thoughtfully down at Cass. "The townhome belongs to my father, however. He could put her out at any time."

"The night of the dinner party she mentioned that he allowed her to live there. That was how she put it. I wondered..." Cass paused.

"Go on."

"Well, I simply wondered if she was afraid he would reclaim it someday. If she worried about it."

"He hasn't shown any inclination to do so. Yet," he added. "Deborah, as I'm sure you have noticed by now, is of a very sanguine nature. If the thought has occurred to her, she's never said a word to me."

"Do you think he might?"

After today, nothing the old bastard could do would surprise Adam. Knowing what a disaster his father's finances were in, the only surprise was that he hadn't already sold it out from under her.

"Adam?"

"My apologies. The truth is, one never knows with my father, which is why I'm grateful Deborah owns this estate. She could live here year-round, if need be."

They walked on, and Cass said, "Are you planning to visit Sir William this week?"

"I am. Your brother wrote to him on my behalf, did you know?" When Cass nodded, he continued. "He'll be expecting me."

As they rounded a curve, a folly came into view, and Cass let out a little squeal of delight. A wide smile broke over her face.

"Oh, look at this! Do the wood nymphs reside there?" she teased, eyes sparkling.

"Only in my wildest dreams," Adam said. Her smile enchanted him, made his breath catch. "Let's walk around to the other side."

Stepping off the path, they wound their way through low-growing foliage until they'd reached the far side. He led her up the few steps into the small, dark interior. A circular stone bench had been built right into the walls, and they sat down on it. Adam let the quiet wash over him. A gentle soughing of the wind was the only sound, and Cass seemed at ease with silence, too.

After they'd rested for a while, he noticed the coolness in the secluded little copse. "Are you warm enough?" he asked.

"I'm fine." She pulled her shawl more tightly about her, though, and he knew she wouldn't be fine much longer.

"Do you ever think about our summers here in Surrey?" Adam asked. He didn't know where that sprang from.

"Sometimes," Cass admitted. "Why do you ask?"

"I always envied you and Jack because you seemed so carefree. Never a shadow of anything disagreeable hanging over you to spoil your happiness."

"It *was* a happy childhood. Aside from the fact that I always wanted to be included in whatever you and my brother were doing, and often was left out. Other than that one tiny flaw, it was close to idyllic, I suppose."

"Now, wait a minute. My memory is quite different. More often than not, we *did* include you in our jaunts about the countryside."

"Only when you took pity on me because I cried. I don't think I've ever properly thanked you for that. Jack did everything he could to prevent it. In hindsight, I can understand why and forgive him, but at the time I hated him for it."

In some ways, Cass was still that girl who used to follow them about and demand to ride and hunt and explore. But Adam was aware, too aware, of her physical maturity. Her undeniable loveliness. He had the feeling that behind the brave face she showed in public, a profound sadness lurked. The tragedy with her fiancé could certainly be to blame for that, curse Bentley, and the loss of both her parents. It wasn't just sadness, but the weight of responsibility, too. He did not understand why Cassie had taken on the education of her sister, and why Jack didn't insist on a governess for the child. He'd pursue that with her later, if an opportunity presented itself.

"What?" Cass said, startling him out of his thoughts. "Why are you staring at me?" Lord, this was the second or third time he'd been so distracted she'd had to prod him back to the moment.

"Forgive me. I was thinking about—"

"Your unhappiness as a boy? I had no awareness of it then, although I did wonder why we saw so little of your parents. And your mother didn't make calls."

Adam had no wish to discuss his father and mother and the shameful circumstances of their marriage. Cass knew too much as it was. So he went with his instinct. "No. I wasn't thinking of that." He glanced at her, holding her gaze, and said, "Actually, it occurred to me that I might be able to think of a way you could properly thank me. You owe me a great deal, you know, and your debt has accumulated interest over the years. It's no small thing now."

Adam had no idea how she would react to his teasing, so a thrill pulsed through him when she laughed. Her face flushed, she said, "You'll have to show me exactly what you mean."

He hadn't expected her to be so brazen. He felt his breath coming faster, his heart pounding. Offering her sensual mouth, her smooth, rounded cheeks, for his delectation, Cass leaned toward him, waiting. Adam desperately wanted to kiss her again, to feel her body with its tempting curves against his. But he hesitated because of the blatant lie he had told his father about her earlier today. She would never forgive him if she knew. He'd feel like a cad if he took advantage of her now. So although he trembled with the effort of controlling his urges, he backed off.

Shock and embarrassment registered on Cass's lovely face. And why not, since he'd been the one who suggested she repay her debt with kisses? She leaped to her feet, but he remained seated, knowing her effect on him was much too obvious in the light colored breeches.

"We had better get back, Adam," she said tersely.

Reluctantly, he rose. "As you wish," he said. They made their way back to the path, and because the silence was no longer comfortable, Adam said, "I've been wondering about how you're getting on, Cassie. You hide it well, but I fear you are troubled." He'd meant it kindly, but she didn't take it that way.

She scowled up at him. "You are mistaken, Adam. Why do you view me thus?"

Deuce take it, now he'd gotten too personal and made her angry. If she were still speaking to him by the end of this walk, it would be a miracle. But he plunged ahead. "Your fiancé's death, for one thing. That would be hard for anyone to bear at such a young age. By your own admission, you sequestered yourself after the tragedy."

"It's in the past. I rarely think of it anymore. I told you that the night of the dinner party."

"That doesn't mean you weren't hurt by it."

She bristled. "Of course I was hurt by it, but it is no longer uppermost in my mind. That is how I prefer it."

He bumbled on. "And—and your parents. They both died

since I last saw you. I wasn't here to offer my condolences. May I do so now?"

At that she softened. "Thank you. My mother's death was hard. She contracted an inflammation of the lung that could not be cured, and she died slowly. At the end, she stayed at Birch Lane with me, and I did all I could to ease her passing." She grimaced. "The one thing she wanted before she died, I could not give her. She was so distraught after Bentley's death, and wanted above all else for me to marry. For her sake, I was sorry it was not to be."

Adam had questions about Bentley, but now was not the time. "And your father?" he asked.

That actually brought a wistful smile. "He died sitting in his favorite chair, reading Homer. The doctor said it was his heart. We found out afterward that he'd experienced some weakness and had been warned to take more exercise and shed some pounds. He didn't follow the doctor's advice."

"If their marriage was as you described to me, he must have missed your mother terribly."

She nodded. "Jack and I think he died of a broken heart."

Adam found himself at a loss for words. And then Cass spoke again.

"The volume he was reading when he died...we lost it somehow. Jack and I sorted through all of Papa's books and disposed of more than a hundred—duplicates, mainly. But this particular book was one he had written, classical mythology for children. He had compiled the stories he used to tell me when I was growing up. There had only been a limited number of volumes published, and most were given as gifts. I must have inadvertently put it with the books to be given away." Her voice caught, and she stopped talking. He noticed she blamed herself, not Jack.

"So it was precious to you."

She blinked away tears. "Oh, yes. I helped him with it. To

get the wording right, exactly as he'd told the stories to me. It grieves me that through my own carelessness, it's lost to me forever."

Adam clutched her hand and squeezed it, but didn't say anything.

"Heavens, Adam, your questions are making me maudlin. Despite everything, I am not unhappy. Please do not think of me that way.

So he simply said, "I'm sorry, Cassie, if I misjudged. Forgive me?"

Her discerning brown eyes studied his face for a long moment. "Of course I forgive you."

God, how he wanted to wrap her in his arms. Resisting the urge was torture. Cursing himself for what Cass no doubt deemed his inexplicable behavior, he guided them toward the house.

· · ·

Get hold of yourself, you ninny. Cass had wanted Adam to kiss her so badly. Kiss her and pull her into his arms as he'd done before. And she'd been sure he was about to do just that. Although she had sensed he wanted the same thing, something had held him back. Maybe he thought her too vulnerable because he believed she was unhappy. *Good God! Do people view me as Miss Dirge? Is that how I appear to the world?*

But something else was amiss. The entire time they'd been together, she'd felt his distraction like a barrier between them. It had made her uncomfortable and overly sensitive, which was why she'd snapped at him when he accused her of being despondent. That and the fact that he apparently had some aversion to kissing her again. And now they walked in near total silence, only the chittering of a pair of squirrels disturbing the quiet. Thank God they didn't have much farther to go.

As they rounded the side of the house, Cass heard the unmistakable sound of carriage wheels. Surprised that anyone would be arriving so late, she said, "Are you expecting someone else?"

"One more guest and her chaperone, I believe. Pardon me, Cass. I must do the honors. I shall see you at dinner." He turned and strode toward the newly arrived equipage as the steps were being lowered.

She started to answer, but Adam wasn't listening. His attention was now completely riveted on the young lady stepping down from the carriage. She was a tall, shapely blonde, and looked even younger than Elizabeth Morgan, if that were possible. Adam had felt no obligation earlier, when she'd arrived. Perhaps the young lady was someone special to him.

He offered his hand to assist her on the last step. "Miss Broxton?" Cass heard him say. "And Lady Broxton," he said to an older woman descending the carriage steps.

Now it made sense. Sir William's daughter and wife. If Adam were to have any hope of gaining the House of Commons seat, he would have to cultivate Broxton's patronage. And what better way to do so than by courting his daughter? Leonora wasn't here, so she may be out of the running. Trying to ignore the prickles of jealousy stabbing at her, Cass hurried up the front steps before she was caught staring. Deborah must have been informed by a footman that the last of her guests had arrived, because she was approaching the front door as Cass entered. "Ta, darling," she said as she swished past.

Cass smiled but didn't answer. She dashed up to her bedchamber to prepare for the evening and get as far away as possible from the scene out front. No doubt she would be forced to endure a scold from Cousin Louisa on how little time she'd left for her toilette.

Chapter Eleven

Cass had no opportunity to speak to Adam at dinner, having been seated at some distance from him. Most of the ladies retired to their chambers after drinking tea. The men played cards and drank, but even they made it an early evening. On Sunday morning, several guests, Cass and her family included, attended church in the village.

For the remainder of the day, most were content with exploring the park, horse riding, or playing croquet on the broad expanse of lawn. Cass, managing to sneak away from Louisa, walked both in the morning and afternoon. It was on that second walk that she spied Adam with Eleanor Broxton on his arm. He appeared to be giving her a tour of the property. Well. Cass hadn't merited such attention from him; in fact, they hadn't even spoken since yesterday, beyond what good manners required.

So it was no surprise to her that she was once again placed nowhere near Adam at dinner. She'd probably have to shout if she wanted his attention. Or throw a piece of food. She vowed not to look his way even once. Miss Broxton claimed the spot on one side of him, while Jenny had the honor of sitting on the other. Cass was seated between Frederick Cochran, Deborah's gentleman friend, and Atherton. At least she'd escaped sitting by Hugh, who was sandwiched between Cousin Louisa and Jenny's mother. From what Cass could observe, however, he was charming them both between sips of soup and wine.

Cass made polite conversation with her dinner partners, although Mr. Cochran was disinterested at best. While she was attempting to converse with him, his eyes invariably strayed toward Deborah. Atherton's interests leaned toward politics, so she talked with him about the Perceval assassination.

"John Bellingham was the assassin, I believe," Cass said. "Have you ever heard of him?"

"Never. Reports say he was seen in the gallery of Commons recently, but there's no law against that. By all accounts the man made no attempt to get away. He admitted his guilt and sat quietly until someone had the presence of mind to convey him to the prison room."

"It was fortunate that the expected mob violence did not occur."

Cass was forced to break her vow and look at Adam, since it was he who had spoken.

"In some parts of the country, the good citizens cheered Perceval's death," Atherton said.

Cass shuddered. She knew people blamed the Prime Minister for the hard economic times, but even so, to rejoice over his murder seemed barbaric. The man had twelve children, for pity's sake. "His grudge against Perceval was over some perceived personal injury, which he blamed on the government," Cass said. "He wasn't connected with the Luddites, or any other dissenters." Sensing Adam's gaze on her long after she'd spoken, Cass felt her cheeks warm. Footmen were serving the second course, so she turned her attention to the portion of fish on her plate.

Atherton said, "Justice was swift. He'll never shoot anyone else."

"Rather too swift," Jack said. "Good God, the man was hanged less than a week after the crime."

"Not much time to mount a defense," Adam said.

Hugh chimed in. "He murdered the Prime Minister. Countless witnesses saw him do it."

"Nevertheless," Cass said, "I agree with Jack and Mr. Grey. Everybody is entitled to a fair trial. How could that have happened in the brief interval between the assassination and the trial?" She looked up to see her cousin's incensed gaze fastened on her. Louisa disapproved of Cass expressing her opinions too freely. She clamped her mouth shut, and opened it only after the beef course was served. From then on, she sneaked furtive glances toward Adam and company. She couldn't help noticing that Eleanor Broxton barely spoke a word, although it seemed both Adam and Jenny were trying to draw her out.

The ladies withdrew while the men drank their port, smoked cheroots, and discussed politics, no doubt. Cass found a seat by herself in a secluded nook. She half-listened to Elizabeth Morgan playing Mozart on the pianoforte. Perhaps Cousin Louisa had been right, and Cass never should have come here. After Adam had kissed her at the dinner party, she'd expected more attention from him, much as it pained her to admit. Yesterday, after he'd teased her and practically demanded a kiss—and she'd shown herself to be so willing—he'd unaccountably changed his mind. And probably, with his mother's help, made sure she was treated like the nonentity she was, both at dinner last night and tonight. Yet at times she had felt his watchful eyes on her. She was…not hurt, exactly, but certainly disheartened.

"Miss Linford?" A timid voice interrupted Cass's woolgathering.

"Miss Broxton, do be seated. And please call me Cass."

"Thank you. I'm Eleanor." She smiled shyly. "I-I feel a little out of place. I don't know anyone, you see."

"Indeed. I have been in your situation and felt the same. But you'll soon make friends and you won't feel so odd."

"I'm not sure why I was invited," she confessed, her blue eyes widening.

"Oh?"

"I might have an idea, though."

"And what is your idea, if you don't mind confiding in me?"

"I think my father wishes me to marry one of the Grey brothers."

"You don't say," Cass said, feigning surprise. "Has your papa made his feelings on the subject known?"

"No, he's only hinted. And Mama won't discuss it with me."

"And what do you think of the idea?" Cass asked, knowing she shouldn't be quizzing this naïve girl, but unable to stop.

"The older one scares me. He's rather frightening, don't you think?"

"Hugh? I wouldn't call him frightening. Some say he is a rake."

"I like Adam," Eleanor said, blushing. "The younger Mr. Grey, that is. He's handsome and seems kind. But I feel dimwitted in his presence. Tongue-tied. I never know what to say."

"Allow me to give you a bit of advice, then. Ask questions. Men love to talk about themselves, and you need only listen attentively and make comments or ask for clarification now and then. Adam has a keen interest in politics, so that is a safe subject."

"But I know nothing about politics! You are well able to join in the men's discussions. I envy that."

"Ask him about standing for a seat in the House of

Commons. He likes to talk about that above all." As soon as the words were out, Cass felt a twinge of guilt. Maybe she'd gone too far. But Adam's plan was no secret, so where was the harm?

"You seem to know him well."

Cass smiled. "He and my brother have been friends for years. I've known him since we were children, but I've only seen him a few times since his return from the Continent."

Just then, the men entered the room. Adam, the last one in, paused in the doorway as though looking for someone. Probably Miss Broxton. "Do you not think him handsome?" Eleanor asked, her gaze fixed on Adam.

Cass couldn't resist. "Oh, very," she said. "One of the handsomest men I have ever known. It will be a lucky woman indeed who weds him." She saw Adam walking toward them and flew up from her chair.

"Ladies," he said.

"Mr. Grey, please take my place," Cass said. "I must speak to Jenny about something."

"But—" He looked flustered. Good. Served him right. He wanted Broxton's seat, and it seemed the daughter came with it. They'd make a grand match.

Cass felt only a little guilty as she wandered off to find Jenny. The Broxton girl was sweet. On the whole, if she wanted to marry Adam, Cass felt she'd given her good advice.

• • •

Adam was having the devil of a time extricating himself from the clutches of Miss Broxton. It seemed she had an endless supply of questions to ask him, and when he answered, she fixed a wide-eyed stare on him, interrupting him now and then to make a comment or ask yet another question. So far they'd covered his plan to stand for Commons (had her father told her?) and moved on to his childhood in Surrey, his European tour, and now the health and well-being of every member of his family. At least she hadn't brought up his military service. Yet.

Under the circumstances, he should be welcoming the opportunity to engage her. And aside from impressing her father, she deserved his kindness. She was young, a guest in his home, and a virtual stranger to all. The problem was…he could not get a word in, even if he'd truly wanted to. When he tried, she spoke over him with another query.

Discreetly, he glanced over at Cassie, who was huddled with Jenny and Jack. A couple of times, he caught her slanting a look at him and Miss Broxton. Both times, he took note of her amused expression before darting her eyes away. Adam strongly suspected she'd somehow engineered his tête-à-tête with the younger girl. Why the hell else had she jumped up as if someone had shouted "Fire!" when he'd strolled over? Cassie was up to something, he was sure of it. And now all he wanted to do was make his escape from Eleanor Broxton and her tiresome questions.

Atherton saved the day. After he joined them, Adam bowed and excused himself. To his dismay, Cass was no longer talking to her brother and his fiancée. She had disappeared. *Deuce take it!* He whirled around in time to see her exit the drawing room. After a discreet pause, he left the room and caught sight of her nearing the end of the passage. He followed cautiously, not wanting her to know he was on her trail. After a few more minutes, it became obvious she was heading for the conservatory. Adam slipped in after her.

The scent of exotic flowers and citrus fruits wafted through the air, which would make it more difficult to locate Cassie by the delicate rose fragrance that always alerted him to her presence. She must bathe in some kind of rose water. *God, don't think about Cass in her bath.* To Adam, she smelled like a rose garden at dawn. Not that he frequented rose gardens at that ungodly hour, but still, that's what her scent reminded him of. The conservatory was in semi-darkness, and he paused to get his bearings. The swish of her skirt told him she was headed toward the open doors leading to the terrace and garden, and the moonlight streaming in guided him. He sneaked up behind her and grabbed her arm.

She let out a shriek. "Adam! You scared me to death."

"My pardon. I didn't mean to frighten you."

"How did you find me?" She frowned at his hand clutching her arm until he let go.

"I followed you," he said, crossing his arms. "I haven't had an opportunity to talk to you all day. And I was tired of entertaining Miss Broxton."

She made a choking noise he thought disguised a laugh. "You have no business following me around. What—why did you? Follow me, that is?"

God help him, he knew he shouldn't, but he took a step toward her. "Because I wanted to do this."

Adam coaxed her into his arms. It wasn't hard, because Cass seemingly had no intention of resisting; she folded herself against him with an audible sigh. Slowly, he lowered his head until his lips brushed her face, lightly caressing her forehead and cheeks, her welcoming mouth. He let go of her with one hand and gently rearranged strands of her hair so that he could kiss the shell of her ear. When a soft moan broke from her, Adam claimed her lips in an aching kiss, and he felt her go limp in his embrace.

He should stop this madness right now, before things got completely out of hand. But it seemed as though he'd been restraining himself for far too long. Primal urge and instinct were controlling him now, and his intense, nearly overwhelming desire for Cass. So instead of stopping, he lowered his head and kissed the rise of her breasts pushing up from her gown. She had entwined her fingers in his hair, and Adam interpreted that as indicative of her own need. He stepped back a little and tugged at her bodice. If he could lower it enough to free her from the confines of her corset, only her chemise would lie between him and her bare skin.

In the moonlight streaming through the glass walls, Adam could see the outline of Cass's breasts. Indeed, the lawn of her chemise clung to her form and only served to enhance his view. At that moment he wanted to consume her, but he knew he must go slowly with her. With the utmost tenderness, he held a breast in each hand, gently kneading and rubbing his thumbs over the tips in the center. Cass leaned into him, so that her breasts pushed more fully into his palms. She glanced down, curious, and when she lifted her head, he kissed her again, fiercely, hungrily. Her breath was ragged.

He'd been afraid she might be embarrassed, but he'd misread her. She was eager. He couldn't get enough of the softness of her lips, of her sweetly exploring tongue, of the smoothness of the inside of her mouth. Lowering his hands until he was grasping the soft flesh of her bottom, he pulled her tightly against his aroused flesh, still kissing her.

Finally, breathless, he released her and stepped back. Her eyes were luminous, an inner light shining through. She looked like a mythological being, a goddess. Aphrodite. He should not be doing this; he had no right. And then she launched herself back into his arms, and he laughed deep in his throat. "You like this, then."

"It's rather obvious, isn't it?" Pause. "You're not laughing at me, are you?"

"Never," Adam whispered. "It was an expression of pleasure." His lips found the silk of her mouth once again, while his hand inevitably found its way back to her breasts. "There are so many things I want to do—"

Wait. Had she spoken?

Cass jerked away from him. "Adam! Someone's coming. I hear voices."

The devil! She was right; he heard them, too. She was already struggling to tuck herself back into her corset. He helped her pull her stays and gown up. If it weren't so dark, Adam knew he'd see pink flaring on her cheeks.

"What should we do?" Cass asked, sounding desperate. The voices were coming closer. He feared the door would burst open any second.

"Outside," he said, grabbing her hand and pulling her in his wake. They raced out onto the terrace, down the steps, and into the garden. After rounding the corner of the house, they stopped, breathless, and Adam led her into the shadows under a grove of trees. "That was close," he said softly.

"If we'd been caught…" Cass said.

"There would have been hell to pay," Adam finished for her. "Your brother would have forced me to marry you."

Bloody hell. That was an insensitive thing to say. He'd blundered badly and he'd pay for it. How could he have gotten so carried away after vowing to keep his distance from her? He'd risked her reputation and no doubt hurt her with such a callous remark.

This wouldn't—couldn't—happen again. He couldn't marry Cass, or any other woman. So what the hell did he think he was doing?

. . .

Cass was glad it was dark enough that Adam couldn't see her face clearly. Not well enough to detect the hurt she knew must be reflected in her eyes. He sounded as if marriage to her would be the worst thing ever to befall a man. It was the way he'd said it, the emphasis he'd placed on certain key words. *Forced* me to *marry* you.

But not for the world did she want him to know how she felt. "What a disaster that would be!" she said, faking a laugh that came out squeaky and high pitched. Suddenly, Cass shivered. In those few words Adam had spoken, her aloneness was defined. Stars spilled into the night sky, their brilliance seeming to mock her sudden despair. *Oh, Adam, why* couldn't *we be happy together?*

Jack had Jenny. Adam had his pick of the myriad eligible young ladies and widows, like Eleanor Broxton and Leonora, who continually sought him out. With Cass he was merely dallying, because he knew her and assumed she would jump at the chance for some attention from him. It was a safe assumption. She'd practically thrown herself at him before, and flinging all caution to the wind, had done so again.

And whom did she have? Cousin Louisa. Yes, her cousin would always be there. They would provide companionship for one another as each grew old. In fact, since Louisa was so much older than Cass, she pictured herself nursing the woman through bouts of illness and infirmity— *Stop this right now, Cassandra Helen Linford. You're being mawkish.* Oh, why had she been so determined to attend this gathering? She had been happier, or at least more at peace, living in the country by herself. She hadn't really recovered from Bentley's death and the blame she'd heaped upon herself for his suicide. Perhaps she never would.

Her hair. She must see to it. Cass did what she could without a mirror, in the dark. She felt Adam's eyes on her, but refused to look at him. She'd meant to steal some time for herself, and instead she'd allowed Adam, who didn't even seem to care about her, to…to take liberties with her person. She was furious with herself for her lack of self-control. For letting her guard down.

Without even glancing at Adam, she said, "I'm going in."

He reached for her. "Wait! It's too soon."

But she did not turn around. Let him stew. What did it matter if somebody saw her? She would hardly be compromised if she were caught strolling by herself. When she reached the house, she entered through the front door and made her way to her chamber. Agnes helped her undress, and she slipped into bed. Before extinguishing the candle on the night table, Cass vowed to give Adam a wide berth for the rest of the week.

Chapter Twelve

Cass was standing before Adam wearing only her chemise. He ripped it off of her, top to bottom, so that she was completely naked. Then his wicked fingers began to massage her breasts. She gasped with pleasure, feeling heated and damp at her center. One thought rang in her ears. Kiss me. Kiss me. *But she couldn't quite see him, not the real man. Only some faceless figure she sensed was Adam. She waited, breathless, for his caress.*

"Morning, ma'am."

Who was intruding? Barging into her room while she and Adam were…Oh, no. She'd been dreaming, a most pleasurable dream from which she'd rather not have awakened. Agnes bustled toward the windows and began opening drapes. "Would you like breakfast in your chamber? Or I can help you bathe and dress, if you'd rather take your meal with the other guests."

"What?" Cass said, voice trembling, still lost in the dream.

"Sorry, ma'am. I'll come back in a bit."

Cass pulled herself up. "No, no, Agnes, it's all right. I

wasn't quite awake when you entered. I shall eat in my room," she said. "Tea and toast, please." At least that would give her time to compose herself.

Furious with Adam after what had transpired last night, Cass couldn't believe she'd dreamed of him so vividly, and in such an alarmingly erotic way. She realized he had disturbed her dreams more than once, she'd jerk awake, hot and sweaty, and, she was ashamed to admit, aroused. It was best to break her fast in her chamber. That way she could avoid seeing him for the present.

When Cass did venture downstairs, she noticed that Adam wasn't with the others in the main drawing room. For a man who was hosting a house party, he seemed to be extraordinarily unconcerned about his guests, who were discussing an afternoon jaunt. Indifferent to the plans, Cass opened a Fanny Burney novel, but was unable to concentrate. Eventually, the other ladies began penning letters, embroidering, or reading; the men departed to play billiards or cards until it was time for their planned outing. Cass hadn't seen Jack either, and when Jenny sat down next to her, she asked where he was.

"He's with Adam, I think. In the library."

Cass drew back, surprised. "Is he? Whatever could they be discussing for so long?"

"Can't you guess?"

Cass laughed. "Of course. The election. I should have known."

• • •

Adam sat behind his desk fiddling with a quill, shaping the nib with a penknife, while he and Jack talked, rather randomly, about his election to Commons. Jack had pulled down a volume of maps and was examining one page, running his finger around coastlines and borders, pausing every so often to give a location a decisive tap. Adam knew he and Jenny were taking a wedding trip to Italy.

"I assume you sent the letter about me to Sir William?" Adam asked.

His friend looked up and smiled. "Of course. I assured him of your many unparalleled qualities, reminded him of your roots here in Surrey, and let him know that you had my support."

"And?"

Jack had picked up a magnifying glass and was bent over, studying, from what Adam could see, the Amalfi Coast. "Got a polite note back saying he'd consider you and requesting the honor of your esteemed self at his home." He dropped the glass and looked up. "You'd better arrange it."

"Of course. I'll ride over sometime in the next few days." He threw down the penknife and scowled. His father's dealings with Sir William would complicate everything. Adam had been operating under the false assumption that the two men were old friends. Now he knew they were anything but. And when he paid his call, would Broxton mention his demand that Adam court his daughter? Even if he hinted at it, it would be damned uncomfortable. Maybe he should be the one to mention it, get it out of the way, but there was nothing he could say that wouldn't amount to falsehoods. *Damnation*.

"What's wrong?" Jack asked. "Is there some difficulty in talking with the man?"

Adam sighed. He supposed he'd better come clean to Jack. And that included everything, even the false betrothal to Cass. "When we met at White's, I mentioned my father wanted to see me."

When Jack didn't say anything, Adam went on. "The news wasn't good. He owes Broxton thousands of pounds in gambling debts."

"Christ almighty."

"There's more."

Jack's brow shot up. "Go on."

"Sir William wants me to marry his daughter, Eleanor. The one who's here at the house party. If I agree, he'll forgive my father's debts, and the old man can start putting money back into the estate, which desperately needs it. You'd be shocked to see how ramshackle it looks, Jack."

"I am sorry to hear it."

Adam took a deep breath and said, "I told him I was engaged to Cass."

When Adam's comment registered, Jack leaped to his feet. "The hell you say."

Adam put his hands up in a placating gesture. "Just hear me out. I knew I had to have a rock solid reason why I couldn't marry Broxton's daughter. Being engaged to someone else seemed unassailable, and Cass sprang to mind." She sprang to mind a great deal lately. And that wasn't all that sprang. Visions of what had happened in the conservatory the night before…but he shouldn't be thinking of that. At all.

Jack began pacing. "There wasn't a single other woman in that bacon-brained head of yours? You had to choose my sister, who has already suffered through one disastrous betrothal? Bloody hell, Adam. What were you thinking?"

"That's what is at issue, isn't it? I didn't have time to think."

"How did you leave it?"

"I agreed to invite Eleanor to the party, but said under no circumstances would I consider breaking my engagement." His friend was watching him closely, and he had a look on his face Adam didn't trust.

"I say, old man," Jack began. Adam had a feeling he knew where this was going.

"Have you never thought about marrying my sister? She's a damn sight too good for you, but you two used to be so close. I've always suspected she harbored a secret *tendre* for you."

Adam's mouth went dry. His throat seemed coated in ashes. "Beg pardon, but what did you just say?"

"You heard me. Why not offer for Cass? Make it real instead of a sham. She's a wonderful girl, and would be an excellent mother. Because of what happened with Bentley, she's a bit reserved, but she could be coaxed out of that, given time. And affection, naturally." He hesitated before going on. "You do have affection for her, do you not?"

Jack deserved to know his feelings regarding marriage. He had the feeling that after last night, Cass already did. "Of course I do. I'm fond of Cass. Always have been. But marriage is out of the question for me."

Jack lifted a brow. "But why? Given your political aspirations, I rather thought you'd be seriously considering taking a wife. Someone who would make a proper hostess for all those dinners and soirees you are going to have to put on once you're an MP."

Adam avoided a direct answer. "I'm looking for a wealthy widow. Somebody like Leonora." When Jack grimaced, Adam continued. "Not her, of course. But a woman experienced with planning dinner parties and balls, and one who would be content with…something less than marriage."

"What if that plan doesn't work out?"

"I may convince Deborah to take on the role."

A corner of Jack's mouth ticked up and he eyed his friend skeptically. "Opposed to love, are you?" he asked. "Just on principle, or has something happened to put you off?" His sarcasm stung, as Adam knew he'd intended it to.

For the first time, Adam felt his temper rise. He fought against it. "Not at all, for most men. Just not for me." The circumstances of his parents' marriage were not known to anyone, even Jack, and Adam wasn't about to explain.

Naturally his friend, probably half the *ton,* if he were honest with himself, knew his mother and father lived apart, and that Adam and his father were estranged, but that was the extent of their knowledge. Nor did he wish to discuss his certainty of becoming, as he grew older, like his father. The less said the better, about any of it, in Adam's opinion.

The rumors and innuendo had always been out there, though. Maybe Jack knew more than Adam believed, and he was goading his friend to make a clean breast of it. But Adam refused to rise to the bait.

"By God, you're a hard headed bastard," Jack said. He muttered something under his breath and lowered himself into a chair. "So what do you expect me to do?"

Adam hesitated. A plan had been forming all along; he simply hadn't wanted to come out with it. He'd need Jack's help to put it into operation. "What if I asked Cass to pretend we're betrothed? Just until after the election. Then, after a few months, she would cry off."

"Oh, for Christ's sake. What possible reason could she have for crying off? She, of all people."

"Women cry off all the time. Nobody need know the reason."

"You know the gossips, Adam. They'll have no compunction about asking her why. Especially after what happened with Bentley."

Adam waved an impatient hand at his friend. "We have plenty of time to come up with a believable reason, one that won't reflect badly on Cass in any way."

"Of course, this is presuming she'd go along with this scheme. I have a strong suspicion she would refuse." He lowered his head into his hands. When he finally looked up at Adam, he said, "As well she should. This can only hurt her."

Jack was right and Adam knew it. Feeling defeated, he kept his mouth shut. He would simply have to admit the lie to his father. It didn't mean he'd have to marry the Broxton girl. He could show an interest in her—hell, he already had—and treat her with respect. Maybe that would be enough to satisfy Sir William. And the more he thought about it, using Cass to further his political ambitions seemed crass. Jack's voice startled him out of his reverie, but it was his words that shocked.

"Ask her."

"Beg pardon?"

"Explain the situation and ask her. If she has any sense, she'll say no. But Cass has a mind of her own, and she's quite interested in politics. It may be that I've got it all wrong and she *will* want to help you."

"And I had just concluded it was a bad idea," Adam said.

"I didn't tell you, but she was miffed that we didn't inform her of your plans to stand for election, that she only found out at the dinner when everybody else did. She likes to be included in political discourse. You heard her talking about the Perceval assassination—I'd wager she knew more about it than most men in attendance."

Adam chuckled. "Probably more than most men in England. So you're withdrawing your objections?"

"I don't like it, and I hope she turns you down. But I agreed to support you. Put the idea to her and see what she says."

Adam was no longer convinced that Cass wouldn't be hurt, maybe irreparably. But she might see it otherwise, and desperation forced his hand. "Agreed. I'll need you to be present when I ask her."

Jack rose, a dark expression stealing across his face. "One stipulation, Grey. You must act the gentleman in all your dealings with my sister. Do you take my meaning?"

Adam stared, not certain he did.

"Come on man, you know what I'm talking about. If I

see you, or hear of you, taking liberties with Cass, you can be sure I'll call you out. Or I may not bother with that. I may just strangle you on the spot."

Adam was speechless. If Jack knew about the liberties he'd already taken with Cass, he'd be a dead man. It was possible that Jack's admonitions would give him the strength to keep his distance from her. Though being in the same house with her, seeing her every day would be torture if he agreed to this demand. Sadly, Adam couldn't seem to control himself when she was near. He was weak, cowardly, and obviously ruled by his cock. What if his rampant desire for her was an indication he was turning into his father?

"Don't just stand there with your mouth open. Do you understand? Your engagement will be a sham, so no stolen kisses, secret embraces, or touching of any kind."

"Fine," Adam bit out. "But people may think it a little strange if we're not the least bit affectionate with each other."

"They can go to the devil," Jack said, glaring at Adam.

"You're being unreasonable, but of course I'll honor your conditions." What choice was there? Adam offered his hand, and they shook on it.

Afterward, when Jack had left, Adam moved to stand by the window behind his desk. What on earth had he gotten himself into? How ironic, that he would be "betrothed" to Cass and instead of bringing them closer, it would drive them apart. He half hoped Cassie would turn him down, because that would be the end of it. He might be done for politically, but at least he wouldn't have a guilty conscience. If he put her out of his mind, perhaps he could forget about his chilling fear that the older he grew, the more Benjamin Grey's tendencies were taking root in him.

Chapter Thirteen

After a light meal, the group made ready for their excursion. Cass had not been part of the decision to explore the Cowdray ruins, but she had long wanted to visit the site, which had burned down sometime in the last twenty years. It was said that the park, and the ruins themselves, were stunning.

Adam was not present at the meal, but when she walked outside wearing her new midnight blue riding habit, she glimpsed him standing outside the stables, helping some of the other ladies at the mounting block. But it was Jack who shouted her name and motioned to her.

"Over here, Cass!"

Obligingly, she strolled toward her brother, who held the reins of a sweet looking little mare. "This is Minerva," he said. "A good mount for you, I think."

Cass had no way of judging, so she would have to trust Jack. She was no horsewoman; in fact, she currently had little opportunity to ride and did not sit a horse with any confidence. As a child, she'd always preferred to ride pillion behind Jack or Adam, and neither of her parents seemed to care that she wasn't developing skills as a rider. The trip to Cowdray would seem like nothing to experienced riders, but to her it would be daunting. She knew it was eight or so miles, so a sixteen-mile trip altogether. She dreaded it.

"I can see by your expression that you are doubting your ability, but have no fear. I've been assured by the stable boys that Minerva is docile, but very responsive."

"Ah, yes. Well, the best I can hope for is that she is also a good follower," Cass said, rolling skeptical eyes at her brother.

And then another, deeper voice intruded. "I'll assist Cass. Why don't you do the same for your fiancée?" Adam said to Jack. When had he approached? He could be as silent as a breath of air, and just as ticklish.

Cass couldn't be sure, but she thought Jack gave Adam a hard stare before he turned to help Jenny. What had warranted that? She had no reason to believe her brother suspected anything improper had occurred between her and Adam.

He gave her his most winning smile. *Why did he have to be so handsome? And why can't I be immune to it?* "Good morning, Cassie. That's a charming riding habit."

"Adam." She was determined to be curt. Even though Cass was pleased he'd noticed her smart new costume, trimmed with gold braid and frogging, she wasn't about to succumb to the first compliment he threw her way. Refusing to look at him, she got on with the business of mounting the horse. Unfortunately, to do so she had to place her hand on Adam's shoulder. Perched on the mounting block, she set a foot in the stirrup and pushed hard against him as he lifted her into the saddle. No man should have such solid, broad shoulders. Shoulders one could lean on. Lean into. *Stop it, Cass. Don't be a ninny.*

After arranging her skirts, she hooked her right leg over the horn and turned her body so she was facing forward. Only then did she look down at her left foot, which now hung suspended above the stirrup. Still, she didn't speak, only waited for Adam to adjust the length for her. To her chagrin, he did no such thing, but turned and marched off without a word.

"Adam! Where do you think you're going?" Cass knew her voice bordered on shrill, revealing her displeasure with her host to all and sundry, but she didn't care. She couldn't ride all the way to Cowdray without her foot in the stirrup. Cass caught a few questioning glances, but she ignored them.

He immediately changed course, circling back to her. "I thought that might force you to speak to me," he said.

"Yes, well so it did. You know I can't ride with my foot dangling."

"Did it not occur to you that your brother would have helped," Adam said sardonically, "or one of the grooms?"

Cass's cheeks warmed. Why hadn't she thought of that instead of humiliating herself by yelling at him? She felt his hand snake under her skirt and grasp her ankle. How dare he, in front of everybody? She knew he was trying to rattle her.

"Raise your skirt for me, my dear," he said, "so I can get to the stirrup." Of course, he made it sound as though he wanted to get to something else entirely. He chuckled, and Cass narrowed her eyes at him. But she hurriedly did as he asked, hoping no curious onlookers would notice. When Adam finished the adjustment, he looked up at her. She recognized by the way his eyes brushed her face gently that he wanted to make peace with her. That he was attempting to tease her out of her hurt feelings. She'd never met a man who could switch from flirtatious to serious so quickly. But she wasn't ready to forgive him for last night. Woodenly, she said, "Thank you, sir."

After testing the tightness of the girths, he looked back down for a final check of the stirrup. Did he yank the strap especially hard, or was it her imagination? Cass threaded the reins through her fingers and watched him walk away.

The ride to Cowdray began uneventfully. Various members of the party slowed their horses to ride with Cass, since she remained entrenched at the rear of the group. Exceedingly grateful that she hadn't yet flown out of the saddle, Cass didn't particularly care. She enjoyed watching the others, though it did not bring her any pleasure when Adam rode alongside Miss Broxton—who appeared to be a skilled rider—for a stretch. There seemed to be competition for a place beside the young girl. When Atherton joined them, Adam rode off. Next up was Hugh, the only one who made Miss Broxton laugh. And from what Cass was able to observe, she actually talked to him. More than one or two sentences. Say what you would about Hugh, he seemed to have an unerring knack for putting people at their ease.

When Jack and Adam cantered ahead, Jenny dropped back to ride alongside Cass. "How are you holding up?" she asked.

"Ha! Are you worried about me?"

Jenny denied it, but looked as if she might break into laughter. They rode in silence for a few minutes, and then Jenny said, "What's going on between you and Adam?"

"Nothing!" Cass said, much louder than she really needed to. Nervously, she reached a hand up to adjust her hat, and the reins, which she had so carefully threaded through her fingers, fell out of her grasp. Giving Jenny a panic-stricken look, Cass made a futile grab for them.

"Carriage approaching," someone shouted.

In seconds it was upon them, traveling at a fearsome speed. Minerva, spooked both by the other horses and the rattling conveyance, bolted. They'd been jogging along at a slow trot until then. Cass knew she couldn't keep her seat for long at this pace, especially without the reins. She grabbed onto the pommel. *Think, Cass!* What did she know about slowing a horse? She was too unnerved to gather her wits. Trees, hedges, fences all seemed to fly by, even though she knew her speed couldn't have increased that drastically.

Cass was dimly aware of surging past other riders and glimpsing shock on their faces. She ought to feel humiliated, but she only felt fear. Her mouth had gone so dry she could barely swallow. Her brain seemed frozen; the only thing that registered was the constant pounding of Minerva's hooves. One of two things was bound to happen—the mare would stop of her own accord, or Cass would go flying off.

She was suddenly conscious of a rider approaching from behind, on her offside. Risking a glance back, she saw that it was Adam. *Oh! Thank God.* He was all concentration and determination. Drawing slightly ahead of her, he leaned down and caught hold of the reins. Cass was disgusted with herself for noticing the play of his shoulders and back muscles.

"Whoa, girl," Adam said while gently pulling back on Minerva's reins. Skillfully, he slowed his own mount while coaxing hers to a gradual halt.

Cass was so relieved she felt faint. Spots danced before her eyes.

"Are you all right?" Adam asked, his brow furrowed. Beads of perspiration shone on his forehead.

"A little shaken up," she said. "I'll be fine once I'm off this horse."

• • •

Adam dismounted and lifted her from the saddle. Cass's face was pale and she was trembling all over. He had to fight down the urge to pull her into his arms and hold her tightly. Just to comfort her, of course. "Let's find you somewhere to sit," he said, taking her elbow and steering her toward a grove of trees.

"Water!" he shouted, "and bring a blanket." A footman rushed forward and handed him a jug. Another stepped in to spread a blanket over the grass. Adam helped Cass to sit, then held the jug to her lips while she took a few sips.

By this time Jack and Jenny had joined them. The others hovered at a respectful distance, waiting to make sure Cass was unharmed.

"Does anything hurt?" Adam asked.

She looked at the three of them, her smile tentative. "My entire body, thank you very much. It feels as though it's been jolted to hell and back."

Adam laughed. Poking fun at herself was a good sign. "You'll be all right. A little sore tomorrow, probably."

"My vanity is wounded, otherwise I think I'm fine." She smiled at Adam, this time a genuine smile, for him alone. Something deep in his gut turned over. Maybe she'd forgiven his callous remarks of last night. When she unexpectedly placed her hand on his chest, her touch burned through three layers all the way to his skin. "Thank you, Adam. You came to my rescue again."

"It was my pleasure," he said, brushing an errant curl behind her ear. "I am available for rescue any time."

Jack hunkered down, spoiling the moment, curse him, and said, "Cass, do you think you can continue on to the ruins?"

"May I have a few moments to decide?"

"Of course," Adam said. He glowered at Jack until Jenny touched his arm and whispered something to him. Jack grumbled under his breath, but walked away with his fiancée. Once they'd ascertained that Cass was all right, the others had scattered. So the couple did indeed find themselves with an unusual amount of privacy, although Adam knew it wouldn't last long. Jack would see to that.

. . .

Cass had been scared out of her wits during Minerva's wild gallop, but now, in the aftermath, felt almost euphoric. She had a ridiculous longing for Adam to kiss her. She'd like to crawl into his lap. Was she hallucinating, or at the very least, having another one of those wicked dreams? She could imagine how good it would feel to have his strong arms circling her waist while she leaned against his shoulder. The very one she'd been admiring such a short time ago, with its muscles bunching and relaxing. Even while in a state of extreme fear, she'd noticed it.

Cass tried to focus on something else she'd noticed. "My brother seems awfully hostile to you," she said.

"A brother's prerogative. He doesn't trust me with you." *With good reason.*

"It's not at all proper, you know. For us to be alone in this secluded spot."

"I don't give a damn. Do you?"

"Not particularly," Cass said, a laugh bubbling up. But immediately she went quiet. "He worries about me, you see. Since the…since Bentley—"

"No need to explain, Cassie." Then he didn't speak for a moment, and Cass thought he must be weighing her words. "Any brother worth his salt would wish to keep you safe. And I should be concerned about your reputation, too."

As much as Cass would have liked to remain hidden from the others, in the hope that Adam would kiss her, she knew it was misplaced. "I'm feeling better," she said.

Adam sprang to his feet. "Up you go, then." Instead of offering his hand, he stooped down and grasped her around the waist, easily lifting her to standing. She reached out and ran her hands down his arms before he could let go of her. He was staring at her with an unguarded expression, one she'd not seen before. It was the way she imagined Antony looked at Cleopatra. The way Paris looked at Helen of Troy. Then she heard Jack's voice, and the moment passed. Quickly, she and Adam stepped away from each other, as though they'd been caught in a compromising position.

"What say you, Cass? Shall we proceed?" her brother asked.

"Please don't ruin the fun on my account," she said. "I'm feeling well enough to go on, truly, I am."

"I don't like it," Jack said, looking skeptical. "After that mad dash, you're bound to be feeling unwell. And I'm not sure I trust your mount. What if we pass another vehicle? Or horses she's unfamiliar with?"

"I agree with Jack," Adam said. "I'll send a footman back for a carriage. I think it's unwise for you to ride any farther."

Cass humphed in disgust. "Why did you ask my opinion if you weren't going to listen to me? How much farther to Cowdray?"

"Can't be more than a mile or so," Adam said. "But still…"

"I'm sure I can ride that far. But I would much appreciate a carriage ride home." In truth, she didn't relish the short ride facing her, but she didn't want to be sent home either. It would feel like a punishment.

In the end it was decided that Cass would ride. Adam would hold Minerva's reins and guide her, making sure she kept to a walk. He would dispatch a footman to bring a carriage to Cowdray, and Cass could decide when she was ready to leave.

She was embarrassed about not being able to control her horse, but she couldn't regret it. What had come after, with Adam, had made her believe that in some small way he did care about her.

Chapter Fourteen

Adam and Cass moved slowly. Unwilling to take any foolish chances where she was concerned, he had urged the rest of the group to proceed at their own pace. The two didn't talk much, but they did pause to admire the view toward the town of Midhurst, and beyond that, the South Downs, chalk hills that extended all the way to the sea.

When they finally arrived at Cowdray, the others were already eating. Adam lifted Cass down. "How are you feeling?"

"Truly, I'm quite recovered. My primary concern right now is food," she said, the tiny mole at one corner of her mouth ticking up when she smiled. Had he noticed it before? It was enchanting. Adam couldn't pull his eyes away.

Cass seemed disconcerted, her eyes darting away. "I could eat a horse." She patted Minerva and said, "Not you, of course. You behaved admirably in spite of being ridden by a very incompetent equestrian."

God, what an idiot you are, staring at her that way! Adam grasped her arm, and they meandered toward the rest of the group, who had arranged themselves on old coverlets spread out on the ground. "What do you think?" He gestured toward the imposing ruins before them.

"I am in awe," Cass said. "They're stunning. Have you seen them before?"

"Never. I'm not in the country very often."

"I love the way they loom right out of the earth, like trees or mountains." When she glanced up at him, her expression was full of wonder. He took great pleasure in the way she could simply give herself over to the enjoyment of something like this. "What a shame it was destroyed by fire."

"Caused by someone's carelessness," Adam said. "As the story goes, the owner was away while renovations were being carried out. Sadly, the workers left a charcoal brazier burning, and the wind did the rest."

They'd reached their friends. Everybody fussed over Cass, who situated herself beside her future sister-in-law, and assured them all that she was feeling fine. Hugh happened to be sitting nearby. He brushed a few crumbs from his hands and said, "Are you certain, Miss Linford? That was rather a nasty ride your mount took you on."

"I'm quite all right, thank you. The carriage spooked her, and I'm to blame as well. I'm a very poor rider."

Hugh turned back to her. "If you would like some instruction while you're staying with us, I would be happy to oblige." While Adam would have loved nothing better than to threaten his brother's life if he tried to make good on the offer, he thought it unwise to do so in company. Besides, he was convinced the comment was meant to goad him.

Cass laughed. "Thank you, but that won't be necessary. At present, I don't have much need to improve."

Jenny had fixed food for them from the feast laid out for the picnic. Cold meat and vegetables, hard-boiled eggs, nuts, Sally Lunns, and apple tarts. Adam passed a plate to Cass, and without another word, she dug in, pausing occasionally to sip at her glass of lemonade. Hungrier than he'd realized, Adam tucked into his own.

• • •

Most of their party had finished eating and were now walking about exploring the ruins. Jack and Adam had their heads together at some distance, so the two girls had a degree of privacy. Jenny nevertheless lowered her voice before saying, "I'm not letting you off the hook on that question I asked earlier."

Cass pretended innocence. "I don't know what you mean."

"Just before your horse bolted, I asked you a question. In fact, I suspect that's what caused you to drop the reins, and for that I apologize." Cass noticed Jenny doing her best to suppress a smile, so she didn't think the other girl was overly sorry. "Surely you can talk to me. We're to be sisters before much longer."

Cass sighed. "What was the question again?"

Jenny groaned in frustration. "What is going on between you and Adam?"

"I told you. Nothing."

Jenny folded her arms and glared. "All indications are to the contrary, Cass. Out with it."

Having decided to be evasive, Cass shrugged. Anything she told Jenny would find its way to Jack, and that was the last thing she wanted. In fact, Jack may have put his fiancée up to this little interrogation. Cass dabbed at her mouth with a serviette and remained silent.

Jenny looked exasperated. "Cass…I have to ask. You're not doing anything, well, unwise, are you?"

"Is kissing unwise?" Cass wasn't about to confess that things had progressed considerably further than that.

To her surprise, Jenny laughed. So she laughed, too. In fact, neither one could stop giggling. Suddenly, two figures towered above them.

"What is so amusing, ladies?" Adam asked.

Cass and Jenny had only to glance at each other before breaking into fresh peals of laughter.

"Oh, let it go, old chap," Jack said. "Let's go exploring." He took Jenny's hand and pulled her up.

When Adam offered his hand to Cass, she rose and brushed off her skirt. They set off behind Jenny and Jack, but Adam quickly steered them in a different direction.

. . .

Whatever they'd been laughing at, Adam knew in his gut it had something to do with him. But he wouldn't press Cassie about it. Ladies had their secrets, just as men did. He pulled her arm through his and they strolled leisurely.

"Oh, look," she said. "Someone's sketching." A young man perched on a large chunk of masonry, probably fallen from the ruin, held a sketchbook in his lap, deftly wielding a piece of charcoal.

"I've heard it's a popular place among the arty sort. They say Turner himself has been here making drawings of it," Adam said.

Their party was not the only group visiting the ruins. Unfamiliar faces passed them as they made their way to the structure. "We must be careful not to disturb anything," Adam said. "From what I understand, debris falls from the ruins on occasion."

"Yes, I believe our artist is sitting on a piece."

They passed through the gatehouse entrance into the courtyard, and from thence wandered from room to room, guessing the function of each. The great hall was obvious—it was the only space large enough for the entertainments that would have occurred there. They located what they thought were the chapel, the kitchens, and what might have been private apartments. From time to time they heard voices calling out or bursts of excited laughter.

When they stumbled upon a deserted room, Adam suggested a short rest. He led her toward the cavernous space that had once been a window and helped her up onto the ledge. Rather than sit, he stood nearby and leaned into the cool, smooth stone. "Both King Henry and Queen Elizabeth stayed at Cowdray, I believe."

"Part of its mystique," Cass said, smiling.

They were quiet for an awkward moment. Adam thought about filling the silence with another trivial comment about Cowdray when Cass spoke. "May I ask you a question, Adam?"

"Of course. I'm not guaranteeing I'll be able to answer, though."

"You and Jack have left me out of your political discussions," she said. "Would you mind telling me why you want to stand for election?"

Jack had warned him, so he shouldn't have been surprised. But politics had been the last thing on his mind. Instead he'd been thinking how much he'd like to kiss her. She looked radiant, framed by the window, the sun highlighting the coppery streaks in her hair. He'd like to step between her legs and pull her into his arms, close enough to feel her breasts against his chest. She'd think he was daft if he did that now, however. He forced himself to concentrate on answering her question.

"It's simple. The war."

"Do you view the war as the greatest problem facing the British people?"

Adam recognized a challenge when he heard it. "Let's say

'greatest obstacle.' Until the war is at an end, the government lacks the money to deal with other problems. We need leaders who will pursue a course of action that can bring that about, sooner rather than later."

"And you're one of those? Leaders, I mean?"

"I hope to be, eventually."

"I see." She cocked her head. "What other causes are you willing to fight for?"

Adam stepped so close to her, he could feel her breath on his neck. "Do you not trust me to make wise choices?" Her irises were slightly darker in color around their edges, something he'd never noticed before. It was what made her eyes so vibrant.

She laughed a little. "I don't know if I trust you. You haven't answered my question."

"Ah, yes. My 'causes.'" He paused, as though thinking about this, but instead of answering, he leaned in and gently kissed the softness of her neck. She smelled divine, her rose scent driving him to a dazed distraction.

She laughed and twisted away from his mouth. "Adam! I believe you're avoiding an answer."

Smiling, he raised his head. "Sorry. It's just that you're… irresistible, Cassie." He put a hand to his head, as though thinking deeply. "Poor relief. Catholic emancipation. Parliamentary reform. Those are some of the issues I care about most. Are you satisfied?" Slowly, he slid his hands up and down her thighs. The slippery feel of her riding costume rubbing against her skin made him wish it were bare flesh he was stroking. He looked in her eyes and saw desire there, and was inordinately pleased. He whispered in her ear. "I forgot one thing, Cassie. Female education." He'd never thought it a nuanced idea before. But now it was about to drive him over the edge.

Her voice sounded raspy. "But…but do you really care

about those things?"

Chuckling, he took a step back. His nearness to her, touching her, wouldn't aid in addressing her concerns. Pacing, his boots scraping against the loose stones littering the ground, he tried to gather his thoughts. *She'll probably be sorry she asked.*

"Do I care that people are barely getting by? That children are laboring in mines? That workers are being replaced with machines? That to gain a seat in Parliament, I have to curry favor with Broxton?" Wound up, he halted abruptly and stared at Cass. "That there's no such thing as a free and fair election?"

He paused to draw in a breath, and Cass waited for him to continue, watching him.

"Yes. I care about all those things. Imagine if my mother, or you and your siblings, were destitute. The wage earner in your family had lost his job and there was not enough to eat. You were desperate. What would you do? Where would you turn?"

"The church, I suppose. But surely they can't help everybody in need."

"Just so. Because of the poor harvests of recent years, the church can't provide for everybody." He gave his head a shake. "Families are starving, so women turn to prostitution. Girls, some as young as ten, are on the streets. And young boys take up thieving and picking pockets. People know this, they denounce it, but nobody does anything about it."

Cass released a soft sigh, and Adam stilled and watched her. "I-I apologize, Adam. I misjudged you. You do care."

"Of course I care!" Anger that she'd thought him so superficial mingled with gladness at her admission she'd been wrong. He hadn't realized her approval was so important to him. And then it occurred to him that this was the perfect moment, when he was certain of her good opinion, to tell

Cass about the false betrothal and ask, beg if need be, for her cooperation. He'd thought Jack should be present, to help smooth the way, but if he couldn't do it on his own the plan was most likely doomed. Ultimately, Adam was the one who must persuade her.

"Cassie. I must beg your help with something."

• • •

Puzzled, Cass regarded Adam with equal degrees of caution and anticipation. He needed her help with the election. He was seeking her advice. At last she could be included in something significant, something that would bring her closer to him.

But why does he look so…guilty?

"You've mentioned to Jack that you wanted to be involved in my election."

She smiled. "Yes, I did. I do."

"A special circumstance has arisen. As it turns out, you are the only person who can help me deal with it."

Odd that she could be the "only person." Now her curiosity was piqued, more than it had been initially. "Go on."

Adam seemed to hesitate. He'd dropped his gaze to the rubble on the floor, and the silence stretched out.

Did he need her encouragement? "If it's my advice you want, I shall be glad to give it."

He looked up and directly at her. "Dearest Cass, it is not your advice I need, precisely."

He was stalling. After years of dealing with a younger sibling, she was able to wait a long time if necessary, though little doubts began to assail her. What could be so difficult to ask of her?

Adam picked up a small fragment of rubble from the floor and rubbed his thumb across its uneven edges. Finally he looked at her. "On my way here I visited my father. It was the first day of the house party, the day you and I came upon each other walking."

"Oh?" She remembered how preoccupied he'd seemed.

"I had not seen him in several years. As you know, we are estranged. But I thought if I were to stand for election, I would need to sort things out with him, at least to some degree." Adam moved toward her, stopping finally and putting his hands behind his back.

Cass wasn't sure if she was meant to respond, but when he did not immediately continue, she said, "And how did you find him?"

"Worse than I expected, but you need only concern yourself with the fact that I told him I was betrothed. To you." He watched her, gauging her reaction.

Cass felt something sink inside her. Was this some kind of monstrous joke? Perhaps she had misunderstood, or hadn't heard him correctly. "I beg your pardon?"

"Let me be perfectly clear. My father is in debt up to his ears, and the person who holds his vowels and mortgages is Sir William Broxton. He as much as promised the man that I would offer for his daughter in exchange for his debts being forgiven. I told my father I was engaged to you so that he would not press me to wed Miss Broxton."

"To me," Cass repeated dumbly. "Why didn't you simply refuse to do it instead of lying?"

"I tried to, I even suggested that the girl marry Hugh. Apparently Sir William wants me. I needed an absolutely unimpeachable reason to refuse. I wasn't about to trade marriage for a seat in Commons, especially since I don't plan to wed. Ever."

Oh. If she'd been in any doubt, that statement cleared things up. Keeping her voice even, she said, "But doesn't he control the seat you want? How do you expect to gain his support if you don't wed his daughter?"

"He can hardly fault me for already being betrothed, nor expect me to break off my engagement to gain his approval. That should put an end to his demands. But if he finds out I lied so I wouldn't be forced to marry Eleanor, he'll never accept me as his candidate." He threw the piece of rubble to the ground and moved closer to her. "I know I've no right to ask it of you, but would you agree to go along with this ruse until after the election?"

Cass bit down on her bottom lip, hard. She wanted to cry. She wanted to scream. But she would do neither. Keeping her emotions in check was paramount. Her hands clasped the window ledge with a ferocity that would no doubt break the skin. There must have been a dozen ladies of the *ton* he could have named, ladies who would have thought it a great lark to agree to such a plan, but when pressed, he'd named her. Had he assumed that she was so besotted with him, she would be the easiest one to persuade?

Now she was the one who stalled. *Keep asking questions. Be rational.* "And if I agree? What then?"

"We keep up the deception until after the election, at which time you will cry off. We would need to make a betrothal announcement, both here to the guests, and in the newspapers." His hand reached out and grasped one of hers, forcing her to let loose of the ledge. "We would have to act the part of a betrothed couple."

Turning her face away from him, she couldn't prevent a laugh from bursting out. But there was no humor in it. "Oh, Adam, did you consider for one moment the repercussions for me? What this would cost me? Another failed engagement. Another reason for me to be shunned by society. It would end any chance I might have for marriage and a family."

"Yes," he said emphatically. "Of course I did. And decided I should not ask this of you, but your brother—"

"Jack? Jack was in on this?"

Cass was pleased to see that Adam looked ashamed. "We—we were talking about my dilemma when the idea occurred to me. He thought it was a terrible notion, for the reasons you just named, and said he wouldn't allow it. And upon consideration, I agreed. I felt it could only lead to further pain for you. But suddenly, unexpectedly, Jack said, 'Ask her.' I had decided not to pursue it, but then he said those two words. 'Ask her.' So, I'm asking."

Cass didn't know what to say. She heard laughter and shouts from far off and could tell by the slant of the sun that the hour was growing late. And still she made no answer.

They both spoke at once. "Cass—"

"Only imagine, I fancied you wanted my political advice! Silly me." Cass found she could not look at him directly, so again she turned her head to the side. "It seems this is the best you can do to involve me in your election."

"It isn't like that, Cassie," Adam said.

Cass's fragile hold on her self-control was slipping away, and she could no longer pretend she wasn't hurt and angry. "Isn't it? 'Keep Cass in her place. The best I can get from her is to pretend she's a love-struck spinster whose dream finally came true. Nobody would have any trouble believing that.'"

"I've never viewed you that way, Cass. Never. And of course I would want you involved in every aspect of my election because I value your opinions, your ideas, your knowledge."

Cass jumped down from her perch on the ledge, landing hard on the uneven surface and stinging the soles of her feet. "But only if I give my consent to this scheme."

He looked miserable, like a man at war with himself. "Yes. No." Holding his hands out in a gesture of surrender, he finally said, "I don't know."

She nodded once, with finality. "Our party will be

wondering where we are." She'd decided not to give him an answer. Let him stew. She brushed past him, leaving him to follow behind her. Once outside, Cass saw that the others were indeed ready to leave, some already mounted. But her brother was pacing nervously, no doubt fighting the urge to go looking for her. The carriage Adam had summoned awaited, and he quickly moved toward it.

He helped her in and saw she was settled. Neither of them had spoken since they'd left their sequestered chamber.

"Cassie—"

"No, don't say anything," she said, cutting him off. He nodded, stepped back, and slammed the door. She thought it sounded like betrayal.

Chapter Fifteen

Adam cornered Jack at breakfast and asked him to come to the library after he'd finished eating. When his friend was settled in the chair in front of the desk, Adam got right to the point. "Yesterday at Cowdray, I spilled the beans to Cass about the lie I told my father, and I asked whether she'd be willing to go along with it until after the election." Adam looked down and began to fiddle with his penknife. "She was not pleased."

Jack looked murderous. "I told you from the start it was a bad idea."

"But when I wanted to back off, you insisted we let her decide! Why? Why didn't you tell me to go to hell?"

Jack crossed his legs at the knee. "Because I'm a fool, I guess." Narrowing his eyes at Adam, he said, "I thought you wanted me there when you asked her. I take it she refused?"

"She hasn't given me an answer yet."

Jack lifted his shoulders. "You've asked. Now give Cass some time to decide."

"I'll be lucky if she even deigns to speak to me again."

Odd that he hadn't been agonizing over the election and what would be a missed opportunity for him if Cass refused, which she absolutely would. What he had been agonizing over instead was a missed opportunity with Cass. He found that he'd been having a great deal of difficulty banishing the false proposal from his thoughts. Banishing *her* from his thoughts. Even taking Jack's caveat into account, the idea that he and Cass could behave like an engaged couple made him smile. Made his blood heat. Jack couldn't watch them every minute of the day, could he? Look what they'd done already, Jack be damned.

"If you weren't so stubborn about marriage…" When Adam glowered at him, Jack did not finish his thought. "Look, old man, do you want me to talk to her?"

Adam didn't even have to think about that. "No. She'll either speak to me about it or not. If she doesn't, I'll take her silence as a 'no.' I'm not going to press her; nor should you."

"Fair enough," Jack said before taking himself out of doors for archery.

• • •

Cass rose stiff and sore from yesterday's ride. She and Adam had not exchanged a single word last evening. She'd slept poorly, ruminating throughout the night about the false betrothal. At one moment furious with Adam for having the gall to ask such a thing of her, at the next wondering why her name had rolled so easily off his tongue. Did he like her? More than like her? But he'd said clearly, leaving no room for doubt, that he would never marry. As though it was some moral imperative or a guiding principle of his life.

Yesterday it had seemed easy to avoid a response. Adam's revelation had been a surprise, and she'd been sad and angry. She still was. She didn't see a future with Adam after the house party, so she supposed she could simply pretend the whole thing had never happened. But Jack's involvement changed everything. He would insist she settle the matter, and probably rightly so. She must give Adam an answer.

After a breakfast of toast and tea, Cass felt ready, albeit reluctant, to face the day. Agnes helped her with her toilette, and then she ventured downstairs. The house was quiet, deserted.

"Where is everyone?" Cass asked the footman posted in the entryway.

"Most are at the archery butts, miss."

He opened the door for her. It was overcast, and she could feel the humidity before she set foot outside. That would wreak havoc on her hair. She could already feel it crinkling up.

"Cassandra!"

She paused in mid-step. *Oh, no.* Cousin Louisa. They'd seen very little of each other since their arrival. Louisa had left Cass to her own devices, and Cass noticed her cousin actually seemed to be enjoying herself, especially while playing piquet with the other chaperones. Yesterday she had chosen to stay home while the younger set visited the ruins.

"Cousin." She tried to put some warmth into her voice.

"Had a lie in this morning, did you?"

Why did she make it sound like sleeping a bit longer than usual was a punishable offense? "I slept later than I intended."

"I've been neglecting you of late. Before you venture out, I wish to speak to you."

Cass averted her eyes so her cousin wouldn't see what she thought of that idea. "Very well." And then she waited, hoping Louisa would be quick and whatever she had to say could be done standing where they were. She expected a short lecture on the cut of her dress, or the way she'd been having Agnes style her hair.

"We'll go to the drawing room."

Resigned, Cass followed the older woman down the hall. When they'd settled themselves on the sofa, Louisa got started. "I warned you about setting your cap for Adam. But it seems as if you've not heeded my advice, and so I must caution you once again. You are making yourself look foolish, and in the end you will be hurt."

Cass's jaw dropped. What had her cousin seen or heard to make her suspicious? And who else thought she looked foolish, besides Louisa?

"Oh, don't look so shocked. I, and probably all the guests, saw Adam follow you from the room the other night. And observed that you did not return."

"I-I went out for a breath of air. I never saw Adam."

"Lie if you must, but I know the truth. I caught a glimpse of you entering your bedchamber. Your hair looked mussed and your gown wrinkled."

How dare she? "What are you implying?" The fact that she was right didn't make her inferences any less insulting.

"Must I spell it out?"

Botheration! The woman had the eyes of a cat on the prowl. Cass should have known better than to lie to her, with her annoying knack for flushing out the truth. She couldn't very well admit to the lie, however, so she forged ahead. "I'd been out walking, Cousin. It was a windy night. And my dress was wrinkled because I'd been wearing it for several hours." This was all true, actually.

"*Hmph.*" Louisa cocked her head and gave Cass a knowing, smug look. "Earlier in the evening, Adam spent a long time with Miss Broxton. Keep in mind that she is much younger than you, and it is very likely that Adam needs her family connections to further his career. He may be contemplating marriage to her."

Don't lose your temper. It's what she wants. "I shall be

the first to wish them happy, if that turns out to be the case. Although I haven't seen any behavior on either of their parts that would make me believe a proposal of marriage is in the offing."

"I understand Adam rescued you yesterday when you lost control of your horse. I told your dear parents many times that you needed to develop your equestrian skills." Then she narrowed her eyes at Cass and said, "Or did you do it on purpose, so that Adam would save you?"

Seething, Cass wondered how much more she could bear. She answered with her teeth almost locked together. "That's outrageous, Cousin, as I think you know. Now, if you'll excuse me, the others will be wondering where I am." She got to her feet and made her way to the door. Louisa was muttering something about ruining her reputation as Cass exited the room.

Practically running, she gained the entryway and strode purposefully toward the door, so fast the footman could barely open it before she flung herself through. Beyond a line of trees, she could see bonnets bobbing around where the archery butts had been set up. Which reminded her, she'd forgotten to retrieve her own bonnet from the footman. She didn't think it would matter, though, because the day was overcast and the air heavy with moisture. Rain would drive them all inside before long.

Going along with Adam's scheme might be crazy, but oh, how she would love to see the expression on Louisa's face when Adam announced their engagement. It would almost be worth it to agree, just for that one moment of triumph.

Cass approached Jenny, who looked up and smiled at her. Jenny should know what kind of evil harridan she was going to be taking up residence with after she married Jack, and Cass would be delighted to inform her. Although she imagined Jenny had already taken the measure of Cousin

Louisa for herself.

• • •

Adam stood off to one side, observing the shooting. Not under the ancient oak, where the chaperones were seated, but not among the guests either. He was surreptitiously watching for Cass. He wouldn't bring up the matter of the false engagement; he simply wanted to be with her, to see how she fared. Would she even speak to him? Did she hate him now?

His eyes wandered to the archers. Jack was showing Jenny how to shoot, but Adam judged his friend was using it as an excuse to press his body close to his fiancée's. Atherton was doing the same for Elizabeth Morgan, more decorously, and Adam was heartened to see that his friend seemed to be enjoying himself. In Atherton's case, this was indicated by the corners of his mouth slightly curving up. Women could be put off by him, but Adam knew he was, at heart, a shy man.

Another quick gander to see if Cass might be walking toward him. But she was nowhere in sight. Adam exhaled an impatient breath and thought he might have to excuse himself and find her. He wondered if he could sneak away without being noticed, but didn't think the odds were good. Just then, an unfamiliar laugh caught his attention. It was Eleanor Broxton, apparently amused at something Hugh had said. They were the third couple at the shooting line. It seemed prudent to wander over and make sure his brother wasn't engaging in anything untoward. He didn't trust Hugh for one minute with a young, virtuous lady. And besides, he should be seen spending time with Eleanor. He ambled over for a friendly little chat.

"Miss Broxton, Hugh," Adam said.

Both Hugh and Eleanor gave a start, as though caught out at something they shouldn't be doing. An uneasy feeling lodged itself in Adam's gut. He decided to ignore it for the time being. "How's the shooting going?"

"She's catching on," Hugh said.

Eleanor cast Hugh an apologetic look. "I'm afraid I'm rather hopeless. But your brother is exceedingly patient."

Adam tilted his head, surprised. He studied Hugh for a moment, considered making a sarcastic comment, but thought better of it. "I am glad to hear it."

And then, in the periphery of his vision, Adam saw Cass. "Excuse me," he said, abruptly turning away. Damn if she didn't look beautiful. She was barreling her way across the grass, her head high, arms pumping, obviously worked up about something. Damn, but Adam wished he *could* marry her. No other woman had yet made him regret his decision not to wed.

She headed straight for Jenny and Jack. It would probably not be wise to horn in on their conversation, but emotion rather than sense seemed to be ruling him. Cass was talking animatedly when he joined their little group. She halted in mid-sentence and glared at him.

"Good morning, Cassie," he said.

"Adam."

"Did you sleep well?"

"Tolerably," she bit out. Jenny discreetly grabbed Jack's sleeve and led him away. Thank God for discerning fiancées.

"Would you shoot with me?" he asked.

• • •

Cass hesitated. Was his purpose to harass her about the made-up engagement? She decided not. Adam looked a bit haggard, as if he, too, had suffered through a difficult night. Despite this, his appearance, as usual, was faultless. Olive green morning coat, ivory waistcoat, fawn britches that showed off his splendid thighs…*Oh, for pity's sake, Cass, stop it.*

She glanced over at the archers, weighing her chances of not looking like an idiot. "I don't know. I haven't had a bow in my hands since we were children."

"I'll help you," Adam said. He placed a hand at the small of her back and half-pushed her toward the shooting line. She wanted to say no, to refuse him for once, but she'd have to explain, which would lead to an argument. Everybody would hear. And it would look odd if she flounced off by herself afterward.

A footman handed Adam a bow and quiver of arrows. He withdrew one and threw the quiver to the ground. After nocking an arrow, he demonstrated the proper form. "Hold the bow like so. And your stance should look thus."

Cass couldn't take her eyes off him, the way his shoulders and back muscles made his coat look like a second skin when he pulled the bowstring back. She couldn't conceive of why it hadn't ripped.

"Cassie," Adam said, and she remembered she was vexed with him. He was holding out the bow.

She accepted it, letting the arrow fall to the ground, and tried to replicate what Adam had shown her. Her feet seemed to remember where to place themselves, parallel to each other, and she squared her shoulders and adjusted her posture. Yes, her body knew what to do. She raised the bow, grasped the string, and pulled back toward her cheek. She'd forgotten how much strength it required.

"It works better with an arrow," Adam said.

Cass's cheeks warmed. "I'm merely practicing. I'll let you know when I'm ready." She pretended to weigh the bow, test the string, and practice her stance for a few minutes before accepting an arrow, while Adam watched, an amused look on his face. Poised to take her shot, Cass grunted when he stepped in at the last second. He placed his hands on her shoulders and pushed down.

"You're hunching your shoulders. Let them relax."

Did he truly believe she'd be able to concentrate while he hovered, watching her, touching her? Cass's first shot went wide of the mark. It was Adam's fault; he'd thrown off her rhythm. "I think my shot would have been true if you hadn't interfered," she said, giving him a petulant look.

"*Unh huh*," he drawled. "Try another."

Two more shots had the same result; a third fell to the ground about ten feet from where they were standing. Cass, already in a foul humor, was all set to slam the bow to the ground and storm off when she felt Adam's hands on her shoulders and his breath tickling her ear. He kneaded her muscles, saying, "You're tense, Cassie. You must relax or you'll never hit the mark."

She'd noticed that Louisa had joined the others, and it wouldn't shock her at all if her cousin marched over to them and pried Adam's hands off her. "Adam, the chaperones will see."

"Has that woman done something to upset you?" he asked, and she could tell by his tone of voice that he was genuinely concerned. It touched her.

She relaxed her face. "Louisa? No more than usual."

He spun her around. "But something? Tell me. I'll speak to Jack, or her, if you say the word."

"I appreciate your concern, truly I do, Adam. But leave it. She's my cross to bear."

"I don't like her having any authority over you."

"Nor do I, but I've learned how to manage her. Most of the time, anyway. Please, do not think of it." She wriggled out of Adam's grasp and resumed her shooting posture. Focusing on the mark, she kept her shoulders down, took her shot, and *voila*! She hit the target! Not in the center, but that didn't matter. She did a little dance of excitement and laughed up at Adam, who gave her a melting smile. And the look. The Antony-at-Cleopatra look.

Oh, damn. Why? Why was he looking at her like that? Adam didn't truly care for her, did he? He only needed her to make things right with Broxton. To help him win an election. If she did not go along with the deception, it was highly likely she would never see him again after the party, except coincidentally. Louisa was probably right; Cass herself had speculated that Adam would marry Eleanor Broxton for political reasons. She thrust the bow at him, so roughly he nearly dropped it. "Please excuse me."

"Cass, wait!" He followed her, reaching for her arm when he caught up. "Let me escort you."

"I'd prefer to be on my own, if it's all the same to you," she said. "We'd need a chaperone, and that's the last thing I want right now." Without waiting for a response, she dipped a half-hearted curtsy and backed away before he could stop her. After she'd walked for a few minutes, she turned around to make sure he wasn't following her. He hadn't moved, but he was watching. Cass intended to head for the lake she'd glimpsed when she and Adam were walking the other day. Momentarily, her path would veer off and she'd be out of his line of sight.

Chapter Sixteen

Adam watched Cass as she stormed off. If she didn't want his company, he couldn't force himself on her. Clearly, he'd hurt her yesterday, nor was she of a mind to forgive him. Hands on hips, he lowered his head and stomped the ground, like a damned horse. Horse's ass was more like it. He never should have asked her. He could see now it was an insult. Telling her he wanted her to pretend to be his fiancée in one breath; in the next, proclaiming loudly that he could never marry. As though saying, "Don't get your hopes up." He cringed just thinking about how it must have sounded to her.

If he was truthful with himself about his motives, he'd admit that part of the reason he wanted her to assent to the plan—a big part of the reason—was so that they could act the part of a betrothed couple. They would be granted more time alone. He could spirit her away to somewhere private and kiss her senseless. Hell, more than kiss her. They'd already progressed to the "more" part, and she'd seemed as passionate about it as he was.

Jesus. His nearly uncontrollable desire for Cass made

him feel as debauched as his father. Or Hugh. Cass deserved marriage and a family, and he was not suited for either. He had to move on. Figure out how to square things with Broxton and get that seat in Commons.

• • •

Cass resisted the urge to look back at Adam, instead concentrating on her destination. The close, muggy air seemed to enfold her, and she guessed the clouds were deviously scheming to pelt her with rain. Nevertheless, she determined to keep on, turning onto a stony path bordered by sweet-scented lavender beds on either side. It led directly to the lake. *Crunch, crunch*. She could feel the stones digging into her feet through her slippers. The lake was only an acre or so, and when she spied a small Grecian temple in the distance, a folly, she decided to keep walking round the perimeter. She moved to the grassy verge, to get away from the stones. There was no lightning, and the few rumbles of thunder that sounded from far off did not seem to pose an immediate threat.

She passed a small boat tied up to a dock and smiled, remembering the rowing competitions of those long ago summers with Adam and Jack. Two of them would race, and the winner would row against the third. She'd even won once or twice, although she suspected it wasn't due to her rowing prowess. If only life could be as simple as it was then. They had all changed since those days of innocence—battered by war, death, and loss. When she'd decided to accept the invitation to the house party, Cass had hoped she'd been given another chance at happiness.

But after yesterday, she felt the thin thread of hope unraveling, disappearing. She could see that her desire, her need, to trust Adam was misplaced. He didn't want to marry. Although she hoped she would find a decent man, one who could forgive her past, she could see now what a pipe dream that was. She'd made a disastrous mistake the first time, and just when she'd thought something might develop with Adam, he'd set her straight. It was for the best. Cass had yet to conquer her guilt over Bentley's death. Her feeling that she was somehow responsible. She had no business contemplating another union.

But did a decision not to marry, on both their parts, mean any chance of physical pleasure was impossible? Thanks to Adam's recent attentions, Cass knew that such pleasures were myriad. There was much she had yet to experience. She understood the generalities of lovemaking, but not the details. Except for the little Adam had shown her. And she wanted more, God help her. With him, to be precise. If she could never have love and marriage and a family, did she have to give *that* up too?

Not if she agreed to the false betrothal. It was common knowledge that engaged couples were permitted more freedoms with each other. They were often allowed to wander off without a chaperone, and who knew what happened then? Anything that both of them wanted, Cass imagined. Well, she knew what she wanted. She was young, healthy, and extremely attracted to Adam. She wanted him to make love to her. The mere thought of it sent a shiver across the back of her neck and made her breathless, shocked at her own boldness. But it seemed to be what Adam wanted, too, judging from his actions of late. And as long as they were discreet and careful…where was the harm?

She laughed out loud at the thought, just as big drops of rain started pelting her. When had the sky gotten so dark, the storm so close? Regretting the lack of her bonnet, she began to run. She was not far from the temple and managed to hurry up the few stairs and under the dome before the full fury of the storm broke. Good heavens, the folly was quite elaborate.

The columns were thick enough to hide behind. And of all things, there was a settee inside. Cass sat down and waited for the storm to pass.

• • •

When it started pouring, Adam knew he'd better find Cass.

He asked Jack to usher everybody into the house while he went in search of her. His friend looked for a moment like he might argue, but then gave a short nod and did as Adam asked.

When he'd last seen Cass, she was turning off onto the path leading to the lake. He now assumed that had been her destination, so that was where he headed. Rain sheeted down, and the wind blew it sideways. He could scarcely see two feet in front of him. The ground squelched every time his booted feet landed. Without warning, the water loomed up before him.

He slid to a stop and shouted. "Cass!" He strained his eyes, but could see nothing. Cupping his hands around his mouth, he tried again. "Cassie!" No answer. Then, in a flash of lightning that struck all too close, Adam got a view of the dock. He had a terrified moment when he feared she might have taken the boat out, but thank God it was still tied up, the waves tossing it about.

A loud clap of thunder, and he nearly jumped out of his skin. *Don't panic, man.* He knew Cassie possessed a good dose of common sense above all else. *What to do?* For lack of a better idea, he began running along the perimeter of the lake, hoping to spot her, calling her name every few seconds. When lightning streaked the sky again, bringing the temple into relief, he breathed easier. Surely she had taken refuge there.

Adam dashed over the rain-slicked grass and up the steps. And there she sat, calm as could be, as though he hadn't been worried to death.

"Adam. Hello."

He rested a hand against one of the columns, panting. "Good God, Cass. I was so worried."

Rising, she said, "I'm fine." And then she laughed, apparently at his expression. "Truly."

Fine. She appeared more than fine. Her damp clothing clung provocatively to every curve of her body. He had to force himself to quit staring.

"Are you warm enough? Let me give you my coat. The lining is dry." She protested, but he quickly slipped it off and wrapped it around her shoulders. They watched the rain for a moment, which was now falling steadily. The worst of the storm had moved off.

"I love the pattering of rain. It's such a lovely, comforting sound," Cass said.

God, this is torture. "Yes. I love waking up to it." He fished in his pocket for a handkerchief and blotted his wet face. Cass was looking at him very intently, as though she wanted to say something. He waited, and finally she spoke.

"Adam, I have an answer for you."

"An answer?" He was at a loss.

Cass laughed again. He loved the sound, so he smiled at her. Some tendrils of her hair had broken loose at her nape, and he couldn't stop himself from reaching out and touching them. Lifting a strand and smoothing it, then laying it back across her skin.

"You asked me a question yesterday. I'm ready to give you an answer."

The light dawned, and he shook his head. "Oh, no, Cass. Please, accept my apology for even broaching the subject. It was a terrible idea, and I was a coward and a fool for telling my father the lie in the first place."

She cocked her head at him. "Perhaps it was not such a terrible idea after all. There might be some advantages to the plan."

He studied her face and couldn't discern any hidden meaning. "To help me get elected, you mean. I can figure out another way. Maybe Broxton—"

She spoke over him. "You said we would have to act like a betrothed couple." She turned her face away, as though embarrassed. "What did you have in mind, exactly?"

Adam hesitated, not wanting to make a mistake. Was he misinterpreting the situation? *Go slowly, man.*

"I think you know what that means, Cassie." He stepped closer. She did not retreat. "We could spend time together, show affection to each other. It's almost expected. Because of our betrothal, we could go off by ourselves. I could kiss you, possibly do…other things." He wasted no time in casting aside the promise he'd made to Jack about this very thing.

"Like what we've been doing?" She removed his coat and laid it on the settee before coming back to stand close to him.

Adam could barely breathe, and his cock was as hard as the marble they were standing on. He leaned in and brushed a kiss across her lips. She closed her eyes and fell against him. "Are you saying what I think you're saying, Cass?"

"We're speaking in riddles, aren't we?" She put her palms against his chest and pulled away a little. "You don't wish to marry. I don't know your reasons, and you don't need to explain them to me." She held up a hand when he tried to interrupt. "No, it's all right. It may surprise you to know that I don't wish to marry either."

Adam was stunned. "But I thought that was why you returned to town. To find a husband. Wasn't it?"

"It is what Jack wants." She smiled wryly. "Sometimes I think I want it, too. But I have barely gotten over the trauma of what happened with my fiancé. I'm terrified of placing trust in another man. You included."

"I see."

"You probably don't, any more than I understand your resistance to marriage. My guess is that it has something to do with your father. Understanding that much will suffice. And you will have to be content with not knowing the particulars of Bentley's death."

"In order to…?"

"In order for us to be lovers."

That did it. "Oh God, Cassie. Are you sure about this?" When she nodded, he drew her into his arms and captured her mouth in a tender, evocative kiss. He wanted her to know all he was feeling. The joy and the excitement. Something deep in his core he couldn't begin to express with words. She opened her sweet mouth, giving up a part of herself to him, letting him in. After a moment, he felt the sun's rays on his back. "Look. The sun has come out. It's a good sign."

Then an unwelcome thought intruded. "Your brother. He'll be out here looking for us any minute."

"No. They were spending the rest of the day in the village. Some of the others, too. I'm certain they would have already gone."

"If you say so."

Cass laughed, and he spun her around and began unfastening buttons. Her dress dropped to the ground in a yellow heap, and then he got to work on her stays. Done. Her chemise felt dry, the moisture not having soaked through the other layers. When he turned her back around, the breath was sucked out of him. Not because she stood before him half naked, but because of the scar beneath her collarbone, on the left side. He'd been in battle, and he recognized a wound from a ball when he saw one. How in the name of Christ had Cass been shot?

His first thought was that he wanted to make absolutely sure she did not feel any less beautiful because of it. And his second: Who did this to her? He knew this wasn't the time to press her, but he intended to find out.

Chapter Seventeen

Despite the sun's reappearance, Cass couldn't help trembling. Adam was looking at her in the strangest way. Then he smiled, slow and simmering, and said, "Do you know how incredibly lovely you are?"

Cass shook her head. She'd never thought of herself as any great beauty. But from the awed look on Adam's face when he gazed at her, she was convinced of his sincerity. And being in his arms felt…perfect. She lifted her face and looked at him, her gaze filled with all the pent-up feelings for Adam she'd kept hidden for so long. She was sure her eyes shone with wanting him.

He seemed to return the feeling. When he covered her lips with his, she lost the ability to think. He coaxed her mouth open and she met his tongue with her own. His kiss stole her breath, her sense, her reason. Adam drew back and pressed kisses along her jaw, and on the tender skin below. In a frenzy, Cass tugged his shirt out of his waistband and slid her hands up his bare chest, skimming over its planes and curves. He felt splendid. Muscled and smooth, just as she'd imagined. Adam's breathing hitched with her touch.

He lowered the straps of her chemise over her shoulders, then slid his hands over the delicate lawn and bared her breasts. If he let go of her, the chemise would slide all the way off and she would be completely naked. He seemed to understand what she was thinking because he said, "I won't let go of you, love." He kissed his way from her shoulders down to the tips of her breasts, and then, to her surprise, took one of her nipples into his mouth and sucked gently.

It was a staggering sensation. She felt it in her belly, and lower, between her legs. It made her weak, and her knees started to buckle. Suddenly, Adam's body tensed and he drew back. She heard him mutter something under his breath, which she thought was "Bloody hell." He pulled the straps of her chemise up around her shoulders, then moved to retrieve her stays, but she grasped his arm. "What's wrong, Adam?"

He gave her a sheepish smile. "*This* is wrong, Cass. I don't want to make love to you here, where any of our guests may decide to take a stroll. We can't be sure they've all gone to the village." His hand drifted up and caressed her cheek, a gesture so sweet and intimate Cass could have wept. "I want our first time to be in a bed, where I can worship you properly."

How could she not smile at that? "You're right, of course." She felt a little foolish for her eagerness, her almost mad desire, to have him take her right here and right now.

He pulled her against him, pressing her against his maleness. "In case you're in doubt of my desires…can you feel that, Cassie? I hope it proves how difficult this is for me."

She gave an embarrassed laugh. "Yes, yes, I see. Now help me get dressed before I make a complete fool of myself."

Walking leisurely back toward the house, they discussed what would come next. "The first thing I must do is talk to Jack. Tell him you're willing to cooperate. Let's hope he hasn't changed his mind about the scheme."

When put in those terms, "willing to cooperate" and "scheme," the whole thing sounded so cold. So opposite of what she'd felt only a short time ago, and it made her think that perhaps they were making a mistake. But she'd known it was a sham, almost a business arrangement, and she must force herself to think about it as such, except for the intimate moments. Then it would be different. "Just to make sure we understand each other," Cass said. "I want to see you get elected, Adam. I'll do whatever I can to help bring that about."

"And I meant it when I said I wanted you involved. You'll be a real asset to my campaign."

"What about your mother? Will you tell her the truth?"

"Absolutely not. I love her, but I'm not sure she could be trusted with the truth. She's in society so much. One slip of the tongue is all it would take, and the news would be all over London in a matter of hours."

Cass nodded and Adam continued. "We can tell our guests tonight at dinner, and I'll send announcements to the papers tomorrow." He paused for a beat. "We may have some difficulty with Jack."

She looked at him, puzzled. "In what way? You said it was his idea to leave the decision to me, which is a miracle of sorts."

Adam stopped abruptly. "He warned me about taking liberties with you. Said there were to be no 'stolen kisses or secret embraces,' or something to that effect, or he'd call me out. When I tried to reason with him, told him that people would expect us to act like an engaged couple, he said they could go to the devil."

"Oh, dear," Cass said. "We'll simply have to be circumspect in his presence. It's not as though we'll be doing anything unseemly in public."

"Don't be so sure about that," Adam said, laughing. "I haven't demonstrated much self-control where you're concerned." Cass thought about the two of them exchanging intimate looks, meaningful smiles, even touches, all with other people about. It made her quiver all over.

"As I said before, he is quite right to worry about your reputation. I respect him for that." He took her by the shoulders and studied her face. "I don't want you hurt by this, Cassie. There is still time to change your mind."

"No," she said. "My mind is made up. I want this, Adam." *I want you.*

. . .

Adam decided to make the announcement in the drawing room, before the assembled guests went in to dinner. After they had returned from the lake, he sought out Deborah while Cass spoke to her disagreeable cousin. He'd yet to have a chance to ask Cass how Louisa had taken the news. Deborah had been thrilled. With tears in her eyes, she'd told Adam that Cass was the very girl she'd hoped he would marry. He could tell she was dying of curiosity, but he cut off any questions, promising he'd explain everything later.

He'd had to wait for most of the day to tell Jack, since he and Jenny had not returned from their shopping expedition to the village until late. Adam asked one of the footmen to alert him when they arrived, and after a cursory greeting, he ushered Jack off to the library. When he'd poured brandies for them both, he said, "Cass has agreed to go along with the false betrothal."

"I don't like it," Jack said. "It could spell ruin for her."

"Have some faith in me, Jack. I swear I won't let that happen." Adam perched on the edge of the desk and studied his friend. "You don't seem surprised."

"I told you she might agree. Not to take anything away from your charms, but Cass does love politics. This will be her first chance to be involved rather than merely reading about it. Louisa will accuse her of neglecting her duties to Pippa because of this."

"But surely the expectation was that Cass would eventually marry. Isn't it time your sister had a governess?"

"Believe me, I have tried to bring Cass around to that view many times. She promised our mother, you see, that she would always look after Pip. She takes it very seriously. But Louisa has a habit of reminding Cass of her duty, and her harping on it doesn't sit well. Did she mention it to you?"

"No, just that she dreaded telling your cousin. I don't like that woman lording it over Cass. She told me that Louisa was her 'cross to bear.' It's not right."

"Cass does a good job of standing up to her, and I step in when necessary."

"What's made the woman so bitter and joyless?"

"Louisa had a failed love affair when she was young. She was once engaged to a military man. He went off to war and returned with a wife. To be honest, every time Cass shows the least interest in society, it's obvious that Louisa is jealous. Since she never married, she doesn't want Cass to."

"I'm glad Cass will be spending more time away from her."

"We can agree on that, anyway," Jack said. He tossed back the rest of his whiskey and rose. "You haven't forgotten about my conditions, have you?" He stood directly in front of Adam and looked him in the eye.

Adam hated lying to his friend, but he couldn't very well say, *Your sister wants me to bed her*, could he? So despite the sharp needles of his conscience pricking him unmercifully, he simply answered, "No. I haven't forgotten."

• • •

Cass stood next to Adam, her nerves as taut as a harp string. Deborah, who had embraced Cass and whispered her sincere joy at the news, waited on his other side. Deborah's reaction was in sharp contrast to her cousin's. When Cass had told Louisa she was engaged to Adam, the older woman plopped down onto the nearest chair and seemed so rattled that Cass rang for a restorative drink.

"No, that cannot be," she'd said. Cass had hidden a grin. Although she hadn't experienced the triumphant feeling she anticipated, she still derived a good deal of satisfaction from the look of disbelief on her cousin's face. That is, until Louisa recovered herself enough to question Cass's commitment to Philippa's education, her suitability as a wife to an MP, and the difficulties of being so much in society as becoming Adam's wife would require. By the time Cass had dealt with all of it, she was feeling much less complacent.

Afterward, Cass had bathed and rested on her bed until it was time to dress for dinner. She'd let her mind drift over all that had happened that day. Overall, she felt...satisfied. Adam had certainly seemed glad of it. More than glad, she thought, when she remembered him practically ripping her clothes off her, and the awed look on his face when he had. In the end, though, she appreciated his consideration of her when he'd temporarily called a halt. Thinking what lay ahead made her heart race and her body flutter with excitement in the strangest places.

But now, when the public announcement was about to be made, she was full of misgivings. What would people think about this sudden turn of events? Would they be happy for her? Would they remember what had happened with Bentley and pity Adam? Even worse, would they think it was a patched-up business brought about by her brother and Adam to ward off a scandal? She was about to find out.

Adam had instructed the butler and one of the footmen

to pour champagne for everyone, and when that was done, he said, "You are probably wondering what we are going to toast. A few weeks ago, I announced that I was standing for election. But this is an even more important—and a much more personal—announcement." He turned and looked at Cass, and had she not known the whole thing was a ruse, she would have believed in the fierce glow in his eyes.

"I've asked Cass to marry me, and she has accepted. I consider myself the luckiest man in Christendom right now."

Well. That might be laying it on a bit too thick. She risked a quick glance at Jack, who wasn't able to prevent one corner of his mouth quirking up.

"So I ask you to raise your glass in a toast to my bride. To Cass and our future together." To her surprise, Adam leaned down and kissed her on the mouth. Was he issuing a challenge to her brother?

Everybody started to talk at once. Jack hugged her— it would have seemed odd if he hadn't. Then Jenny. Cass wondered if she knew and decided from her subdued manner that she did. Hugh came up and kissed her cheek. "My brother has a lot more sense that I gave him credit for," he said, smiling. She spoke to everyone, and only felt a little guilty when Eleanor Broxton approached her looking sheepish.

"Miss Linford, may I wish you happy? I am so embarrassed…what I said to you about Mr. Grey. I-I didn't know."

Cass thought it best to be truthful. "Neither did I, that night. No apology is necessary." She squeezed the girl's hand before letting it go.

They went into dinner, and ironically, she was finally seated next to Adam.

• • •

"All of Christendom, eh?" Cass asked. "Not just England, or London? Or this little corner of Surrey? That was quite a pronouncement, Adam."

He chuckled. "Too much? I thought it sounded rather dashing, actually." The after dinner rituals over, Adam had steered Cass toward the terrace when he'd judged that she had enough of congratulations, well wishes, and nosy questions for one evening. She looked enchanting in some sort of clingy confection that outlined all her curves. Adam didn't think she was wearing stays. He glanced around, hoping they were alone.

"My brother and Jenny are just a few feet away."

"Ah. We don't want to bring Jack down on our heads this soon. How are you, Cass?"

"It has been a strange evening. The fact that we're lying to everybody spoils things a bit."

"I've suffered pangs of guilt all night, if it makes you feel any better. We must remember that our friends will soon be gone and then we can do some real work towards the election and not worry about other people."

"Speaking of the election…I have a question for you. At Cowdray I wanted to ask you about the war, but didn't have a chance. Would you tell me about Walcheren, Adam?"

He blinked, not expecting this. He thought she might want to know what the first steps would be in the campaign. But the war? He'd given her and her cousin a summary of what Walcheren had been like. Why did she need to know more?

"You wish to talk about the war? Tonight?" He studied her face, obviously puzzled. "You surprise me, Cass. There's not much more to tell than I already described to you."

"Surely that's not true. Jack said you left out a great deal."

He gave her a wry grin. "Remind me to thank him for that."

Cass had been leaning with one arm propped against the stone railing, but now she stood straight and looked at him directly. "You told me at Cowdray that the main reason you wanted to stand for election was the war. As your... what shall we call me, in private, that is? Your assistant? Your helpmeet?" She laughed, but he didn't hear any humor there. "I need—want—to know more, Adam."

"In the end, you may wish you hadn't asked," he said. "Walcheren was hell, a mosquito infested swamp, and ultimately, a graveyard for English soldiers. The invasion was intended to help the Austrians in their fight against the French. But by the time we got there, they had been defeated and were negotiating with Bonaparte." He caressed her hand while he spoke, rubbing his thumb along her palm and up her fingers. His gaze remained focused on their hands, but Cass's never left his face.

"We attacked Flushing, hoping to destroy, or at least weaken, the French Navy, but we only succeeded in chasing them out. The siege on Flushing—that's when I was wounded. The French removed their fleet to Antwerp. And then, men began to sicken from fever. Thousands died, in the most appalling conditions, and nobody knew what to do. I was terrified I'd die from it, too, especially in my weakened condition. In the end, we lost all those good men and gained nothing."

He dropped her hand and stepped back. "When I returned to England, I learned about the panorama depicting the bombardment of Flushing, for the amusement of the Prince Regent and his friends." He released a clipped laugh. "It sickened me. That's when I decided to escape to the Continent for a time. Which turned out to be two years."

"One last question. How did you get out of Walcheren?"

"The army began evacuating as many of the sick as they could, and since they were so short of medical men, they allowed me to leave, to help on board ship. Having been wounded, I wasn't of much use to them. The fighting was over by then, in any case. The army had only stayed on because of the sickness."

Tears glistened in her eyes. "Thank God you didn't catch the fever. It seems a miracle that you did not."

Her words were a balm to his wounded heart. Adam pulled her into his arms, kissing away the tears poised on her eyelashes. "My sweet Cassie, don't cry." He was in dangerous territory here, showing his emotions, but he couldn't seem to stop himself. Jack might still be nearby, but right now he didn't give a damn. Never had he been so attracted to her, or any other woman. He wanted her right now, with a fierceness that robbed him of breath. Hell, of reason. Before he could overthink it, he said, "I will come to you tonight, Cass." When she didn't answer immediately, he said, "We can wait if you're not ready, but know I can't resist you for much longer."

She shook her head and smiled at him. "I'll be waiting. And I'm ready."

Chapter Eighteen

Restless, Cass had moved from her bed to the window embrasure. Clad only in her night rail, she sat with her knees up, her arms encircling them, staring out into the darkness. *What does one do while waiting for a lover?* She'd finally ruled out trying to sleep; she was far too jittery. Images of what she was about to do with Adam were playing havoc with her peace of mind.

Never before had she contemplated becoming a man's mistress.

Of course, she wouldn't be Adam's mistress in the true sense of the word, but there were definitely similarities. Heaven forbid if he tried to give her a jewel, or some other extravagant gift. That brought a smile, because she was certain Adam wouldn't dream of treating her like some doxy he would pay for her favors.

She knew Adam didn't love her, yet she believed he was fond of her and undeniably desired her. But still he didn't want to be married to her, or anyone, so he said. When she'd told him she thought this had something to do with his father, he hadn't denied it. Perhaps one day he'd tell her more. She chose not to dwell on her own feelings about marriage. Better not to analyze it too closely, at least not tonight.

Cass raised her head when she heard a tapping on her door. It was so faint, she decided she'd imagined it. Then, unmistakably, she heard the door click open, felt a cool rush of air flood the room, and a thrill of anticipation raced through her. She lowered her legs to the floor and quickly walked over. It wouldn't do for him to be caught loitering in the passage.

"Adam," she whispered, beckoning him in. He was holding a decanter and two glasses. He wore only britches and shirt.

"Hello, Cassie. You look fetching."

The rogue. She couldn't help smiling. Her night rail was not what a bride might wear on her wedding night, but she'd had the seamstress make up one of the finest lawn, with embroidery across the top and thin straps.

"Let's sit in the embrasure," Cass said.

Adam poured them each some wine. "I thought we should have a private toast," he said, raising his glass. "To the loveliest lady in Christendom—"

"Stop teasing me," Cass said, chuckling.

He laughed softly. "I wouldn't dream of it. You *are* the loveliest woman of my acquaintance, and the sweetest and smartest. I'm grateful to you, Cassie, for everything. Not just this."

They clinked glasses and drank. The moonlight limned him, and Cass thought what a beautiful man he was. His thick, dark gold hair, his strong, proud profile. She reached out a hand and ran it across the back of his cheek, feeling the stubble. It excited her.

"I thought about shaving for you, but decided my valet would think I'd lost my mind."

"I am glad you did not." Nervously, she swallowed her

wine and was grateful for the slow warmth spreading through her chest and abdomen. After a minute, Adam took the glass from her hand and scooted closer to her. He placed his hands on her arms, sliding them slowly downward.

"It's not too late to change your mind, Cass," he said. "We can carry off the pretense of being engaged without making love."

"Would that be all right with you?"

"Hell, no. It would kill me."

And me as well. Cass knew she wasn't interested in the pretense without the lovemaking. "It's what I want, Adam. I may never experience it otherwise."

Adam's breath hitched, then his mouth found hers. Pulling her into his arms, he whispered, "Cassie, I want you so much. You and no other. It's driving me mad." He rose and brought her with him.

She answered with her body, molding herself against him, wrapping her arms around him and pressing into his chest, so that her breasts rubbed against him. Now there was nothing between them but the fine gauze of his shirt and the thin fabric of her night rail. In the moon-drenched room, she lost herself in his kiss. Cradled in his arms, Cass felt absolutely safe. She had no hesitation about entrusting her body to him.

· · ·

Adam's cock strained against his britches. He nibbled the corners of her mouth before smothering her forehead, cheeks, and ears with his kisses. He couldn't resist running his hands through her lustrous hair, drawing handfuls of it up to bury his face in. He hadn't seen it down since they were children. After he luxuriated in the feel of it, the scent of it, he moved his hands to her breasts, gently teasing her nipples.

"Oh," she said. *"Oh."*

He groaned deep in his throat. God, she smelled good. The rose scent she always wore, now faint at the end of the day, was intoxicating. It was so Cass. Impatient now to see her, all of her, he reached down and lifted her gown over her head, tossing it aside.

Cass drew in a sharp breath.

"You're so lovely, Cassie. Your hair, your creamy skin." And then he paused. The moonlight had struck her in such a way that he could see her wound. The one he'd wondered about this morning. "Some day you will tell me about this, how it happened, who was responsible. I'll probably have to kill him." That last bit came out fiercely, gutturally.

She shook her head, clearly signaling she didn't want to discuss it. "Now I wish to see you without your clothes, Adam."

He let out a short bark of laughter. "I am yours to command, madam." He yanked his shirt over his head. So aroused he couldn't comply fast enough, he was reduced to hopping around so as not to lose his balance while he tugged off his boots and britches. He could hear Cass giggling. How to romance your intended. He could write the book on how not to.

• • •

When he was finally still, Cass stared unabashedly. She stepped behind him and ran her hand down his powerful back and over the taut curve of his buttocks. He was long of thigh, and his calves bulged with muscles. "Explore all you want, love. It's only making me want you more."

Adam spun around, surprising her. Cass stepped back in shock when she caught her first glimpse of his arousal. Truly, she didn't see how that part of him was going to join with her...part. But since she only had a vague idea about the particulars, she decided to let him be her guide,

"Having a change of heart, are you?" Adam asked, smiling.

"Maybe. A little." She trembled slightly.

"Don't worry, darling. It will be my pleasure to make you ready for me."

I love hearing you call me darling. And love. She'd never be able to resist him if he kept that up.

He lifted her and carried her to the bed. Easing his body alongside hers, he resumed kissing her, while stroking her tenderly and whispering endearments. Cass told herself to relax. This was her beloved Adam, the man she'd adored most of her life. He wouldn't do anything to hurt her. Gradually, with his kisses and his touch, her trembling subsided.

"What would you like me to do?" Cass asked.

"More of what you were doing when we were standing. Touch me."

So she did, this time exploring the bands of muscle across his chest, even massaging his nipples gently, as he had done to her. Adam gasped, all the while continuing his gentle stroking of her.

His hands moved to her inner thighs, and then to her most intimate place. He worked magic on her sensitive flesh with his fingers, caressing, stroking, and gliding inside her until she couldn't help making soft gasping sounds. Maybe that was something a lady shouldn't do, but she couldn't help it. And Adam seemed to like it, since he said, "That's it, love, tell me." Arching, she felt close to coming apart, and when she finally did, her body shook with unexpected tremors. Crying out with pleasure, she hurled herself into his arms. "I didn't—I never knew…"

Adam framed her face with his hands and kissed her so sweetly, she ached inside. Feeling more confident, Cass reached out and put her hand on his rigid flesh. "Oh, sweet Jesus!" Adam cried. "Don't!"

She jerked her hand away, embarrassed. "I'm so sorry. I thought you would—"

"Yes, darling, it feels heavenly, it's just that…never mind." In one fluid move, he was above her, lifting her knees and opening her to him. She felt him at her entrance, yet he hesitated.

"Are you sure, Cassie? Are you sure you want this, too?"

"Very sure." She had no intention of stopping now. Reaching toward him, she ran her palms over his chest, delighting in the feel of his hard, sinewy flesh.

Laughing softly, Adam began to push himself inside her. At first, she felt only joy in the claiming of her body by this irresistible man she'd desired for so long. Then the feeling changed, became uncomfortable, even painful, and at its worst, she cried out once, sharply. Adam paused, mumbling an apology. He waited a moment before he began to slowly withdraw and then slide back inside her.

"Cassie," he whispered, his breath caressing her ear. "You are exquisite. So sweet. Everything a man could want." Maybe Adam's words helped ease the pain, because suddenly she was moving her hips in rhythm with his, and it felt good. *So good.* Cass was caught up in the ancient dance between male and female. She and Adam were joined together, performing an act common to all of humanity. Yet it was unique to them, because the way they felt, what they meant to each other, belonged to them alone. The idea affected her profoundly.

All she could hear for a few minutes was their breathing and their bodies brushing against the sheets. Adam's eyes were glazed and his face looked as if he were far away. A moment later, a primal noise erupted from his chest and he did something that shocked Cass. He spilled his seed on the bed and not inside her. Then he dropped down onto her, kissing her and enfolding her in his arms. "I'm sorry for hurting you, Cassie."

She felt giddy, too sated to talk. They lay in silence for a time, until she came back to herself. "Adam, why did you—"

"We can't risk you getting with child." He rose and walked over to the washstand. She heard a splash of water and after a minute realized he must be washing himself. Then he came back with the wet cloth. Embarrassed, she rolled to the side while he cleaned the sheet as well as he could.

And she wondered, couldn't help wondering, had it been pleasing for Adam? She needed reassurance, because she would have been devastated if she'd disappointed him. He climbed back in bed and spooned himself around her, kissing her neck and ear.

"You were magnificent, darling."

Cass breathed a sigh of relief. "Truly? You're not just trying to make me feel good?"

"I hope you already feel good, so no, I'm not. Do you think you'd like to do this again sometime?"

She knew he was teasing her, but twisted around to face him anyway. "Yes! Good God, yes." They both laughed. Much later sometime during the night, Cass felt her night rail sliding over her skin, and the covers being drawn up around her body.

When she woke up in the early dawn, shivering, Adam was gone. She felt an ache, an empty place inside, and wondered why this seemed like the end of something rather than the beginning.

• • •

Nothing in particular had been scheduled for the following day. Some of the men went off to hunt hare and squirrel. Others chose angling. Jack and Adam, Cass noticed, both opted for riding. Their horses probably did need a good gallop, she thought, and no doubt Jack wanted to talk privately to Adam. She'd like to be privy to that conversation. *Then again, perhaps not.*

The ball was planned for that evening, and tomorrow, everybody would take their leave. Cass was not at all sure what lay in store afterward for her and Adam. He had yet to speak to Sir William, and before making any further plans, he must do so. He wouldn't need her for that, so she would probably return to London and not see Adam again until he, too, had returned. Cass dreaded the thought of being cooped up in the carriage with her cousin. She could travel with Jenny and her mother, although that would leave Louisa by herself, something her cousin would never countenance.

Most of the ladies remained in the salon, reading, writing letters, or talking about their ball gowns, jewelry, and the styling of their hair. Seated near a window, Cass tuned them out and gazed outside. She couldn't keep Adam out of her thoughts. And when she allowed him in, she couldn't prevent a little twitch of a smile pulling at her lips. When Jenny approached her and asked if she wanted to walk around the park, she had to drag herself back to the present. Aware that the other girl would have questions, Cass was not particularly enthusiastic about the idea, but she would not decline. She loved Jenny, looked forward to having a sister her own age. She would have to be as honest as she could without betraying the true nature of her arrangement with Adam.

Tying their bonnet strings as they left the house, they decided to take the gravel path that led to the wood. Both girls wore sturdy half boots. It had rained during the night, leaving the air clean and clear. Cass inhaled deeply, drawing the freshness into her lungs.

"Forgive me if I am intruding on your privacy, Cass, but will you tell me what in heaven's name persuaded you to agree to Adam's scheme?" Cass could sense Jenny's eyes on her, but she kept her own gaze forward.

Nothing like getting right to the point.

"Surely my brother explained," Cass said, hoping foolishly that might put an end to it.

"He explained Adam's reason for telling his father he was engaged to you. I understand Adam's thinking, to a point. It is your decision I cannot fathom."

Cass was irritated, though she tried not to show it. Would she ever reach a point at which she no longer had to justify her decisions and actions to Jack and Jenny, or Louisa? "My life is dull and predictable, Jenny. I wanted to do something exciting. Something daring. Is that so difficult to comprehend?"

"Forgive me, Cass. I didn't realize you were so dissatisfied." Her apology sounded sincere, and Cass felt bad about her sharp response. "My fear is that at the conclusion of this, you will be hurt once again."

"It may seem unthinkable to you, but I'm willing to take that risk." Cass stopped walking and looked squarely at her friend. "Your life is settled. You know its course exactly. You will marry Jack and bear his children. You will be Lady Linford and take your place in society."

"You make it sound so tedious," Jenny said, scrunching up her face.

"I didn't mean it that way. I know you and Jack want me to find a husband, because you think that is the path to happiness. I'm not convinced marriage will make me happy. I've been betrothed, and it led to heartbreak. I'm not sure I can go through it again."

"But Bentley was ill. He was not right in his mind."

"Wasn't he? I don't know. Perhaps it was my own failings that contributed to his breakdown. Something in me that makes me unsuitable for marriage."

Jenny shook her head, then said, "I hope you know how preposterous that sounds."

Cass lifted a shoulder, wishing this conversation would come to an end.

"Exactly what are you getting out of this arrangement, Cass? How will it benefit you?"

Cass wasn't sure of the answer to that question. Although she'd all but sworn to Adam that becoming his lover and political advisor was all she wanted, she had doubts. It angered her that Jenny's question forced her to confront them. Was she kidding herself? Why had she felt so lost and alone after they'd made love, if all she wanted was an affair?

Jenny was staring at her, and Cass knew she must answer. "I can't explain it further. You will have to accept what I've already said. Now, may we speak of something else?"

"Of course. One more comment, and then I promise not to bring the matter up again." She paused, and Cass could see her considering what she wished to say. "I don't believe you. I don't believe that you don't want love and marriage and a family. In fact, I don't believe Adam, either. If he didn't want to marry you, why did your name spring to mind during the discussion with his father? There, I've said it, and now I'm finished." She inhaled deeply, as if she'd been waiting to draw breath.

Cass was stunned. How dare she presume to know Cass's deepest feelings? And Adam's? Jenny continued to chatter away, and Cass provided short, disjointed responses. As they neared the house, her friend said, "Why not come to Italy with Jack and me? We would love having you."

Cass laughed. "Oh, yes, you would love having me on your wedding trip. Kind of you, dear, but no, thank you."

"Many couples take family members, you know. It is not unusual."

"I don't want to risk my brother's ire for the rest of my life, so I politely decline." Cass linked arms with Jenny, appreciating her sweet nature and her desire to help. It was time to talk of less weighty topics.

"What are you wearing to the ball tonight?"

Chapter Nineteen

The end-of-house-party ball had been officially declared Adam and Cass's betrothal ball. Adam had protested that they didn't want the fuss, but he knew it was wise to go along with his mother's wishes on this. Hopefully, hosting it here in Surrey would put paid to the idea of repeating the ordeal in town. And it would be beneficial to reacquaint himself with some of the more distinguished citizens who would be in attendance. He was sure Broxton would be joining his wife and daughter for the festivities, and it would afford Adam a good opportunity for an informal meeting with the man prior to the more official one.

After making love to Cass last night, it was difficult to focus on politics. Adam wished he could have revealed his true feelings to her, could have told her it had never been that good before. He'd lost himself in her. Nearly lost his soul. To his astonishment, her gratification had been paramount to him. But he couldn't tell her. Couldn't let her believe they could be more to each other than lovers.

Cass was distressed about the ball, as he knew she would

be. He wasn't sure he understood her reluctance, although he knew it was related to Bentley's death. Someday he would insist that she tell him the story. The real story, not the one the gossips bruited about. "I danced with you at the Mainwaring ball, and you were perfectly at ease," Adam had told her when she protested.

"Because I could go unnoticed. Practically. At this ball I'll be the center of attention."

Nevertheless, she had given in, and now they stood side-by-side with Deborah to greet their guests. For a time, the line seemed to go on forever, although Adam knew not that many people had been invited. He wanted to get the celebration underway so that he and Cass could open the dancing. Later he'd have a chance to waltz with her and hold her close. He was having trouble suppressing visions of her naked body, especially since her elegant ball gown showed off the tops of her creamy breasts.

"Adam," his mother was saying. "You remember Sir William, of course?"

Of course...not. He'd asked his mother to be the first to receive guests for this very reason. He hadn't seen the man for so long, he was afraid he wouldn't recognize him. Broxton cut an imposing figure, tall with an upright posture, despite his somewhat dated style. His hair was powdered and pulled back into a queue, and his evening clothes would have been fashionable ten years ago. Not that Adam cared.

He thrust out a hand. "Sir William. Glad you could join us. We've been enjoying the company of your wife and charming daughter all week." Broxton smiled stiffly.

"May I introduce my fiancée, Cassandra Linford?"

The older man turned to Cass and bowed. She curtsied and they shook hands. "Welcome, Sir William. A pleasure to make your acquaintance." Adam had instructed her not to mention the election unless Broxton did. An awkward silence ensued, during which he seemed to be studying Cass.

"You're the Viscount's sister? Good man. I like him."

"Yes, my brother is Viscount Linford." She laughed nervously. Adam could sense her discomfort.

Finally Broxton said, "Must look around for my wife and daughter," and quickly walked away. Cass turned to Adam, brows raised.

"He's a somber old gaffer, isn't he? Nothing much to say to any of us." Adam wondered if he should read anything into that, but greeting the remainder of the guests distracted him, and he did not think about it again.

At last the flow of people dwindled, and Deborah conferred with the orchestra and announced the dance. Cass and Adam stood at the top, closest to the musicians. And the evening officially began.

· · ·

After she and Adam had gone down the middle, Cass had a chance to truly survey her surroundings. He took her hand and pulled her closer so they could hear each other over the music. "The ballroom looks beautiful," Cass said. "Deborah has outdone herself."

"And it smells like you. Like roses. I told her they were your favorite. Deborah could do this in her sleep, I imagine."

Still, Cass was impressed. The room had been aired and the wood floors polished. At the far end, the huge stone fireplace was festooned with greenery, which had been intertwined with roses and dianthus. Huge bouquets rested on every table, made up predominantly of roses. Pale pink, deep scarlet, yellow ones, white ones. Every shade imaginable. Candlelight glowed from the chandeliers and sconces, highlighting the gleaming dark wood paneling. And every woman there showed to advantage in the soft glow.

"How are you feeling, Cassie?" Adam asked.

She shrugged. "Fine. This was never going to be easy. I knew that." In truth, she'd been grappling with her feelings ever since her talk with Jenny earlier.

"Have I told you how stunning you look?" Adam's eyes swept her from head to toe. Cass was wearing her new sage green ball gown with tiers of vandyked lace at the hem. The neckline plunged into a V, deeper than was customary for her and she knew her bosom pushed up provocatively. This was the dress that had caused her to row with Louisa. Cass's only worry had been that the design would hide her scar, and the clever dressmaker had been able to achieve that.

The next set was a cotillion. Deborah had thought that the country neighbors would be more likely to be familiar with its figures and changes than they would for those of the quadrille, and Cass agreed. Her partner was Squire Remson, a very agreeable man who danced quite capably.

Adam had asked her before the ball to save the first waltz for him. After the cotillion, the squire had escorted her to the edge of dance floor to stand with Jack and Jenny. Cass had no idea where Adam was. She'd caught a glimpse of him dancing with Miss Broxton—she supposed he felt obligated to dance with her—and was now sneaking glances around the room to see if she could spot him.

Jenny distracted her. "It's a lovely ball, Cass."

"Yes." Cass could hear the unspoken words. *If only it weren't such a sham.*

Then she felt a hand at her back, and Adam was there. He leaned in and whispered in her ear. "May I have the pleasure of this dance, Cassie?"

She could have melted, simply at his light touch at the small of her back, his breath at her ear, his nearness. A liquid warmth spread through her body, and she wished that she did not always have such a visceral and immediate reaction to him. It made thoughts of eventually separating from him all the more painful. But now was not the time to think about that, so she smiled and laid her hand on his arm.

As they spun around the floor, Cass noticed Hugh dancing with Eleanor and wondered if he had an interest there. The two seemed to get on well. After that, she simply allowed herself to be caught up in the moment. Adam held her close, and now that they were "betrothed," she did not care what people might think.

"I've been watching you all evening, darling." His voice was low and seductive. "You're quite the vixen in that dress. Consider yourself lucky that I haven't swept you into my arms and up to my chamber."

Cass laughed. "I wish you would. This is torture."

"You're so beautiful, Cass. Every man in the room is drooling with envy."

"Ha! You exaggerate. Every woman is wondering why you chose me."

"Only if they're fools." His eyes were warm, holding a sweet promise, and he leaned down and brushed a kiss across her lips.

When she realized that some sort of ruckus seemed to be occurring near the door, Cass tore her eyes away from Adam's. She heard shouting, and gradually the orchestra ceased playing. Adam hurried to the musicians and urged them to continue, then did the same with the dancing couples. Cass followed him to the main door where she saw a slovenly looking older man arguing with Hugh. Adam's brother had a firm hold on the man's arm and was urging him into the hall. This could be none other than Benjamin Grey. *Oh, no. He'll ruin the evening.*

Adam spun around and said, "Cass, return to our guests. This is a private matter that Hugh and I must deal with."

She nodded and realized she was not alone. Deborah had

come up to stand beside her. "I have not seen him in years," she said. "What a sad sight he is."

"Did you invite him?"

Deborah's laugh was harsh. "Certainly not. I would like to know how he found out."

"Probably village gossips." Cass linked arms with the older woman. "Come, let's get some ratafia. If we stand here watching, sooner or later so will all the guests."

"You are right," Deborah said. "But I need something much stronger than ratafia."

Before they could steal away, matters deteriorated. Despite his drunkenness, and the fact that his two grown sons—both large, strong men—were attempting to wrestle him out of the ballroom, Benjamin Grey managed to stand his ground. "Marry the Broxton chit, Adam. I'm ruined if you don't."

"Come out in the hall, Father, and we'll discuss it," Adam said. It was as though the old man were frozen in place. Eyes bulging, he reddened with the effort to stay put. Cass worried he might suffer a heart seizure and collapse on the spot.

"Won't have Hugh." He looked at his older son, who was sweating with the effort of removing his father from the room. "Sorry, boy. Won't have you. Wants Adam, war hero." He paused and looked around for a moment, then said, "Christ almighty, where am I?" Suddenly he went limp.

His sons used the opportunity to carry him to a nearby chamber. The ballroom had gone quiet, even though the musicians had valiantly tried to play on, and Cass wondered how much of the exchange the guests had heard. Most of them had deserted the dance floor and flocked toward where the action was taking place. The Broxtons, Cass noted with horror, were front and center. What must Sir William be thinking? In a few moments, she heard Broxton bidding Deborah a good evening. Then he turned to his wife and daughter. "Get your things. We're leaving."

"But Papa," Eleanor said, "we are not packed."

"You will be in the time it takes to pull the carriage around. See to it!"

Cass and Deborah glanced at each other, both with a knowing look in their eyes. This would not end well for Adam.

Deborah turned to the guests, clapped her hands, and said, "Come, everybody! This is a night of celebration. Let's resume dancing." She signaled the musicians, who immediately started a new piece. Dancers crowded onto the floor, willing, apparently, to do what they were told.

Cass edged her way toward the corridor and the closed door. Retreating to the shadows, she leaned against the wall and waited. Adam would no doubt need propping up after this, and she wanted to help. In a minute or two, the door opened. She heard him instructing Scott, Deborah's butler, who must have been in the room with them, to have Benjamin Grey's carriage brought round. Just after, Hugh came out with his father, supporting him with an arm about his shoulders, and they walked slowly down the hall. Soon Scott reappeared and grabbed hold of the drunken man's other arm.

Cass was uncertain. Should she go to Adam, who hadn't yet left the room, or wait for him to exit? She took a step forward, and suddenly there he was. He closed the door, then sighed deeply and leaned his forehead into the wood. After a few seconds, he stood up, then brushed his clothes off and ran a hand through his hair. Cass felt as though she were spying on him.

"Adam," she said, stepping out where he could see her.

"Stay put, Cass," he said. He walked over to her and wrapped her in his arms. "I'm sorry you had to see that. Here, let's go through these doors. They lead to the conservatory. We can get outside for a breath of air for a few minutes."

They passed through the conservatory and out the doors

leading to one end of the terrace. Adam steered Cass toward a large potted shrub, and they kept to one side of it, where any guests exiting from the ballroom could not see them.

"I'm so sorry, Adam. I didn't realize he was…"

"Hard to find the right word, isn't it?" He left her side and began to pace. "Do you see now why I can't marry?"

"Because of your father's behavior? Granted, it's appalling, but most women have been exposed to drunkenness, Adam. It wouldn't be such a great burden."

"You don't know everything, Cass. What I wouldn't give if that were the only problem. There are things about my family…I'd rather die than expose you to them." He stopped his pacing and watched her.

Cass saw a man who looked defeated. He had such a look of despair on his face, she wanted to weep. She stepped forward and framed his face with her hands. "You are a grown man. A good man. He can't hurt you anymore."

Adam grabbed her wrists. "No? Broxton has left."

When Cass didn't say anything, he said, "It's true, isn't it?"

She nodded. "Yes, I'm afraid so. But we already knew your father had made an enemy of him. Don't assume Sir William puts you in the same category."

"How could he not? I would, under the same circumstances." Before Cass could respond, Adam said, "We must return to the ballroom. We're the guests of honor, after all. I know it's a lot to ask, but could you put this incident out of your mind for the rest of the evening?"

"I'll try," Cass said.

Somehow, they made it through the supper, the announcement of their betrothal and accompanying toast, and several more dances. By the time the carriages had departed and the house party guests had retired, Cass was exhausted. She couldn't help wondering, though, if Adam would come to her chamber tonight. She would not turn him away if he did.

But at the end of the night he walked her to her room and gave her a chaste kiss good night.

"It's been a long evening, Cassie. I'll see you in the morning."

That cleared things up. He did not turn around as he strode down the hall. She watched him all the way, a handsome, brooding figure, though she noticed he was limping slightly. Once inside her chamber, Cass dropped onto the bed and lowered her face into her hands. She remained that way until Agnes arrived to help her undress.

Chapter Twenty

When Cass first glimpsed Adam at breakfast, she knew a night's sleep hadn't helped his mood. His expression was stony, his jaw set. He looked up from his paper long enough to nod a greeting to her. While a footman poured her tea, she filled her plate with rolls, shirred eggs, and bacon. Nibbling half-heartedly, she listened to Jenny's description of some of the items she'd purchased on the recent trip to the village. An unusual clasp for her hair. A new bonnet. A copy of Lord Byron's latest volume of poetry, *Childe Harold*.

Most of the guests were preparing to leave and did not linger over breakfast. Finally, Jack, Jenny, Adam, and Cass were the only ones left. Adam folded his paper and set it aside.

"I intend to visit Sir William this morning."

"The timing is unfortunate," Jack said.

Adam nodded. "I am not optimistic, but he has said he would consider me, and I must have his answer, whatever it is."

Cass said, "He and your father were at odds before Jack even wrote to him about you. Last night's antics couldn't have come as a great shock to him."

"You're right, of course. But Sir William heard what my father said in a crowded ballroom about Eleanor. The man probably felt humiliated."

"I don't think too many people could make out what he was saying," Jenny said.

"Enough did to get his back up," Jack said. "And all the gossips will soon get wind of it. Then there is the matter of your engagement to Cass." Cass felt heat rise in her cheeks.

Adam stood. "We could discuss it all morning and still not know where things stand. I must be on my way."

"Should we wait for your return before we depart?" Jack asked.

Adam had turned to go, but spun back around. "Would you mind? We'll need to settle some things once we know Broxton's decision. In fact, I think you should stay over tonight."

As soon as Adam's footsteps could no longer be heard, Cass said, "I must tell Louisa we aren't leaving today. She's been supervising the packing. She'll be angry."

"And I should tell Mama," Jenny said.

"I was wondering," Cass said, "if there was some way I could get out of riding home with Louisa. I rather wanted to strangle her on the way here." She looked at Jack imploringly.

"My mother is quite fond of Louisa," Jenny said.

Simultaneously, Cass and Jack said, "She is?"

Jenny laughed. "She has a few redeeming qualities, you know. Why don't I suggest that the two of them ride home in our carriage, and you and I can ride in yours? Jack, what do you think?"

"As long as I don't have to ride with her, whatever you decide suits me."

Both girls gave him a quelling look before taking themselves off to find the two older women.

. . .

Adam was accorded a cordial welcome by Sir William and led into a drawing room with tall sash windows and comfortable groupings of furniture. Eleanor rang for tea. "Mama is out making calls," she said. Once the tea was poured, she excused herself.

"I'm glad you called, Grey," Sir William said as soon as they'd resumed their seats. The Viscount tells me you wish to stand for Commons as my candidate." There was a hardness around his mouth that made Adam uneasy.

"Yes, sir. Linford supports my election."

"I was inclined to give you a chance. My current man is ready to retire. To say the truth, he hasn't been worth much for several years. Too old, and in his cups more often than not. Don't even think he attends sessions on a regular basis."

Adam had not missed his use of the past tense, and so waited with dread to hear the rest. Despite what had happened at the ball, he'd hoped the man could separate the election from his troubles with Adam's father.

"But I'm afraid the stand-off with Benjamin over the debt he owes me, combined with his actions of last night, have changed my mind." Looking like he'd just been poked with a cattle prod, he tilted his head forward and peered at Adam. "I detested my Eleanor witnessing his unseemly behavior. And half of Haslemere looking on, too. It's an outrage."

Broxton sat back in his chair and kept his accusatory gaze fixed on Adam, who felt like a schoolboy about to be sent down. "Given your parentage, I'm not sure I can trust you to do your duty as an MP. I've concluded that all the Grey men are alike."

"I am not my father, sir," Adam said stiffly, using every ounce of self-control he possessed not to rage at the unfairness of this statement. It was one thing for *him* to fear he might turn out like his father, but another matter altogether for someone else to accuse him of it. Interesting that Sir William had made no mention of his wish for Adam to marry Eleanor, which was what had set all of these events in motion. Apparently, he'd had no qualms about Adam's character when he suggested that.

Sir William continued as though he hadn't heard. "Your conduct in the war was exemplary. I'd assumed you might work toward ending this interminable conflict."

Adam leaned forward. "That's exactly what I wish to do, sir. It's the foremost reason I want a seat in Commons."

Sir William made no response, merely sat staring at Adam with his arms crossed over his chest. Very carefully Adam placed his teacup on the table. Above all else, he wanted to depart with his dignity—what little he apparently had left— intact. "My apologies if Miss Broxton was in any way hurt by my father's actions." Adam wanted to make it clear that he wasn't responsible.

Sir William shifted in his chair and spoke at last. "I had hoped you might make a match with my Eleanor."

Ah, there it was at last. "But I am betrothed to Miss Linford. Surely you would not have expected me to break my engagement. What kind of man would that make me?" Adam cringed inside at his own hypocrisy.

"That is not what your father led me to believe."

"You must understand, Sir William, that I have had no contact with my father. Until a few days ago, I hadn't seen him in years."

His brows shot up, and hope rose in Adam's chest that he might reconsider his decision. But no. Sir William got to his feet and said, "I am sorry we could not have concluded this in a way that was satisfactory for us both."

That I marry your daughter in exchange for a seat in Commons? Adam was certain that if he offered to jilt Cass there and then and marry Eleanor, Broxton would agree.

When the man did not offer to shake hands, Adam bowed and said, "I'll see myself out."

He couldn't really blame anybody else for his father's behavior; yet all the way home he wondered why Sir William had continued to gamble with the old man. At some point, Broxton must have known he couldn't honor his debt. It was as if he had wanted to force Benjamin Grey into a hole he could never crawl out of.

As soon as he arrived at the estate, Adam retreated to the library. He knew the others were probably waiting for him, but he badly needed some time alone to mull over all that had happened today. He poured himself a whiskey and sank into his chair. God, but he was tired. Tired of everything.

He drank a long swallow and ruminated. On the way home, he'd begun to think about Cassie. What he had said to Sir William about being engaged to her. Christ, he felt like a scoundrel. And a liar. He'd said to the man, "I'm not my father," but was it true? He was certainly acting like him.

It struck him that he was using Cass in the worst sort of way imaginable. Adam should never have agreed to her plan for them to be lovers. If she'd agreed to play the part of his betrothed, that would have been one thing. Even asking that was less than honorable. But when she'd raised the possibility of more, well, that had changed everything. The fact that he hadn't been strong enough to reject it out of hand spoke volumes about his true character. He had allowed her to persuade him that she didn't want marriage because she didn't trust men. Well, she'd been right not to trust him. A decent man would have put paid to her plan before anything had occurred. A decent man would have figured out a way to help her rather than sleep with her. Instead, he'd thought only of himself.

It sickened Adam to draw this conclusion, but the evidence was undeniable. He was turning into his father. He wasn't good enough for Cass. Would never be good enough for her. The whole scheme hadn't felt right from the outset. Lying to his mother, Hugh, and his friends. And after making love to Cass, he hadn't allowed himself to express his true feelings to her. Not when their engagement was a sham.

There was only one thing to do, and that was to end the whole scheme with Cass, before she was hurt beyond repair. She was a lady, and one whom he admired and respected. Yes, and lusted after. As long as they allowed the pretense of an engagement to go on, that would be the case, and he wasn't sure if he could resist her. He would seek Cass out right now, before he had time to change his mind, and tell her it was over. There was just enough time to get it done before they had to dress for dinner.

• • •

Cass had been keeping watch for Adam for the past hour or so. Earlier, she had been out for a walk; afterward she'd joined in a game of piquet with Jenny, Jenny's mother, and Deborah. Cousin Louisa sat nearby embroidering, and when Cass had said she was tired of cards, her cousin happily took her place.

She tried to read, but couldn't concentrate. Nevertheless, she resolutely held the book out in front of her and hoped nobody would notice that she turned the page very infrequently. Just when she thought she might lose her mind, she glimpsed Adam in the doorway. He seemed in a good enough humor, but she knew it could be for show.

"Good evening, ladies." After some desultory talk about nothing, he made his way over to Cass and said, "Come to the library with me?" The others, absorbed in their game, hardly gave them a second glance.

She nodded and followed him from the room. Adam poured himself a whiskey and she accepted a glass of sherry. Instead of sitting behind the desk, he seated himself next to her on the settee. He was quiet, sober, and Cass concluded that the news could not be good.

Adam swallowed a good measure of his drink before speaking. "Sir William intends to look elsewhere for a candidate. Having concluded that 'all the Grey men are alike,' he has rejected me."

Cass set her glass down. "Oh, Adam, no. I am so sorry."

"I've made my peace with his decision, Cassie. Don't distress yourself." He reached for her hand and gently enfolded it in his much larger one.

"But your hopes and dreams, all you wanted to accomplish, lost! I can't bear it, for your sake. How can you be so calm about it?"

Adam raised her hand to his lips and kissed it softly. "There is nothing I can do short of marrying his daughter. Despite his apparent dislike of the Grey men, I had the distinct impression that if I'd suggested breaking my engagement to you and offering for Eleanor, he would have changed his view quite readily."

"What a hypocrite."

Adam poured himself another whiskey and walked over to stand by the windows. "Perhaps. I'm extremely disappointed in not being his candidate, but the greater anguish is to have someone accuse me of being like my father."

"Broxton doesn't know you, Adam. If he did, he wouldn't accuse you of something so blatantly false."

He glanced at Cass, his expression so desolate she wanted to weep. "Are you certain?" He tossed back his drink and set the glass down. "Look at what I've done to you. First asking you to pretend to be engaged to me. That was bad enough, but then when you suggested we become lovers, instead of doing the gentlemanly thing and refusing, I slept with you." He paused and rubbed a hand over his face. "You say I'm a good man, but a good man would not have agreed. He would have been more concerned about your reputation, your happiness, and would have tried to help you overcome your mistrust of men before bedding you."

Cass rose, shaking her head. "No, Adam. You're wrong. I asked for this arrangement, and as far as I'm concerned…" Her voice petered out. She knew there were aspects of it that made her uncomfortable, too, partly due to her own indecision about whether she would be happier with marriage. Yet she was not at all ready to give up the intimacy she had just found with Adam because of a few lingering doubts.

"See? You're not convinced either."

She walked over to him and grasped his arm. "Doesn't intimacy always involve a degree of uncertainty, by its very nature? I know it's made me more vulnerable, but I will never regret what we did. Never."

Adam smiled, that sweet, closed-mouth smile she believed was for her alone. "I'm glad of that, at least." He pulled her into his arms, pressing rough kisses on her mouth. Electrified by his touch, she molded herself against him, trying to fit her curves to his flat planes and angles. When his hands clutched her bottom, she felt his tumescence and thought she might scream with her need for him.

Then, with a curse, he backed away from her. "No," he said. "No."

Cass knew he desired her, but he'd apparently made up his mind to resist her. "I'm sorry that wanting me makes you feel…corrupted, somehow," she said, her throat thick. "Will you now wish to forget what we did? Never think of it again?"

"You are a lady, Cassie. I stole something precious from

you. Your innocence."

"Now you're being ridiculous. I *asked* you to make love to me, Adam. I was a willing—more than willing—participant." She probably should have stopped herself, but now she was angry as well as hurt. "If you truly believe you stole my innocence, isn't it far worse that you did so and now wish to forsake me?"

He grabbed her by the shoulders. "That's not...I'm not..."

He couldn't even finish his sentence.

Don't cry. Do not cry, she commanded herself.

Adam's jaw was set stubbornly. They were at an impasse, and she would have to be the one to give way. She must accept his decision and try to salvage their friendship—and her dignity. Drawing back, she forced herself to say, "Fine. No more of this, then. But I am not giving up on your political career. What will you do now that Sir William won't have you?"

"I'm not giving up either, Cass. As soon as I'm back in town, I'll start inquiring about other constituencies that might be in need of a candidate. I am not without connections. Somebody's bound to know."

Cass was only half listening. She was forming her own plan. "I think I shall stay in the country for a few more days. Possibly longer."

Adam cocked his head at her. "Why? What can be done here?"

"If you must know, I would like some time by myself. Do you think Deborah would mind if I remained here, or should I decamp to Birch Lane?"

Adam's eyes softened. "Of course you can stay here. Birch Lane is twice the size of this place. You'd be lost there, all by yourself."

Cass nodded. "What about the engagement? What should we do? Jack will need to know if we're calling it off."

Adam sat on the edge of the desk. "I'll inform Jack of Sir William's decision. As to others, for now, we do nothing. The announcement has just been in the papers. It would look exceedingly odd if you cried off this quickly." He paused. "If you wouldn't mind, there may be some matters you can assist me with when you come up to London."

"Of course. I said I wanted to help, and I meant it." And she did, even though her heart was breaking. She turned to leave, then thought she might as well ask what was uppermost on her mind. "One question, Adam. Did your father have affairs? Is that what scares you about us? About marriage?"

She was standing close enough that she could see the pulse at his temple jumping. "I never discuss it, Cass. Don't ask it of me."

She nodded. "Very well, but it's difficult for me to understand without knowing the truth." Just as she was about to exit the room, she heard his voice.

"The truth is far worse than you can imagine." Cass spun around and looked at him straight on, waiting for him to elaborate. He did not. She shut the door quietly behind her.

Cass was so distracted while Agnes was helping her dress that the poor woman had to repeat questions a second and third time: "Which necklace do you wish to wear? How shall I arrange your hair? Oh, there's a spot on you slipper." Her answer to everything was, "Do what you think best, Agnes."

Cass was thinking about Adam and his father. The broken down man who had disrupted the ball. Try as she might, she could see no evidence to support the idea that Adam was anything like the man. But she understood that it did not matter what she, or anyone else, believed, but only what Adam believed about himself.

Chapter Twenty-One

Adam parted from Cass with a virtuous kiss on the cheek. It worried him that she seemed so tranquil. Was she hiding her true feelings? He'd had difficulty holding back his own, reining in his urge to hold her and kiss her and never let her go. Jack had accepted her decision to remain behind with equanimity, not questioning it, only asking if she was sure it was what she wanted.

Because he was driving his curricle, Adam was able to make better time than the others. The traveling arrangements had made him chuckle. It had finally been worked out that Jenny's mother would ride with Cass's cousin. Jenny would travel in her coach, with Jack riding alongside. Adam knew, though, that Jack would end up inside the coach with his fiancée at intervals. And that was what made him laugh. Jack was a lucky devil.

Cass staying on in the country for a time was for the best. Until he knew what the next steps were for him, there would not be much she could do to help, if indeed she truly wanted to do so. Tomorrow, Adam would sit down and make a plan for finding another constituency. Other options open to him held no appeal. He wasn't titled; his only hope for Parliament was in Commons. He had no estates to manage. Perhaps some MP, or a lower-level cabinet minister, needed a secretary. But oh, hell, was that really how he wanted to spend the rest of his life?

· · ·

After he'd been in town a few days, he was ready to put his plan in motion. He'd spend time at the coffee room at the House of Commons, where he could rub elbows with MPs, and would probably run into some with whom he was already acquainted.

One rainy afternoon when he'd grown tired of lying passively in wait for influential MPs, he dashed out to Hatchard's Bookshop in Piccadilly. They did not have what he wanted, but the helpful proprietor gave him a list of other shops to try. It was a start.

Evenings found him musing before the fire in his library, sipping a whiskey before he dined alone. Oh, he had the usual number of invitations, but he wasn't very enthusiastic about any of them. He would have to start accepting some, however. He needed the exposure.

His thoughts turned to Cass most nights, and at odd moments during the day. What was she doing all alone in Deborah's house? *Damnation!* Unconsciously, he would compare the sound of some other woman's voice to hers. Her sweet face, glossy hair, splendid body preoccupied him, whether awake or dreaming. How had he thought he could simply put her out of his mind? He was beginning to realize it wouldn't be possible.

Adam decided to write her a letter. That would be better than nothing.

. . .

Cass's true motive for staying in the country was to devise a plan to persuade Sir William Broxton to change his mind about Adam. She had no idea whether he had a chance at finding another sponsor, but she knew it would not be easy. She'd thought it best that she keep what she was doing to herself. Although Adam had accepted readily enough that Sir William had cast him off, the cause had pained him. Telling him that all the Grey men were alike. Cass knew trying to reason with Adam about it would be for naught, so she would see what she could accomplish on her own.

She was determined to do whatever she could so he was well informed in case things changed. Immersing herself in political news was one way to do that. Even if she could not find an opening to use with Sir William, the information would prove useful for Adam's efforts in town.

Realizing she hadn't looked at any of the papers since she'd been in the country, she asked that the *Post* and *Chronicle* be brought to her with her breakfast. On the first morning, she read with horror about the Felling Mine explosion, near Newcastle. It was suspected that several children were among the dead, although no bodies had been recovered yet. Cass recalled that Adam was quite passionate about child labor, and she thought he might wish to know the facts as they came to light. She went to the writing desk and drew out a sheet of parchment. Recording the pertinent details was no trouble, and she could do the same with other news.

Cass ventured out of doors as often as she could, roaming all over Deborah's park. One morning she walked around the lake and paused when she came to the temple. Today the surface of the lake was flat, mirror like. Nothing at all like it had been on that day when Adam had made her forget everything except her own desperate need for him. The day she had told him she wanted them to be lovers. The mere thought of his touch, his kisses, made her heart race, her skin hot. She missed him, longed for him, and wondered if he thought of her at all.

The Grey family was a puzzle to her. What had driven them apart? What was so awful that Adam couldn't tell her about it? Was it simply Benjamin Grey's drinking, or was he a gambler, too? Had he kept mistresses? She could only speculate, since Adam refused to talk about it. All of these failings were common in families of the *ton*, but most of them remained together, despite less than idyllic marriages. Surely the elder Grey couldn't always have been the wastrel he appeared to be now. If only Adam would tell her about it, she could help heal the wounds his father had inflicted on him.

And then, a few days later, she received a letter from him in the post. She left off flower arranging to read it.

5 June
London

Dearest Cass,

I hope this letter finds you in good health.

I am writing to ask if your needs are being met by Deborah's staff. I entrusted them with your care and have every expectation they will do their best for you. Please inform me if there is anything not to your liking.

The weather in London is foul. A miasma drifts up from the river, making the air more oppressive and dank than usual. Be glad you are not here because it is ~~bloody~~ terribly unpleasant.

I've been spending afternoons at the coffee room in the House of Commons and have made some new acquaintances. What I've learned so far is not encouraging. The easiest and fastest way to

*gain a constituency is to possess a full purse. Next
easiest: be under the patronage of a landowner, as
I had hoped to be with Sir William. On the whole,
local candidates are preferred—outsiders are not
welcome. I am beginning to wonder if I should
give up. My new friends tell me that introductions
to the "right" people, if timely, could make all the
difference.*
    We shall see.
    Yours,
    A.

Cass threw the letter down in frustration. The tone
was formal and impersonal, but hadn't Adam made it clear
that was how he wanted things to be between them? Still,
it disheartened her. She read the letter a second time, but
could find nothing hopeful about it. Gazing out the window,
she thought it would behoove her to speed up her search for
an opening with Sir William. Returning to her flowers, she
picked up some gladioli stems and inserted them into her
arrangement. She was deep in thought when Scott entered
the room.

"Very nice, Miss Linford," he said, eyeing the flowers.
"You have visitors."

"I do?" Cass couldn't imagine who. She tucked the last
stem into the vase and looked up.

"Viscount Linford and Miss Pippa Linford."

Philippa came crashing into the room. "Cassie!"

Cass knelt down and hugged her sister tightly. "Hello,
my darling girl! Let me look at you." She held Pippa at arm's
length. "Why, I believe you've grown at least a few inches in
the short time I've been away."

"I have so much to tell you," the little girl announced.
"Cousin Louisa's gone, Jack rowed with her and sent her

away. And I have a governess."

"What on earth?" Cass said, frowning at her brother.

Pippa continued. "She's very beautiful, Cass. That's why Louisa didn't like her."

Cass choked back a laugh. The butler was still hovering in the doorway. "Scott, could you send Mrs. Wetherby to me, please? And tea for all of us."

Jack and Cass sat down and allowed their younger sibling to roam about the room, examining Deborah's knickknacks. "Don't—"

"I know, I know. Don't touch."

Cass eyed her brother quizzically. "You, brother dear, have some explaining to do."

Jack looked sheepish. But before he could begin, the housekeeper arrived.

"Mrs. Wetherby, aren't there some new kittens in the stables? I think my sister would love to see them," Cass said. "Do you have a girl in the kitchen who could be spared for a few minutes?"

"Of course, Miss Linford."

Cass called Pippa over and introduced her to the housekeeper. "How would you like to visit some new kittens, Pip?"

"Oh, yes! I'll be so careful. I won't squeeze them, I promise."

"Good girl. I know you'll be very gentle."

When Pippa had left and they were settled with tea, sandwiches, and biscuits, Cass said, "Tell me everything."

"I've been thinking a lot about this, Cass. After Mama died—and Bentley—tutoring Pippa filled a void in your life. At least I always thought it did."

Cass nodded and he went on. "And I know you made a promise to our mother. Well, I think you've more than fulfilled that promise. If you're going to be busy helping Adam, it seemed like a good time to make a change." Jack snatched a sandwich from the plate and stuffed the whole thing into his mouth. "You are still intending to help him, I assume?"

"If I can. And you're right about a change. I only wish you'd consulted me first."

"I would have, believe me. But Miss Stanton was available and came highly recommended. I didn't want to risk losing her."

"I want to meet her, of course. Does she understand that Pippa isn't a book learner?"

Jack had moved on to the sweets. "These biscuits are wonderful. What's in that filling? Almonds?" He brushed crumbs off his coat and continued. "Yes. She thinks our little sister is delightful. Says she's naturally inquisitive. She's already taken her to the British Museum, one of the parks, the zoo. That's what caused the row with Louisa."

"That's no surprise. Go on." Cass narrowed her eyes and looked suspiciously at Jack.

"Let's say our cousin took a strong dislike of Miss Stanton almost immediately. She disapproved of everything the woman did." He rubbed a hand over his face. "You know how she is, Cass. She couldn't force you into a traditional style of teaching, but she was determined to do so with Miss Stanton. I'm afraid I lost my temper. Rather badly."

Cass held back a smile. "Did you ask her to leave?"

"No. I didn't go that far. Later in the day she came to me and said she wanted to go north, to the home of a distant cousin. Nobody we've ever heard of. She arranged it and was gone within a few days."

"I'm away for, what, not even a fortnight, and look what happens. The household falls apart!"

"I thought you'd be happy. About Louisa, anyway."

"I'm teasing, Jack. I think you've made excellent decisions all around. Louisa was never truly content with us, and I was becoming less and less tolerant of her." Cass rested her head on the back of her chair. "How peaceful our house will be. I must return home just to have the pleasure of it."

"You'll write to her?"

"Certainly. I have the feeling it will be much easier to communicate with her by post than it ever was in person." They both laughed, and then Cass turned serious. "I do hope she will be happier in her new home."

Talk turned to Adam, and Cass told Jack what little she'd learned from his letter.

"I'm afraid it's going to be a rough go," Jack said.

Cass paused in the middle of pouring more tea. "I've just now had a thought. Could you intervene, Jack? I remember Papa discussing candidates with Sir William on occasion."

"I'm afraid it wouldn't work in this case. The debt Adam's father owes Broxton is a huge obstacle. Men can owe money all over town, but they must always settle debts of honor. It's not hard to see why he wouldn't want Adam for his candidate."

"Didn't seem to stop him from wanting Adam as a husband for Eleanor."

Jack gave his head a shake. "Odd, that. Still, I don't think I could change his mind."

"*Hmm*. I suppose not."

Before Pippa and Jack left in the morning, he said, "Are you sure you don't mind about the governess, Cass? If you don't like her, we can find somebody else, or you can return to duty, if you prefer."

She put a hand on his shoulder and squeezed. "No. I loved teaching Pippa, but it is time for me to find other interests. I shall be happy simply being Pippa's sister again."

Jack nodded. "When are you coming up to Town?"

"I don't know yet. Soon, I hope."

His jaw hardened. "There is something you should know before you return."

"What is it? What's wrong?"

"There are some fools about town saying nasty things about you. Exactly what I was afraid of when Adam came up with his idea that the two of you pretend to be engaged."

Cass couldn't keep the exasperation from her voice. "Jack. Tell me precisely what is being said."

He shrugged, and she realized he couldn't bear to have her know. "Ridiculous nonsense. 'Adam had better watch his back.' 'It was Cass Linford's pistol that killed Bentley.' That kind of thing."

Cass felt the blood drain from her face. "Some people will always be mean-spirited, Jack. We must ignore them."

"I know. But it's hard when they've put it in the betting books at White's."

"You must be joking."

"No. A wager on whether Adam will survive the engagement. The odds are against it, I'm afraid." When he saw the stricken look on her face, Jack said, "I shouldn't have told you. I'm sorry, Cass. Will you be all right?"

"I'm fine." Her legs were trembling, and she badly needed to sit down, but she must see them off first. "Thank you for telling me. I know it wasn't easy." She called to Pippa, who'd been chasing one of the dogs, and hugged her. When her brother and sister were settled in the carriage, Cass gave them what she hoped was a convincing smile. "I'll see you again soon. Don't worry about me." Jack patted her hand and signaled the coachman to move. As the carriage made its turn onto the approach road, Pippa hung out the window and waved. Cass waved back, laughing. Until she was crying. She hurried inside and grabbed a bonnet and spencer, then informed Scott she was going to walk for a while. She roamed aimlessly, blinded by her tears. A false engagement to her was making Adam a laughing stock. Brilliant. He must have heard the gossip, too. What must he be thinking? She would have to cry off soon, to spare him ridicule as he was trying to find his way politically.

After Bentley's death, she'd been dimly aware that there were whispers that she'd shot him, but having been injured herself, and in shock after the tragedy, she hadn't paid close attention. No doubt Jack and her mother had protected her from the worst. No wonder they hadn't minded when she sequestered herself in the country for two years.

When Cass looked up, she was near the folly in the woods. She sat down on the stone bench and thought about the fact that she had never told either of them about Bentley's final words to her, just before he shot himself. In her mind's eye, Cass could see him clearly, even now. His darkly handsome face ravaged by some inner demon, his shaking hand pointing the pistol at her. And then he'd said, *You're to blame for this*, before turning the gun on himself.

She had never understood what he had meant, and so she'd carried a burden of guilt in her heart for her fiancé's death. Dabbing at the tears trailing down her cheeks, Cass truly believed she must have been responsible for Bentley taking his own life. If only she knew what she had done or said to drive him to such a desperate act. And now it was all being dredged up again, and she and Adam weren't even truly engaged.

Chapter Twenty-Two

Adam had indeed heard the rumors. He'd like to strangle the bastard who had entered the wager about Cass into the betting books, but he had to find out who it was first. Atherton had promised to tell him if he learned anything. His other friends and acquaintances seemed to be avoiding him. Probably some of them were among the scandalmongers.

Scowling, Adam dragged his attention back to the document before him. Parliament was conducting a second inquiry into the disaster at Walcheren to follow up on some matters not addressed previously. He'd been summoned to give testimony, since he'd been out of the country the first time. He was loath to take part, hating the thought of dredging it all up again. Reluctantly, he concluded it was incumbent upon him to do his duty and answer questions, but he dreaded it.

He set the summons aside and picked up the letter he'd been writing earlier.

11 June
London

Dearest Cassie,

I miss you to distraction. I dream about having you: in my bed, on my desk, atop the library table, under the dining room table. On the bench in the garden. In an opera box. At Vauxhall Gardens, our own ecstasy far surpassing the fireworks.

Thoroughly disgusted with himself, he crumpled the paper and lobbed it toward the grate, where it landed with a soft crackle to settle among all the other discards. Almost a fortnight had passed since Adam had seen Cass. She'd sent him a short note in response to his first letter, assuring him that she was being well taken care of. But that was all. She gave no hint of missing him. It wasn't fair. Why should he be longing for her when she was apparently quite content to rusticate without him?

Shoving his chair back, he got to his feet and commenced pacing about the room. He'd hit a brick wall in his attempts to find the book he was seeking. The one he so desperately wanted to give Cass. And that was the least of his problems. Despite his best intentions and a great deal of time and effort, Adam had accomplished very little since he'd arrived in town. He was discouraged about his chances of finding another constituency, and now he had these rumors about Cass to contend with. People were petty and cruel. They were bored and had nothing better to do than invent lies that hurt innocent people. He knew that, so why couldn't he simply get out among them and show the *ton* that the gossip was so ridiculous as to be beneath his notice. Instead he hid at home like a coward.

Adam desperately needed someone to confide in, from whom to seek advice. Ironically, Cass was the only person he trusted enough to fill that role. He missed her so much that his ability to concentrate had gone to hell. He needed her, in every way. Cass would know what to do, how to proceed. Adam had lost his confidence and didn't think he could find it again without her. God, if things were different, he would marry Cass in a heartbeat. If she would have him, that is, and he wasn't at all sure she would. By her own admission, she didn't trust him any more than other men, and he didn't blame her. The chances were excellent that he would turn out like his father, in any case, and he would never subject Cass to what his mother had gone through.

After a while, Adam removed to his chamber. He crawled into a bottle and got as drunk as a lord. Dinner came and went. He remained. When his valet dared to come through, Adam shooed him out. When Flynn rapped on the door and said he was leaving a tray, Adam leaped up—if a staggering little hop could be called a leap—and yanked the door open. "Take that away. Bring another bottle of this." He thrust the empty brandy bottle into his butler's hands. "Make it two, no, three more bottles. Leave them in the hall."

Flynn, trained to keep his expression impassive, said, "Very good, sir."

Adam gathered up the bottles when they were delivered. Ah, he was a happy man. He drank long into the night, and over the next week continued in the same manner. He choked down a few bites of food each day, so his stomach could handle the liquor. Occasionally, he went for middle-of-the-night rambles around the townhouse. He turned away his valet (easy), and Flynn (harder), who at one point told Adam he was being bloody stupid.

Adam was perfectly content locked up in his chamber, drinking himself into a stupor every day. And perfectly miserable.

• • •

A week after Jack and Pippa's visit, Cass had decided on a course of action.

She might be the object of ridicule in the *ton*, the woman who could never be free of her past, but there was no reason, while living in the country, she could not follow through with her plan. After all, it was the reason she had remained here when everybody else had decamped for town.

One afternoon while walking around the lake, she rested on the temple steps to think. The day was warm, and the bees buzzing around the abundant periwinkle made a pleasing sound. She needed to speak with Sir William, but before she could do so, she must learn something more about him that would help establish a bond between them. In these matters it was often the heart rather than the mind that won people over. As soon as she returned from her walk, she would talk to Mr. Scott. If he were the least bit like other butlers she'd known, he would be a font of local information. And Mrs. Wetherby as well. Surely one of them would know some small tidbit, some trifling detail about the baronet, that would help her.

On her return to the house, she found Mrs. Wetherby in the entryway instructing a new housemaid in her duties. Cass watched for a moment. *Heavens, who knew there was such intricacy to dusting?* "Pardon me, Mrs. Wetherby," she said. "When you are finished here, may I have a word?"

"Certainly, miss. Would you like to drink tea with me? We might sit in the downstairs drawing room. It's Mrs. Grey's favorite."

They made themselves comfortable in the rose and white room, Cass on the sofa and Mrs. Wetherby in a damask chair. In a few minutes, one of the kitchen maids brought the tea and some biscuits. Cass poured. Handing the woman a cup, she asked, "How long have you worked for the Greys?"

The housekeeper smiled, her face lighting up. Obviously,

talking of the family was something she enjoyed. "Oh, many years now. I've done any number of jobs. I was a maid at Longmere when the boys were born. I was Master Adam's nursemaid for a time. Then Mrs. Grey asked me to be her lady's maid."

Ah. Cass leaned back and sipped her tea. Thoughts of Sir William flew right out of her head. She could likely learn something about Adam from this woman. About the Grey family. But she didn't want to seem too eager. "When did you take on the housekeeper's duties? Were you still at Longmere?"

"No, no, that was after we left. That is, Mrs. Grey and young Adam left, and I went with them. I couldn't bear to leave her, not in her..." It was obvious Mrs. Wetherby was struggling for the right word. Cass supplied it.

"Situation?" she prompted.

"She was expecting another child, you see."

Cass sucked in a breath. "I had no idea."

Mrs. Wetherby went on. "I swear, I don't know how she stayed with that man as long as she did." Her face flushed, she leaned forward and lowered her voice, and Cass knew she was priming herself to share further secrets. "It was after he, the master, tried to get his sons involved in his nonsense. That was when she finally left."

"I see," Cass said, even though she didn't have an inkling.

"His wild goings-on, with women and gambling and such," she said, giving Cass a knowing look. "He wanted the boys to take part in the parties, forcing his sons to do, well, you know, with the lowest of women. And they, so young. Hugh sixteen and Adam not yet fifteen. Their father said that was how they'd learn to be men. Mrs. Grey caught him red handed."

Cass felt herself blush. Surely she should not be privy to such information. But that did not stop her from asking, nearly in a whisper, "What happened afterward?"

"We left the next morning. Took only what we could pack in a few bandboxes before Mr. Grey woke up. Hugh came, too."

"How horrible." *And how revealing.* It explained so much. After learning this, how could she even think about Sir William? It would have to wait. "Mrs. Wetherby, would you mind terribly if we continued this conversation another time? I'm feeling a bit fatigued."

"Oh, my, I've rattled on too long."

"Not at all." Cass hesitated, then asked, "How did Hugh end up back at Longmere with his father?"

"A mother has no rights as far as her children are concerned, you know. That man threatened to take her to court if she tried to keep Adam and Hugh both. By rights, he could have demanded to have both sons with him but he'd always been partial to his firstborn, so Mrs. Grey had to give Hugh up. It took her a long time to get over that."

"And the baby?"

"Stillborn. She came too early, and to this day I swear it was because of all the turmoil Mrs. Grey had to bear.

"Thank you for telling me," Cass said.

Mrs. Wetherby gave her a rueful smile. "You're going to be part of the family, my dear. You stay here now and rest. Would you like me to leave the tea?"

"Please," Cass said, wishing she had some brandy instead. That might be the only way to obliterate the deep sadness for Adam, for all of them, taking root inside her. What she still did not understand, though, was why Adam was so certain he would end up being the same kind of man as Benjamin Grey. Why, in his mind, was it so inescapable?

• • •

Adam had lost track of time. Had he been holed up in his chamber for hours, or days? His scalp was beginning to itch and he was repulsed by his own rank odor. Over the last few days he'd gradually stopped drinking. A bath and a shave seemed like a good idea. He walked over to the door to holler for his man, but when he heaved it open, Hugh was standing there, looking pristine in a shirt so white it practically glowed. His forest green coat looked new and superbly tailored.

"Well, if it isn't Beau Brummell's little brother." Adam slammed the door and retreated to his chair. Hugh opened it and walked in, looking repulsed.

"You stink like a rutting pig." Before Adam could protest, Hugh hollered for Flynn, who was told to find Adam's valet and order a bath. The entire household must have been on alert, in case the master decided to bathe, because the tub and hot water were brought in record time. And Grissom appeared almost immediately, with razor and fresh towels in hand.

"I'll make myself at home until you're presentable," Hugh said. "By the way, where is Deborah?"

"Last I knew, she and Freddie were off in the country visiting one of his new grandchildren. His daughters seem to breed like rabbits."

When Adam sank into the tub, he felt sanity returning. The amount of grime dissolving around him was appalling. After a minute, he dunked his head and then gave his hair and scalp a good scrub. He had his valet pour fresh water over his hair to rinse it, and then over his whole body.

He'd barely tucked his shirt in before Hugh returned. "When did you last eat?" his brother asked. When Adam didn't answer, Hugh said, "You sure as hell look like you could use a decent meal. You can eat while we're talking."

"I have nothing to say to you, brother."

"Bollocks. You drowned yourself in drink and remained

locked up in your bedchamber for days on end. I think you need to talk to somebody, and it looks like I'm the only man available for the job."

Apparently Hugh didn't discourage easily. When Adam motioned to the chairs in front of the fireplace, Hugh scowled, surveying the room with a look of disgust. "Oh, no. We're not staying in here."

Adam had to admit the room was indeed an unholy mess. Dirty clothes and linens lying around. Plates of uneaten food that had been moldering for days. Empty bottles of whiskey. An unmade bed. He chortled. "I can't argue that point. We'll use the library." He signaled Hugh to lead the way. Once they were settled, Flynn brought in plates of eggs, kippers, toast, and rolls, along with plenty of coffee. The mere scent of the food, odors mingling, nearly drove Adam over the edge. Ravenous, he filled a plate and took a seat behind his desk. Hugh watched him eat, an amused look on his face, drinking coffee and eating a roll.

Adam finished, pushed his plate away, and poured himself a fresh cup of coffee. He had no experience with brotherly confidences and only wanted to get this unwelcome visit over with so Hugh would leave.

Hugh stretched his long legs out and gave his brother a sardonic look. "I don't give a damn about you, Adam, or the reason you're holed up here. But I happen to think Cass is a lovely and intelligent woman. I've heard some rumors since I've been in town. A few idiots have even made comments to my face. What's going on?"

Adam sighed. He'd better start at the beginning. "Cass's fiancée, Bentley, the Earl of Wilton's heir, committed suicide while he and Cass were at Drury Lane. He shot himself."

"Jesus. I didn't know. When?"

"I only recently found out about it myself, from Deborah. It was a few years ago, around the time I left for the Continent.

At Jack's insistence, Cass only agreed lately to return to society." Adam took a swallow of coffee. "What have you heard?"

"That Cass killed someone. How long until she kills you? That sort of drivel. I had no idea what it all meant."

"It's in the betting book at White's. I'm itching to get my hands on the man who made the original wager."

"Have you talked to Cass about it? About the night it happened?"

"I don't know any of the details of the night Bentley died, but I'm sure Cass has never fired a pistol. She couldn't hurt anyone any more than Deborah could." Since he'd come this far, Adam decided to tell Hugh the rest. He related the whole sorry tale of how and why he'd lied to the elder Grey about being engaged to Cass.

"Father wanted you to marry Miss Broxton." It was a statement, pronounced in a voice cold as ice. "I wasn't under consideration as a husband for Eleanor, I take it?"

Hugh's eyes had darkened and his jaw looked set in stone. So that was the way the wind blew, Adam thought. *What a fool I was, not to have picked up on it.* He recalled that his brother and Miss Broxton seemed to get on so well during the house party. Hugh had shown endless patience with her during the target shooting, and she had sung his praises. Blinded by his determination to despise his brother, Adam's only thought had been to keep him away from Eleanor.

"I—I did not wish to be married to Miss Broxton, nor she to me, I'm sure. Sir William thinks I'm a war hero, or some such nonsense. That is why he chose me."

Hugh nodded brusquely in acknowledgment. "I see. So in order to get out of the marriage, you said you were engaged to Cass. And somehow got her to go along with it."

Adam cringed. When put like that it seemed so sordid. "I know how it sounds. But I will never marry, and I don't believe

Cass wishes to either. After what happened with Bentley, she doesn't have much trust in men."

Hugh frowned. "Why do say you'll never marry? Don't politicians need a wife?"

Adam snorted. "Because of Father. I may end up exactly like him. I spent the last week drinking myself to oblivion. If that's not following in his footsteps—"

"Don't be an arse. You had good reason. I may be mistaken, but I'd guess indulging in a drunken binge is a rarity for you." Hugh leaned forward, hands on thighs. "You're nothing like the old man. In case you've forgotten, I'm the one with that reputation."

"That's as may be, but it doesn't change my feelings on the matter. I can navigate politics without a wife." He couldn't fathom why Hugh didn't understand. "Our father's debauched life destroyed our family. Damaged Deborah almost beyond recovery. Separated us. It's in our blood." Adam shoved his chair back violently and stood up. "Frankly, I'm surprised you don't feel the same way. I take it you're back in town to find a wife."

Hugh straightened. "Ostensibly. I've not much interest in it at the moment."

Adam edged toward the door, hoping his brother would take the cue and leave. "And just so you know. Broxton decided against me. Because of the old man's debt, and his shenanigans at the ball. Thinks we're all alike."

A laugh burst from Hugh. "How that must have galled you. What will you do now?"

"I'm trying to find another constituency, but not having much success."

"What about you and Cass?"

"After a time, she'll cry off."

"Christ. What an unholy mess you've gotten yourself into."

"How astute of you. And now, I'm sure you must have someplace else to be," Adam said.

Hugh rose and walked toward Adam. Standing eye to eye with him, he said, "Someday you may like to know exactly what life with our father was like for me. It may set you straight on a few things." He brushed past Adam and opened the door.

Right before stepping through, he spun back around and said, "Do you love Cass?"

Adam wasn't sure if he wanted to answer. But finally he said, "I think perhaps I do."

"Then you're a bloody lunatic if you don't beg her to marry you."

As soon as Hugh was gone, Adam began composing a new letter to Cass.

Chapter Twenty-Three

After what she had learned from Mrs. Wetherby, Cass was even more determined to speak to Sir William about Adam. In the end, it was the morning papers that provided her with the information she sought. She had taken to eating breakfast at her writing desk, skimming the news as she nibbled on toast and drank tea. A few days after her talk with the housekeeper, both papers carried an updated list of the dead from the Siege of Badajoz, which had occurred last spring. Although it was ultimately a victory, thousands of British soldiers had been killed, and afterwards, the men had gone crazy, rampaging throughout the town, killing innocent Spanish citizens, even killing some of their own comrades. It had taken days to restore order.

Among the list of the dead she found one name she recognized:

Captain Benedict Broxton, Light Division, Haslemere, Surrey

Cass dropped a piece of toast halfway to her mouth. She had the opening she needed with Sir William. As soon as she'd finished eating, Agnes helped her dress and she called for a conveyance. There was no time like the present.

Seated in the carriage, Cass had a chance to study the Broxton home as she approached. The house was newly constructed, and, in Cass's opinion, did not fit into its surrounding park at all. It was stucco, ornamented with a good deal of wrought iron and an elaborate fan light over the front door, which featured patterned surrounds. A house much more suited to town than country.

She handed the butler her card, and Eleanor herself came to greet her, walking briskly over the parquet floor. "Miss Linford. How nice to see you!"

Cass held out her hand. "I am glad to see you, too, Miss Broxton." Eleanor turned and looked around, as though she wasn't sure what came next. "Please, do join us in the drawing room."

Cass followed her down a corridor leading off the central rotunda. They entered a room, fitted up quite beautifully in maroon and cream, and Sir William immediately got to his feet to greet her. "Miss Linford." He looked at his wife, whose face bore a tight smile. "My dear?"

"How do you do, Lady Broxton?" Cass offered her hand to the older lady, who clasped it, albeit reluctantly. She spoke not a word. Cass decided to act as if she hadn't noticed the bordering-on-rude greeting.

"Please, be seated," Eleanor said. "Will you take tea with us?"

Certain the elder Broxtons would prefer that she did not, Cass nevertheless assented. If she refused, her visit would be over before she'd accomplished her mission. She racked her brain for a topic of conversation and finally settled on the décor.

"What a lovely room this is," she said, glancing around. "Did you fit it up yourself, Lady Broxton?"

At this, Eleanor's mother perked up. "Yes. Eleanor helped me. She has a great eye for color and design."

"I particularly like your drapes, and the upholstery on the Sheraton armchairs is elegant. Well done, Miss Broxton," Cass said. "Have you put your talents to work in other parts of the house?"

"Only in a small way. My interest lies chiefly in fashion design."

"It is Eleanor's little hobby," her mother said.

Well. How condescending.

Maybe this isn't the best topic of conversation. She would hate to find herself on Sir William's bad side before she'd even had a chance to speak to him about Adam. Rather than pursue it further, Cass simply smiled at the girl. Fortunately, the tea arrived and Eleanor busied herself pouring and passing the cups around. Cass swallowed the strong brew, hoping it would shore up her confidence.

Lady Broxton started to say something else, but Eleanor cut her off, asking Cass how long she planned to remain in the country. Cass said her plans were not firm.

At last Sir William stood. "If you will excuse me, Miss Linford, I have some business to take care of." Obviously, he thought Cass wished to visit with the ladies of the house. She leaped to her feet. It was now or never.

"Sir William, I wonder if you could spare me a few moments to speak to you privately." She could see the wheels turning as he thought over his response. He nodded to his wife and Eleanor, who took their leave, the latter shaking Cass's hand most enthusiastically.

"Goodbye, Miss Linford. Please do call again."

"It would be my pleasure. And I hope you will call upon

me. I am presently in residence at Deborah Grey's home." She remembered Eleanor asking her for advice—about Adam. But later she'd seemed interested in Hugh and comfortable with him.

Sir William waited for Cass to return to her chair before seating himself. "What may I do for you?" he asked. His graying hair was combed back from his high forehead. She thought the style made him look perpetually surprised.

Cass took a steadying breath. "Sir William. I-I've come to ask, what is your opinion of the war?"

He grunted in surprise. "Is this a serious question, Miss Linford?"

"Quite serious, sir."

"I've no idea what brings you to my door to ask me such a thing. It's not women's business. But since you ask, I'm damned sick of it. I want it over and done with, and I want men in Parliament who will get the job done. Allocate more money, whatever it takes."

"I thought you might feel that way. Before we talk further, may I offer my sincere condolences on the loss of your son, Sir William? I saw his name in the paper, on the list of dead from the Siege of Badajoz, in the Peninsula."

He looked down, and she thought maybe he was trying to get his emotions in check. "Not my son, Miss Linford, but like one. My nephew. My only brother's boy, who lived with us after his parents died. He was a captain in the Light Division."

"When Adam—my fiancé—first returned to London and told me he wanted to stand for Commons, I grilled him. You see, sir, I've always had a keen interest in politics. It turned out that he was passionate about ending the war."

"*Humph.* So that is what this is about. I've already told him I won't support him."

Cass scooted to the edge of her chair and went on as though he hadn't spoken. "Do you know about Walcheren?

About what happened there? Adam was wounded in the siege on Flushing. No good ever came of it—they chased the French navy out, but did no real damage. Afterward thousands of our own men died from a fever. Adam helped care for them during the evacuation. It's his view that countless men lost their lives for naught."

Broxton's eyes sparked, and Cass knew she'd struck a chord. "That is how I feel about Badajoz. The victory came at too great a price. And would you like to know the ultimate irony, Miss Linford?" Abruptly, he stopped talking and his gaze settled somewhere over Cass's head.

She waited. It would be best to give him the time he needed. He cleared his throat after a moment and said, "Benedict was killed in the rampaging after the battle. Killed by one of his own men."

"Oh, no!" Involuntarily, her hand shot out and covered his. Of course, she'd just read about it in the morning papers. The men so demoralized by the vast number of their dead brothers, they'd gone about the town looting, rioting, breaking into homes, and shooting their own officers who tried to stop them. "I am so sorry."

He patted Cass's hand, his eyes shining with tears. "Tell your fiancé I will reconsider my decision. If he can help stop this damned, endless war…but I make no promises."

• • •

It was Adam's second letter that decided Cass. It was time to go to Town.

When she returned from the Broxton's, the post was waiting in its usual place, a silver tray on the chest in the entryway. Happiness rippled through her when she saw Adam's handwriting. Carefully, she broke the seal and unfolded it, hoping there would be more than just platitudes this time.

She was disappointed at first.

16 June
London

Dearest Cassie,

The weather here in London has improved. I've returned to my daily gallops on Rotten Row, and walks about town are once again possible. I detest going everywhere by coach.

I trust life in the country is tranquil and you are well. I ran into Jack at White's. He told me that he and Pippa visited you and that he informed you of the nasty bit of gossip circulating here. Please try to put it out of your mind, Cass. When I find out who is responsible, I'll send him to kingdom come.

Sorry to say, I've made no further progress on finding a constituency. All the talk here is about the war with America. For us to be involved in another conflict is a grave mistake, I fear.

The remainder of the letter caused her heart to jump in her chest, stopped her breath:

But to hell with all of that. Here is the truth of things, my darling. I am unable to get a decent night's sleep. Because you, Cassie, are there in all my dreams. I find myself in the awkward position of longing for you when in fact it is I who separated us. Ironic, isn't it?

My desire for you is threatening my sanity. Images of your lush body are what unsettle my dreams and keep me awake. If it weren't for my

father and our family curse, I would worship you as
you deserve. I have been trying to write you another
of those meaningless letters for days and have
succeeded only in filling the grate with crumpled
parchment. It came down to this: I couldn't write
without telling you how I miss you and ache for
you, in every possible way.

> *Yours, as ever,*
> *A.*

Cass felt as if she were floating somewhere above herself. Was that her, Cass, Adam was talking about? He hadn't said it outright, but weren't these the words of a man in love? At least, she thought they were, never before having been the recipient of a love letter. Had she been fooling herself these last few weeks? Was she in love with him, too?

Cass began to laugh and cry all at once. After a minute, she gathered herself and considered what to do. The letter allowed her to hope that there might be a future for them. She wasn't fool enough to believe his fears of becoming like his father had suddenly vanished. Nor had her deep reservations about marriage. But wasn't their chance at happiness worth fighting for? Cass hastened upstairs, narrowly avoiding a collision with one of the footmen. "Oh, sorry!" she said, rushing past him.

Wrenching open the door of her chamber, she called out for her maid. "Agnes! Start packing. We're going to London."

Chapter Twenty-Four

Adam stood at the perimeter of the ballroom, talking in a desultory manner with a couple of his new acquaintances. Both were MPs. He had spent his afternoon at Peele's perusing as many newspapers as he could digest at one sitting and drinking an excessive amount of coffee. Later, he'd dined at Offley's Tavern on Henrietta Street, where he'd run into Jarvis and Howell, the two men now standing beside him. Only one of them, Howell, had an invitation to the ball, but they sneaked Jarvis past the footmen with no problem.

"I believe I shall ask that blond-haired chit over there to dance," Jarvis said.

Adam sipped his wine. "I don't think that's a good idea unless you've been introduced. She looks quite young. Aren't wealthy widows more your line?"

Jarvis laughed. "I'll find somebody to properly introduce me," he said, wandering off.

Howell looked at Adam and shrugged. "He's hopeless. But he's not a complete fool. He won't do anything untoward."

"Glad to hear it," Adam said. He watched the couples

who were dancing the current set and remembered the last time he'd danced with Cass, at their betrothal ball. She'd been wearing that enchanting green dress that had pushed up her breasts so provocatively. He wondered if she'd received his letter yet, and if she had, what she must be thinking. He must have been suffering from temporary insanity to write such things to her. Not to write them, but to actually send the letter. Stirring up feelings he had tried, apparently unsuccessfully, to banish.

Adam looked up, astonished, when he heard the footman announce the newest arrivals. "Viscount Linford and Miss Cassandra Linford."

• • •

Cass waited at the top of the steps, clinging to her brother's arm.

When she'd reached Linford House, only a few hours ago, she had sent a message round to Adam telling him of her arrival. Jack had taken tea with her and insisted she attend the Cowper ball with him and Jenny that evening.

"But I've only just gotten here," she protested. "Isn't there some event I could attend tomorrow? And I would rather hear from Adam first."

Jack looked sympathetic. "I know, my dear. But to my knowledge, there are no balls tomorrow. The season is nearly at an end, you know. And it is vital that you be seen in public." He stuffed a biscuit into his mouth and washed it down with a long gulp of tea.

"With Adam!" Cass said, frustrated. "What good will it do to be seen if we're not in each other's company?"

"I have a feeling he'll be there. From what I understand, he spends most days at the coffee houses seeking patronage. He probably arrived home with only enough time to change and didn't receive your message."

Cass had reluctantly agreed. Her first reaction to any public appearance, since the disaster at Drury Lane, was first to avoid it, and if that wasn't possible, to remain in the shadows. Now Jack wanted her to attend a ball, the chief purpose of which was to be seen by the entire *ton*. As fate would have it, however, she wasn't sorry.

Because as they stood there, waiting to be announced, every nerve ending told her Adam was in the room. She felt it, knew it instinctively. She'd made the right decision. Or had she? A sea of faces was upturned, staring at them. Was she daft? In her state of wild anticipation over seeing Adam, she had forgotten all about the innuendo, the nasty rumors circulating about Bentley's death.

It seemed to Cass, despite the music, that the room had gone silent. Excited voices, laughter, the typical sounds of a ball had ceased. Her legs felt suddenly stiff, and she hoped she would make it down the stairs without stumbling.

"We have friends here, Cass. All of them ready to stand by you," Jack whispered. "Be brave and smile, for God's sake." A cloying scent, probably caused by the huge bouquets of summer flowers placed about the room, made her stomach roil.

We have enemies, too. Cass could see some of them, heads together, whispering, casting sly glances in her direction. One woman, for the amusement of her friends, held out her hand and pretended to shoot a pistol. But Cass stretched her lips into a semblance of a smile anyway. When they reached the ballroom floor, after what seemed like hours, Atherton was there waiting. Eyes welcoming, he bowed over Cass's hand. "Miss Linford. Town has been a dull place without you."

"My lord," she said with a genuine smile. "How good to see you again." Now she heard whispers, rising to a hum, and when Atherton stepped aside, a path had opened up behind him. To make room for Adam, who was slowly walking toward her, eyes smoldering and looking devilishly handsome. As though he wanted to show them all that she was his and he was coming to claim her. And they could all be damned. His gaze never left her face.

• • •

A thousand thoughts vied for Adam's attention, but he was preoccupied with only one at the moment. He was so damned happy to see Cassie. He forgot about the fact that she hadn't bothered to tell him she was coming. That he hadn't had time to quash the rumors. That he never should have written that damned letter before he'd figured things out. She looked stunning, in a deep blue silk gown that draped enticingly around her body and showed off its tantalizing curves.

She was staring back at him, her head cocked, and for a moment he couldn't tell if she was glad to see him. And then she smiled. A glowing, heated smile she was trying to temper, to hold back a bit, but could not. He drew closer, and she let go of her brother's arm and stood alone, waiting for him. Adam walked right up to her and placed a palm to one side of her lovely face. Then he kissed her on the mouth. Not just a skimming of the lips, but an open-mouthed, deep kiss. He hadn't meant to be so brazen, but what was a man to do when met with the woman of his dreams, from whom he'd been separated far too long?

There were cheers from the men, clapping, and nervous laughter. And then the ballroom got back to normal.

She sounded breathless. "Adam."

He smiled. "Cassie. Come with me." He grabbed her hand and tugged.

Jack was scowling at them both, but if he dared stop them, Adam would probably punch him. He ushered Cass out of the room and down a corridor lighted with branches of candles. All the doors were closed. He knocked on one, cracked it open, and heard a little scream. "Not this one," he said.

They finally found an unoccupied room, which was lit by a single candle as well as a fire in the grate. Adam locked the door and then pulled Cass into his arms, kissing her long and deep and savagely. God, how he'd been longing for this. Her hands slid up his chest and she pushed. Enough so that he knew she wanted him to stop. Grudgingly, he ended the kiss. But he still held her close.

"Hello, Adam," she said.

"Damn, you're beautiful. My pardon. I can't help myself." He rested his forehead on hers for a beat, then drew back and said, "Why didn't you tell me you were coming?"

"It was a spur-of-the-moment decision. When I got to Town, I sent a note—I guess you didn't see it."

"I've been gone all day. Dashed home to change for the ball, then right back out."

"Well," Cass said. "Here I am."

"Yes." *Thank the gods, my own Aphrodite is here.* "I've missed you Cass."

She wrenched out of his grasp. "What has changed, Adam? When we were last together, you said you'd used me and you were afraid of becoming like your father. Now…your letter. And this." She waved her arm about. "All this…passion."

He looked intently at her for a moment. How could he explain it when he did not fully understand it himself? "Hugh," he said at last.

"Hugh, your brother? What are you talking about?"

Adam laughed. "I was, let's say, in a bad way. Hugh came to check on me. He said something I haven't been able to get out of my mind. Actually, more than one thing."

Cass started to speak, but he interrupted her. "I need to pay a visit to my father." Yes, that was it. It had just come clear.

"You recently saw him. Twice, I believe. It did not go well."

Adam scrubbed a hand over his face. "I have some questions for him. It's time he answered them."

Cass nodded. "When will you go?"

"In a few days. I'm not about to leave until we've had some time together." When he tried to wrap his arms around her again, she protested.

"We must get back. It is probably about time for supper. A good opportunity to talk to other guests and show everyone what a devoted couple we are."

"Don't laugh," Adam said. "I am devoted to you."

• • •

Supper was torture. Cass sat between two of Adam's new friends, Sebastian Jarvis and Wesley Howell. Jarvis had rogue written all over him. Tall, well formed, and quite handsome. He had the look of a man who took no pains with his toilette — dark stubble and mussed hair — but Cass was reasonably sure it was a look he cultivated.

Mr. Howell was more serious and Cass found him easy to talk to. He was an MP for Newcastle, near where the Felling mine disaster had occurred. He told her a little bit about his concerns regarding mine safety and child labor.

"As far as I'm concerned, sending children down a mine is a criminal act," Cass said. "Will they be able to recover the bodies?"

"The pits are closed now, so the fires will go out. At some point, when it's deemed safe enough, they'll attempt it. Probably not for another month or so."

Adam was conversing with her brother on one side and Jenny on the other. She felt his eyes on her throughout, and a couple of times his slow, simmering smile caused her to squirm. It made her hot, damp between her legs, and left her feeling light headed. For pity's sake, she couldn't concentrate on what was being said when he looked at her like that. And all she could do was fasten her eyes on him and try not to break into that daft smile that reflected the joy she was feeling.

Later, when they parted, Adam whispered in her ear. "Dream of me tonight. I promise I'll be dreaming of you."

Cass shivered.

· · ·

Cass spent the next morning helping Agnes with the unpacking. After that, she ventured up to the nursery to visit Pippa and meet her new governess. She braced herself for the worst, as she fully expected to dislike the woman who was taking on the role Cass had performed for the last few years.

"Cassie!" Philippa shouted when she glimpsed her sister.

"Pip, pip!" Cass knelt down and Pippa ran into her arms.

"Hooray! I missed you so much, Cassie."

"I know, dearest, I missed you, too." Then she leaned in and whispered something in her sister's ear. Suddenly shy, Pippa looked back and forth from Cass to her tutor.

"Cassie, may I present my new governess?"

Cass suppressed a grin and nodded.

"I should like to introduce Miss Annis Stanton to you." The little girl turned toward the governess then and said, "Miss Stanton, this is my sister, Miss Cassandra Linford."

Cass, who'd still been kneeling, rose and stepped forward, offering her hand. She was so taken aback by the very lovely face before her, she barely managed to stammer out a greeting.

"It is a pleasure to meet you, Miss Linford," the woman said.

"Likewise, Miss Stanton." Cass turned and spoke to Philippa. "I should like to have a private word with your governess, Pip."

Pippa skipped out of the room, but could not resist turning back and making a face at Cass.

"Please, let's do sit down," Cass said, gesturing toward the table and chairs. When they were settled, Cass said, "Tell me about yourself, Miss Stanton."

"I'm from Devon, originally. My mother died when I was quite young, and my father raised me and educated me. He employed masters for music, drawing, and dancing. When he died, I came to London to live with relatives, but...that did not work out. I placed an ad in the papers."

Cass wondered how often she'd had to recite this autobiography. It sounded memorized and made the details of Annis Stanton's life seem insignificant. She had an arresting face, set off by deep green eyes that carried a hint of mystery. There was something about her that Cass identified with.

"And how are you and Philippa getting on?"

"She's delightful!" Miss Stanton said. "I love her spirit and her youthful enthusiasm. She's inquisitive about so many things."

"I am relieved to hear you say it. Pippa is not cut out for a traditional education—at least not a steady diet of it. She needs to be up and moving about and exploring. Visiting museums and parks, taking walks, anything that results in her learning something without even being aware." After a discreet pause, Cass said, "I am sorry my cousin tried to impede your efforts."

The other woman blushed. "I feel responsible for her hasty departure. It was rather awkward."

Cass sighed. "Please, do not. Louisa was never quite at home in our household. I am afraid she did not approve of our method of doing...anything." Cass laughed. Miss Stanton covered her mouth with her hand to hide her own smile.

"Are you settling in to life at Linford House?"

"It is certainly the best post I have ever had. The staff is kind and welcoming, and I'm beginning to feel at home here. I attended church this morning with the housekeeper."

Cass smiled. "Good. If you wouldn't mind, I would enjoy accompanying you and Pippa on some of your excursions. I have been her tutor for the last few years."

"So your brother told me. I wouldn't mind at all, and I'm certain Pippa would be thrilled."

Before taking her leave, Cass's eyes roved around the schoolroom. It held so many memories, not only from her own childhood, but from her years of tutoring her sister. She had expected to feel a pang of regret or sadness, but oddly enough, she did not. It felt like part of her old life. Like a skin she was shedding in order to begin anew.

Chapter Twenty-Five

Monday evening Cass was reading, her book propped up on a cushion so she could brush out her hair at the same time. After Agnes had helped her undress, she'd dismissed her for the night. She'd neither seen nor heard from Adam since the ball and was having trouble concentrating. Why hadn't he called on her?

Her chamber door opened and Adam came through. Cass was so shocked she dropped the hairbrush and stammered. "How did you get in here?"

"*Shh*." He kissed her softly, then bent down and retrieved the brush. "Allow me the pleasure."

Obligingly, she turned in her seat so that he could attend to her hair. "You haven't answered my question." She kept her voice low.

"When Jack and I fancied ourselves a couple of young Corinthians, we often sneaked into the house through a window near the kitchen. It was never kept locked. It still isn't. Must have a word with Willis about that."

Every stroke of the brush felt divine, making her scalp

tingle with sensations only Adam could arouse in her. After a moment, Cass leaned back against his chest. He snaked one arm across her breasts and encircled her waist with the other, her hair forgotten for the moment. She turned her face around to kiss him.

"Not yet. I want to tell you about my day first."

She laughed. "Go ahead. Just…don't move."

Adam chuckled. "I had to give testimony before a Parliamentary committee on Walcheren."

Cass gave him a questioning look. "I thought that inquiry had been held a few years ago. How was it?"

Adam smiled. "You're right, of course. This was a separate inquiry to receive testimony from those of us who were not available at the time. Tying up loose ends, I suppose. Setting the seal on the lessons-learned column. I've been dreading it, to say the truth. But I thought about that evening at the house party. You forcing me —"

"I did not force you!"

"Urging me, then. You said if you were going to help me get elected, you needed to know about my experience in the war."

"That much I admit to."

"My testimony was exactly the same as what I told you that night, and I was so glad you'd pressured me — my pardon, *encouraged* me — to be forthcoming. It helped me to summarize it concisely before the committee." He moved away from her, taking his warmth with him, and she immediately felt chilled. "Of course they asked me much more detailed questions and dredged up horrors I would have preferred to forget."

"I'm sorry, Adam." Cass realized he was not comfortable talking about Walcheren, perhaps never would be.

He ran his hand up her arm. "If it helps prevent such a disaster happening again, it will be worth it. The rest of the day I spent in my usual futile attempts at finding a constituency.

I lingered in the coffee room at the House of Commons—God, I'm sick of that place—and had dinner at Offley's. To no avail."

Cass rose, feeling dread in the pit of her stomach. *Nothing from Sir William, then.*

Adam was talking again. "But as it turned out, I had no need to look further. A letter from Broxton came in today's post."

She could not tell from his expression whether the news was good or bad. But from what he'd said, it must be good, mustn't it?

He cocked his head at her. "Why didn't you tell me what you'd done, Cassie?"

She waited, but he didn't say more. "So, was it good news, then?" When he nodded, her profound sense of relief made her giddy. "I—he made no promises. I didn't want to raise your hopes only to have you disappointed again."

Adam was gazing at her in the strangest way. "How did you do it? He didn't give me any details, only said that what you'd told him cast me in a more favorable light."

"I'd been studying the newspapers and discovered that his nephew was killed at Badajoz. That gave me an opening. When I visited, I offered my condolences and then asked him his opinion of the war. I told him about what you'd experienced at Walcheren. I hope that was all right—I only gave him the basic facts. But Badajoz and Walcheren have certain similarities."

"Indeed they do. You're a remarkable woman, Cassandra Linford. I stand in awe of your political acumen." He paused, looked at her suspiciously, then said, "That's why you wanted to stay down in the country, isn't it? To try to mend things with him."

When she nodded, he said, "Come here, my heart." Cass walked straight into his embrace.

Adam drew back and said, "Is your brother at home?"

She blushed. "No. He and Jenny are —"

"I don't give a damn where they are. I only want to know if it's safe for me to show you how deeply I appreciate what you did." He crushed her against him and rocked her in his arms. "May I?"

Cass was suddenly aware of his body, his broad shoulders and powerful thighs, which she could feel pressing against her. She felt something else, too. His arousal. Happiness surged inside her, knowing she could do that to him. "I've been waiting all day, Adam. I'm yours." Her body desired him with everything she had, and she would deny him nothing.

• • •

Adam kissed her slowly, seductively. Cass kissed him back, opening her mouth to his gentle coaxing, and for a moment they made love just with their lips and tongues. When that was no longer enough, he gently pushed her away and rained tender kisses across her face and down her neck, until he came to the delicate hollow at her throat. He laved it, then blew lightly on it.

When Cass murmured, "*Mmm*," he smiled.

Adam slipped her dressing gown off her shoulders, but before he could get her naked, she stopped him, pulling at his coat until he tugged it off. She helped him unknot his cravat, and then he pulled his shirt over his head.

When they'd made love the first time, the room had been in darkness. Now, soft, fading daylight streamed through the windows and outlined Adam's chest and abdomen. He stood still and let her drink it in. Her eyes followed the line of dark gold hair that disappeared into his britches. While she was still watching, he sat down on the bed and pulled his boots off. Finally, enjoying her blatant study of him, he removed his pants. His cock sprang out, and he stood and reached for her, his eyes blazing. "I meant every word of that letter, Cassie."

• • •

Adam lifted her night rail over her head, so that she stood before him perfectly naked. She closed her eyes, wanting to block out everything except Adam's touch. His hands moved slowly, languorously, over her breasts, then up to her neck and shoulders and down her arms. Her skin felt heated from his caresses. He knelt, pulling her closer, and began kissing her belly, moving his lips down and down. Cass moved her legs apart, allowing him access to her most intimate part. When she felt his tongue, she released a long sigh of pure pleasure.

When he stood, she nearly screamed *no*, but the sight of him, of his naked shoulders and chest, aroused her. She wanted to feel the curve of his every muscle. If she were an artist, she'd make him pose for her. She'd like to sculpt him, so he would be hers to gaze upon whenever she desired.

Adam backed her up to the bed, their bodies still touching, and laid her down with tenderness. Stretching out beside her, he traced a path from her neck, down her side to the indentation at her waist, up over the curve of her hip, over her flank, as far as he could reach. Now his voice caressed her. "I love touching you, Cassie. Your skin is all satin and silk." He buried his face between her breasts.

Cass sank her fingers into his hair while he took the tip of one breast into his mouth and caressed it with his tongue, teased it with his teeth. She was all nerve endings now, nothing but a mass of sensitivity. Warmth gathered in her belly and desire made her moist and a little mad with wanting him. She moved restlessly.

"Is this what you want, my darling?" He slid his hand up her thigh, grazing her flesh ever so lightly as he moved closer to her center. For a long time, she was lost in the silken touch of his fingers. Adam brought her to the top of an abyss and left her suspended. Once, twice. Finally, when she thought she could bear it no longer, her body refused another ebbing. Her hips rose from the bed and a piercing sweetness possessed her. Owned her. She gasped and clung to him, crying his name over and over again.

When she opened her eyes, she caught him looking at her unguardedly, with so much naked emotion in his eyes it shocked her to her core. She threw her arms around his neck and kissed him deeply.

Adam moved her hand to his penis. "Will you touch me, darling?" And he showed her exactly how to stroke him. To her wanton delight, he said, "Oh yes, you wicked girl. More." Cass rose up and straddled him so she could take in the wonder of his swollen flesh, watch as it trembled with her touch. Amazed at her own daring, she bent down and ran her tongue over the head glistening with a drop of his seed. When Adam nearly shot off the bed, she kissed him there until he begged her to stop. "Where did you learn that?" he asked in a choked voice, but Cass didn't think he really wanted an answer. In any case, she didn't have one. She was acting on pure instinct.

He pulled her down and kissed her mouth, then lifted her at the waist and set her over him so that her opening was aligned with his swollen flesh. "We—we're going to…like this?" Cass asked.

Adam laughed. "We are indeed." His fingers slid into her folds and found her sensitive spot, stroking her until she moaned and cried out for him. Then he pulled her down onto his shaft in one swift motion. She felt a momentary pain and gasped.

"Are you all right? Should I stop?" Adam asked.

"Don't you dare."

...

Adam chuckled low in his throat. His hands at her waist, he urged her up and down, until she began to move on her own. He could tell the exact moment when her pleasure began to mount. Her mouth formed a silent *O*. He was aware he must look like the village lad who'd just stolen the pie. Adam was thrilled to be bringing Cass such sensual delight, holding his own at bay when it was killing him. Reaching for her breasts, he massaged the tips gently, while she drove toward her climax. Just before it happened, she stilled. And then he felt the contractions inside her, felt the waves of bliss wash over her.

Adam held her for a moment, then laid her on her back and knelt between her bent knees. Cass grasped him and guided him toward her opening. "Wrap your legs around my hips, love." Propping himself on his arms, he lowered his body toward hers, and letting himself go at last, thrust in and out until he convulsed with a loud cry. He collapsed onto her, kissing her, holding her, before withdrawing and moving to her side. Strange, he hadn't even considered spilling his seed anywhere but into her body.

He was breathing hard; they both were. Before he could change his mind, he said, voice trembling, "You. You, Cassie, are everything to me." Her eyes were liquid, and he thought she might weep. With tears of joy, he hoped. Quickly, he kissed her forehead and rolled off her. Feeling elated, he padded over to the basin. In a minute he returned to her with a wet washing flannel. When she reached for it, he said, "Let me."

Afterward Adam climbed into bed with her and pulled her against his chest. In seconds, he felt her body relax, felt her sinking into sleep. He wished they could stay like this all night, but that couldn't happen. Yet. After a while, he eased away from her, retrieved his clothing, and dressed. When he was done, he sat on the edge of the bed, waking her. She smiled sleepily up at him, looking endearingly mussed and thoroughly sated.

"I must leave, darling, before Jack gets home. I'm going down to Surrey tomorrow to see my father."

"How long?" Cass asked.

"I should be back in a few days. I'll come to see you as soon as I can."

She lifted up enough to throw her arms around his neck, and holding him fiercely to her, kissed him deeply. "Goodbye, Adam."

Sensing a finality in her words, he felt a momentary panic. "What is it Cass? Is something wrong?" She shook her head and burrowed back under the covers, and he thought perhaps she'd not been quite awake.

• • •

When he'd gone, Cass got out of bed and put on her night rail and dressing gown. She was restless. After a while she padded softly downstairs and poured herself a glass of sherry. She sat in the darkness of the drawing room and sipped it.

Every time she thought about Adam, she felt as if a swarm of butterflies had been let loose inside her. She couldn't put a name to the feeling.

Yes you can, you fool. It's called love. You're in love with Adam.

How could she have been so blind to her own feelings? She'd loved him almost since that first day he'd come home with Jack. How could she ever have thought, if given a choice, she could bear to live her life without him? But now it seemed that was exactly what she must do.

After Adam came to terms with his long held beliefs about his father, assuming he could, Cass was nearly positive he was going to propose. But she couldn't marry him. She'd been responsible for Bentley's death; he'd told her so just before he died. Adam had referred to "the family curse" in his letter, but what if *she* was the one who was cursed?

She could never live with herself if she somehow caused Adam's death, or hurt him irreparably. So she would say a loving but firm "no." She'd lived without him since she was eighteen, and she could do it again. And it would be far better for him to wed a woman who had a spotless reputation, one whose past was not tainted with her fiancé's suicide.

Tears overflowed and rolled down her cheeks. She sat for a long time, crying and sipping at her drink between sobs.

Chapter Twenty-Six

Adam, so ebullient after last night, felt his spirits sinking the closer he got to Longmere. Over and over he reminded himself to think only of Cassie and how she'd turned his world upside down and sideways. It had been coming on gradually, ever since he'd first seen her that day Jack had brought him to Linford House. He was in love with her; he knew that now. He wanted to marry her. Visiting his father was, he hoped, a means of discovering if he was destined to end up the same way, or if there was hope for him and he could propose to Cass.

This time Wesley opened the door before Adam even knocked. Someone must have seen him riding down the drive.

"How are you, Wesley?" The old man appeared confused by the question. Adam passed him his hat and gloves and said, "Is my father in?"

Adam found Benjamin Grey seated at his desk, spectacles on his nose, poring over a ledger book. Was he trying to find a sum of money that had been overlooked? When he raised his head and saw Adam, he slammed the book shut. "To what do

I owe the honor?" he said petulantly.

Before answering, Adam asked Wesley if there was anybody around who could make them a cup of tea. His father said, "None for me; I'm drinking whiskey."

"Bring it anyway, Wesley, with some sandwiches, biscuits, whatever you've got. I'm starving. Is Hugh around?" Adam asked his father.

"He's out at one of the farms, helping a tenant with a new roof." The old man chuckled, then said, "He's not hiding from you."

Adam thought that was a strange comment, but he wasn't about to rise to the bait. "Hugh came to see me in town recently." Adam finally sat down, although his parent hadn't invited him to. "While he was there, he said a few things that puzzled me. I wanted to ask you about them."

His father carefully removed his spectacles and set them down. "I have a question for you first. Are you still determined to marry the Linford chit?"

Adam barked a caustic laugh. "I am." At least now it wasn't a lie.

"I heard Broxton wouldn't take you. You could fix that by marrying his girl."

"He's had a change of heart. He wants me to stand as his man after all. Unlike you, he understands there's no chance of my marrying Eleanor."

His father's color rose, and he started to say something. But Wesley came in with the tea tray. Adam was impressed that it was neatly laid out, with fresh sandwiches and apple tarts on a platter next to the teapot.

Adam poured, recalling that his father took his tea plain. He put some sandwiches and a tart on a plate for him as well, then stood up and placed everything on the desk.

"I said I didn't want any."

"Well, maybe you'll change your mind." Adam tucked

into the fare, washing everything down with tea. After a minute, he noticed his father sneaking a sandwich from the plate and eating it rather quickly. He drank some tea also.

"Say what you came for, Adam. I haven't got all day."

Adam thought possibly that his father did, but he decided not to offer his opinion on the matter. Brushing the crumbs from his hands, he said, "How did you and Hugh get on after Deborah and I left?"

His parent looked at Adam coldly. "Why are you asking now, after all this time?"

"I need to know, Father. Did you keep on with your tawdry pursuits, and did you get Hugh involved?"

The older man didn't answer, but got to his feet and poured himself a brandy. He swallowed a long draught and then turned to Adam. "You've never cared before." A shank of his long hair fell over one eye and he shoved it out of the way.

"Please, just answer my question." Adam was close to losing his temper, but knew that would ruin any chance he had of learning anything. So he forced himself to remain calm, his hands gripping the arms of the chair.

His father seemed to be thinking over what to tell him, because he said nothing for a long time. Eventually, he refilled his glass and resumed his seat. "Deborah leaving and taking you nearly killed me."

Christ, how could he not respond to that? Did his father have any idea how it had affected Deborah? How she had cried for Hugh every night for months? But he maintained his silence, jaws clamped tight as a vise.

"I knew if I wanted to keep Hugh, I'd have to change. So no more women, at least not here. I gave up drinking and gambling, too, until Hugh was older. He kept on with his tutor. Your brother is a smart man, could have gone to university, but chose not to. Said it wasn't for him.

"I started gambling again at the tavern in the village, five or six years ago, mostly with Broxton. He goaded me. Always loved your mother, you see. Couldn't stand that she'd married me and not him."

"What?" Adam couldn't keep the shock from his voice. "Why have I never heard this before?"

"How many parents make their children privy to their love affairs?"

Adam leaned back in his chair, stunned by the revelations. "Why did you do it? Flaunt those women under Deborah's nose and try to force Hugh and me…"

For the first time, Adam sensed despair in his father's eyes. "Because I was not a fit husband or father. I always felt your mother was above my touch, and it made me miserable. I behaved in such a way that she soon was. And I couldn't stop myself until it was too late."

Adam knew, then, that his father was a weak man, and that they were in no way alike. He would never behave like that to Cassie. By all that was holy, he would never risk losing her, because he loved her too damn much.

Coolly he said, "Why does Hugh have a reputation as a rake, if things were as you say?"

"Because he is my son and I raised him. Oh, he had his share of peccadillos with the ladies, but no more than any other young man feeling his oats. You and Hugh take after your mother. You'll probably never hear me say it again, but I'm proud of both of you. All the good in you is from Deborah."

Adam rose, his legs feeling a bit unsteady. His father said, "Did you get what you came for?"

"You ruined our family. You separated Hugh and me, and very nearly destroyed Deborah. To this day, I don't know how she had the strength to go on, after losing Hugh and then the baby she carried. Your baby."

His father looked ashamed then. "It was unforgivable, I know. I am sorry for it."

Adam nodded. "That's something, anyway. I'll see myself out." He had wanted to rail at the man. To vent his anger until his father cowered in the corner. Maybe even punch him. But he could not. Benjamin Grey was a broken man already.

Adam hurried down the stairs, all the things his father had told him competing with thoughts of Cass. He wanted to heal, as Deborah had, from the pain the old man had caused. He didn't want to be obsessed by it anymore. He wanted to marry Cass and start his own family, a family he would love and protect and safeguard, and he hoped to God that was what she wanted, too.

Adam retrieved his gloves and hat from Wesley and bolted through the door, nearly plowing right into Hugh. Sweating profusely, his brother was wearing workmen's trousers and a rough-woven shirt.

"Adam. What the hell are you doing here?"

"Walk to the stables with me and I'll tell you." They strode alongside each other for a moment in silence, and then Adam began. "You said some things to me that got me to thinking maybe I wasn't like Father. And that you're not either. I came down here to get some answers."

Hugh snorted. "And did you?"

Adam ignored the question, but abruptly stopped walking. "When I asked the old man where you were, he said I shouldn't worry, that you weren't hiding from me. What the hell did that mean?"

Hugh shrugged. "When you used to visit Father, didn't you think it odd that I was never here?"

"He said you were helping tenants or visiting neighbors. There was always a ready excuse. I believed him."

Hugh laughed and shook his head. "Those were lies, Adam. I didn't want to see you. I was hiding, either in my room or somewhere outside. You and Deborah abandoned me, left me here with him, without so much as a by-your-leave. If you'll recall, I didn't visit you in town either."

Adam was thunderstruck. He felt a sadness deep in his core. All these years, and he'd never once made an effort to understand how his brother felt about the break-up of their family. He should have sought Hugh out, attempted to find something they could do together. They might have found common ground and begun to forge the kind of relationship brothers should have.

He put a hand on Hugh's shoulder. "I am sorry. So very sorry."

Hugh flinched, as though Adam's hand had burned him. His voice was a snarl. "I don't want to be your friend, brother. Let's keep going our separate ways. It's worked fine for years."

Adam held out his hand, hoping the gesture would be a new beginning for them. But Hugh ignored him, turning to walk back toward the house.

So be it. But he couldn't help hoping things might be different someday. He wasn't ready to give up on Hugh.

• • •

Cass and Pippa were taking tea together in the drawing room. It was Miss Stanton's afternoon off, and Cass was happy to have her sister to herself. "I think you've had enough of those raspberry tarts, Pip," Cass said.

"Last one," Pippa said, nearly unintelligibly, since she'd stuffed it into her mouth before Cass could stop her. "Why do you keep looking at the door, Cassie? Is Adam coming to see you?"

Cass's cheeks flamed. She'd felt edgy all day. She couldn't wait to see Adam; she dreaded seeing Adam.

A change of subject was in order. "Pippa, there is

something I've been wanting to ask you."

Pippa had resumed sketching after finishing her tea. "Let me see," Cass said. "Move over." Her sister was drawing some of the flowers she'd seen at the Royal Zoological Gardens the day before, and making quite a beautiful job of it. Although Cass did not recall seeing any fairies or elves peeping through the foliage. Or that the leaves themselves had brilliant stars etched on them. She loved that Pippa seemed to feel freer to express her whimsical nature now that Louisa was gone.

"What do you want to ask me?"

"Is it quite all right with you that I'm not your teacher any longer?"

Pippa looked up from her sketchbook. "I was afraid at first, when Jack told me."

Cass's heart dropped. "Afraid you would not get on with Miss Stanton?"

Her sister nodded. "But I like her. She's a good teacher, like you. And Jack explained to me about you. Now that you're old, you have more important things to do. Like helping Mr. Grey to be in Parliament."

Cass laughed. "I'm not *that* old, dear heart."

"You know what I mean."

"Come here and give me a hug." Pippa dropped her sketchbook and curled up next to her big sister, and that was how Adam found them when he entered the room a short time later.

• • •

"Well, if it isn't my two favorite ladies," Adam said, ruffling Pippa's hair.

"You're in time for tea," Cass said. He studied her, noticed that she looked a little strained around the eyes.

"Pippa, be a dear and give your sister and me some

privacy, would you?"

She leaped off the sofa and grabbed her sketchbook. "Would you like to see my flower sketches, Adam?"

"Very much, but another time."

"Miss Stanton isn't home. That's Pippa's new governess." Cass turned to her sister. "Go to the kitchen, dear. Cook will entertain you for a while." Pippa skipped off and Adam claimed the place next to Cass.

He raised a brow. "When did this happen?"

"When I was in Surrey. I knew nothing about it until their visit."

"And it's all right with you? I know you've loved teaching your sister." He lifted her hand, kissed it, kept on holding it.

"It's fine. Jack was right; it was time for a change. There's something else, too. Louisa's gone."

Adam smiled. "I'm glad, Cassie. I hated the way that woman treated you."

"Apparently she and Jack got into a row over the new governess's teaching methods. Jack lost his temper, and she decided to leave."

"I only wish it had happened sooner." He paused and looked down at their entwined hands. "I didn't come here to talk about Pippa or your cousin, darling. I came to talk about us."

Cass didn't say anything. She kept her quiet, dark eyes fastened on him.

"I talked to my father. For the first time in years, I saw him clearly. I'm not like him, Cassie." He shook his head and laughed, as though he could hardly believe it. "Not at all. And I suspect that Hugh isn't either."

Cass threw her arms around his neck. "Nobody ever thought you were, Adam. Only you did." She backed away enough to see his face and said, "He answered your questions?"

"My father hasn't lived the kind of life I had imagined. No women or gambling, or even drink, until Hugh was a grown man. And my brother was not involved in any of it." Adam smiled, still holding her. "Father even told me about the marriage. He thought Deborah was above his touch, as he put it. It was a self-fulfilling prophecy, evidently."

He kissed Cass on the mouth, hard, and then drew back. "I'm not afraid anymore."

"I'm so glad for you." Tears wound their way down her cheeks.

Adam rubbed them away with his thumbs. "Don't cry, love. I spoke to Hugh, too. He's angry, resentful of Deborah and me because he thinks we abandoned him."

"But that's not true! Mrs. Wetherby told me…" Cass flushed, looked down.

"Cass. What did my housekeeper tell you?"

"Oh, God, I'm sorry, Adam. I had no intention of prying. I wanted to talk to her about Sir William, to see if she knew anything that might help me approach him. Somehow the conversation evolved into the situation between your mother and father at the time you left Longmere." She bit down on her lip. "Once she started, I didn't know how to stop her." Cass looked miserable. "That's not entirely the truth. I didn't want to stop her. I thought it would help me understand you if I knew as much as possible about all of it."

"I should fire the woman," Adam said.

"Oh, no, please do not. She loves all of you! It was not malicious. She said I was going to be part of the family and I should know everything."

"Well, that much is true."

A quietness came over her. Adam didn't know if that was a good sign or bad. He lifted her hands to his lips and kissed each one. "I love you, Cassie. I want to marry you. Please say you'll be my wife."

She was quiet for so long, he knew something was terribly wrong. "I can't marry you, Adam." She stood and slowly backed away from him.

Adam sprang to his feet. He hadn't expected this. Maybe some hesitance, but not this curt, absolute rejection.

"Why not, Cass? You love me, too. Do not deny it." Fear made his voice strident. He moved toward her and reached for her hand, but she buried it in her skirt. Her face had gone colorless and her eyes were glossed with tears.

"My reputation. It will damage your career, strip you of respect."

He tried to argue, but she showed him her palms. "Be realistic, Adam. The wagers in the betting books prove the *ton* hasn't forgotten what happened to Bentley. It will only get worse. It will never go away."

"Do you think I give a damn about that? It's not the end of the world if I'm never a Member of Parliament." Every time he took a step closer to her, she took another one back, until they'd reached the door. He could not find the right words to convince her, to banish the anguish from her face.

"So you will give up on us simply because of some ridiculous rumors that don't hold a grain of truth?"

By this time, her back was against the door. "They do, though. Hold a grain of truth." Her eyes held such pain, he ached for her. He didn't move, only waited to hear what she would say. He had the feeling he was about to learn the true reason for her refusal.

"I *was* responsible for Bentley's death, you see."

Ice settled around his heart. "What? That's nonsense. Have you begun to believe the lies people have made up about you?" He tried to laugh, as if he thought she was joking, but he knew better.

"Oh, I didn't shoot him. Of course I did not do that. But he died because of something I did. Something that was wrong with me."

With that unfathomable statement, she fled the room, leaving Adam bewildered. He thought back to when Cass had suggested they become lovers. She was adamant that she didn't wish to marry. She had been traumatized by what had happened with Bentley and didn't trust men. Himself included. Christ, why hadn't he paid more attention to that? Why hadn't he, at some point, insisted she tell him more? He walked over to the drinks tray, poured himself a whiskey, and knocked it back in one swallow.

And then he went in search of Jack.

Chapter Twenty-Seven

Cass tarried in the window seat for a long time. At length, from the slant of the light, she could see it was time to dress for dinner. And she would need to help Pippa. She wondered if Adam had left and felt such emptiness inside, she dropped back down. It was possible she would never see him again. It was an idea she would have to accustom herself to, after she recovered from her broken heart.

She was about to ring for Agnes when she heard a soft knock at her door. When she opened it, there stood Jack. He hadn't bothered to put his coat on; he must have rushed right up to her after Adam…

"May I come in, Cass?"

"Of course," she said. Two chairs stood facing each other before the grate. Cass sat with an upright posture and tried to appear composed. Her brother perched on the edge of his seat and leaned so far forward, she thought he might slide right off.

"Adam said you refused his offer of marriage. Why, Cass? He doesn't understand your reasons. Nor do I." He paused a moment. "It's the real thing this time, Cass. Not a sham."

"I can't marry him. You don't know everything that happened that night. The night Bentley died."

Jack grasped one of her hands. "Then it's time I did. And Adam certainly deserves more of an explanation than you offered. He loves you, Cass."

Big, wrenching sobs burst out then. Jack simply let her cry. She sat there hugging herself until her tears were spent. "Is... is Adam still here?" she finally asked, dabbing at her eyes with a handkerchief.

Jack grimaced, shaking his head. "He's discouraged, though not ready to give up on you. But we must get this sorted. Patience has it limits, you know."

In a wobbly voice she said, "I wouldn't want anything more to do with me, were I he."

Jack let go of her hand and got to his feet. "Don't be maudlin, Cass. Wash your face, my dear. Do whatever it is you ladies do to repair the damage done by excessive tears, and then join me in the library."

"But I have to see to Pippa. And it's nearly supper time..."

"Pippa's capable of dressing herself, and I've already spoken to Miss Stanton. She's offered to eat with Pip in the nursery if we are delayed." He lowered his chin and gave Cass a look that told her he would not accept any more excuses.

"I won't be long," she said.

· · ·

When Cass entered the room, Jack, now dressed for dinner, rose from behind his desk and guided her toward the sofa. After he'd seated himself beside her, he spoke. "Will you tell me exactly what happened the night of Bentley's death? I'm ashamed I've never pressed you for the details."

She pulled in a deep breath. "Yes. All right. Where should

I begin?" she said, half to herself. Cass could feel the familiar sense of dread building. The dread that nearly paralyzed her whenever she thought of that night. She'd never discussed the circumstances of Bentley's suicide with anybody save her mother, and then only in the immediate aftermath. As she'd healed from her wound, neither Jack nor her parents ever mentioned it. Bentley died, was buried, and they never discussed him again, nor the fact that he'd nearly killed her. It was a taboo subject, even in the privacy of their own home.

Cass began speaking. "As you're aware, we were at Drury Lane. It was the interval, and Bentley suggested we stroll in the corridor. There was a crush, and I clung to his arm for fear of becoming separated from him." She laughed humorlessly. "I remember being glad of the noise and the crowd because I wouldn't have to worry about making polite conversation with him."

"You did not deal easily together." It wasn't a question, just a confirmation. "I always worried about that."

So Jack had noticed something not quite right between herself and Bentley. "In the beginning I tried to draw him out, to contrive a way to get him to speak to me in other than the most obligatory manner. But by this time I'd given up. The closer it drew to our wedding day, the less interested in me he seemed."

Jack nodded and Cass continued.

"We carried on to the fringes of the crowd and he asked if I wanted lemonade. He left, and I stood there trying not to dwell on my doubts and misgivings." She hesitated, because suddenly the sadness she felt over the tragedy of that night seemed too fresh and too unbearable.

"If you need to stop, Cass, just say so. Would you like a fortifying drink?"

"It might help."

After Jack had poured them each a libation, she

continued. "How could I wed a man who clearly did not love me and barely tolerated my company? That's what was tormenting me. During the interval at the theater, that is what I was thinking of."

Jack looked stricken, but she pushed on, staring straight ahead, almost trancelike. "I distracted myself by looking at the crowd. I remember spotting you standing with a group of your friends." She gave him a sardonic look. "Widow-watching. At least, that's what I called it. I was having a laugh to myself about it when I heard Bentley's voice saying my name. I looked around, wondering how he'd made his way back so quickly. He was standing quite close, holding a pistol and pointing it at my chest." A lump in her throat as big as Astley's Amphitheater nearly prevented her from continuing.

Jack squeezed her hand, encouraging her. "I was so terrified my mouth went dry. Bentley was staring directly at me, his eyes wild looking. His face was twisted into a kind of mask."

"Did he say anything?"

"Only to warn me not to say a word. As if I could. He grabbed my arm and forced me down a deserted hall. Away from anybody who might help me. I thought about screaming, even wondered if I'd be heard above the din. But before I could decide what to do, he shoved me against the wall. When he spoke, I couldn't make sense of what he said."

I still cannot.

She was quiet for so long that Jack had to prompt her. "Cass?"

She gave her head a shake. "It was only, 'You're to blame for this.' I was utterly at a loss, not to mention crippled with fear. I finally said, 'For what? What have I done?' certain he truly meant to kill me. Suddenly he whirled me around, so that he was against the wall, and then he turned the gun on himself and fired. I did scream then, but that wasn't what brought people running. It was the retort of the gun. My head rang with it for days."

Cass paused to sip her sherry before going on. "You know the rest. Someone found you. You'll recall I was covered in blood and trembling all over, and you wrapped me up in an opera cloak and escorted me out of there. It wasn't until we got home, and Mama and Agnes were cleaning me up, that we discovered I'd been hit by the same ball that had killed Bentley. I hadn't felt any pain until then."

"You were in shock. Did you ever see any of Bentley's family again?"

She shook her head. "When I heard the rumors that they blamed me for his suicide, I was devastated. Especially because of his final words to me. It was my fault that he died, Jack. I know it was. But to this day I don't understand what I did to cause him to end his life." She exhaled a long, shuddering breath.

When she looked up, Cass was shocked to see tears on her brother's cheeks. He brushed them away and said, "Papa and I attended his funeral to pay our respects. It was obvious we weren't welcome."

Cass resumed speaking. "When the rumors started, I couldn't bear living in town, not after I heard about the gossip. Which is why I stayed at Birch Lane for two years. It was healing for me to be there, with Mama and Pippa. It was when I began to tutor her."

"Cass, I—"

"No, wait. Let me finish. Bentley's suicide made me feel I wasn't fit to be his wife. Anybody's wife. There was something lacking in me, and I haven't changed, Jack. That's one of the reasons I'm afraid to marry Adam."

"My dearest sister, there is nothing in your character that would cause a man to wish to die. You must not think it." Jack patted her hand and rose to replenish their drinks.

Cass thought it was a miracle she'd been able to hold herself together during this recitation. A feeling of exhaustion swept over her. She rested her head against the back of the sofa, believing this difficult discussion was all but over.

Jack handed her a fresh sherry and resumed his seat. "Why did you never tell me about this, Cass?"

She smiled sadly. "Jack. You know you and our parents never wished to discuss it."

Her brother sighed and set his glass down. Kneeling before Cass, he grasped her hands in his own and gave her a pleading look. "I hope you can forgive me. I should have talked to you about this long ago. I convinced myself that if we simply put the whole sordid thing from our minds, all would be well. I never thought of the anguish you might be suffering."

"Well, I didn't tell you, so you couldn't have known."

"Ruralizing for two years should have tipped me off," he said ruefully. He gave her hands a final squeeze and returned to his seat. "I have an idea of what Bentley may have meant by his comment."

Cass choked on the swallow of sherry she'd just imbibed. "You do?"

"It may be related to the marriage settlements. Papa made some puzzling remarks during the process, but I never thought to question him. It was none of my business. Now I wish I had."

Baffled, Cass said, "But why would Bentley's last words have anything to do with the marriage settlements?"

"You would be surprised at the range of matters spelled out in those documents. Believe me, I've just been through it for my own engagement to Jenny."

"We still use the same solicitors as Papa, do we not? Surely somebody will remember. And they'll have copies, won't they?"

"I probably have a copy somewhere, come to that. But

I'd feel better if I spoke to someone at the firm. Give me a few days, Cass. We'll get to the bottom of this. I'll not stand by and see you sacrifice your happiness because of some cruel comment Bentley made before he died."

It was probably foolish to hope, but she couldn't help it. Finding out what her former fiancé had meant would bring her some peace of mind, if nothing else.

• • •

Adam, having gone directly to White's after leaving Linford House, now sat in a secluded corner nursing a brandy and pretending to read the *Chronicle*. With any luck, the newspaper would discourage those who wished for convivial company.

The news was of little interest to him, at least at present. Repeal of Orders in Council had been finalized. It looked like Napoleon was on the brink of invading Russia. There was a short piece about the Walcheren inquiries. It was all depressing as hell. *Turn the page, man. Make it appear you're really absorbed.* He kept his eyes trained on the print, but his mind was elsewhere.

Why? Why had Cass rejected him? What on earth made her believe she was responsible for Bentley's death? "He died because of something I did. Something that was wrong with me." He'd never heard such rubbish in his life. Adam had wanted to persuade her, make her see reason, but she'd fled before he had the chance. He couldn't very well follow her to her chamber, so he'd gone in search of her brother. Adam had simply told Jack she'd turned down his proposal. He hadn't revealed what she said, thinking it would be better for him to learn everything from Cass.

He dropped the paper into his lap and closed his eyes. A vision of Cass standing nude before him last night sprang to his mind. Why had she allowed him to make love to her if she didn't love him? If she knew in the end she would reject him? He had sensed finality in her goodbye, and he'd been right.

Someone was hovering nearby. Maybe if he didn't open his eyes, whoever it was would go away. But no. The fool claimed the chair across from Adam and waited, apparently watching him. Reluctantly, Adam looked up. He wanted to see who he was going to have to kill.

Atherton. *Christ.* The man was too good, too gentlemanly, to throttle. Adam gave him a sardonic look before saying, "Join me?" He signaled the waiter to bring him another brandy and one for his friend. Former friend.

"If you don't want company, you need only say."

And too perceptive by half. "You're here, so you may as well stay." Now that Adam looked more closely, Atherton had the manner of a man with something on his mind, his eyes fairly sparking with anticipation. Obviously, there was something he wished to tell Adam. "What is it, then? Don't hold back."

Atherton guffawed. "How did you know?"

That response made Adam smile. "I've known you a long time, friend. Now spill."

The waiter brought their brandies, and after he'd disappeared, Atherton leaned forward and spoke in a low voice. "You asked me to keep an ear out for who might have placed the wager about Miss Linford in the betting books." He glanced around furtively, as though he were about to impart state secrets.

It was entertaining, so Adam let him take his time. "And?"

"I overheard a conversation in the card room at the Gilchrist ball the other night. Players at a table adjacent to mine were far into their cups, discussing the bet. I gathered from what was said that it was Brandon who made the wager and placed it in the book."

"Brandon." Adam was at a loss. "Don't know the man."

"But you do. He's a member here. It's just that you hardly ever see him, because he's always gambling in one of the private rooms. Middle-aged fellow, tending toward fat. In debt up to his ears, it's said."

Adam finally conjured up an image of the man. "I know who you're talking about. But why? What has he got against Cass?"

Again, the surreptitious look around the room. "He was a crony of Bentley. If he were looking for someone to blame for the man's suicide…" Atherton's voice trailed off.

"Ah. I see," Adam said.

"Will you call him out?"

With a jolt, Adam realized that everyone, except Jack and Jenny, still thought he and Cass were betrothed. She hadn't yet cried off, as they had planned. Disconcerted, Adam shook his head. "Miss Linford and I…well, Cass has decided she doesn't want to marry me. We haven't yet announced it, but we must do so soon. It would seem odd if I called Brandon out under those circumstances."

Atherton's brow wrinkled. "Sorry to hear it, old man. I thought you two made an ideal couple."

So did I.

"My thanks. I'm glad to have the information, in any case. Who knows when the opportunity may present itself to visit revenge upon him, even if private and unofficial."

Hell, Adam would like to strangle the man. People like him were the ones who encouraged the notion that Cass was to blame for Bentley's death.

They finished their drinks in silence. Adam thought about the bleak evening ahead of him and found he didn't want to face it alone. "Join me for dinner?"

Atherton agreed, and Adam drank steadily before, during, and after they'd eaten. Late in the evening, his friend put him in a hackney, as he was too drunk to make his way home on his own.

Chapter Twenty-Eight

Seated at her library worktable, Cass finished reuniting a page with its book, slid her finger down the seam to secure it, and slammed the volume shut. Pippa and Jenny lounged nearby on the floor, playing Jackstraws. Rising, Cass hunched and relaxed her shoulders, trying to release the tension that had been plaguing her since she...since Adam. All her thoughts began and ended with him, even when she made a determined effort to think about something else entirely.

Prowling about the room, she glanced at the collection of books lining the shelves. Even though she and Jack had sorted through them after their father's death, there were hundreds remaining, and they needed organizing. Perhaps this would be a good time to start.

Jenny's voice broke into her ruminations. Cass hadn't realized the other girl had come up behind her. "Are you going to isolate yourself forever, my dear?"

Cass raised her brows. "It hasn't been a week yet."

Jenny pulled Cass's arm through hers, and they began a slow circling of the room. Pippa was still playing with the

Jackstraws, not paying them any attention. "Adam was at the Chartley's musicale last night. Did I tell you?"

Cass sighed, something within her breaking apart at the thought of him in society, speaking cordially with people, some of whom would be eligible young ladies. "That is to be expected, Jenny. He asked me to marry him. I said no. Of course he wishes to…to socialize."

"Just so you know, he looked bored and left early."

"Oh." Cass tried to sound as though it didn't matter to her, but she couldn't help getting a little boost from that news.

"You should do likewise, Cass."

"Look bored and leave early? That doesn't sound very entertaining."

Jenny stopped walking in mid-step, abruptly pulling away from her friend. "You are exasperating."

"So says my brother. You've been spending entirely too much time with him. All his opinions are rubbing off on you."

"Which of my opinions do you speak of?" Jack said. He was standing in the doorway, looking smug. "Of course, as my wife, Jenny must agree with me in all matters and spout my opinions whenever the opportunity presents itself, so I'm gratified to hear she's already doing so."

Both women glared at him, even though they knew he was teasing.

"Jack!" Pippa ran to her brother, leaving Jackstraws scattered hither and yon. "May we go out to the park? I am exceedingly bored."

"What say you, ladies? Shall we indulge the little imp?"

"You go," Cass said. "I've an idea for a project I want to undertake."

"Oh, no," Jack said. "You must join us, or we'll not go at all."

"Please, Cassie," said Pippa. "Why are you so mopey lately, anyway?"

Her spirits had indeed been low. At times a desperate loneliness seized her, with her future so unsettled and nothing to look forward to with any excitement. With any hope. But for Pippa's sake, she must hold herself together.

"I'm sorry, dearest. Of course I'll come, and we may depart just as soon as you've put the Jackstraws away."

Pippa performed the task quickly, and they all went off to gather their wraps. Jack grabbed Cass's arm before she got far. "I've had a letter from the solicitor, Cass. Mr. Fairbrook, the oldest partner, has returned from a trip and will see me tomorrow."

"Ah." A rush of hope spread warmth through her chest.

"I'm confident he'll recall the particulars. In any event, he will examine the marriage settlements with me, and that should tell us something."

"Should I come?"

Jack's lips twitched. "No, absolutely not. You know how these old fellows are. Women belong at home, and all that. This is better dealt with by me."

Cass nodded. She didn't like it, but knew he was right.

They rode to the park in the town carriage. The coachman let them out near the entrance, and Cass grabbed Pippa's hand before she could dart away. It was early yet, but still there were many walkers, riders, and conveyances circling about. Easy for a little girl to become lost, or be easily overlooked by a coachman or rider.

The usual jockeying for position was underway, something Cass found amusing. Dowagers peeked out their windows to engage in conversation. Young bucks rode spirited mounts and cast their eyes about for young ladies. In turn, the young ladies, their maids hovering discreetly behind, tried to catch the eye of one of the gentlemen.

By unspoken agreement, Cass and her family stayed off Rotten Row, choosing instead to stroll around the park's perimeter. Cass half hoped she would see Adam, even though any contact with him could only deepen her sadness.

"Let go of me, Cassie," Pippa begged.

"Only if you promise not to run ahead of us. And you must be very careful to watch out for riders and—"

"Can we go to the Serpentine?"

Her brother and Jenny had stopped to wait for them, and Jack said, "Why not?"

• • •

After spending much of the day brooding, Adam asked for his mare to be saddled. He and his horse needed a good gallop, and it was just early enough that Rotten Row, with any luck, would not yet be clogged with other riders. He set off from Cavendish Square to Oxford Street. Without conscious thought, he normally tuned out the jarring noises of the city, but today the clattering of iron wheels, calls of street peddlers, and raised voices of pedestrians jangled his already frayed nerves.

Earlier, Adam had made repeated attempts to write to Sir William Broxton, but he found himself unable to complete a missive to the man. He was torn between requesting a meeting to discuss his election or, on the opposite end of the spectrum, telling the man he'd decided he didn't want to stand for Commons after all. Losing Cass had changed everything. What good was his dream of becoming an MP without her?

He entered the park at Cumberland Gate and proceeded south, soon regretting his choice. Lady Leonora came alongside him before he'd ridden ten yards. If only he'd continued down Park Lane to Hyde Park Corner, he might have missed her.

"My lady," he said, inclining his head. She was wearing a ridiculous looking riding habit with caped shoulders, like a man's greatcoat, and military braiding. It was the only time he could recall thinking her fashion sense had failed her.

"Hello, Adam. Riding alone today? Where is your charming fiancée?"

He knew she was goading him, and he was not about to fall prey to her tricks. "At home, I assume. We do not keep track of each other's movements."

"I see." When he did not speak, she plunged on. "What a shame about the wagers. It seems Cassandra's unfortunate past will forever provide fodder for such mischief. Not to mention for the gossips." Her face wore a snide look that Adam, were he not a gentleman, would have happily slapped away.

"You're an expert in that area, are you not? Isn't gossip your stock-in-trade, Leonora?" Adam halted his horse and dismounted, hoping she would ride on. But, worse luck, she did the same. The woman was impervious to insults.

"Really, Adam, I've never repeated anything that wasn't already being bruited about by everybody else. If a woman chooses to make herself an object of ridicule, she has only herself to blame."

Enough. He would not tolerate any more from her. Abruptly, he stopped walking to turn and face her, standing closer to her than was strictly polite. "Except, of course, Cass did not make that choice. Since you are not privy to her personal affairs, I'll say only that she is entirely blameless in the matter of her fiancé's death. Former fiancé. If you are so innocent in the spreading of *on-dits*, perhaps you should defend her when you hear gossip about her. Now, please take your hack and get out of my sight."

She flinched, as though he had slapped her. "How dare you speak to me that way?" She drew herself up and puffed out her bosom. "I am a countess."

Adam resisted the urge to laugh.

Ignoring her, he took a step back, and when he spun around to make his way toward Rotten Row, somehow the entire Linford family stood before him. Jack and Jenny and Philippa. And Cass, standing a little apart from the others, her face completely drained of color.

Bloody hell. Could this day get any worse?

• • •

Kneeling on the floor of the library, surrounded by books, Cass was making every effort to block out the memory of Adam in the park yesterday, deep in conversation with Lady Leonora. Standing so close to her, they might as well have been embracing. All the way home, Jack had tried to persuade Cass they were arguing. She hadn't stayed around long enough to judge, but grabbed Pippa's hand and fled. She had no doubt it was exactly what she thought, and if she tried to convince herself otherwise, more fool her. Her anguish weighed heavily on her, leaving her breathless.

Impulsively, Cass had decided to rearrange the library shelves, to place the books in alphabetical order by author, to be precise. It was a much bigger chore than she'd anticipated. But the Lord only knew, she needed a huge task to fill up the space in her head she instinctively reserved for Adam. And she was trying not to think about the fact that Jack was, even now, at his appointment with the solicitor.

A knock on the door, and she swiveled around to see who was there. "Beg pardon, Miss Linford. Flowers for you."

"For me? You'd better bring them to me, Meg. I'm not sure I can stand up among this mess I've made." The girl handed her a bouquet of roses, their hue a deep, luxurious red. A note fell out and landed on top of a book. Cass snatched it up, thanking the departing servant. Laying the roses down, she sat back on her heels and tore open the note. It was short, and after she'd read it, her resolve to put Adam out of her thoughts shattered into a million pieces. Or it may well have been her heart that shattered.

"Cass, Believe in me, my love. Believe in us. Yours, A."

She lowered her face to her hands. *Stop tormenting me, Adam. Just stop it.* Why was he making her love him more, when she'd already said she couldn't marry him? She simply must harden her heart against him. Carefully, she refolded the note and then heaved it across the room. It landed atop the stack of 'S' authors before sliding to the floor.

The door pushed open. Jack said, "What on earth?"

. . .

After brother and sister had decamped to the drawing room and Cass rang for tea, Jack waved her to the sofa. "That's quite a project you've taken on," he said, chuckling.

"Yes, well, I needed something to do. Most of the time, Pippa is at her lessons with Miss Stanton, Jenny is either with you or occupied with her trousseau..." Her words petered out. A footman brought in the tea, Meg following on his heels with the roses. Cass thought she would scream if Jack made her wait much longer to hear what the old solicitor had said.

While she poured, he finally spoke. "Shall I tell you what I learned today?"

Her head bobbed up. "I might kill you if you don't. Is it good news?" She didn't know if she could handle more bad.

"It is...illuminating, let's say."

Cass stared at Adam's roses and willed herself to be strong. Whatever Jack had learned, it may not make a difference, in any case. She steeled herself. "Go ahead."

"At the time the settlements were negotiated, Mr. Fairbrook hired an investigator to look into Bentley's affairs. Seems he had vowels out all over town. Fairbrook says he'd been reputed to play deep, and his friends confirmed it."

"Did Papa know?"

"According to Fairbrook, Papa acknowledged he'd heard the rumors, but hadn't given them much credence." Jack looked sheepish. "I'd heard them too, Cass, and I hadn't put much store in them, either. I hadn't pegged him as one of those aristocrats who squandered his own fortune and needed to marry for money."

"Looking back, I probably should have realized—"

Jack shook his head. "You were young and naive. Do not blame yourself."

"Tell me the rest."

"Fairbrook urged Papa to take the situation seriously. Said he'd seen too many dowries drained away by lords who gambled, speculated, or kept multiple mistresses."

How many mistresses did Bentley have? Perhaps more than one. Cass cringed at the thought.

"On Mr. Fairbrook's counsel, they requested a final meeting with Bentley, during which Papa informed him he wished to make some changes in the agreement." Jack drew a piece of paper from his pocket. "Fairbrook's clerk copied this for me. I was afraid I wouldn't remember it correctly. The settlement was amended so that a much greater sum was set aside for you and your children, Cass."

"What was Bentley's reaction?"

Jack shrugged. "He made no objection. How could he, without seeming crass?" After glancing down at his paper, he continued. "They also added a stipulation that Bentley could not pay, out of your dowry, any sum greater than five thousand pounds at one time, and only once per year, for the first five years of your marriage."

Cass moved to the edge of her chair. "But how would we have known it was money from my dowry rather than his own money?"

"Bentley was at a stand, Cass. He was barely getting by on the allowance he received from his father. Your money would have been required for personal and household needs, for children, maybe a trip or two a year. Any large expenditures by your husband would have been immediately obvious to anybody who was paying attention, and Papa, with Fairbrook's help, intended to do exactly that."

"I can't imagine that sat well with Bentley, if matters were as bad as you say."

"Mr. Fairbrook said he went into a rage. Even threatened to call off the engagement. In the end, however, some of your money served him better than none."

Cass released the breath she'd been holding and fell back against the sofa cushions. "Mystery solved, then. He blamed me for his financial woes. He wouldn't be able to settle his considerable debt using my money."

"I'm sorry, Cass. I'm sure Papa had no idea Bentley would take his life, let alone blame you for it."

"No." She'd thought she would feel elation. Vindication. Instead, it was as though a huge empty space had opened up in her chest.

Jack, perhaps sensing her odd reaction, rose and knelt in front of her, taking her hands in his. "You can marry Adam now, Cass. No more obstacles."

Again she said, "No."

His eyes searched her face. "What? Whyever not?"

Cass withdrew her hands and mustered herself. Jack needed a reason why she would still refuse Adam, and it was down to her to make it clear. "I would be an embarrassment to him, Jack. My reputation as the woman who caused my betrothed's death will always be there, just waiting to be stirred up by gossips and rumormongers. It's a relief to have this explanation—possible explanation—of Bentley's motives, but it doesn't change my standing in society."

"But that's based on a lie!"

"Possibly. But we're only going on assumptions. And besides, we can't very well announce the truth, or what we believe to be the truth, to the *ton*."

Her brother threw his hands up. "You're making a mistake if you don't accept Adam, Cass. He loves you."

"But does he love me enough? In the end I might cost him his career. I can't let that happen. I will not allow that to happen."

Cass leaned her head against the cushions, and after a moment, the door closed quietly. She did not move until it was time to dress for dinner.

Chapter Twenty-Nine

One week. One entire week had passed since Cass had refused Adam's marriage proposal. His inability to change anything, and his corresponding level of frustration, were making him crazy, so when he spotted Brandon sauntering through the main room of White's, he saw red. Literally. Streams of crimson rippled in his vision. How dare the man stroll about as though he bore no responsibility for rekindling the rumor and innuendo about Cassie?

Brandon stopped here and there to greet his cronies, as though he were the goddam Prime Minister. It turned Adam's stomach. He wanted to pommel the bastard until he couldn't get up. When he was within range, Adam stood and blocked his way.

"Hullo, Grey." Brandon looked Adam up and down contemptuously. "What can I do for you?"

"You will remove the wager relating to my fiancée and myself from the books. Now."

"It's just a bit of fun, man. Where's your sense of humor?" He laughed, brayed like a donkey, although Adam could tell he was uneasy.

Adam's hand shot out and fisted the front of Brandon's fine lawn shirt, pulling him close. "I don't find it in the least amusing."

Not content with the degree of ire he'd already raised, Brandon plunged in further. "You're insane if you marry that chit. Everybody knows it will ruin your prospects."

Adam hauled off and punched him.

Conversations soon ceased, and the members began to gather round. By the time management intervened, telling them to take it outside, Adam had thrown several more punches and deflected a few from his opponent. Now breathing heavily, both men were carried along in the tide of their crazed friends who were hungry for blood, and ended up on St. James Street, beneath the bow window.

They circled each other, fists raised. Brandon lunged, landing a glancing blow to Adam's jaw. *Hell and damnation, that hurts.* Adam sucked in a breath and threw a solid punch to Brandon's chest, knocking the other man backward. He stumbled and fell on his arse. Adam knew it was time to call a halt, but his temper was still raging. He threw himself atop the other man and pounded his ribs and chest, face and head. Blood poured from Brandon's nose.

That was when somebody clasped Adam from behind and separated him from his prey. Two somebodies, as it turned out. "Are you crazy, man? Do you want to kill him?" The voice belonged to Jack, and Atherton was with him.

"As a matter of fact," Adam said between gasps, "I do."

The crowd quickly dispersed. Brandon went off with his friends to God knew where, and Adam made no further protest when his rescuers escorted him to down the street to the York Coffeehouse.

Jack heaved him onto a bench, then left to order coffees for all of them. Atherton stopped a serving girl and asked for water. He dipped his handkerchief into it and passed it to Adam. Wiping his face, Adam was surprised to see his adversary had drawn blood.

"I think it's Brandon's blood," Atherton said. "Christ, Adam, if I'd known you were going to do something like this, I'd never have told you who put the wager in the books."

"Too late now," Adam said.

Jack returned with the coffees and started in on him. "Have you lost all reason? You'll be kicked out of White's. Branded as a lunatic. What got into you?"

By now, Adam was cooling off. He knew he'd acted stupidly. Christ, he might have killed the man if his friends hadn't come along when they did. "It was Brandon who put the wager in the books."

Jack tried to suppress a grin, but couldn't quite manage it. "Ah. Well, at least you had a reason for acting like a maniac."

They drank their coffee in silence for a few minutes. Jack turned to Atherton and said, "Look, old man, Adam and I have some private matters to discuss. Do you mind?"

"Not in the least," Atherton said, always the accommodating gentleman.

When he'd gone, Jack said, "I have some information for you." Adam's attention never wavered while his friend related everything Cass had told him about Bentley's death, including his final words to her.

"That bastard," Adam said. "Too bad he's already dead. I'd love to kill him myself."

"Calm yourself. There's more." Jack filled him in on the details he'd learned from Fairbrook.

A little flicker of optimism kindled in Adam's weary soul. "What did Cass say? Has this convinced her she bears no blame for Bentley's death?"

"I think it has. But being relieved of that burden doesn't seem to have changed her mind about accepting you.

Stubborn girl believes marriage to her will ruin your political prospects."

Given what Brandon had said mere moments ago, Adam understood. Cassie was too smart not to know what the *ton* thought about a marriage between them, and her instinct was to protect him. It was part of the reason she'd refused him in the first place, and part of the reason he loved her. There had to be something else he could do to change her mind, to win her over despite her misgivings.

"If only there was some way to alter society's perception of her. Or to convince her it *could* change." If only somebody close to Bentley could stand up for her, defend her. But the man was too long dead. It seemed hopeless.

"I don't see how we could bring that about." Jack said, his brow furrowing.

Adam remained quiet for a moment, pondering, his disjointed thoughts careening into each other. Then, in a blinding flash of inspiration, he had it. It was a long shot, but it was worth a try.

He leaned closer to Jack. "Is the Earl of Wilton still living? Bentley's father?"

• • •

Sun streamed through the windows of the small dining room. Cass and Jack were eating breakfast and leafing through the morning papers. When Willis brought in the post on a salver, Cass glanced up. "A parcel for you as well, Miss Linford," he said, placing it before her.

Curiosity getting the better of her, Cass put aside her tea and scone and gave her full attention to the parcel. Hurriedly, she untied the string and ripped off the paper. When she recognized the contents, tears welled in her eyes. Where was the note? She found it under the wrappings and unsealed it.

6 July

Dearest Cassie,

I began to search for your father's book after the house party, when I came up to town by myself. This volume led me on a merry chase, my love, from Ludgate Hill, to Paternoster Row, and St. Paul's Churchyard. It gave me great joy to find it for you, and I hope it makes you happy.

Yours always, A.

Somehow, despite the odds against finding one of the few existing copies of her father's myths, Adam had done it. When she opened the cover, her heart nearly leaped from her chest. Her initials were on the flyleaf. It was her own copy.

She must have made a sound, then, because Jack looked up, obviously alarmed. "What is it, Cass?" Emotion crowding her throat, she couldn't speak. She handed Jack the book and the note.

A huge grin popped out on her brother's face. "If you think finding that book is the best thing he's done, you must read this." He held out the Morning *Post*. "The man adores you, Cass. You're a fool if you don't marry him."

"What are you talking about?" she asked, wiping her eyes.

He lifted his brows. "Read it and see."

She sat, spreading the paper out on the table. The piece Jack was referring to was on page three, directly under a list of the comings and goings of various worthies of the *ton*.

A FATHER SETS THE RECORD STRAIGHT

IT HAS RECENTLY COME TO MY ATTENTION THAT VICIOUS RUMORS CONTINUE TO CIRCULATE REGARDING THE MANNER OF MY SON'S DEATH, WHICH OCCURRED MORE THAN TWO YEARS AGO. I WISH TO LAY THEM TO REST ONCE AND FOR ALL. I HAVE LEARNED

THAT AMONG SOME MEMBERS OF THE TON, MISS CASSANDRA LINFORD, HIS FIANCÉE AT THE TIME, HAS BEEN BLAMED FOR HIS DEMISE. BE ASSURED THAT NOTHING COULD BE FURTHER FROM THE TRUTH. MY SON, OLIVER, VISCOUNT BENTLEY, TOOK HIS OWN LIFE BY SHOOTING HIMSELF WITH A PISTOL. MISS LINFORD WAS THE UNFORTUNATE WITNESS TO THIS SAD EVENT, BUT BEARS NO RESPONSIBILITY WHATSOEVER FOR HIS SUICIDE. SHE ACTED WITH INTEGRITY DURING THE AFTERMATH, NEVER SPEAKING OF IT PUBLICLY, NOR OFFERING UP THE PARTICULARS TO THE NEWSPAPERS OR SCANDALMONGERS.

AFTER MY SON'S DEATH, MY FAMILY AND I UNDERSTANDABLY WERE MIRED IN GRIEF. I GOT WIND OF THE RUMORS ABOUT MISS LINFORD AND ASSUMED THEY WOULD FADE AWAY, AS THESE THINGS USUALLY DO. I SHOULD HAVE PUT PAID TO THEM THE MOMENT THEY SURFACED, AS THEY WERE NOT ONLY UNFOUNDED, BUT CRUEL. TO THIS DAY, I REGRET THAT I DID NOT. MY ONLY SON, MY HEIR, HAD JUST DIED, AND I WASN'T ABLE TO SUMMON THE COURAGE IT WOULD HAVE TAKEN TO SET THINGS RIGHT.

ALLOW ME TO DO SO NOW. MISS LINFORD HAS SUFFERED ENOUGH. SHE IS BLAMELESS IN MY SON'S DEATH. I PRAY THAT LONDON SOCIETY WILL WELCOME HER FULLY AND CEASE ANY FURTHER BASELESS SPECULATION REGARDING HER INVOLVEMENT IN VISCOUNT BENTLEY'S DEATH.

WILTON

7 JULY

When she'd finished reading, Cass looked up at her brother. "I must go to Adam. Call for the carriage while I change."

"He's not in town, Cass. He told me he was spending a week in Haslemere to help with the haying on the home farm."

"Do you mean at his father's estate?" she asked.

"Yes. But he's staying at his mother's place."

Cass leaped to her feet. "Then that's where I'll go." When Jack started to protest, she interrupted. "Don't you dare try to stop me, Jack. Agnes will accompany me, and there will be plenty of servants around. You need not worry."

• • •

Every muscle in Adam's torso ached. Despite that, he loved the feeling of accomplishment helping with the harvest brought. He hadn't been around to do it in years. And in his current state of mind, the wielding of the scythe also brought him a physical release he badly needed. When he'd returned to Deborah's home at the end of the day, he stopped only long enough to grab a bar of soap and a towel before hurrying to the lake and diving into the water. He'd washed and dried himself, then dressed in clean buff britches and a linen shirt.

Sitting on the steps of the folly, elbows on knees, he ruminated about his day. It was Hugh who'd sent Adam a note inviting him to come down for the haying. Perhaps unduly optimistic, Adam viewed this as a tentative step toward reconciliation. He hadn't seen his brother since their unpleasant encounter at Longmere. Today, Hugh had been civil, if not overly friendly. Adam knew Hugh needed time, but that did not stop him wishing things were different between them. He could use a friend right now. In the future, he would try his best to mend their relationship, and conceivably, at some point, his brother would meet him halfway.

And then Adam's thoughts drifted to Cass. Had she received the book? Many times he'd imagined her opening it, the look of joy that would light up her face when she recognized it. And the article. Had it appeared yet? He'd gotten back in touch with the Earl to make sure the old man had arranged everything with the *Post*, but left London before the piece was published. There was nothing to be done now except wait until he returned to Town. Then he would know everything. The book and the article, they were his last, best hope.

He glanced up. A figure was walking toward him. Was it… could it be? He couldn't take his eyes off her. And she was hurrying toward him. Practically running. He rose and went to meet her.

• • •

A thrill rippled through Cass at the moment Adam recognized her. She quickened her pace, a laugh bubbling up from her chest.

When she neared him, he held his arms out. "My love," he said, crushing her against him and sending Cass's heart spinning. "Come." They walked back toward the folly, still clinging to each other.

Her heart was so full. She wanted to thank him for all he had done, but he stopped her. "A moment, darling. First let me say something." They were still standing. Adam untied her bonnet, removed it, and threw it down on the steps. Then he grasped her arms and pulled her closer to him.

"Do you remember our first meeting here?"

Her face heated at the memory. How she'd thrown herself at him, telling him she wanted him to make love to her. "Of course."

His gaze was steady, never leaving her face. "When we met here the first time, it was about desire."

She felt the heat in her face grow more fierce, if that were possible.

"Now it is about something more than that. Make no mistake, I want you back in my bed, Cassie, but not unless you love me. Not unless you'll marry me."

The tears started. Placing her hands on his chest, she said, "The book. Thank you, Adam. It's the nicest gift anyone has ever given me. I love you even more for it. And Wilton's article in the *Post*. I don't know how you convinced him to — "

He cut her off. "These things are nothing unless they caused you to have a change of heart." He led her to the steps and they sat down. Enfolding her hands in his, he said, "Let's never again let my father or Bentley control us. They hurt us, scarred us in more ways than one. That's over. From now on, nothing matters except you and me and our love. Agreed?"

She nodded, her throat too thick to respond.

"I did not expect to see you here, Cassie, but it means the world to me that you came." He gave her a roguish grin. "Does this mean you'll marry me?"

She reached up and cupped his face in her hand. "Yes. For the love of God, yes."

Adam's eyes strayed to the folly. "There's a settee in there," he said. "I've always wondered what it would be like to make love on it."

Cass laughed. "There's no time like the present to find out."

Epilogue

Cass and Adam were married in Haslemere, in the village church, a month or so after Jack and Jenny's nuptials. Their wedding was a simple affair, with family and close friends in attendance, and Cass thought it was perfect. They remained in Surrey until the election, so that Adam could entertain men in the pub, meet citizens at local events, and visit schools, churches, and charitable establishments.

He took his seat in the House of Commons in November. That evening, instead of the soiree they might have been expected to host, he and Cass celebrated with a special evening at home, by themselves. During their candlelit dinner, she couldn't help gazing at him with a quiet pride, repeating how proud she was of him until, laughing, he insisted she call a halt.

They withdrew together after their meal. Adam stood before the mantel, sipping port, and Cass sat on the sofa. It was a chilly night, and a fire burned in the grate. "Were you pleased with your first day?" she asked.

"In the main, it consisted of formalities, plus a good deal

of back slapping and joking. It will take time to fit in."

"There are more than a hundred new members, so you're not alone in that. Selecting allies from that group would be a good beginning." Her mind began churning with ideas, but she had more important matters to discuss with Adam tonight.

"As usual, your advice is right on target." He joined Cass on the sofa. "I couldn't have done this without you, love." Adam gazed at his wife. He would never quite believe this gift he'd been given. This wonder that was Cass.

She smiled. "I don't believe that for a minute, but cannot deny that we are a good fit."

"In more ways than one." And he lifted her onto his lap.

"Adam! The footman will be bringing the tea tray any minute."

"No, he won't. I told them to wait an hour." He had a wicked gleam in his eye. But when he bent to kiss her, she stopped him.

"Actually, there is something important I've been wanting to talk to you about."

"Oh?" He kissed her lips before she could say another word, then her neck, then the rise of her breasts before she stopped him.

"Adam! You're going to want to hear this."

"I'm sorry, darling." He set her off his lap and turned to face her. "What is it?"

"I would like very much to have Philippa live with us. That is, if you approve."

"I didn't know you wanted this, Cassie. If it will make you happy, of course we'll have Pippa. But no tutoring! You've done enough of that."

"I've no intention of it, and besides, Pippa has a governess, as you well know."

"And your brother has approved of this?"

"Yes, wholeheartedly, and Jenny, too." Cass gave him a sly

grin. "I shall soon have my own reason to spend time in the nursery."

A log shifted in the hearth, sending a shower of sparks up the chimney. "Ah, you wish to fit it up to your own design, to make it ready for your sister. Whatever you want."

"Well, yes, but that's not why." She placed a hand on her abdomen and pointedly glanced down. By the look on his face, she saw the light dawn at last.

"You are with child," he said, springing to his feet. An incandescent joy shone in his eyes and spread over his face. "Cassie. Are you sure?"

"I am," she said, laughing. "As sure as I can be. We will be parents, unless we suffer pestilence, famine, flood, or some other unforeseen disaster."

He knelt in front of her, and setting his fingers on her lips, said, "Don't. Never say or think such things again. Promise me." He cupped her face with his hands and began kissing every available expanse of her delicate skin. "I love you, I love you, I love you…shall I go on?"

"Never stop," Cass answered, putting her lips to his.

Acknowledgments

As always, many thanks to my agent, Steven Chudney, for finding this book a home. Thanks also to the members of my critique group who read the manuscript, found the flaws, and helped fix them.

I would also like to thank Erin Molta, my editor, for knowing exactly what this story needed to make it the best it could be. My gratitude also goes to the Entangled production and marketing teams for all their work on behalf of *A False Proposal*.

My husband, Jim Mingle, read the manuscript more than once, as did Lisa Brown Roberts, my friend and critique partner. I am so grateful to them both.

About the Author

Pamela Mingle has spent much of her professional life in libraries and classrooms. With a lot of hard work and a little luck, she's found a new career as a writer. Pam is the author of *The Pursuit of Mary Bennet, A Pride and Prejudice Novel*, and *Kissing Shakespeare*, winner of the 2013 Colorado Book Award for Young Adult Fiction. A self-proclaimed Janeite, Pam is Regional Coordinator for the Denver/Boulder region of the Jane Austen Society of North America.

Pam lives and writes in Lakewood, Colorado. She and her husband enjoy walking in England, which has proved to be a wonderful way to discover new settings for her books.

Discover more historical romance...

To Love a Libertine
by Liana LeFey

When Miss Eden Lowther catches the eye of Lord Percival Falloure, Marquess of Tavistoke, she's delighted, for his wicked lordship is anything but boring. The canny coquette sets out to capture the infamous "Terror of the Ton" but he is not at all what she expects. Having suffered heartbreak and humiliation two years ago, Lord Tavistoke is wary of love. Determined to avoid the marriage yoke, he looks to reestablish his rotten reputation with a rousing scandal. His mark: Miss Eden Lowther, a tearing beauty reported to have left devastation in her wake last Season. If anyone has asked for ruination, it is the heartless "Hellion of Holker Hall."

Viscountess of Vice
a *Regency Reformers* novel by Jenny Holiday

Lady Catharine wants a little excitement. Bored of playing the role of the ton's favorite slightly scandalous widow, she jumps at the chance to go undercover as a courtesan. Social reformer James Burnham is conducting a study of vice in England's capital. Catharine is the last sort of woman James should want, but want her he does. When Catharine and James are forced to band together, they'll be drawn into a web of secrets and lies that endangers their lives—and their hearts.

Bayou Nights
by Julie Mulhern

Matthias Blake is as out of place in New Orleans as a raven in a flock of hummingbirds. He has serious work to do and Christine

Lambert is a distraction he doesn't need. But how can he resist a lady in distress—even if that lady can win a fight armed with a hat pin? Together they must overcome their pasts and defeat dark forces sent by a shadowy evil. In the process, they just might find the greatest treasure of all…

COME TO ME
by Oberon Wonch

Comte Grégoire FitzHenri, the new Earl of Shyleburgh is one of the Norman Conqueror's favored warriors…but he isn't known for his romantic sensibility or his command of the English language. He looks forward to his imminent marriage to his longtime betrothed. But as a rough-hewn soldier, he wishes to enchant the elegant lady before taking their wedding vows— which means much-needed lessons in courtly love. The clever Bridget of Shyleburgh has been secretly in love with Grégoire since he was promised in marriage to her sister and is determined to help him. But Grégoire's heated missives tempt a fair maiden to stray down a path filled with forbidden pleasures. But his words are meant for another…aren't they?